LEADERSHIP SUCCESSION
IN THE WORLD OF THE PAULINE CIRCLE

New Testament Monographs, 5

Series Editor
Stanley E. Porter

LEADERSHIP SUCCESSION
IN THE WORLD OF THE PAULINE CIRCLE

Perry L. Stepp

SHEFFIELD PHOENIX PRESS

2005

Copyright © 2005, 2006 Sheffield Phoenix Press

First published in hardback, 2005
First published in paperback, 2006

Published by Sheffield Phoenix Press
Department of Biblical Studies, University of Sheffield
Sheffield S10 2TN

www.sheffieldphoenix.com

All rights reserved.
No part of this publication may be reproduced or transmitted in any form or by any means, electronic or mechanical, including photocopying, recording or any information storage or retrieval system, without the publishers' permission in writing.

A CIP catalogue record for this book
is available from the British Library

Typeset by Forthcoming Publications
Printed by Lightning Source

ISBN 1-905048-10-6 (hardback)
ISBN 1-905048-73-4 (paperback)
ISSN 1747-9606

To Elizabeth, who is my heart

28 July 2004 — 2 Corinthians 5.17

Contents

List of Figures and Tables	ix
Preface	xiii
Abbreviations	xv

Chapter 1
INTRODUCTION — 1
1. Justification of this Study — 2
2. Methodology—Reading from the Perspective of the Authorial Audience — 8
3. This Study's Argument — 13

Chapter 2
THE ANCIENT UNDERSTANDING OF SUCCESSION, PART 1:
BACKGROUND AND GRAECO-ROMAN TEXTS — 15
1. Describing the Function of Succession — 17
2. Graeco-Roman Texts Describing the Function of Succession — 19
3. Summary of Graeco-Roman Texts Describing the Function of Succession — 55

Chapter 3
THE ANCIENT UNDERSTANDING OF SUCCESSION, PART 2:
SUCCESSION IN JEWISH AND CHRISTIAN TEXTS — 60
1. Succession in Jewish Texts — 60
2. Jewish Texts Describing the Function of Succession — 62
3. Summary of Jewish Texts Describing the Function of Succession — 88
4. Christian Texts Describing the Function of Succession — 91
5. Summary of Christian Texts Describing the Function of Succession — 108

Chapter 4
SUCCESSION IN THE PASTORAL EPISTLES, PART 1:
FIRST TIMOTHY — 111
1. Paul's Succession from Christ — 113
2. The Function of the Succession from Christ to Paul — 114
3. Timothy's Succession from Paul and from the Elders — 135

4. The Function of the Successions to Timothy	137
5. Timothy as Paul's Successor and the Elders' Successor in 1 Timothy	147
6. Other Leaders' Succession from Paul or Timothy	150
7. The Function of Succession from Paul or Timothy to Other Leaders	151
8. Summary: The Function of Succession in 1 Timothy	152

Chapter 5
SUCCESSION IN THE PASTORAL EPISTLES, PART 2:
SECOND TIMOTHY AND TITUS 153
1. Evidence of Succession from Christ to Paul in 2 Timothy 153
2. The Function of the Succession from Christ to Paul in 2 Timothy 155
3. Evidence of Succession from Paul to Timothy (and on to the Faithful) in 2 Timothy 166
4. The Function of the Succession from Paul to Timothy (and on to the Faithful) 169
5. Evidence of Succession from Christ to Paul in Titus 179
6. Evidence of Succession from Paul to Titus in Titus 180
7. Conclusions 182

Chapter 6
SUCCESSION IN THE PASTORAL EPISTLES, PART 3:
READING THE PASTORAL EPISTLES FROM THE PERSPECTIVE
OF THE AUTHORIAL AUDIENCE 183
1. Titus 184
2. First Timothy 185
3. Second Timothy 188
4. Summary and Conclusion 191

Chapter 7
CONCLUSION 192
1. Summary of the Evidence 192
2. Conclusions Drawn from this Study 197
3. Avenues for Future Research 205

Bibliography 208
Index of References 218
Index of Authors 225

LIST OF FIGURES AND TABLES

Figures

1.	Illustrating the Primary Act of Succession	17
2.	Illustrating both the Primary Act and the Function of Succession	18
3.	Illustration of Hypothetical Succession, Showing both the Primary Act of Succession and the Function(s) of Succession	19
4.	The Function of Succession in Herodotus 3.53	22
5.	The Function of Succession in Herodotus 5.90-92	22
6.	The Functions of Succession in Plato, *Laws* 6.769c	25
7.	The Functions of Succession in Aristotle, *Politics* 1293a.13-30	27
8.	The Functions of Succession in Aristotle, *Athenian Constitution* 28.1-4	27
9.	The Function of Succession in Diodorus Siculus 15.8-11	29
10.	The Function of Succession in Diodorus Siculus 15.93.1	30
11.	The Function of Succession in Diodorus Siculus 17–18	32
12.	The Function of Succession in Strabo, *Geography* 11.13.9	33
13.	The Function of Succession in Strabo, *Geography* 13.1.3	34
14.	The Functions of Succession in Livy 23.27.9-12	35
15.	The Function of Succession in Pausanius, *Description of Greece* 7.12	36
16.	The Functions of Succession in Dio Chrysostom 64.20-22	37
17.	The Functions of Succession in Dio Cassius 53	39
18.	The Functions of Succession in Aulus Gellius, *Attic Nights* 13.5	40
19.	The Function of Succession in Diogenes Laertius 4.67	42
20.	The Function of Succession in Diogenes Laertius 9.115	42
21.	The Functions of Succession in Diogenes Laertius 10.9	43
22.	The Function of Succession in Iamblichus, *On the Pythagorean Way of Life* 36	44
23.	The Function of Succession in Lysias, *Pension* 6	46
24.	The Function of Succession in Xenophon, *Anabasis* 1.5.2	47
25.	The Function of Succession in Aristotle, *Sophistical Refutations* 34.27-35	48
26.	The Function of Succession in Pliny the Elder, *Natural History* 30.2.4-5	48
27.	The Functions of Succession in Tacitus, *Annals* 15.62	50
28.	The Functions of Succession in Demosthenes, *Aphobus* 2.19	52
29.	The Function of Succession in Plato, *Laws* 5.740b	53
30.	The Function of Succession in *Diodorus Siculus* 10.30.1-2	54
31.	The Function of Succession in Lucian, *Alexander the False Prophet* 5	55
32.	The Functions of Succession in Numbers 27.12-23 and Joshua 1.2-9	64

33.	The Functions of Succession in 1 Samuel 9–18 (LXX 1 Kingdoms 9–18)	67
34.	The Functions of Succession in 1 Kings 1–2 (LXX 3 Kingdoms 1–2)	69
35.	The Function of Succession in 1 Kings 11.43, etc. (LXX 3 Kingdoms 11.44, etc.)	70
36.	The Functions of Succession in 1 Kings 19–2 Kings 2 (LXX 3 Kingdoms 19–4 Kingdoms 2)	72
37.	The Function of Succession in Sirach 47.11-13	74
38.	The Function of Succession in Eupolemus (in Alexander Polyhistor, in Eusebius, *Preparation for the Gospel* 9.30+447c-d)	75
39.	The Function of Succession in 1 Maccabees 2.65-66; 3.1	76
40.	The Function of Succession in 1 Maccabees 6.14-15	77
41.	The Functions of Succession in 2 Maccabees 9.22-27	79
42.	The Function of Succession in Pseudo-Philo, *Biblical Antiquities*	80
43.	The Functions of Succession in *Testament of Moses* 1.6-10; 10.15	81
44.	The Function of Succession in Josephus, *Jewish Antiquities* 7.14.2+337	83
45.	The Function of Succession in Josephus, *Jewish Antiquities* 9.2.2+27-28	83
46.	The Function of Succession in Josephus, *Life* 1.76+428-29	84
47.	The Function of Succession in Josephus, *Against Apion* 1.17+110	85
48.	The Function of Succession in Josephus, *Against Apion* 1.8+41	86
49.	The Function of Succession in *3 Enoch* 48D.6-10	87
50.	The Function of Succession in Josephus, *Life* 1.1+3, 6, and *Against Apion* 1.7+31	88
51.	The Function of Succession in Matthew 16.13-20	93
52.	The Function of Succession in Luke 22.28-30	94
53.	The Functions of Succession in Acts 6–7	96
54.	The Functions of Succession in Acts 24.27 and 25.9	97
55.	The Functions of Succession in 1 Clement 42–44	98
56.	The Functions of Succession in Athenagoras, *Legatio* 37	100
57.	The Function of Succession in Hegesippus (in Eusebius, *Ecclesiastical History* 4.21-22)	100
58.	The Function of Succession in Clement of Alexandria, *Stromateis*	102
59.	The Functions of Succession in Apollinarius of Hierapolis (in Eusebius, *Ecclesiastical History* 5.14-19)	103
60.	The Function of Succession in Luke 1.1-4	104
61.	The Function of Succession in Athenagoras, *Legatio* 28	105
62.	The Function of Succession in Irenaeus, *Against Heresies* 3.2.1-2	106
63.	The Function of Succession in Irenaeus, *Against Heresies* 3.3.1-3	107
64.	The Functions of the Succession from Christ to Paul in 1 Timothy	134
65.	The Functions of the Succession from Paul to Timothy in 1 Timothy	149
66.	The Function of the Succession from the Elders to Timothy in 1 Timothy	149
67.	The Functions of the Succession from Christ to Paul in 2 Timothy	165
68.	The Functions of the Succession from Paul to Timothy in 2 Timothy	178
69.	The Functions of the Succession from Christ to Paul in 1 Timothy	186

List of Figures and Tables xi

70.	The Functions of the Succession from Paul to Timothy in 1 Timothy	187
71.	The Function of the Succession from the Elders to Timothy in 1 Timothy	188
72.	The Functions of the Succession from Christ to Paul in 2 Timothy	189
73.	The Functions of the Succession from Paul to Timothy (and on to the Faithful) in 2 Timothy	190

Tables

1.	Graeco-Roman Texts Describing the Passing-On of Leadership/Rule	58
2.	Graeco-Roman Texts Describing the Passing-On of the Headship of a Philosophical School	58
3.	Graeco-Roman Texts Describing the Passing-On of a Task	59
4.	Graeco-Roman Texts Describing the Passing-On of Knowledge or Tradition	59
5.	Graeco-Roman Texts Describing the Passing-On of Possessions	59
6.	Jewish Texts Describing the Passing-On of Leadership/Rule	90
7.	Jewish Texts Describing the Passing-On of Tradition/Knowledge	90
8.	Jewish Texts Describing the Passing-On of Possessions	90
9.	Christian Texts Describing the Passing-On of Leadership/Rule	110
10.	Christian Texts Describing the Passing-On of Knowledge or Tradition	110
11.	The Functions of Succession in 1 Timothy	152
12.	The Functions of Succession in 2 Timothy	179
13.	*Texts Describing the Passing-On of Leadership/Rule*	194
14.	Texts Describing the Passing-On of the Headship of a Philosophical School	195
15.	Texts Describing the Passing-On of a Task	196
16.	Texts Describing the Passing-On of Knowledge or Tradition	196
17.	Texts Describing the Passing-On of Possessions	197

Preface

My love affair with the Pastoral Epistles began one afternoon in 1984, when I spent time meditating on 2 Tim. 2.20-21 in my devotions. Since that time, these letters have been a frequent source of guidance and frustration for me. I am honored to have the opportunity to study, teach, and write about these texts.

In this study, I attempt to build on and extend the work of my professors Charles Talbert, Mikeal Parsons, and Alan Culpepper. These scholars taught me to pay attention to literary theory, ancient and modern, and to read the New Testament against the literary cultures in which it was written and received. This study is a small and imperfect monument celebrating their work.

This monograph is a revision of my PhD dissertation, written at Baylor University 1999–2002 under the direction of Charles Talbert, my mentor and teacher and friend. Dr Talbert sparked my interest in genre and succession. After reading *What Is a Gospel?*,[1] I stopped Dr Talbert in the hallway and asked him, 'What about succession in the Hebrew Bible? Does it present succession in the same kind of ways as the Graeco-Roman sources?' And at that moment the jaws of a trap sprung shut, the course of my life since that day was determined.

I have had the distinct privilege of working with Dr Talbert on two projects, my dissertation and a separate project which lay groundwork for it. As his student I have observed '[his] teaching, [his] conduct, [his] aim in life, [his] faith, [and his] patience'. As a scholar, I am honored to now have the opportunity to 'entrust to faithful people what I have heard' from him. As a professor and teacher of the Bible, I know no more judicious or reliable guide to the meaning of New Testament texts than Dr Talbert. I am blessed and humbled to have worked with him.

Many people have contributed to this study, too many for me to thank them all by name. At the risk of offending by omission, I wish to single out the following:

First and foremost, let me express my love and gratitude to Beth, my wife, and our children, Kayla, Anna, and Joshua: you mean the world to me. The

---

1. Charles H. Talbert, *What is a Gospel? The Genre of the Canonical Gospels* (Philadelphia: Fortress Press, 1977).

fact that I've survived to write this study is a testament to your faithfulness, love, and sacrifice.

I am grateful to Stan Porter and David Clines at Sheffield Phoenix Press, and to Duncan Burns of Forthcoming Publications for their loving attention to my manuscript. I want to thank the other anonymous readers who have read the manuscript and offered helpful and constructive criticisms. I also want to thank my professors and colleagues at Baylor University, other than those named above, who also contributed directly to this study: Bill Bellinger, Stan Harstine, and Martin Culy. I also want to thank my colleagues at Kentucky Christian University. My appreciation goes to Trey Anastasio and Jerry Garcia: without the backdrop provided by your wizardry, this study would never have been written. I also want to thank my students at Dallas Christian College, Christ for the Nations Institute (Dallas, TX), George W. Truett Seminary, Baylor University, and Kentucky Christian University, for your encouragement and for all that you have taught me while I was teaching you. Special thanks go to my friend and colleague at Kentucky Christian University, Rob Ford, who generously shared of his professional development funds to underwrite the preparation of indices for this book. Finally, I want to thank Amber Davis, my student worker at Kentucky Christian University, for her assistance with this project.

In closing, I owe a great debt of gratitude to my parents, Errol and Joyce Stepp, for their support and love, and for the inheritance of intellectual curiosity that they passed on to me.

ABBREVIATIONS

AB	Anchor Bible
ABD	David Noel Freedman (ed.), *The Anchor Bible Dictionary* (6 vols.; New York: Doubleday, 1992)
ACW	Ancient Christian Writers
AnBib	Analecta biblica
ANET	James B. Pritchard (ed.), *Ancient Near Eastern Texts Relating to the Old Testament* (Princeton, NJ: Princeton University Press, 3rd edn, 1966)
ANF	*Ante-Nicene Fathers*
ASV	American Standard Version
BAGD	Walter Bauer, William F. Arndt, F. William Gingrich and Frederick W. Danker, *A Greek–English Lexicon of the New Testament and Other Early Christian Literature* (Chicago: University of Chicago Press, 2nd edn, 1958)
BTB	*Biblical Theology Bulletin*
CBQ	*Catholic Biblical Quarterly*
CEV	Contemporary English Version
EDNT	H. Balz and G. Schneider (eds.), *Exegetical Dictionary of the New Testament* (3 vols.; Grand Rapids: Eerdmans, 1990–93)
HTKNT	Herders theologischer Kommentar zum Neuen Testament
HTR	*Harvard Theological Review*
ICC	International Critical Commentary
JBL	*Journal of Biblical Literature*
JSNTSup	*Journal for the Study of the New Testament*, Supplement Series
JSOT	*Journal for the Study of the Old Testament*
JSOTSup	*Journal for the Study of the Old Testament*, Supplement Series
JTS	*Journal of Theological Studies*
KJV	King James Version
LCL	Loeb Classical Library
LEC	Library of Early Christianity
LSJ	H.G. Liddell, Robert Scott and H. Stuart Jones, *Greek–English Lexicon* (Oxford: Clarendon Press, 9th edn, 1968)
NCBC	New Century Bible Commentary
NCV	New Century Version
NIV	New International Version
NKJV	New King James Version
NLT	New Living Translation
NRSV	New Revised Standard Version
NTL	New Testament Library

OCD	*Oxford Classical Dictionary*
OTP	James Charlesworth (ed.), *The Old Testament Pseudepigrapha* (2 vols.; Garden City, NY: Doubleday, 1983)
RNT	Regensburger Neues Testament
RSV	Revised Standard Version
SBLDS	SBL Dissertation Series
SBLMS	SBL Monograph Series
SBLRBS	SBL Resources for Biblical Study
SNTSMS	Society for New Testament Studies Monograph Series
TDNT	Gerhard Kittel and Gerhard Friedrich (eds.), *Theological Dictionary of the New Testament* (trans. Geoffrey W. Bromiley; 10 vols.; Grand Rapids: Eerdmans, 1964–)
TynBul	*Tyndale Bulletin*
WBC	Word Biblical Commentary
WUNT	Wissenschaftliche Untersuchungen zum Neuen Testament

1

INTRODUCTION

Ancient Mediterranean texts often contain mentions or accounts of *succession*, a phenomenon by which an important person's power or greatness lived on in an heir or successor after the important person died. Witness three examples: when Alexander the Great died, the society and empire (and culture) he championed could have died with him. When near death, Alexander provided for their continuation by appointing Perdiccas to be his regent, leaving him a list of instructions and giving him authority to bequeath responsibility and territory to 'the strongest' (τῷ κρατίστῳ) of Alexander's generals (Diodorus Siculus 17.117.4, 18.3-4 [Welles, LCL]).[1] These heirs were historically referred to as 'the Successors' (Διάδοχοι).[2] When Aristotle died, his school (and thus his learnedness and understanding of the world) could have died with him. But he provided for its continuation: when he was near death, he chose a successor to lead his school (Aulus Gellius, *Attic Nights* 13.5). When Moses became concerned about who would lead Israel after his death, God prompted him to choose Joshua to be his successor, so that the people of Israel would not be 'like sheep without a shepherd' (Num. 27.12-23).[3] In these and hundreds of other examples,[4] we find the retelling of events in which succession took place. These retellings come from a variety of texts, Graeco-Roman, Jewish, and Christian. Because these texts use various matrices of fixed terminology and types and phenomena,[5] ancient readers/hearers would have understood from these texts that succession had taken place.

---

1. When the story of Alexander's death is repeated at the beginning of Diororus's accounts of the Διάδοχοι, Alexander leaves his kingdom to 'the best' (τῷ ἀρίστῳ) (Diodorus Siculus 18.1.4).
2. 'Διάδοχοι', *OCD*, 271: cf. Diodorus Siculus 18.4.1; Plutarch, *Demetrius* 5.1.4; Appianus, *Syriaca* 343.1; Herodianus 6.2.6.7; Dio Cassius 40.14.2.5; etc.
3. Unless otherwise noted, English Bible quotations are from the NRSV.
4. The most complete catalog of texts in which succession plays a major role is Charles H. Talbert and Perry L. Stepp, 'Succession in Mediterranean Antiquity, Part 1: The Lukan Milieu', and 'Succession in Mediterranean Antiquity, Part 2: Luke–Acts', *Society of Biblical Literature Seminar Papers, 1998* (SBLSP, 37; 2 vols.; Atlanta: Scholars Press, 1998), I, pp. 148-68, and pp. 169-79 respectively.
5. Talbert and Stepp, 'Succession: Part 1', pp. 149-54, 160-67.

In the literature of the New Testament, succession is central to several texts, none more than the Pastoral Epistles. A proper understanding of succession in the Pastorals is particularly important for understanding the relationships between Paul and Timothy and Paul and Titus described there, and how those relationships affect their tasks as Christian leaders. Yet these documents have never been examined against a solid historical understanding of how succession functioned in the ancient Mediterranean literary milieu. These texts have often been discussed and appealed to in arguments over the nature of ministry, church leadership and church unity, but such discussions have always proceeded from a stance more dogmatic than historical.[6] The need for a historical study of these documents, how succession functions and the implications of such function for our understanding of the first-century Church, is self-evident.

1. *Justification of this Study*

From New Testament times, the discussion of succession as it relates to church leadership has always been a polemical discussion carried on in an ecclesial (rather than academic) context. A brief survey of the history of this discussion shows this to be the case. The earliest mentions of succession—in the Pastoral Epistles and in 1 Clement 42–44—are polemically charged: in these texts, the authors argue against the dangers presented by false teaching and insurrection within the church, respectively. Further, since the middle of the third century, discussion of succession and church leadership has always meant discussion of *apostolic succession* (i.e. the passing on of the apostolic office in the office of the bishop, particularly in the papacy) as opposed to discussion of other types of succession within the Church. This trend differs from the successions in view in the earliest references, which are not successions of apostolic office. In 1 Timothy and 2 Timothy, what is passed from Paul to Timothy is responsibility for and authority over the teaching and propagation of Paul's gospel. In 1 Clement 42–44, what is passed on are the offices of elder/overseer and deacon. None of these first-century documents speaks of perpetuation of the apostolic office.

Responses to Gnosticism 180–225 CE
Three documents from the struggle with Gnosticism in the late second and early third centuries refer to apostolic succession. These continue the trend

---

6. Regarding church leadership and the nature of ministry, see Hans von Campenhausen, *Ecclesiastical Authority and Spiritual Power* (Stanford, CA: Stanford University Press, 1969), particularly pp. 106-19; regarding church unity, see Hans Küng (ed.), *Apostolic Succession: Rethinking a Barrier to Unity* (Concilium, 34; New York: Paulist Press, 1968).

noted above: as with 1 Clement and the Pastorals, these documents do not argue that the apostolic office is passed on from the apostles to their successors, but rather that teaching/responsibility/ministry/knowledge was passed on.[7]

In *Against Heresies* 3.2.2 and 3.3.1, Irenaeus (d. c. 200) attacks the Gnostic proposition of secret tradition passed on from the apostles. Irenaeus counters by asserting that what the apostles passed on was the apostolic teaching, not secret knowledge. He writes of previously referring the Gnostics 'to that tradition which originates from the apostles [and] which is preserved by means of the succession of presbyters in the Churches'.[8] Further, if the apostles had possessed secret knowledge, they would have passed this on to those to whom they passed on the leadership of the Church:

> We are in a position to reckon up those who were by the apostles instituted [as] bishops in the Churches, and [to demonstrate] the succession of these men to our own times; those who neither taught nor knew of anything like what these [heretics] rave about. For if the apostles had known hidden mysteries, which they were in the habit of imparting to 'the perfect' apart and privily from the rest, they would have delivered them especially to those to whom they were also committing the Churches themselves.[9]

Note that the successions (of both elders *and* overseers) referred to in this passage were of both leadership *and* teaching and tradition. The passing on of leadership is not defined as the passing on of apostolic office but of apostolic mission—leadership and care of the Church. But equal in importance to the succession of leadership is the succession of teaching, which ensures that the doctrine preached in post-apostolic churches was faithful to the gospel which the apostles themselves preached.

Tertullian (d. c. 220) makes a similar argument in *Prescription against Heretics* 20–21. Jesus delivered the gospel to his apostles, and sent them to serve as his witnesses throughout the world. They went, founding churches in every city. The doctrine which they planted in those churches in turn spread to other places through the founding of other churches. In this way, all churches are apostolic, because all partake of the apostolic doctrine. The only legitimate preaching is that which descends from the apostles, those whom Jesus sent. The only legitimate test of preaching is whether it agrees with the doctrine taught in the churches founded by the apostles. Therefore:

---

7. For the remainder of this reconstruction of the history of the doctrine, I have followed Carlos Alfredo Steger, *Apostolic Succession in the Writings of Yves Congar and Oscar Cullmann* (Andrews University Seminary Doctoral Dissertation Series; Berrien Springs, MI: Andrews University Press, 1993), pp. 15-57.
8. Irenaeus, *Against Heresies* 3.2.2 (*ANF* 1.415).
9. Irenaeus, *Against Heresies* 3.3.1 (*ANF* 1.415).

> All doctrine which agrees with the apostolic churches—those moulds and original sources of the faith—must be reckoned for truth, as undoubtedly containing that which the churches received from the apostles, the apostles from Christ, Christ from God.[10]

Note again that it is the apostolic mission and tradition which are passed on, not the apostolic office.[11] The connection of all true churches with the apostolic teaching, as determined by the canon of teaching from the churches directly founded by the apostles, makes those churches true and apostolic.

Hippolytus of Rome (d. 236) also focuses on the passing on of mission and tradition rather than office, although he is the first to write specifically of the bishops as the apostles' heirs. In the prologue of *Refutation of All Heresies*, he refers to the bishops in their struggle to defend the apostolic teaching against heresy as 'their [the apostles'] successors'. He contrasts this with the leaders of the heretics, who did not derive their teachings from the Scriptures nor 'from preserving the succession of any saint'.[12]

Identification of the Bishops with the Apostles
By the time of Cyprian (d. 258), however, the Church claimed that the bishops held the apostolic office. In his third letter, Cyprian asserts the superiority of the bishop over the deacon by noting that: 'it was the Lord who chose Apostles, that is to say, bishops and appointed leaders, whereas it was the Apostles who, after the ascension of our Lord into heaven, established deacons to assist the Church and themselves, in their office of bishop'.[13] Likewise, Cyprian later writes to Florentius, who opposed him: 'You are now appointing yourself judge over God and Christ, and He did say to the apostles, and thereby to all the leaders who are successors to the apostles, appointed to replace them: "He who hears you hears me, and he who hears me hears Him who sent me. And he who despises you despises me and Him who sent me."'[14]

The doctrine of apostolic succession reaches its full traditional articulation with Leo the Great (d. 461). In his third sermon, Leo speaks of Peter receiving the keys of the kingdom from Christ:

> Blessed Peter does not relinquish his government of the Church... He now manages the things entrusted to him more completely and more effectively. He

---

10. Tertullian, *The Prescription against Heretics* 21 (*ANF* 3.252).
11. Likewise, Tertullian in ch. 25 of *Prescription against Heretics* describes the deposit which Paul passed on to Timothy in 1 Tim. 1.18 and 2 Tim. 1.12-14 as the pure Pauline gospel, not Paul's apostolic office.
12. Hippolytus, *The Refutation of All Heresies*, prologue (*ANF* 5.10).
13. Cyprian, *The Letters of St. Cyprian of Carthage* 3.3.1 (trans. G.W. Clarke; *ACW* 43; New York: Newman, 1984), p. 56.
14. Cyprian, *Letters* 66.4.2 (*ACW* 46), p. 119.

carries out every aspect of his duties and responsibilities in him and with him through whom he has been glorified.

So, if we do anything correctly or judge anything correctly, if we obtain anything at all from the mercy of God...it comes about as a result of his works and merits. In this see his power lives on and his authority reigns supreme...
In the universal Church, Peter says every day, 'You are Christ, Son of the living God'.[15]

The doctrine remained in this form, basically unchanged except to grow more entrenched, until after Vatican II. Roman Catholicism has historically and consistently viewed as not valid those churches outside of the unbroken succession of the laying-on of hands. For example, in 1896, Leo XIII asserted that 'ordinations carried out according to the Anglican rite have been and are absolutely null and utterly void'.[16] Vatican II served only to affirm these views, officially identifying the college of apostles with the college of bishops.[17] Divine revelation and supernatural ability to lead were passed on through the unbroken pipeline of the laying-on of hands.[18] Writing of how the doctrine so quickly became entrenched and intractable, Everett Ferguson notes,

> Apostolic succession arose in a polemical situation as an effective argument for the truth of Catholic tradition against Gnostic teachings. As so often happens to successful arguments, it came to be regarded as an article of faith, not just a defense of the truth but a part of the truth itself.[19]

The Responses of the Reformers
The Reformers took issue with the locating of apostolic authority and truth in men linked to the apostles only by an unbroken pipeline of the laying-on of hands. Martin Luther wrote that 'the people of God are not those who have the physical succession but those who have the promise and believe it'.[20] Calvin similarly wrote that continuity with the apostolic church is preserved by maintaining the pure apostolic doctrine, not by 'succession in persons

---

15. St Leo the Great, *Sermons* 3.3 (trans. Jane Patricia Freeland and Agnes Josephine Conway; Washington, DC: Catholic University of America, 1996), pp. 22-23.

16. Leo XIII, *The Great Encyclical Letters of Pope Leo XIII* (New York: Benziger Brothers, 1903), p. 405.

17. Second Vatican Council, 'Dogmatic Constitution of the Church', in *The Documents of Vatican II* (ed. Walter M. Abbott; New York: Guild, 1966), Article 19; see also Articles 20 and 22.

18. Second Vatican Council, 'Dogmatic', Article 21.

19. Everett Ferguson, 'Apostolic Succession', in *idem* (ed.), *Encyclopedia of Early Christianity* (2 vols.; New York: Garland, 2nd edn, 1997), I, pp. 94-95.

20. Martin Luther, *Lectures on Genesis*, vols. 1–8 of *Luther's Works* (ed. Jaroslav Pelikan; trans. George Schick; 55 vols.; St Louis: Concordia Publishing House, 1958), IV, p. 33.

alone'.[21] These two positions—that apostolicity rested either in the faith of the Church or in the pure teaching and doctrine of the Church—remain the two major ecclesiastical alternatives for churches who do not accept apostolic succession.

Baptism, Eucharist, and Ministry
In 1982, the Faith and Order Commission of the World Council of Churches issued a broad challenge to the traditional views of apostolic succession by publishing the Lima document, *Baptism, Eucharist, and Ministry (BEM)*.[22] This document is a significant achievement for the ecumenical movement in the World Council of Churches, the culmination of work which began in Lausanne in 1927.

Five sections of the document deal with the issue of apostolic succession, Ministry 35–38 and 53(b). Ministry 35 notes that apostolic succession is found in the apostolic tradition of the Church universal, rather than in any one group: 'This succession is an expression of...the continuity of Christ's own mission in which the Church participates'. The pipeline of the laying-on of hands is 'a powerful expression of the continuity of the Church throughout history'. Ministry 36 further asserts that apostolic succession was one of the expressions of the apostolic tradition in the earliest centuries of the Church.[23] Ministry 37 notes the increasing recognition, among churches practicing apostolic succession, of the validity of churches outside their line of succession, which may or may not hold to the episcopal ministry. Ministry 38 notes that this recognition 'does not diminish the importance of the episcopal ministry'. Instead, such churches can 'appreciate the episcopal succession as a sign, though not a guarantee, of the continuity and unity of the Church'.

All in all, Ministry 35–38 draws a rather irenic picture of consensus in the World Council of Churches regarding apostolic succession. The reality was more difficult, however. Most respondents applauded the way *BEM* distinguished between apostolic succession and apostolic tradition, but the approval was not unanimous. Some of the major respondents surveyed took issue with these distinctions. In their official responses, the Roman Catholic and

---

21. John Calvin, *Institutes of the Christian Religion* 4.2.3 (trans. John Allen; 4 vols.; Philadelphia: Presbyterian Board of Christian Education, 1986), II, pp. 304-307.
22. *Baptism, Eucharist, and Ministry* (Faith and Order Paper, 111; Geneva: World Council of Churches, 1982).
23. In the commentary on Ministry 36, the writer appeals directly to 1 Clem. 42–44: 'Clement of Rome linked the mission of the bishop with the sending of Christ by the Father and the sending of the apostles by Christ. This made the bishop a successor of the apostles, ensuring the permanence of the apostolic mission in the Church.' As stated above and demonstrated below, this is a misreading of Clement's statements regarding succession.

Orthodox Churches expressed strong reservations about giving recognition 'to other forms of an orderly transmission of ministry'. Further, they also bridled at the implication that episcopal succession did not guarantee 'continuity and unity': 'Episcopal succession as a guarantee and "effective sign" must be safeguarded as a condition for unity and recognition of ministry'.[24] As a group, Reformed Churches had opposing reservations. The official response of the Church of Norway read in part: 'We cannot see that the validity of ministerial acts performed by ordained persons is dependent on being able to trace back to the first apostles a formal succession of the laying on of hands'.[25]

Ministry 53(b) proved even more controversial. It recognizes as valid the ministries of churches outside the pipeline of succession who are nevertheless 'living in faithful continuity with the apostolic faith and mission'. It then goes on to make the following suggestions to those churches, however:

> These churches [those without episcopal succession of ministry] are asked to realize that the continuity with the Church of the apostles finds profound expression in the successive laying on of hands by bishops and that, though they may not lack the continuity of the apostolic tradition, this sign will strengthen and deepen that continuity. They may need to recover the sign of the episcopal succession.

Reformed and Free Churches found this suggestion disproportionate: churches practicing episcopal succession are 'merely asked to make an act of recognition', while those not practicing episcopal succession are asked to make a structural change by becoming 'grafted into' someone else's line of episcopal succession. The Roman Catholic Church, for its part, refused to recognize the validity of ministries not practicing the succession: 'We believe that ordained ministries require sacramental ordination by a bishop standing in the apostolic succession'.[26]

In summary, the Faith and Order commission noted that, 'For many on both sides of the issue the question of episcopal succession remains the most difficult problem for further dialogue on ministry'.[27]

---

24. *Baptism, Eucharist & Ministry 1982–1990* (Faith and Order Paper, 149; Geneva: WCC Publications, 1990), p. 84. See also the official response of the Roman Catholic Church in Max Thurian (ed.), *Churches Respond to BEM. IV. Official Responses to the 'Baptism, Eucharist and Ministry' Text* (Faith and Order Paper, 137; Geneva: World Council of Churches, 1987), p. 32.

25. *Baptism, Eucharist & Ministry*, p. 84. See also the Church of Norway's full response in Max Thurian (ed.), *Churches Respond to BEM. II. Official Responses to the 'Baptism, Eucharist and Ministry' Text* (Faith and Order Paper, 132; Geneva: World Council of Churches, 1986), p. 121.

26. *Baptism, Eucharist & Ministry*, p. 86. The quote is from the official Roman Catholic response in Thurian (ed.), *Churches Respond to BEM*, IV, p. 35.

27. *Baptism, Eucharist & Ministry*, p. 128. Similarly, 'Behind this criticism [criticism from both sides of the suggestions in 53(b)] lies the fact that there is not an agreement on

The Present State of the Discussion

At present, all sides of the debate remain entrenched in positions that were set in stone centuries ago. The history of conflict over the issue of apostolic succession, and the history of conflicts between the groups which found expression in statements regarding the issue of apostolic succession, has thrown up a fence which keeps the sides from examining the historical and textual evidence from a fresh, open, unbiased (or less biased) perspective. Hear again the words of Everett Ferguson: 'As so often happens to successful arguments, it [the doctrine of apostolic succession] came to be regarded as an article of faith, not just a defense of the truth but a part of the truth itself'.[28]

In sum: the discussion about succession has been and continues to be in an ecclesial context rather than an academic one. The discussion has been and continues to be polemical rather than historical. The need for an academic and historical approach to the problem justifies this study.

2. *Methodology—Reading from the Perspective of the Authorial Audience*

In this study, my approach is essentially redactional, but it differs from traditional redaction criticism in an important way. Instead of seeking authorial intent, I approach these documents from the perspective of the authorial audience, an approach outlined and practiced by Peter J. Rabinowitz and Hans Robert Jauss.[29] This way of reading avoids some of the weaknesses of traditional, 'author-centered' reading by treating intention 'as a matter of social convention rather than of individual psychology':

> In other words, my perspective allows us to treat the reader's attempt to read as the author intended, not as a search for the author's private psyche, but rather as the joining of a particular social/interpretive community...the acceptance of the author's invitation to read in a particular socially constituted way that is shared by the author and his or her expected readers.[30]

---

the necessity of the episcopal ministry and especially of episcopal succession in the church and on its necessity for the sake of mutual recognition of ministries. Such recognition is acknowledged by all to be an essential element in the unity we seek' (p. 129).

28. Ferguson, 'Apostolic Succession', I, pp. 94-95.

29. Hans Robert Jauss, *Toward an Aesthetic of Reception* (Minneapolis: University of Minnesota Press, 1982), pp. 3-45; Peter J. Rabinowitz, 'Truth in Fiction', *Critical Inquiry* 4 (1977), pp. 121-41.

30. Peter J. Rabinowitz, *Before Reading: Narrative Conventions and the Politics of Interpretation* (Ithaca, NY: Cornell University Press, 1987), p. 22. See also *idem*, 'Whirl without End: Audience-Oriented Criticism', in *idem*, G. Douglas Atkins and Laura Morrow, *Contemporary Literary Theory* (Amherst: University of Massachusetts Press, 1989), pp. 81-100.

Rabinowitz defines four audiences for every piece of literature. First is the *actual audience*, external to the text, the flesh-and-blood person(s) experiencing the text. Second is the *authorial audience*, the audience the author envisioned as he/she wrote, which presumably has the knowledge and background needed to understand the text. Third is the *narrative audience*, discrete to the text, to whom the narrator communicates directly. Fourth is the *ideal narrative audience* ('ideal from the narrator's point of view'), discrete to the text, who believe everything the narrator says and see things from his/her point of view.[31]

The authorial audience is thus the author's intended audience, which he/she envisioned while writing. The authorial audience differs from the *implied reader*. The implied reader is discrete to the text, constructed wholly from features therein. The authorial audience (Rabinowitz also refers to this audience as the *intended reader*), on the other hand, is constructed by an interplay between the literary conventions of the text and the conventions of texts and culture around the production and reception of the text. The intended reader is a '[historically] contextualized implied reader'.[32] 'The intended reader may not be marked by or present in the text at all, but may rather be silently *presupposed* by it.' This audience therefore 'is not reducible to textual features but can be determined only by an examination of the interrelation between the text and the context in which the work was produced'.[33]

Likewise, the authorial audience is not the actual historical audience, but a hypothetical audience contemporary to the historical audience. The critic reading a biblical text from the perspective of the authorial audience constructs that audience by reading the biblical text against texts from the milieus surrounding it, comparing the literary conventions in the biblical text with the conventions of contemporaneous texts and society. The critic makes this comparison in hopes of defining the audience the author envisioned while he/she wrote.

The central question the critic will ask regarding this hypothetical audience is: *What allusions does this text make to knowledge external to itself?* In other words: What does this audience know that is pertinent to this text? What do they believe that is pertinent to this text? What values do they hold that are pertinent to this text? With what texts must they be familiar to understand this text? This allows the critic 'to pose questions that the text gave an answer to, and thereby to discover how the contemporary reader [contemporary to the author] could have viewed and understood the work'.[34]

---

31. Rabinowitz, 'Truth', pp. 126-34, quotation from p. 134.
32. Rabinowitz, 'Whirl', p. 85. Jauss, *Toward an Aesthetic*, p. 20, writes that the basis for this type of reading is the historically reconstructed 'experience of the literary work by its readers'.
33. Rabinowitz, 'Whirl', p. 85.
34. Jauss, *Toward an Aesthetic*, p. 28.

Turning to the Pastoral Epistles, I ask: What allusions do the texts make to knowledge external to themselves? First, the texts allude to literary conventions, presupposing that the audience would have knowledge sufficient to decode genre-signals and typological signals so as to read the texts properly. Second, the texts allude to historical and cultural knowledge external to themselves, presupposing that the audience has sufficient knowledge to understand these allusions. I turn my attention now to outlining briefly these allusions, first the allusions to literary conventions and second the allusions to historical and cultural knowledge.

Allusions to Literary Conventions
The Pastoral Epistles presuppose that the authorial audience has knowledge of two specific sets of literary conventions. The texts first presuppose that the authorial audience of the Pastorals understands succession terminology and typology. I will explore this set of conventions in Chapters 2 and 3 of this study.

Second, the texts presuppose that the authorial audience understands standard Graeco-Roman epistolary conventions, particularly regarding the different letter types represented among the Pastoral Epistles. William A. Richards has written the most comprehensive recent study of these conventions, in which he also applies the result of his exploration to the Pastorals.[35] Building on the works of David Aune[36] and Stanley Stowers,[37] which are themselves built on the work of the ancient epistolary theorists, Richards does two things pertinent to this section of my study. First, he proposes a new two-part system of categorization for ancient letters. The first part of the system, based on Aune's work, accounts for 'the audience the text presumes for itself'. The second part of the system, based on Stowers's work, accounts

---

35. William A. Richards, *Difference and Distance in Post-Pauline Christianity: An Epistolary Analysis of the Pastorals* (Studies in Biblical Literature, 44; New York: Peter Lang, 2002).

36. David Aune, *The New Testament in its Literary Environment* (LEC, 8; Philadelphia: Westminster Press, 1987), pp. 161-62. Aune lists the following letter types: '(1) letters of friendship; (2) family letters; (3) letters of praise and blame; (4) hortatory letters; (5) letters of recommendation (or mediation); and (6) accusing, apologetic, and accounting letters'.

37. Stanley K. Stowers, *Letter Writing in Greco-Roman Antiquity* (LEC, 5; Philadelphia: Westminster Press, 1986), pp. 49-173. Stowers lists the following letter types: Letters of Friendship, Family Letters, Letters of Praise and Blame, Letters of Exhortation and Advice, Letters of Mediation, and Accusing, Apologetic, and Accounting Letters. He subdivides the Letters of Exhortation and Advice into seven subgroups: Paraenetic Letters (Exhortation and Dissuasion), Letters of Advice, Protreptic Letters (Exhortation to a Way of Life), Letters of Admonition, Letters of Rebuke, Letters of Reproach, and Letters of Consolation.

for the apparent function of the letters.[38] Second, Richards analyzes the content/rhetoric and the apparent presupposed audience of each of the Pastorals and classifies each of the letters. In terms of content, he finds each of the letters to be deliberative and primarily paraenetic, although Titus does have some epideictic elements.

In terms of audience, Richards notes that all three are public letters (i.e. they presuppose an audience larger than just the individual named as the recipient), but each approaches this audience differently. *First Timothy* focuses on first-person instructions and admonitions for both the recipient (second-person) and the Church the recipient leads (third-person). The balance of first-, second-, and third-person matches Stirewalt's description of the Letter-Essay.[39] Thus Richards classifies 1 Timothy as a Deliberative (paraenetic) Letter-Essay, which contains instruction and admonishment for both the recipient and the larger audience (the community) behind the recipient.[40] *Second Timothy* carries a more personal tone, with friendly clichés (e.g. 'I long to see you') and terms of endearment in the opening (e.g. ἀγαπητῷ τέκνῳ). Yet the titles that Paul needs to claim for himself and the second-person plural verb in the closing evince the letter's public nature. The letter does not contain the same third-person admonitions as 1 Timothy (thus it is not a Letter-Essay), and it is too personal for an Official letter. Richards thus classifies 2 Timothy as a Literary Deliberative (paraenetic) Letter. The audience is more focused than the entire community (which is in view in 1 Timothy), however: 2 Timothy aims at those in the community who 'can put [themselves] in the recipient's place', namely those serving and leading in the community or aspiring to do so.[41] *Titus* has an expanded opening, weighted with terse allusions to topics and issues which will be explored in the letter—and all before the recipient is even named. Titus is an 'Official communication in which a superior authorizes a subordinate for work entrusted to him or her...[which] "paves the way" for the agent acting on the letter-writer's behalf'. Richards thus classifies Titus as an Official Deliberative (paraenetic) Letter, an open letter to the community written to authorize Titus for the work entrusted to him.[42]

38. Richards, *Difference and Distance*, pp. 55-57, 59-60, respectively.
39. Martin L. Stirewalt, 'The Form and Function of the Greek Letter-Essay', in K.P. Donfried (ed.), *The Romans Debate* (Peabody, MA: Hendrickson, rev. edn, 1991), pp. 147-71, writes, 'The letter-setting behind the letter-essay is triangular, I-thou-they...the writer of the letter-essay holds both the "thou" and the "they" in mind'. Other features in 1 Timothy that fit the Letter-Essay sub-genre are the statement of purpose in the opening, the *parousia* statement (3.14-15; 4.13), and the use of the vocative case to address the recipient when moving from the body of the letter to the closing.
40. Richards, *Difference and Distance*, pp. 179-82.
41. Richards, *Difference and Distance*, p. 133.
42. Richards, *Difference and Distance*, pp. 93-96.

Each of the letters—1 Timothy as a Deliberative Letter-Essay, 2 Timothy as a Literary Deliberative Letter, and Titus as an Official Deliberative Letter—requires different interpretive moves on the part of its audience. In using the different epistolary types, the author assumes that the audience is competent to make these moves. In other words, when the text calls for different 'games' (by using different epistolary types), it assumes that the audience will know the different rules of play for each.

Allusions to Knowledge External to the Text
The Pastorals not only presuppose the audience's knowledge of the literary conventions discussed above. Each of the texts also alludes to knowledge external to the text which the authorial audience must have to read the letters properly. The texts make these allusions without offering sufficient explanation for a reader who is unfamiliar with the objects involved. These allusions leave a gap. The texts thus presuppose that the authorial audience possesses the necessary information regarding those objects to fill in those gaps.

Among other items of knowledge external to the text, 1 Timothy presupposes that the readers have knowledge of Paul's pre-Christian life, his conversion and commissioning, and his missionary practices, including his working relationship with Timothy. Among other items of knowledge external to the text, 2 Timothy presupposes that the readers have knowledge of Paul's missionary career, particularly his suffering and his working relationship with Timothy. Among other items of knowledge external to the text, Titus presupposes that the readers have knowledge of Paul's authority, his missionary career and praxis, and his relationship with Titus. In Chapters 4 and 5 below, I will explore how these allusions function, and show how the knowledge that the authorial audience brings to the text—their knowledge of Paul and Timothy and Titus, and their knowledge of literary conventions relating to succession and of epistolary conventions—intersects with the text of the Pastorals itself.

Summary
In this section, I have started exploring the knowledge that the authorial audience brought with them to the text, knowledge essential for their proper understanding of the text. The text presupposes that they brought with them knowledge of Paul and his work, his conversion and commissioning, and his praxis and authority. They also brought with them knowledge of Timothy and Titus, how Paul used his associates in the course of his ministry. The text further presupposes that they brought with them knowledge of ancient Graeco-Roman epistolary conventions. This knowledge kept them from misreading the types of letters which the Pastorals present—they knew the rules of reading the different types, so they played the game properly. Finally,

the text presupposes that they brought with them understanding of literary conventions dealing with succession. In the next two chapters, I outline and define those conventions.

3. *This Study's Argument*

In this study, I will use Rabinowitz's approach to analyze the function of succession in the Pastoral Epistles, and the contribution this analysis makes to understanding each of the documents in entirety.

This study contains six chapters. In the present chapter, I have provided a standard introduction to the project. I have outlined goals and methodology, sketched a history of the debate, and summarized the project's contribution to scholarly understanding and application of the New Testament. I devote the remainder of this chapter to outlining the balance of the monograph.

In the second and third chapters, I survey ancient texts which describe the function of succession. Succession is mentioned or appealed to in a number of ancient texts. In this study, my textbase includes 60 ancient Mediterranean texts, distilled from Graeco-Roman, Jewish, and Christian sources from before 200 CE, which not only refer to succession between people but also have as a central and explicit concern the *function* of succession (what succession achieved, its desired outcome). This theme (that succession functioned to achieve or accomplish something) is not the only way the authorial audience would have understood succession, since I do not find it explicitly present in all references to succession. The theme may indeed be implied in other references to succession, but I chose to treat only those passages in which the function of succession is prominently referred to, either explicit or strongly implied. But it is one significant way in which the authorial audience would have understood succession.

In these chapters, I show how ancient Graeco-Roman (Chapter 2) and Jewish and Christian texts (Chapter 3) all appealed to succession in much the same way. I show that succession had much the same functions across the milieus. I outline the textual and typological features common to succession stories, and explore the function of succession in several ancient texts from various milieus. At the end of the chapters, I compare and contrast the different texts against one another within and across the milieus. I will show many significant similarities and one significant difference between the function of succession in the Graeco-Roman texts and the function of succession in the Jewish and Christian texts.

Chapters 4, 5, and 6 comprise my treatment of the Pastoral Epistles. In the fourth and fifth chapters, I examine the letters from the perspective of the authorial audience, specifically against the background provided by Chapters 2 and 3. I treat 1 Timothy in Chapter 4 and 2 Timothy and Titus in Chapter 5.

With regard to each of the letters, I ask two central questions. First: Would the authorial audience have found evidence of succession in this document? And if so, which relationships would they have read/understood in terms of succession? Second: If the authorial audience would have inferred succession in a relationship, how does that succession function? What would they have understood that succession to achieve for the people involved in the succession and for the people around it? *Prima facie*, the Pastoral Epistles are letters from Paul to Timothy and Titus, young missionaries who were engaged in work Paul had assigned to them. All three letters center on the importance of safeguarding the integrity of the Church's teaching, although they emphasize different aspects and prescribe different actions with regard to that teaching. In two of the letters, the authorial audience would have heard immediate cues that succession was in play: these include technical language and typological features germane to succession. In these letters, Paul's relationship to the recipients would have been understood in terms of succession. The third letter, by contrast, contains fewer of the features from which the authorial audience would have inferred succession and does not develop to the same depth the description of Paul's relationship to the recipient.

The sixth chapter is the conclusion of my treatment of the Pastoral Epistles. In that chapter, I offer a brief reading of the letters to Timothy and Titus from the perspective of the authorial audience, based on the knowledge and expectations they would have drawn from their texts. Here I will suggest a central theme that can provide a unifying center for reading the Pastorals. This theme is Paul's departure and the problems and issues his absence raises for his churches. The center of my reading is how the Pastorals utilize succession to meet those challenges.

In the seventh chapter, I will draw conclusions from the study. I will outline the results, and their implications for current discussion of the Pastoral Epistles, other early Christian literature in which succession plays an important part (e.g. 1 Clement, Irenaeus), church leadership, and the nature of Christian ministry. I will also formulate a list of issues raised by the study which require further research.

2

THE ANCIENT UNDERSTANDING OF SUCCESSION, PART 1: BACKGROUND AND GRAECO-ROMAN TEXTS

In the penultimate section of the previous chapter, I began to describe the authorial audience of the Pastoral Epistles. I noted that the text of these letters assumes that their audience has knowledge, external to the epistles themselves, of cultural and historical data, epistolary conventions, and literary conventions relating to succession. In the present chapter, I turn to defining these literary conventions relating to succession. I will here explore the way succession was used in ancient Mediterranean texts, and through that exploration gain an understanding of how an ancient audience, such as the authorial audience of the Pastoral Epistles, would have reacted when receiving texts in which succession features prominently.

Ancient Mediterranean writers often appealed to succession when describing the interrelationships of rulers and leaders (political, military, judicial, scholastic, religious), practitioners of a craft or skill (such as magic, rhetoric, fishing), monastics, and possessors of knowledge or tradition. They also occasionally used the concept when describing the relationships between groups and nations, which is of a piece with the ancient application of βίος to groups as well as individuals.[1]

To date, the most exhaustive description of the ancient Mediterranean literature referring to succession is a project on which I collaborated with Charles Talbert.[2] In those articles, we noted that succession stories tend to have a set form and similar typological features. The three consistent components are: first, naming what is passed on (i.e. the object of succession); second, describing 'the symbolic acts which accompany the succession (e.g. transfer of clothing or other possessions; transfer of glory, spirit, authority/ rule; laying on of hands; anointing)', to which we later added a speech of

---

1. Three examples of ancient biographies of groups (instead of individuals) are Dikaiarchus's *Bios Hellados*, Varro's *De vita populi Romani*, and Iamblichus's *On the Pythagorean Life* (Περὶ τοῦ Πυθαγορείου βίου).
2. Talbert and Stepp, 'Succession' (see p. 1 n. 4, above).

commissioning;³ and third, describing phenomena that confirm 'that the succession has taken place (e.g. the people's acclamation; repetition by the successor of acts that replicate the type of thing performed by his predecessor)'.⁴

We also noted that references to succession in such literature tend to be marked by certain characteristic expressions.⁵ First are references to the successor, who is described as the one who comes after (μετά) a predecessor, or the one who takes a predecessor's place (the one ἀντί the predecessor), or the one who succeeds a predecessor (διαδέχομαι, to be διάδοχος); or the one who follows a predecessor (to be a hearer [ἀκούω or διακούω] or disciple [μαθητής] of a predecessor).

Second are references to the predecessor's action in passing on the object of succession to the successor. Writers refer to this act in terms of giving/delivering (παραδίδωμι); bequeathing (διατίθημι, ἀπολείπω, καταλείπω); appointing (καθίστημι, συνίστημι, χειροτονέω, ἀναδείκνυμι, ἀποδείκνυμι); entrusting (παρατίθημι, πιστεύω, ἐγχειρίζω); or casting/putting something on the successor (ἐπ' αὐτόν). Third are references to the act of receiving what is passed on in the succession. Writers refer to this in terms of receiving (διαδέχομαι, ἐκδέχομαι, παραλαμβάνω, λαμβάνω) or taking upon himself/herself (ἐπ' αὐτόν).

Fourth are references to the object of succession, what is passed on. Some important objects mentioned in succession are a kingdom (βασιλεία, τυραννίς); rule/authority/leadership (ἀρχή, ἡγεμονία, μοναρχία, δυναστεία, ναυαρχία); a succession (διαδοχή); a school (σχολή); disciples (μαθηταί); instruction (παραθήκη); tradition (παράδοσις); ministry (λειτουργία); and priesthood (ἱερωσύνη).

Using the tools that Talbert and I have provided, I can describe and compare succession stories in a couple of different ways. First, I can analyze and compare their forms and typological features. Second, I can analyze and compare the language that is used to describe the actants in the primary act of succession.

I can render some of the features of this second type of analysis graphically:

---

3. Talbert and Stepp, 'Succession: Part 2', p. 171.
4. Talbert and Stepp, 'Succession: Part 1', p. 163. The examples and quotes are from their summary of Jewish texts, which precedes an analysis of Graeco-Roman and Christian texts in which they find the same components. After surveying texts from all three milieus, they conclude: 'Since the same three components are found in all the stories of succession, whether they be Jewish, Greco-Roman, or Christian, it seems reasonable to conclude that there was a conventional form of a succession story in Mediterranean antiquity' (I, p. 167).
5. Talbert and Stepp, 'Succession: Part 1', pp. 149-54.

2. Background and Graeco-Roman Texts

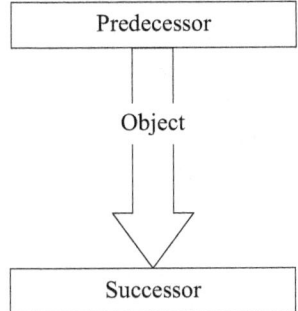

Figure 1. *Illustrating the Primary Act of Succession*

1. *Describing the Function of Succession*

This second type of analysis opens the door for a third way of describing and comparing succession stories. To this point, I have discussed the primary act of succession itself (Predecessor → Object → Successor). But wrapped up in this exchange between predecessor and successor, I sometimes find a second exchange that speaks of the purpose or result of the succession. This second exchange sometimes involves the same parties as the primary exchange, and sometimes it does not. It must be described functionally: What did the succession event achieve? Why was it necessary? What did the predecessor hope to accomplish? How were people affected by this succession? This second exchange is not always referred to, explicitly or implicitly, in ancient accounts: texts *can* simply mention the fact of succession. Those texts that do mention both the fact and the function of succession are the object of the remainder of this inquiry.

To illustrate how a second exchange can be included in a simple account of succession, allow me to propose a hypothetical situation. Suppose I am the president of my neighborhood homeowners association. As president, I have successfully crusaded to protect the appearance of my neighborhood by forbidding basketball goals in driveways, unmowed lawns, old cars and trucks parked on the street, etc. When my time in office expires, I ensure that my neighborhood will continue to be tidy by choosing a successor who will carry on this agenda.

This hypothetical succession event involves at least *two* exchanges, two transactions, not one. In the first exchange, the act of succession, I (the predecessor) pass the presidency of the homeowner's association (the object) on to the next president (the successor). I also pass on a second object to my successor, namely my intention or agenda for the neighborhood, which I hope the successor will continue to realize: thus the act of succession has a complex object, two objects intertwined, office *and* agenda. In the second exchange, which must be described functionally, I (the sender) give a well-kept appearance (a benefit/consequence) to the neighborhood (the receiver).[6] The two exchanges are wrapped together. No analysis or discussion of this succession is complete which does not account for both exchanges, and no comparison of succession accounts is complete which does not consider how succession functions in those stories.

Allow me to borrow and adapt another device from structuralism to illustrate. The two exchanges can best be described in terms of axes and actants:

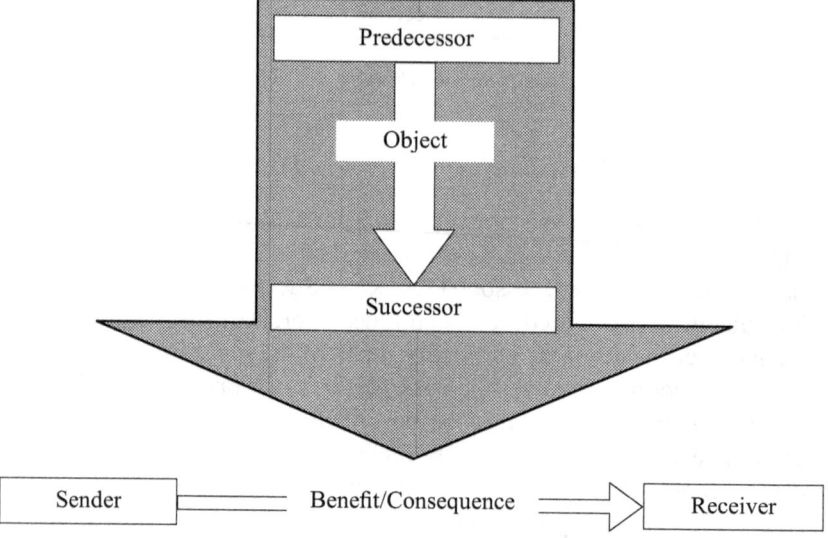

Figure 2. *Illustrating both the Primary Act and the Function of Succession*

The boxes in the diagram designate the *actants*, the entities in the narrative that act. The clear arrows designate the *axes* along which their transactions take place. The axis that runs from the predecessor to the successor is the axis of succession, which describes the succession act itself, be it simple (i.e. involving a single object) or complex (i.e. involving multiple objects). The axis that runs from sender to receiver is the axis of function, which describes the purpose or result of succession. With this model, I can more completely render the facts and function of a succession story.

I can illustrate the above hypothetical succession story graphically:

---

6. Here, I use structuralist language ('sender', 'receiver') as a descriptive tool, but I am not here using or endorsing structuralism. For the terminology, see Daniel Patte, *The Religious Dimensions of Biblical Texts: Greimas's Structural Semiotics and Biblical Exegesis* (Atlanta: Scholars Press, 1990), pp. 54-60.

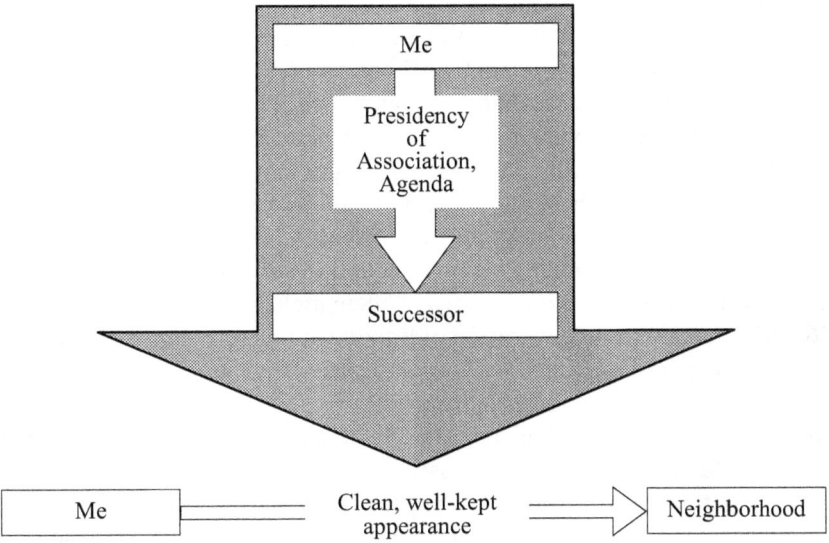

Figure 3. *Illustration of Hypothetical Succession,
Showing both the Primary Act of Succession and the Function(s) of Succession*

As the illustration shows, in this scenario I passed on two objects to my successor, not one: my office and my agenda. Through this passing on, I achieved a particular function—I gave a benefit to the neighborhood, a continued clean and well-kept appearance. I stated explicitly that the neighborhood had enjoyed this benefit under my leadership, and I hoped that it would continue to do so under my successor. Thus succession in this case functions to ensure *continuity of effect*, the effect of my leadership continues.

Thus far in this chapter, I have shown two things. First, I have shown that succession can involve not one but two actions, for example both the simple passing on of office or place and also a function or a purpose which is achieved through the passing on of office or place. Second, I have shown that these actions can together be illustrated graphically, in terms of axes and actants.

2. *Graeco-Roman Texts Describing the Function of Succession*

Several years ago, in preparation for the articles referred to above,[7] I began gathering ancient Mediterranean texts that referred to succession. I searched for references roughly antedating 200 CE, choosing that time period so as to best reflect the ideational world of the New Testament. I gathered references by looking for texts in which I suspected succession to be part of the picture

7. Talbert and Stepp, 'Succession'.

—for example, stories about rulers and philosophers, especially relating to their deaths; stories about Joshua and Moses. I also gathered references by searching for key terms (such as those outlined on p. 16, above) in the *Thesaurus linguae graecae*.[8] For this study, I gathered a textbase of 60 passages in which the function of succession is a prominent (explicit or strongly implicit) and primary concern. These passages comprise this study's comparative sample. This is not to imply that the function of succession is not a concern in the other passages referring to succession but not included in the sample.[9] I simply did not regard the function of succession as being prominent enough in those texts to warrant their inclusion. For example, Gen. 36.33-39 contains a succession list of Edomite kings. The entirety of Genesis 36 focuses on how God blessed Esau and made him a nation. In context, the successions in the list apparently function to realize God's agenda/promise. But in the text itself I find no explicit or strongly implicit information regarding the function of the succession, and have therefore not included this passage in this study's comparative sample. I selected for this study's comparative sample only those passages where the function of succession is an explicit (or strongly implicit) and primary concern.

In the remainder of this chapter, I survey the 28 Graeco-Roman texts from my textbase which describe the function of succession. I have arranged them in categories according to their object. They describe the passing on of leadership or rule, the passing on of headship of a philosophical school (a special subset of the first group), the passing on of a task, the passing on of knowledge or tradition, and the passing on of possessions. I address each group of texts in chronological order within the categories. I will survey each text in hopes of defining the functions that succession served. In this chapter and the next, I have numbered each text sequentially across the chapters. I hope thereby to facilitate comparisons within the textbase.

Texts Describing the Passing on of Leadership/Rule
Text 1: Herodotus 3.53. Herodotus was a Greek historian of the fifth century BCE. In 3.53 of his *History*, he records the story of Periander's relationship with his youngest son and chosen successor, Lycophron. Lycophron hated Periander because he (Periander) had killed Lycophron's mother, Melissa. Unable to reconcile with his son, Periander exiled him to Corcyra.

---

8. *Thesaurus linguae graecae* (Thesaurus Linguae Graecae; California: Irvine, 1996).

9. Nor am I asserting that function as I have defined it would be the only reason for which an ancient Mediterranean text would appeal to succession. For example, in *Gallic Wars* 6.13, Caesar tells the story of how, when a Druid chieftain dies, his potential successors fight one another for the right to take his place (to succeed him, Lat. *succedit*). There seems to be no prominent causal or functional emphasis in the mention of succession here, other than to show a general sense of connectedness.

Years later, Periander realized that his ability to lead and govern was slipping away because of his age. He regarded his oldest son unfit to inherit the τυραννίς, but Lycophron—though estranged from him—he regarded as having more fit character and intelligence. He attempted to find a way for Lycophron to succeed him in Corinth, so as to keep the throne in his family and lineage. One of his attempts involved sending his daughter to persuade Lycophron to reconcile with his father:

> Brother, would you see the sovereignty pass to others, and our father's house plundered, rather than come hence and have it for your own?... Despotism is a hard thing to hold; many covet it, and our father is now old and past his prime; give not what is your estate to others. (Herodotus 3.53 [Godley, LCL])[10]

This passage centers on Periander's property—his tyranny—and the means by which he seeks to maintain possession of it. He desires a successor who will inherit the property, thus (in a sense) maintaining his ownership after his death. If Lycophron refuses to succeed his father, or if that succession is thwarted by a third party (as actually happened),[11] the τυραννίς and the property will fall out of the family's possession or into chaos. The passage does not focus on Periander's manner of ruling, nor on the effect of his rule, nor on any specific agenda of his. The focus is squarely on who will possess his property when he dies. Thus, in this passage, succession of leadership/rule ensures continuity of possession.

Figure 4 (see next page) maps the exchanges Periander envisions.

Text 2: Herodotus 5.90-92. In 5.90-92, Herodotus records a debate between the Spartans, Lacedaemonians, Corinthians, and others, over whether or not they should support Hippias in his quest to be set up as tyrant over Athens. The parties are at war with Athens, and are afraid of her growing power and independence. Further, they have received oracles indicating that the Athenians cannot be trusted. Some had hoped, by setting up a despot, to weaken Athens's threat to themselves, her neighbors. As the debate unfolds, Socles the Corinthian protests any support for Hippias by recounting a part of Corinthian history, the story of the bloodthirsty Corinthian tyrant Cypselus and his even more bloodthirsty son and heir, the aforementioned Periander.

---

10. For commentary, see James Romm, *Herodotus* (New Haven: Yale University Press, 1998).

11. As Herodotus tells it, Lycophron finally consented to succeed his father when Periander offered to exile himself to Corcyra if Lycophron would come to Corinth and take the τυραννίς. When the people of Corcyra heard of this plan, they put Lycophron to death in hopes of keeping Periander from taking residence in their city. Note that the fact that the succession is thwarted does not stand in the way of our analyzing its hoped-for function.

22 *Leadership Succession in the World of the Pauline Circle*

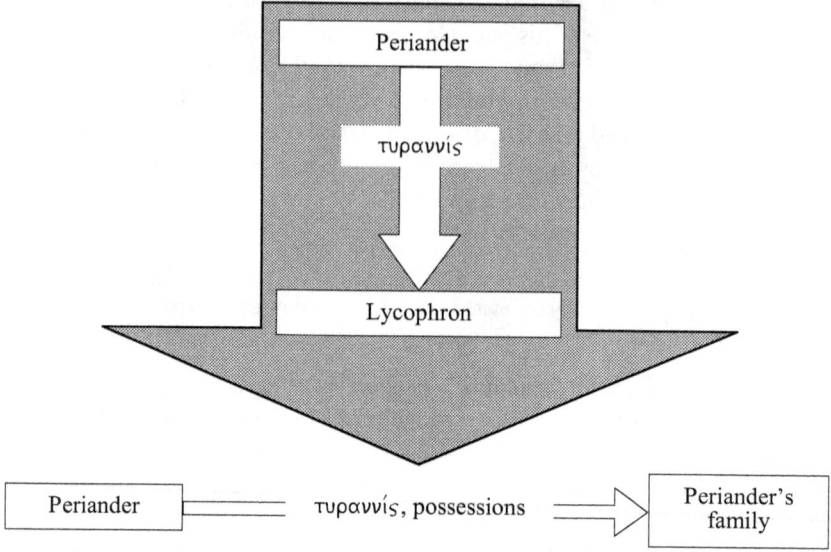

Figure 4. *The Function of Succession in Herodotus 3.53*

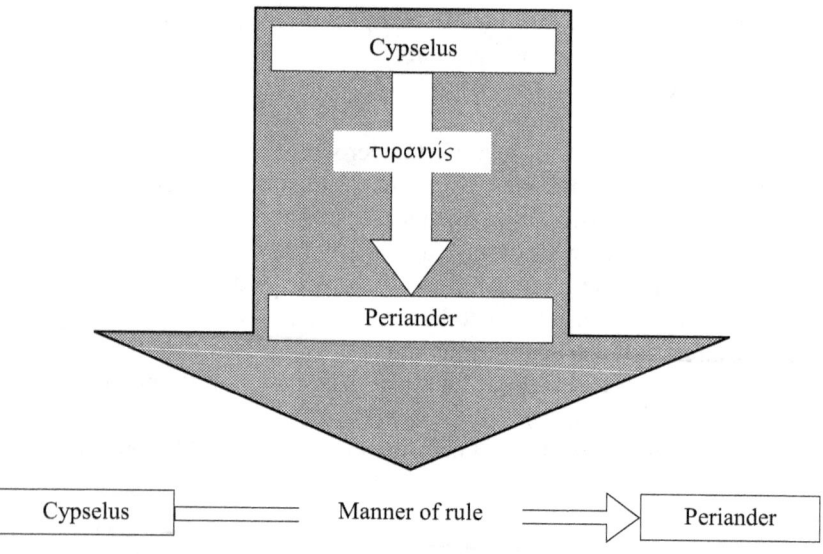

Figure 5. *The Function of Succession in Herodotus 5.90-92*

2. Background and Graeco-Roman Texts

Cypselus was a violent and harsh ruler who killed and robbed his own people. Periander, upon succession to the throne (διάδοχός τε τῆς τυραννίδος ὁ παῖς Περίανδρος γίνεται [5.92]) was at first not so harsh, but he soon fell under the influence of Thrasybulus of Miletus. Periander sent a messenger to Thrasybulus, asking how he (Periander) could best rule his kingdom. In response, Thrasybulus took the messenger out into a field that was nearly ready to harvest, and as he walked along and talked to the messenger, he systematically destroyed the best stalks of grain, rendering them useless.

The messenger returned and told Periander about Thrasybulus's behavior, and Periander understood the message: the safest way for Periander to rule was to destroy any Corinthian who might challenge him. And so Periander became a true successor of Cypselus, his father, by inheriting both his father's τυραννίς and his father's manner of ruling.[12] Immediately after the story of Thrasybulus's message to Periander, Herodotus has Socles say, 'Whatever act of slaughter or banishment Cypselus had left undone, that did Periander bring to accomplishment... Know then, ye Lacedaemonians, that such a thing is despotism and such are its deeds' (5.92).

Compare this text with Text 1: Herodotus 3.53 above. Whereas the above passage dealt with an intended consequence of succession, there is no indication of the predecessor's intention here. Thus succession may or may not involve intent/purpose, and may produce unintended (or not particularly intended) results. As for the result itself: not only is the τυραννίς passed from father to son, the son also inherits his father's violent temperament and manner of rule. The center is the characteristic attitudes and actions shared by predecessor and successor, not the property or the effects of the rule on its subjects (although the effect is central to the framing story).

In this passage, succession of leadership/rule ensures continuity of manner (i.e. it ensures that the successor will share characteristic attitudes/actions of the predecessor). By the change in his manner of ruling to a style more like his father's, Periander truly becomes his father's successor.

The two exchanges in this succession event can be illustrated as in Fig. 5.

Text 3: Plato, Laws *6.769c*. In *Laws*, Plato expands on themes from his *Republic*. He shows a greater concern for what laws should be and how they should be administered (thus the title) than in the earlier work. In 6.769, the Athenian is describing the proper administration of laws. He uses this parable:

> You know the endless labour which painters expend on their pictures—they are always putting in or taking out colours, or whatever be the term which artists employ; they seem as if they would never cease touching up their works, which are always being made brighter and more beautiful.

12. In structuralist terms, Thrasybulus would not be Periander's predecessor but rather a helper in the exchange between Cypselus and Periander.

> ...Suppose that someone had a mind to paint a figure in the most beautiful manner, in the hope that his work instead of losing would always improve as time went on—do you not see that being a mortal, unless he leaves some one to succeed him (καταλείψει διάδοχον) who will correct the flaws which time may introduce, and be able to add what is left imperfect through the defect of the artist, and who will further brighten up and improve the picture, all his great labour will last but a short time?
>
> *Cleinias*: True.
>
> *Athenian*: And is not the aim of the legislator similar? First, he desires that his laws should be written down with all possible exactness; in the second place, as time goes on and he has made an actual trial of his decrees, will he not find omissions? Do you imagine that there ever was a legislator so foolish as not to know that many things are necessarily omitted, which someone coming after him (ἃ δεῖ τινὰ ξυνεπόμενον) must correct ([δεῖ] ἐπανορθοῦν), if the constitution and the order of government is not to deteriorate, but to improve in the state which he has established? (Plato, *Laws* 6.769c [Jowett])[13]

Note first that there are two succession stories here—that of the painter and his successors, and that of the legislator and his successors. In terms of the function of succession, the stories are the same—which is, after all, central to Plato's analogy. Note second that the primary act of succession in the main story (of the succession of legislators) has a complex object: the legislator passes on both the authority to test and rewrite laws (leadership/rule) and his agenda for constantly improving the laws and making them appropriate for situations beyond their original conception and beyond his lifetime and ability to personally oversee the laws' appropriateness.

Compare this text with Texts 1 and 2 above. The first text focused on the object of succession (property), how possession was to be kept. The second text focused on characteristic attitudes/actions shared by the predecessor and successor. This third text focuses again on the object of succession. And again, the primary story (the legislator, not the painter) references succession of leadership/rule. But what are its functions?

The text accents the benefit that succession gives to the law itself, or laws in general: through the succession of legislators, the institution (the law) will always be kept appropriate for the different situations the society it serves must face. Thus succession serves to ensure continued institutional vitality. The text also accents the continued effect of appropriate laws, which is only possible because of succession. Further, the text implies that the successor will share the predecessor's characteristic attitude toward the law (namely the predecessor's desire that the law always be appropriate, and thus should be 'fine-tuned' as the situation warrants).

---

13. The Greek text is from Plato, *Laws* (trans. R.G. Bury; LCL; Cambridge, MA: Harvard University Press, 1952). For commentary, see R.F. Stalley, *An Introduction to Plato's Laws* (Indianapolis: Hackett, 1983).

2. Background and Graeco-Roman Texts

Note that the difference between continuity of effect and continued institutional vitality is rather nuanced: in fact, continued institutional vitality seems to be a subset of continuity of effect, separated only by point of view. From the perspective of the sender, the law is kept appropriate, thus the institution is benefited. From the perspective of the receiver, the benefit continues to be enjoyed. Further comparisons will perhaps help better define these categories.

Succession in this text appears, then, to serve three functions. It ensures continued institutional vitality by ensuring that the law is kept appropriate. It ensures continuity of effect, in that the people enjoy the benefits of appropriate laws under both the predecessor and the successor(s). It also ensures continuity of manner, since the predecessor and successor share a characteristic attitude or activity.

I can map the primary exchanges thus:

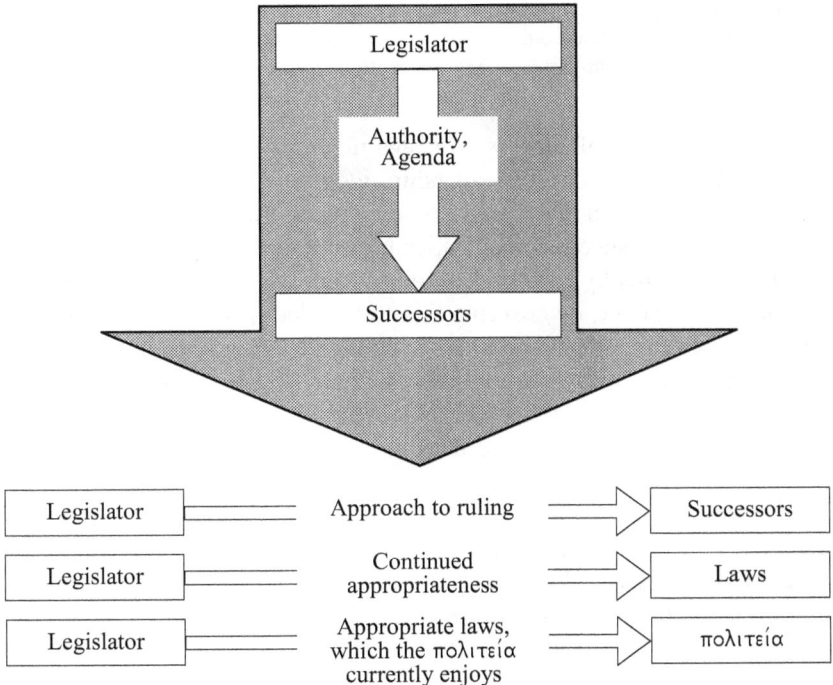

Figure 6. *The Functions of Succession in Plato,* Laws *6.769c*

Text 4: Aristotle, Politics *1293a.13-30.* In *Politics* 1293a.13-30 §4.5.6, Aristotle describes the different kinds of oligarchies. In the first, many people possess property, but no one has a very large amount. Every property owner participates in government, and since there are many participants (none of whom is rich enough to be idle, none poor enough to need to be cared for by the state) and since all work, they must depend on the laws to rule. The result is a government of laws rather than a government of men (1293a.13-20 §4.5.6).

In the second kind of oligarchy, fewer people possess property and each owner possesses more. These 'select' the people who will go into government. They are not strong enough to rule without the law, so they make laws that conform with their best interests (1293a.21-26 §4.5.7). In the third kind of oligarchy, there are even fewer property owners, and each has a proportionately greater share of wealth. These keep offices to themselves by proclaiming through law that the offices are hereditary:

> [Speaking initially of the second type of oligarchy]... The stronger they are, the more power they claim, ...they make the law represent their wishes. When this power is intensified by a further diminution of their numbers and increase of their property, there arises a third and further stage of oligarchy, in which the governing class keeps the offices in their own hands, and the law ordains that the son shall succeed the father (κατὰ νόμον δὲ τὸν κελεύοντα τῶν τελευτώντων διαδέχεσθαι τοὺς υἱούς). (Aristotle, *Politics* 1293a.23-30 §4.5.7-8 [Jowett])[14]

Note that the object of succession is again complex: what the predecessor passes on is both office (thus leadership/rule) and a particular agenda, self-benefiting rule, by which the predecessors seek to '[keep] the offices in their own hands'. Here, succession of leadership/rule serves three functions. First, it promotes stability by ensuring continuity of possession. Second, it ensures continuity of manner, by ensuring that the predecessor(s) and successor(s) approach characteristic tasks with the same attitude, in the same manner. Third, succession ensures continuity of effect—those who are in power are able to continue using their power to benefit themselves.

Figure 7 (opposite) illustrates the central exchanges in this succession.

Text 5: Aristotle, Athenian Constitution *28.1-4*. In his discussion of the Athenian Constitution, Aristotle remarks on the quality of leaders who served Athens over the years. When Pericles led the δῆμος things went well, but after his death the quality of leaders steadily declined (28.1). Cleon was the next head of the δῆμος after Pericles. He was 'impetuous' and improper in his conduct, and did 'the most to corrupt the people' (μάλιστα διαφθεῖραι τὸν δῆμον) (28.3). Subsequent leaders instituted the dole, and so on, further corrupting the people by buying their votes.

---

14. Greek text from Aristotle, *Politics* (trans. H. Rackham; LCL; London: William Heinemann, 1932); see also J.T. Bookman, 'The Wisdom of the Many: An Analysis of the Arguments of Books III and IV of Aristotle's "Politics" ', *History of Political Thought* 13 (1992), pp. 1-12; Michael Davis, *The Politics of Philosophy: A Commentary on Aristotle's Politics* (Lanham, MD: Rowman & Littlefield, 1996).

2. Background and Graeco-Roman Texts

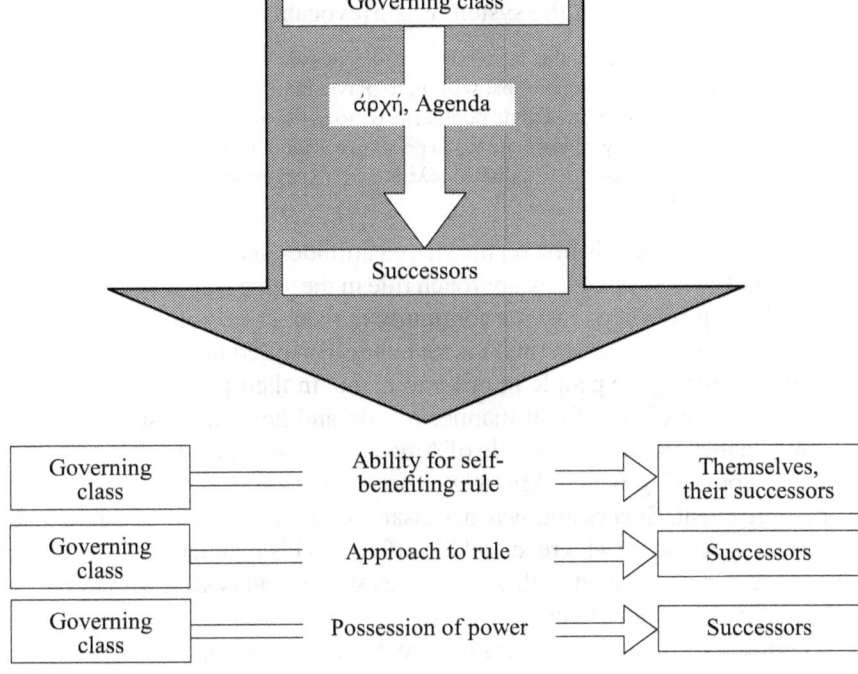

Figure 7. *The Functions of Succession in Aristotle,* Politics *1293a.13-30*

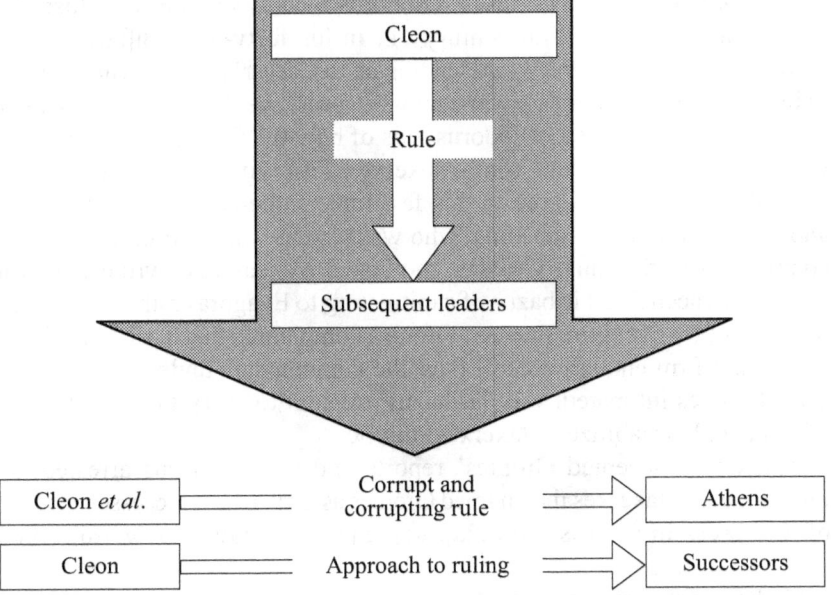

Figure 8. *The Functions of Succession in Aristotle,* Athenian Constitution *28.1-4*

Once the citizens discovered they could vote largesse from the public treasury for themselves, the system was irrevocably broken:

> From Cleon onward, the leadership of the people was handed on in an unbroken line by the men most willing to play a bold part and to gratify the many with an eye to immediate popularity (ἀπὸ δὲ [Κλέωντος] ἤδη διεδέχοντο συνεχῶς τὴν δημαγωγίαν οἱ μάλιστα βουλόμενοι θρασύνεσθαι καὶ χαρίζεσθαι τοῖς πολλοῖς πρὸς τὸ παραυτίκα βλέποντες). (Aristotle, *Ath. Cons.* 28.4 [Rackham, LCL])[15]

The focus in this text is first on the shared attitudes and actions of the predecessor and successors—they approach rule in the same way. Thus succession of leadership/rule here ensures continuity in manner (of rule). True successors of Cleon not only inherited his seat, they also ruled in the manner that he ruled, corrupting the people in order to maintain their power. The text also focuses on the effect of that manner of rule and how succession served to complete that effect—the people of Athens were corrupted by this approach to rule, something which Aristotle clearly views as a process and not as a one-time event. Succession was necessary to that process, if Cleon had not had real successors (who received his office and his manner), Athens would not have been corrupted in this way. Thus succession is seen here to ensure the realization of an effect.

Figure 8 (previous page) sets out the exchanges wrapped up in this succession.

Text 6: Diodorus Siculus 15.8-11. Diodorus Siculus was a Roman historian who wrote during the first century CE. In his forty-book Βιβλιοθήκη, he recounts the history of the world leading up to Caesar's Gallic War (54 BCE). In his description of Persia's war against Cyprus, events that took place in the early fourth century BCE, Diodorus tells of how the Cyprian king Evagoras won a favorable settlement from Artaxerxes. Tiribazus, Artaxerxes' supreme general, was about to agree to this favorable settlement, when Orontes—another of Artaxerxes' generals, who was also the king's brother-in-law—complained to the king. Orontes, motivated by jealousy, wrote letters to Artaxerxes accusing Tiribazus of capitulating to Evagoras rather than pressing for victory over him. Further, Orontes complained that Tiribazus did not maintain a firm enough control over the commanders under his authority. This, Orontes intimated, was Tiribazus' attempt to curry favor with them, which could destabilize Artaxerxes' throne.

Artaxerxes accepted Orontes' reports and had Tiribazus arrested and imprisoned. Artaxerxes then named Orontes as Tiribazus's successor as leader of the forces in Cyprus (διαδεξάμενος τὴν ἡγεμονίαν τῶν ἐν τῷ Κύπρῳ

---

15. For commentary, see J.M. Moore, *Aristotle and Xenophon on Democracy and Oligarchy* (Berkeley: University of California Press, 1975).

δυναμένων). But Evagoras proved to be tougher than Orontes had anticipated, and Tiribazus's men hated Orontes for betraying their old commander. So Orontes was eventually forced to make peace on the same terms that he had urged Artaxerxes to arrest Tiribazus over. After his trial, Tiribazus was eventually restored, and Orontes was expelled in shame (Diodorus Siculus 15.8-11 [Sherman, LCL]).[16]

As with Text 5: Aristotle, *Cons. Ath.* 28.1-4, this text focuses on the effect of succession. A comparison between the two is instructive, however: in the previous text, the effect was the culmination of a process intertwined with the succession. Here, the effect apparently would have been realized without the succession, it is seen as being simply handed on from predecessor to successor. Orontes succeeded Tiribazus as military leader, and the outcome of his leadership was the same as the outcome that almost certainly would have come from Tiribazus's leadership—a result favorable to Evagoras.

Thus what we see in this text is how succession of leadership/rule can ensure continuity of effect—the successor achieves the same result that the predecessor would have achieved had the succession not taken place, whether the result is planned for or desired, or not. This differs from realization of effect, as in Text 5: Aristotle, *Cons. Ath.* 28.1-4, because there the effect/result would not have taken place at all without the succession.

I can map the exchanges contained here thus:

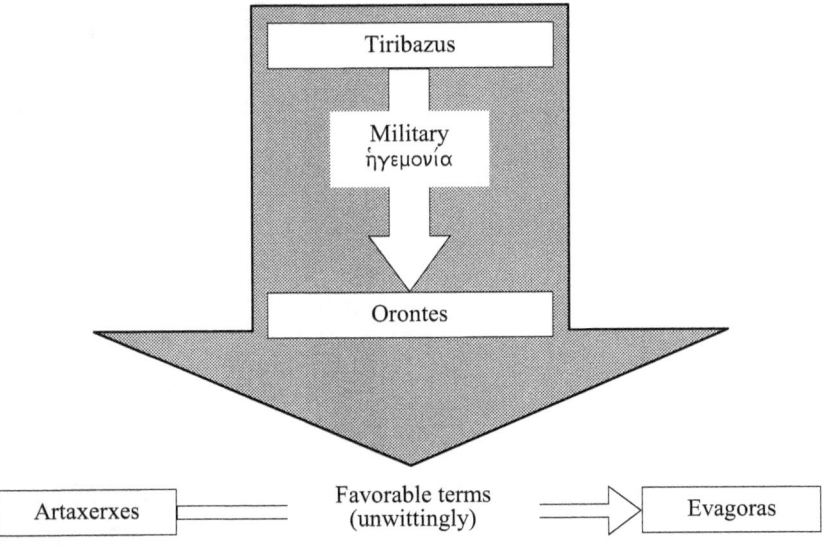

Figure 9. *The Function of Succession in Diodorus Siculus 15.8-11*

16. For commentary, see P.J. Stylianou, *A Historical Commentary on Diodorus Siculus, Book 15* (Oxford: Clarendon Press, 1998); Michael Grant, *Readings in the Classical Historians* (New York: Charles Scribner's Sons, 1992).

Text 7: Diodorus Siculus 15.93.1. In a section on the Persian throne, Diodorus tells of the succession of Artaxerxes I. When that king died, according to Diodorus, he passed on both his name and his βασιλείαν to his successor: 'The King of Persia (Artaxerxes I) died, …and Ochus, who now assumed a new name, Artaxerxes, succeeded to the kingdom' (βασιλεὺς τῶν Περσῶν ἐτελεύτησεν…τὴν δὲ βασιλείαν διεδέξατο ˀΩχος ὁ μετονομασθεὶς Ἀρταξέρξης). The people, because of their respect for Artaxerxes I, had asked Ochus his successor to take the same name. In so doing, they hoped to get for themselves continuing skilled, benevolent rule in the tradition of Artaxerxes I. The predecessor 'ruled well' (καλῶς βεβασιλευκότος) and was 'altogether peace-loving and fortunate' (παντελῶς εἰρηνικοῦ καὶ ἐπιτυχοῦς), so 'the Persians changed the names of those who ruled after him and prescribed that they should bear that name' (Diodorus Siculus 15.93.1 [Sherman, LCL]).

Diodorus is mistaken regarding the order of succession after Artaxerxes I. Artaxerxes I was in reality succeeded by his son Darius II, who was succeeded by Artaxerxes II (Mnemon), who was *then* followed by Ochus. But the point is clear, regardless of the mistake. The people asked the successor to take the name of a king who had ruled them well, in hopes that the successor would also rule well.

I can map the exchanges envisioned here thus:

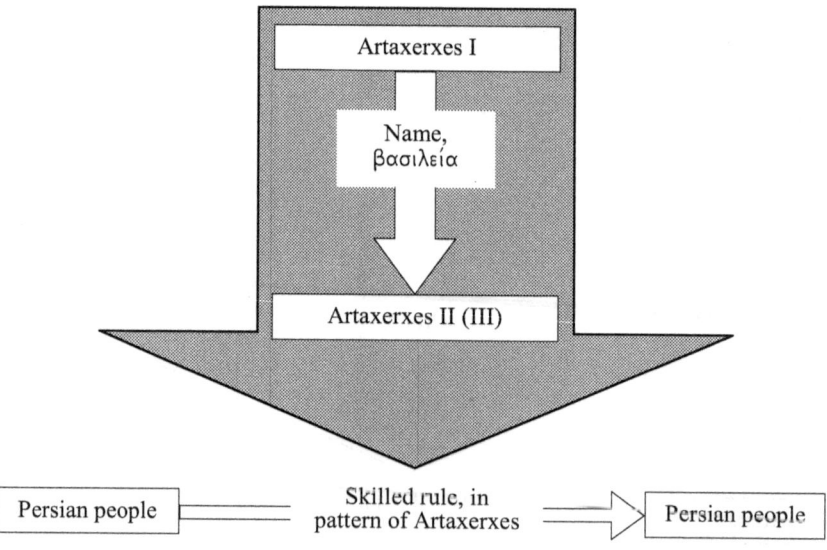

Figure 10. *The Function of Succession in Diodorus Siculus 15.93.1*

Note the symbolism involved in the name change: Ochus is not simply receiving Artaxerxes' property or throne, he is taking Artaxerxes' place. The focus here is either on the manner of rule (a shared characteristic activity) or on the effect of the rule. But which? Diodorus gives explicit attention to the fact that Artaxerxes ruled well (καλῶς βεβασιλευκότος). Therefore, as with Text 2: Herodotus 5.90-92, and Text 5: Aristotle, *Ath. Cons.* 28.1-4 above, succession of leadership/rule here ensures continuity in manner of rule. True successors will continue to rule in the same manner (i.e. with the same characteristic attitudes/activities, as their predecessors).

Text 8: Diodorus Siculus 17–18. In Books 17–18, Diodorus writes of the death of Alexander the Great and the subsequent actions of his generals:

> When he [Alexander], at length, despaired of life, he took off his ring and handed it to Perdiccas. His Friends asked: 'To whom do you leave the kingdom?' (τίνι τὴν βασιλείαν ἀπολείπεις) and he replied: 'To the strongest' (τῷ κρατίστῳ). He added, and these were his last words, that all of his leading Friends would stage a vast contest in honor of his funeral. (Diodorus Siculus, 17.117.3-4 [Welles, LCL])

In 18.4.6, Diodorus turns his attention to how τοῖς διαδεξαμένοις τὴν βασιλείαν carried out (or did not carry out) Alexander's agenda (18.4.6). His first prominent example is Craterus, who

> ...received written instructions which the king had given him for execution; nevertheless, after the death of Alexander, it seemed best to the successors (διαδόχοις) not to carry out these plans. (18.4.1)

Perdiccas also failed to follow Alexander's plans: when faced with the cost of building a tomb for Alexander, he demurred: 'The other designs of Alexander, which were many and great and called for an unprecedented outlay, he (Perdiccas) decided that it was inexpedient to carry them out'. So also Cassander, who was 'plainly disclosed by his own actions as a bitter enemy to Alexander's policies. He murdered Olympias and threw out her body without burial, and with great enthusiasm restored Thebes, which had been destroyed by Alexander' (in 17.118.2) (18.4.3).[17]

Figure 11 (next page) maps the exchanges in Diodorus's narrative.

This text focuses on Alexander's legacy, which he attempted to realize on his own terms after death through his successors. He hoped, by succession of leadership/rule (the passing on of his kingdom, which also involved the passing on of a second object, Alexander's agenda), to build the name and glorious legacy he wanted to leave to the world (in a sense, a monument to himself). Alexander had begun to build this legacy, but he did not finish it, it was the hoped-for effect of succession, an effect which would not have been realized without the succession. But his Διάδοχοι failed to live up to their

---

17. See also Plutarch, *Alexander* 72.3. For commentary on Diodorus's treatment of Alexander, see N.G.L. Hammond, *Three Historians of Alexander the Great: The So-Called Vulgate Authors, Diodorus, Justin, and Curtius* (Cambridge: Cambridge University Press, 1983).

title: they received the kingdom but did not fulfill the agenda as Alexander had wished.[18]

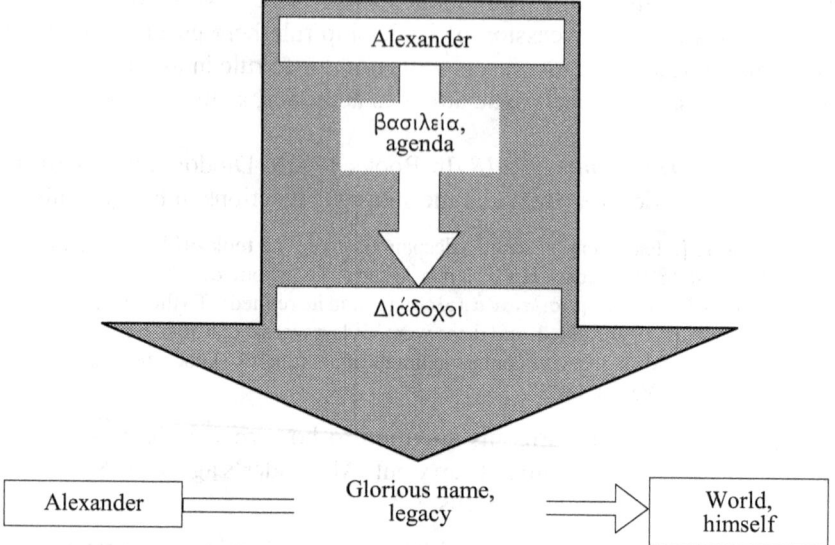

Figure 11. *The Function of Succession in Diodorus Siculus 17–18*

Note also that the fact that Alexander far outstrips his successors in terms of glory and achievement does not negate the succession. Thus a successor can fail to achieve what the predecessor achieves, fail to accumulate the same amount of honor, and still be a successor. The successor need not parallel the predecessor in every way. They can differ in degree of importance, glory, achievement, and succession would still have been inferred.

Text 9: Strabo, Geography *11.13.9*. Strabo flourished at the turn of the eras. In his *Geography*, he describes the terrain and history of the world of his day. In describing Media, Strabo notes the similarities between the Medes' culture and that of their neighbors, the Armenians. Strabo asserts that these similarities exist because the Armenians took their culture from the Medes. Further, the Persians, who 'were their [the Medes'] masters and their successors in the supreme authority over Asia' (τοῖς ἔξουσιν αὐτοὺς καὶ διαδεξαμένοις τὴν τῆς Ἀσίας ἐξουσίαν) also took much of their culture from the Medes. Strabo then lists several 'Persian' customs—their clothing, 'their zeal for archery and horsemanship', and so on—which they inherited from the Medes, their predecessors as supreme rulers over Asia (Strabo, *Geography* 11.13.9 [Jones, LCL]).

---

18. For a different perspective on how Alexander's Διάδοχοι succeeded/did not succeed to Alexander's legacy, see Text 13: Dio Chrysostom 64.20-22 below.

This text speaks of two nations, two cultures, one succeeding the other. While this may seem odd, it is not really unique: above I have shown how indefinite groups of people—legislators, for example—can have as their successors another indefinite group of people, and I will show other examples below. Strabo here ignores the difference in scope and describes the two cultures in the same terms he later uses to describe individuals, focusing on characteristic activities/attitudes that were shared by the predecessors and successors. Note that the exchanges do not need to be intentional for the text to speak of it in terms of succession. Regardless of the predecessors' intentions, the successors not only took their land and authority, they also took on their customs, characteristic activities of the predecessor. Thus succession of leadership/rule here ensures continuity of manner.

I can map the exchanges in this text thus:

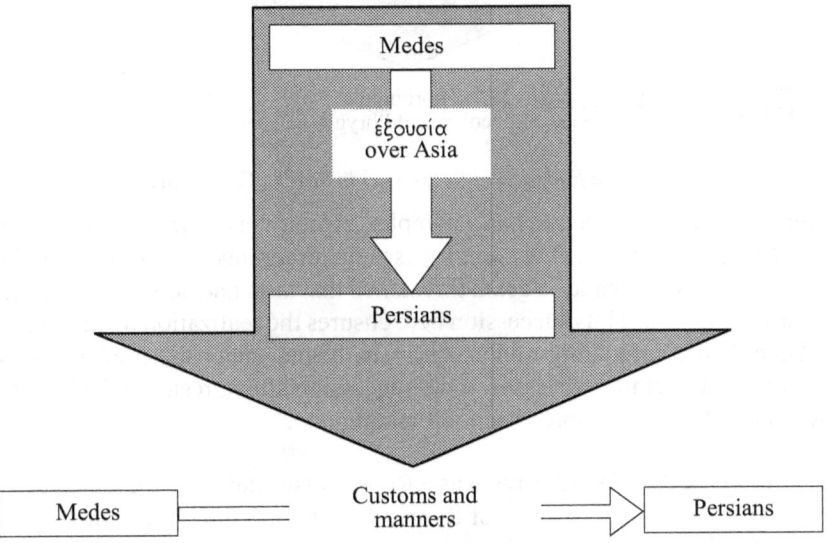

Figure 12. *The Function of Succession in Strabo,* Geography *11.13.9*

Text 10: Strabo, Geography *13.1.3.* In Strabo's description of Phrygia, he recounts how that area was explored and colonized. The colonists most responsible for the settlement of Phrygia were the Aeolians, who approached colonization slowly and methodically. Their activities in the area, led by Orestes (Ὀρέστην…ἄρξαι τοῦ στόλου) were almost derailed by Orestes' death. But Orestes' son, Penthilus, succeeded him (διαδέξασθαι τὸν υἱὸν αὐτοῦ Πενθίλον, 13.1.3). As a proper successor to Orestes, Penthilus led the colonization and completed his father's work. Penthilus was succeeded by his son Archelaus, and Archelaus was succeeded by his son Gras, each inheriting his father's place of leadership and each continuing his father's work. In this way, the whole area was thoroughly colonized.

I can map the exchanges in this narrative thus:

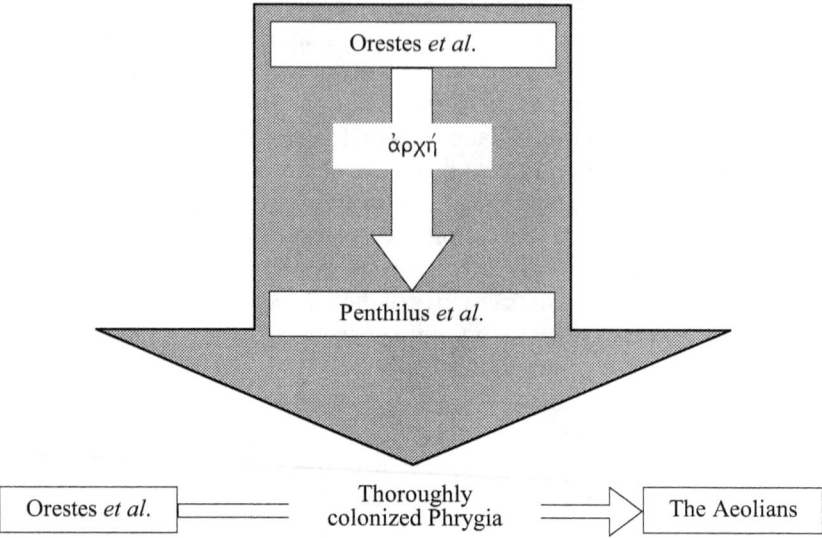

Figure 13. *The Function of Succession in Strabo,* Geography *13.1.3*

Note that succession again has a complex object: the predecessor passes on leadership and agenda. This text focuses on an unfinished task (colonizing Phrygia), how the leader's death threatened that task, and how succession led to its completion. Thus succession here ensures the realization of an effect— a benefit (the colonizing of Phrygia) was begun under the predecessor is completed under the successor. If the succession after Orestes had failed, the Aeolians' task would have been left incomplete.

Text 11: Livy 23.27.9-12. Livy was a Roman historian who flourished at the turn of the eras. In his history of Rome, *Ab urbe condita* ('From the Founding of the City') 23.27.9-12, he wrote of the Carthaginian general Hasdrubal. Early in the second Punic War, Hasdrubal established Carthage's control of Spain, a stepping-stone in Hannibal's planned invasion of Rome. The Spanish proved difficult to rule, but Hasdrubal was able to maintain control. Then orders came from Carthage, which directed Hasdrubal to move his army on to Rome at first opportunity. When news of these orders spread among the Spanish people, they became more openly defiant of the Carthaginians and began openly to support Rome:

> Accordingly, Hasdrubal at once sent a letter to Carthage, showing what a loss the mere report of his departure had caused; that if he were actually to leave the country, Spain would belong to the Romans before he should cross the Hiberius.[19] For besides the lack of both an army and a general to leave in his

19. The Hiberius was the northern boundary of Spain.

place, so able were the Roman generals that they could scarcely be resisted if the forces were evenly matched. And so, if they had any regard for Spain, they should send him a successor with a strong army (*successorum sibi cum valido exercitu mitterent*). (Livy 23.27.9-12 [Moore, LCL])[20]

As with Strabo's story of the colonizing of Phrygia (the text immediately preceding), succession here has a complex object—both leadership and agenda are passed on. This story focuses on an effect/benefit which Carthage desires—controlling Spain—and a second effect/benefit that Hasdrubal aims to derive from the first benefit—the hoped-for ability to invade Rome. That second benefit will not be become a reality unless the first benefit is maintained (i.e. unless Carthage through Hasdrubal or his successor maintains control of Spain). Thus succession of leadership/rule here functions to ensure both continuity of effect (Carthage maintains control of Spain) and realization of a second effect (Carthage is able to invade Rome). From Hasdrubal's point of view, if his superiors would send him a proper successor then Carthage might yet keep control in Spain and maintain a favorable position for attacking Rome. But if a proper successor was not sent, Carthage would lose the tenuous benefit that they had thus far maintained.

I can map the exchanges Hasdrubal envisions thus:

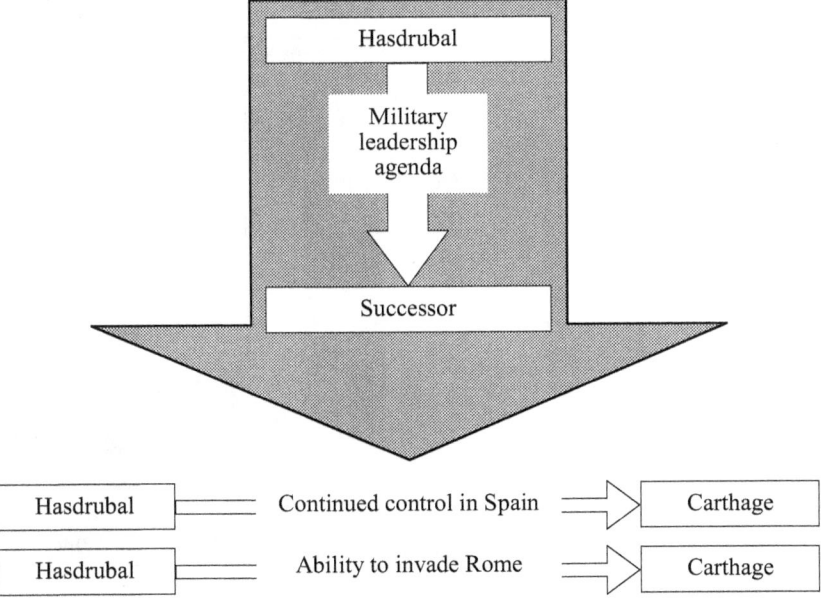

Figure 14. *The Functions of Succession in Livy 23.27.9-12*

---

20. For commentary, see Andrew Feldherr, *Spectacle and Society in Livy's History* (Berkeley: University of California Press, 1998).

Text 12: Pausanias, Description of Greece *7.12.* In his *Description of Greece*, the second-century CE writer Pausanias surveys Greek history. One of the stories he relates is that of the Achaean general Menalcidas and his compatriot, Callicrates.

Menalcidas was a scoundrel, who cheated fellow-scoundrel Callicrates (to whom Pausanias refers as 'the worst rascal of his time, one who could never resist a bribe of any kind' [ὃς ἐλάσσων παντοίου καὶ ἐπὶ οὐδενὶ οἰκείῳ κέρδει], Pausanias, *Description of Greece* 7.12.2 [Jones, LCL]) out of money from a bribe they had agreed to split. In return, Callicrates had Menalcidas charged with treason, a capital crime.

For help, Menalcidas turned to Diaius of Megalopolis, who had succeeded him as general in service of Achaea. He bribed Diaius, paying him three talents so that Diaius would use his influence to save Menalcidas's skin. Diaius 'on this occasion was so active, because of the bribe, that he succeeded in saving Menalcidas' (7.12.2).

This text focuses on characteristic activities/attitudes shared by the predecessor and his successor. Thus succession of leadership/rule here again ensures continuity of manner. Diaius was Menalcidas's successor in more ways than one—as general, scoundrel, and taker of bribes.

I can map the exchanges thus:

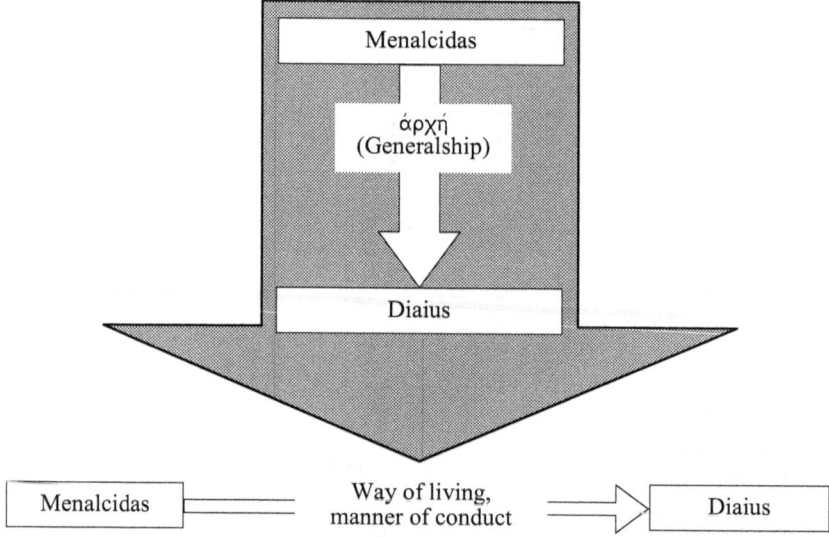

Figure 15. *The Function of Succession in Pausanius,* Description of Greece *7.12*

Text 13: Dio Chrysostom 64.20-22. Dio Chrysostom was an orator of the second century CE. His sixty-fourth discourse, usually regarded as pseudonymous,[21] is an encomium to the goddess Fortune (Τύχη). In it, the orator describes how different cultures and historical and mythical figures were humbled or exalted by the whim of Τύχη.

In 64.20-21, the orator tells of Alexander's sins of ὕβρις, and how Fortune (through Alexander's untimely death) humbled him. In the next paragraph (64.22), the orator describes how Alexander's successors (τοὺς διαδεξαμένους τὴν βασιλείαν) also committed the same sins of ὕβρις, and how Fortune humbled them as well (Dio Chrysostom 64 [Crosby, LCL]).

I can illustrate the exchanges in this succession thus:

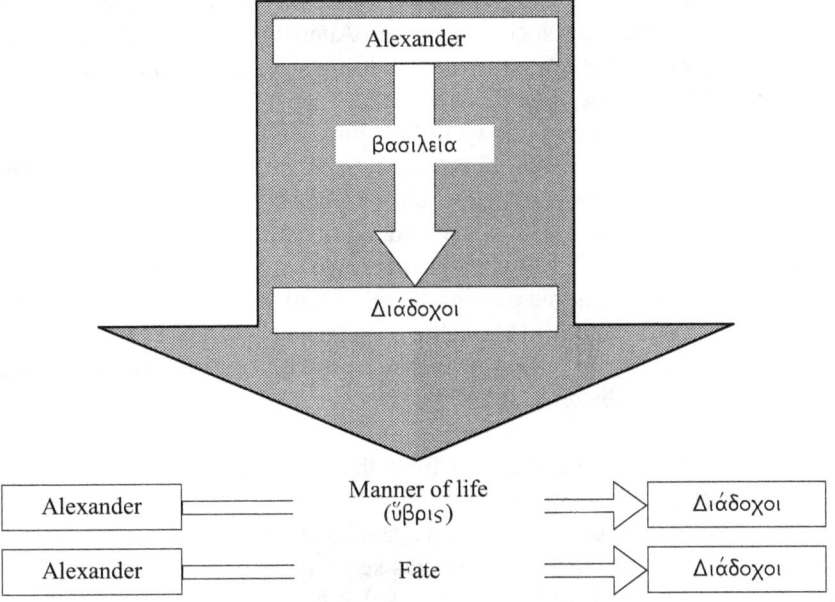

Figure 16. *The Functions of Succession in Dio Chrysostom 64.20-22*

Note that here, as with Text 8: Diodorus Siculus 17–18 above, equivalence of achievements between predecessor and successor is not necessary. The fact that the successors never equaled their predecessor in glory does not negate the fact of succession.

This text focuses on characteristic actions/attitudes shared by predecessor and successors, and on the shared effect. Therefore, succession here functions to ensure both continuity of manner and continuity of effect. This text gives us a clear illustration of how the function of succession can include either the

---

21. George Kennedy, *The Art of Rhetoric in the Roman World, 300 BC–AD 300* (Princeton, NJ: Princeton University Press, 1972), p. 566.

purpose of succession (i.e. what the predecessor or the sender intended to achieve as described by the text) or the *result* of succession (i.e. what came out of the succession, regardless of the predecessor's or the sender's intentions). In this example, the writer implies no intentionality on Alexander's part, no indication that he wanted his successors to emulate his hubris and receive the comeuppance he received. But by emulating him, intentionally or not, they acted as the true Διάδοχοι of Alexander.

Text 14: Dio Cassius 53. Dio was a Roman politician and historian of the third century CE. He wrote several works, including biographies and religious literature, but is best remembered for his history of Rome, which tells its story from its beginnings through 229 CE. In 53.30-31, Dio tells the story of how Augustus chose his successor. When Augustus was thought to be near death, he appointed Agrippa to follow him as emperor. This choice was unexpected: Marcellus, thought to be the heir apparent, was Augustus's son-in-law, and Augustus was known to love him dearly (Dio Cassius 53).[22]

Why did Augustus make this unexpected choice? He apparently chose Agrippa because he felt Agrippa would be a better ruler. Consider: first, the people loved Agrippa (53.31.4). Second, Agrippa was of moderate temperament (53.32.1; 54.11.6). Third, Augustus made his choice after talking to the leaders of the people 'about public affairs' (53.30.2). Fourth, Augustus 'was not confident of the youth's (Marcellus's) judgement' (53.31.4). Fifth, Augustus attempted to read his will (in which he chose no successor) to the Senate, but they would not listen to it (53.31.1).

Dio notes: 'He either wished the people to regain their liberty or for Agrippa to receive the leadership from them' ('Αγρίππαν τὴν ἡγεμονίαν παρ' ἐκείνου λαβεῖν ἠθέλησεν).[23]

Note that succession of leadership again involves passing on not just office or authority but also agenda: Augustus seeks to make sure that the people continued to be ruled well. He believes that he has himself ruled well and benevolently, and seeks a successor whom he believes will rule in the same way. Here, succession serves to ensure continuity of manner of rule (from Augustus's perspective) and continuity of effect (from the people's perspective, assuming as Augustus did that they felt they were being ruled well).

I can map the exchanges in the passage thus:

---

22. For commentary, see J.W. Rich, *The Augustan Settlement: Roman History 53–59/Cassius Dio* (Warminster: Aris & Phillips, 1990).

23. Marcellus is further shown not to be Augustus's successor by the story of Augustus's near-fatal illness. Augustus, when gravely ill, went to the healer Musa and recovered. Marcellus later similarly fell ill, went to Musa, and died of his illness. True, Agrippa also preceded Augustus in death, but not before serving as his co-regent.

2. Background and Graeco-Roman Texts

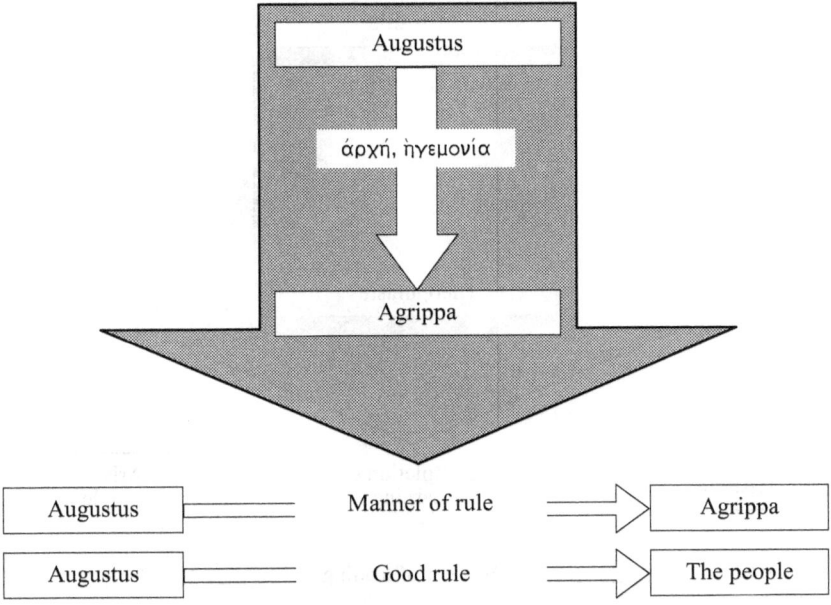

Figure 17. *The Functions of Succession in Dio Cassius 53*

Texts Describing Succession of Headship of Philosophical School
Text 15: *Aulus Gellius*, Attic Nights *13.5*. In Book 13 of Gellius's collection of anecdotes and notes, we encounter the story of Aristotle choosing a successor. When the philosopher was near death, his students came to him and asked him to choose a successor to lead the school after he died. They feared that his death would leave their education incomplete, and so asked for someone 'to whom, as to himself [Aristotle], they might apply after his last day, to complete and perfect their knowledge of the studies into which he had initiated them'.

So Aristotle agreed to choose a successor. The two leading candidates were Theophrastus of Lesbos and Eudemus of Rhodes. A few days later, Aristotle asked his disciples to bring him wines from Rhodes and Lesbos. After tasting both, Aristotle said, 'Both are very good indeed, but the Lesbian is the sweeter'. Everyone understood that this was Aristotle's way of choosing Theophrastus as his successor. And when Aristotle died, they became disciples of Theophrastus (Aulus Gellius, *Attic Nights* 13.5 [Rolfe, LCL]).[24]

The exchanges in this scene are mapped in the following figure:

---

24. For commentary, see Leofranc Holford-Strevens, *Aulus Gellius* (Chapel Hill: University of North Carolina Press, 1989).

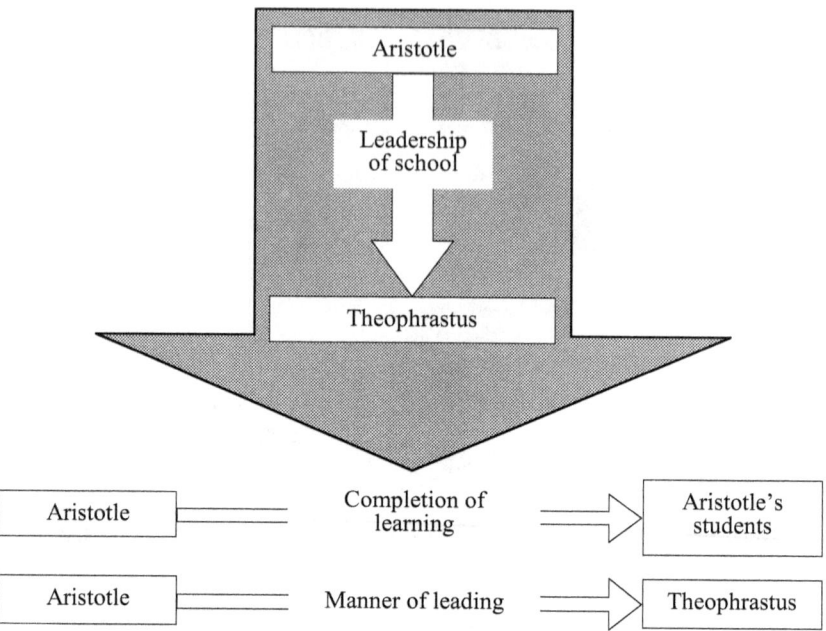

Figure 18. *The Functions of Succession in Aulus Gellius,* Attic Nights *13.5*

As with some of the texts showing succession of leadership/rule above, this text has a complex object: leadership of the school is passed on, and interwoven with it is Aristotle's agenda (the thorough education of his students). This text focuses on the effect of succession: Aristotle 'began a good work' in his students, and they, knowing that he was near death, asked him to pass on his place as their teacher to a successor who would carry it on to completion. An aspect of Aristotle's work was understood to remain unfinished as long as his students remained immature, and a successor was needed to finish it.

Thus, succession of the headship of a philosophical school here ensures the realization of an effect. Succession allows the work which Aristotle began to realize—the education of his students—be completed by his successor. Why is this not continuity of effect rather than realization of effect? Because the text explicitly states that the student's hope was for someone 'to complete and perfect their knowledge of the studies into which [Aristotle] had initiated them'. Thus the work was unfinished when Aristotle passed it on to Theophrastus. A second function is also in view: Aristotle led the school by teaching (a characteristic activity), his successor is also to lead the school by teaching. Thus succession here ensures continuity of manner.

Note that Aristotle's greatness in comparison to Theophrastus does not lessen the need for or the legitimacy of succession, or of the successor finishing his predecessor's unfinished work. Theophrastus was fit to complete the education of Aristotle's students and to perpetuate Aristotle's school.

2. Background and Graeco-Roman Texts
41

Text 16: Diogenes Laertius 4.67. In the third century CE, Diogenes Laertius wrote a collection of short βίοι of the differing philosophical schools and philosophers leading up to his day. In Books 3–4, Diogenes covers the lives of Plato, the Academy: Speusippus, Xenocrates, and so on. In his βίος of Clitomachus (who led the Academy from 129 BCE), he notes that Clitomachus succeeded Carneades as head of the Academy. After he succeeded Carneades, Clitomachus wrote prolifically—Carneades left nothing in writing (4.65). 'He [Clitomachus] succeeded Carneades in the headship of the school, and by his writings did much to elucidate his [Carneades'] opinions' (διεδέξατο τὸν Καρνεάδην καὶ τὰ αὑτοῦ μάλιστα διὰ τῶν συγγραμμάτων ἐφώτισεν) (Diogenes Laertius 4.65-67 [Hicks, LCL]).[25]

Where does this text focus? It appears at first to focus on the effect of succession—Clitomachus succeeded Carneades as head of the school, with the result being that Carneades' teachings were preserved and propagated. But succession does not figure in that effect in the ways I have seen to this point—no continuity of effect from predecessor to successor, or the successor's completion of the predecessor's unfinished work.

Instead, this text focuses on the object of succession—Carneades' teachings—and how succession ensures the continued vitality of that institution (the teachings). Succession here results in those teachings continuing to spread and be studied. If there had been no successor, or if Clitomachus had been a different kind of successor—one who shared his predecessor's antipathy toward writing—Carneades' teaching would not have been preserved and spread.

Figure 19 (next page) maps the exchanges.

Text 17: Diogenes Laertius 9.115. In Books 8 and 9 of his βίοι, Diogenes sketches the 'Italian' (Diogenes' term) philosophers, from Pythagoras to Epicurus. As part of this group, he mentions the skeptic Timon, who was active during the early third century BCE. Timon was a good writer, but left no successor for his branch of the skeptical school: 'He left no successor, but his school lapsed (Τούτου διάδοχος...γέγονεν οὐδείς, ἀλλὰ διέλιπεν ἡ ἀγωγή) until Ptolemy of Cyrene re-established it', Diogenes Laertius 9.115 [Hicks, LCL]).

Again, the focus of the contemplated succession is the object—the school. Nothing is said of possession of property or the effect of the succession, and so on. Thus succession in the headship of a philosophical school here ensures that the institution (the school) continues to thrive. If Timon had had a proper successor, his school would not have fallen into inactivity.

The contemplated exchanges are mapped in Fig. 20 (next page).

25. For commentary, see Jørgen Mejer, *Diogenes Laertius and his Hellenistic Background* (Wiesbaden: Steiner, 1978).

42   *Leadership Succession in the World of the Pauline Circle*

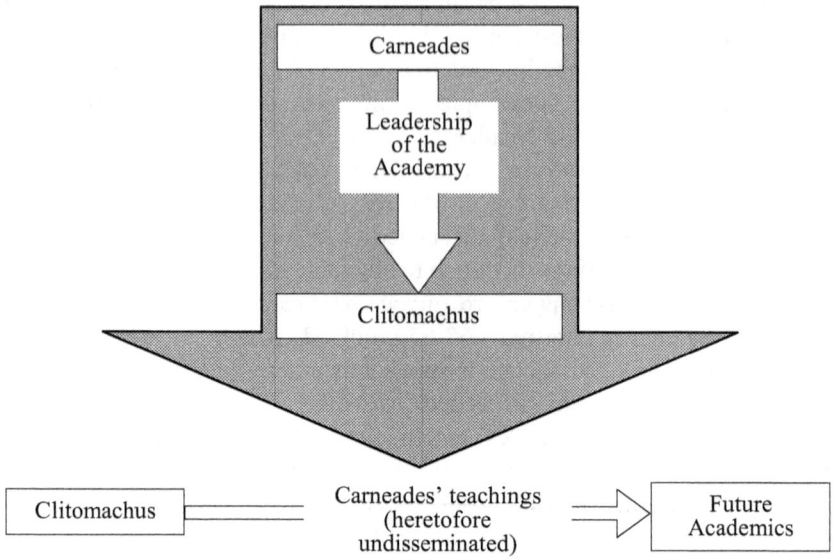

Figure 19. *The Function of Succession in Diogenes Laertius 4.67*

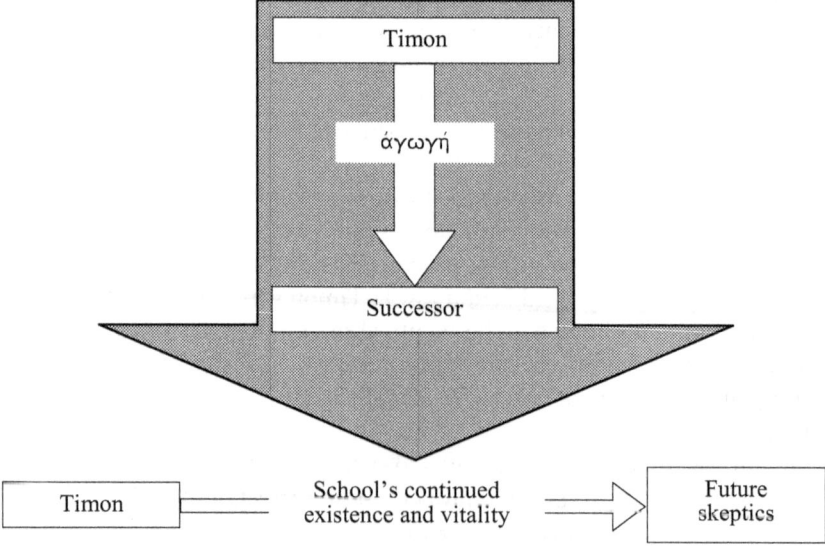

Figure 20. *The Function of Succession in Diogenes Laertius 9.115*

Text 18: Diogenes Laertius 10.9. Here, Diogenes describes his favorite philosopher, Epicurus. He asserts Epicureanism's superiority over all other schools of philosophy, noting that 'the School itself (ἡ διαδοχή)..., while nearly all the others have died out, continues forever without interruption through numberless reigns of one scholarch after another' (10.9 [Hicks, LCL]).[26] Further, Diogenes notes that Epicurus in his will dictated that his heirs must 'place the garden and all that pertains to it at the disposal of Hermarchus,[27] ...and the members of his society, and those whom Hermarchus may leave as his successors (οἷς ἂν Ἕρμαρχος καταλίπῃ διαδόχοις τῆς φιλοσοφίας), to live and study in' (10.17).

The following figure illustrates the exchanges:

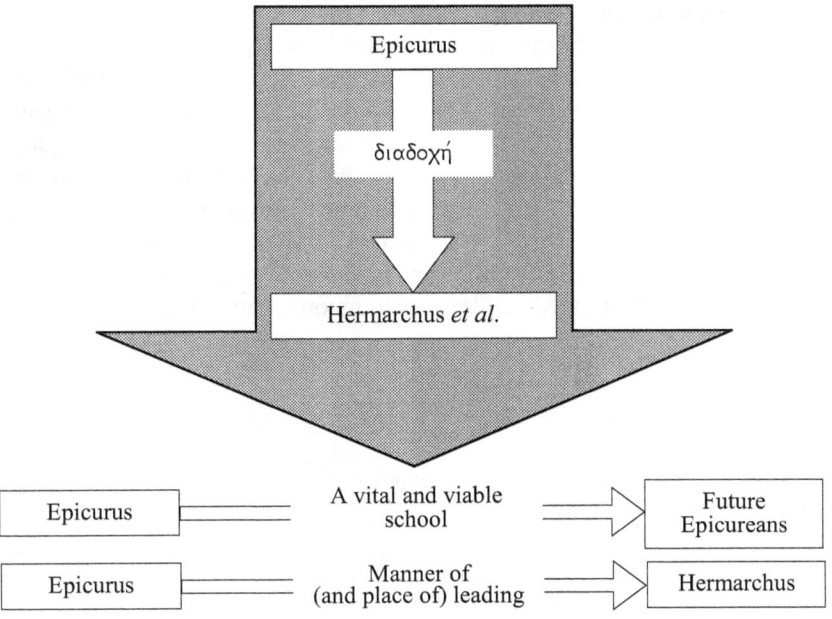

Figure 21. *The Functions of Succession in Diogenes Laertius 10.9*

At first glance, this text seems to contain two succession stories, two objects —the headship of the school and the bequest of property—but that is in fact not the case. The property is not deeded to Hermarchus but to Amynomachus, on the condition that he in perpetuity allows Hermarchus and those who follow him in the school to use the property. Thus the conditions in the will are part of Hermarchus's succession of Epicurus as head of the school.

And the focus is on that single object—headship of the school—and how succession serves to ensure the continued vitality of the institution (Epicurus's

---

26. Diogenes uses διαδοχή as a synonym for σχολή here and 1.20; 2.108-109.
27. Hermarchus was Epicurus's successor: DL 10.15, τήν τε σχολὴν διαδέξασθαι Ἕρμαρχον.

school). Other schools, which had no continuing succession, had died out by Diogenes' time. The conditions of the will are attached to this succession, dictating the continued use of Epicurus's property by his successors, so that future members of his school might continue to learn, study, and teach there. This description also centers first on institutional vitality. Second, Hermarchus is expected to share his predecessor's characteristic activity (and location) by teaching in Epicurus's garden: thus succession not only ensures continued institutional vitality, it also ensures continuity of manner.

Text 19: Iamblichus, On the Pythagorean Way of Life *36*. Iamblichus's *On the Pythagorean Way of Life* is a biography of Pythagoras that includes a large survey of Pythagoras's teachings and a short biographical section covering Pythagoras's successors. In ch. 36, Iamblichus lists the succession from Pythagoras. He notes that Aristaeus was considered worthy to succeed to leadership of the school because he 'had full command of their doctrines' (διὰ τὸ ἐξαιρέτως περικεκρατηκέναι τῶν δογμάτων, Iamblichus, *Pythagorean* 36.265 [Dillon and Hershbell]). In the next paragraph, Iamblichus comments on how two of the movement's later adherents 'spread abroad Pythagorean sayings' (διέδωκε τὰς Πυθαγορείους φωνάς) and 'published the secret teachings of Pythagoras' (κρύφα ἐκφέροντα τὰ Πυθαγόρου δόγματα, 36.266).[28]

The exchanges wrapped up in this succession scene can be illustrated thus:

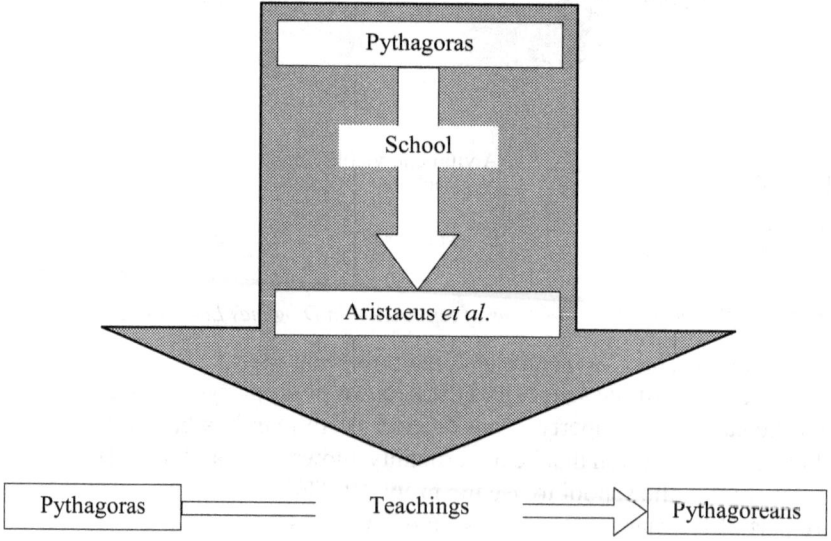

Figure 22. *The Function of Succession in Iamblichus,* On the Pythagorean Way of Life *36*

28. See Tomas Hägg, Philip Rousseau, and Christian Høgel, *Greek Biography and Panegyric in Late Antiquity* (Berkeley: University of California Press, 2000).

2. Background and Graeco-Roman Texts

Among the record of Pythagoras's successors, the three statements given above are the *only* descriptions of philosophical activity. Thus the text's focus in the section on the successors is the object of succession—the Pythagorean way of life, hence the book's title—and the continued existence and propagation of that teaching. Thus succession here ensures continued institutional vitality.

Texts Describing Succession of Task
Text 20: Lysias, Pension 6. Lysias was an Athenian orator of the late fifth century BCE. In *Pension*, he speaks for a disabled client who was in danger of losing his public pension. Such assistance was reviewed every year, and citizens could challenge the pensioner's request for assistance at the review. Someone had raised such a challenge to Lysias's client. In his argument, Lysias describes his client as being unable to support himself. He has no children to support him, nor can he purchase a slave to succeed him in the work: 'I am unable to procure someone to relieve me of the work' (τὸν διαδεξόμενον δ' αὐτὴν οὔπω δύναμαι κτήσασθαι, Lysias, *Pension* 6 [Lamb, LCL])—such a successor would take over the work but pay the pensioner.

This passage focuses on the effect of the proposed succession, how said succession would allow the effect of the predecessor's work (to wit, his paycheck) to continue. The text focuses not on the work, but on the effect. The predecessor, were he able, would have worked at his trade to support himself. Due to his disability, he needs a successor who can work at the same trade to the same effect. Since the hypothetical succession has not taken place, Lysias's client requires public assistance.

As with the discussions of Alexander and his successors in Text 8: Diodorus Siculus 17–18 and Text 13: Dio Chrysostom 64.20-22 above, note here that the successor does not need to be the predecessor's equal for succession to have been inferred. In fact, this example differs from the above-mentioned in a very specific way. In both discussions of Alexander and his Διάδοχοι, the difference between predecessor and successor(s) was a difference of degree—both Alexander and his successors were rulers and generals, but Alexander was more glorious and successful. But here, the parties do not even occupy the same stations in life or society—one is free and master, the other is the first's slave. The slave can be his master's successor, even though he remains a slave and is never his master's equal. Here, the successor is not a replacement for the predecessor but is rather his delegate, a delegation that is described in the language of succession.

In this text, hypothetical succession in a task ensures continuity of effect. If he had the means to afford a slave, the sender (the client) would give a living wage (the benefit) to the receiver (himself) and not need the public's support.

Figure 23 (next page) maps the exchanges in this hypothetical succession.

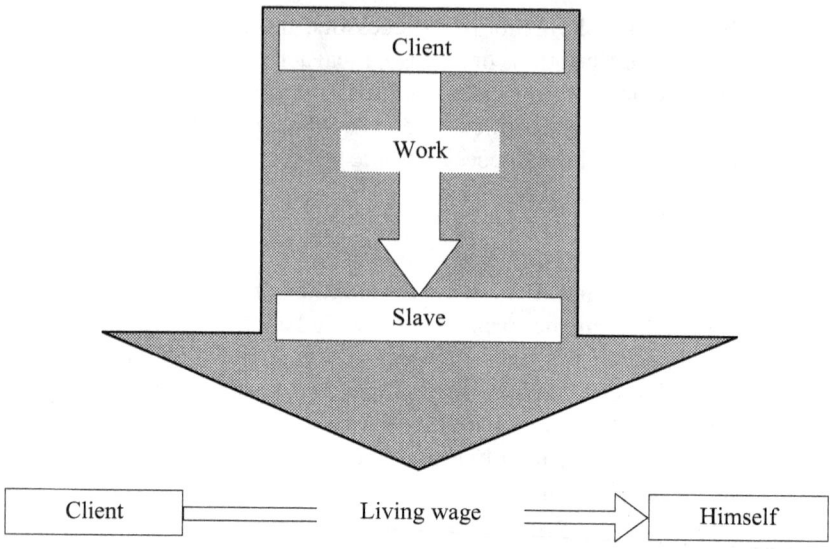

Figure 23. *The Function of Succession in Lysias,* Pension 6

Text 21: Xenophon, Anabasis *1.5.2*. Xenophon was an Athenian soldier and writer of the third century BCE. In *Anabasis*, he writes an account of Cyrus the Younger's attempt to overthrow his brother, Artaxerxes II (Mnemon). This uprising took place in about 400 BCE, and Xenophon was himself one of the mercenaries hired by Cyrus. In 1.5.2, Xenophon tells how Cyrus's men would hunt wild donkeys in the desert for food. Because the donkeys ran faster than the soldiers' horses, the only way to catch them was to chase them in shifts: 'The horsemen posted themselves at intervals and hunted them in relays' (διαστάντες οἱ ἱππεῖς θηρῷεν διαδεχόμενοι, Xenophon, *Anabasis* 1.5.2 [Brownson, LCL]).[29]

This passage focuses on an unfinished task and how succession allows that task to be completed. If the succession had not taken place, the soldiers never would have gotten their meal of donkey flesh—they would not have been able to catch their supper. But because the succession took place—because the task was passed on from horseman to horseman—the predecessors' work was taken up by the successors, and the wild donkeys were worn down, caught, and eaten. Thus a task that was difficult or impossible for one person to accomplish was accomplished through succession, through the efforts of several successors, who completed the predecessors' work. Thus succession of task ensures the realization of an effect—the donkeys are finally caught.

I can map the exchanges in this narrative thus:

---

29. For commentary, see Steven W. Hirsch, *The Friendship of the Barbarians: Xenophon and the Persian Empire* (Hanover: University Press of New England, 1985).

2. Background and Graeco-Roman Texts

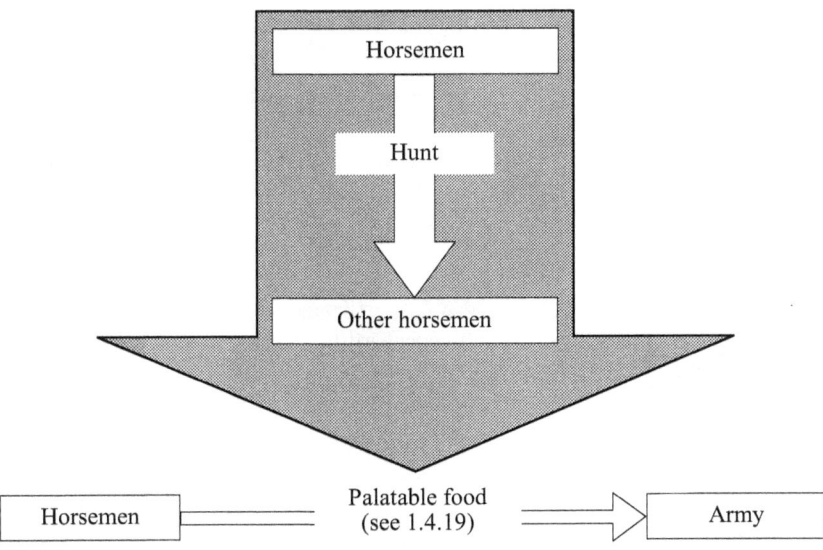

Figure 24. *The Function of Succession in Xenophon,* Anabasis *1.5.2*

Texts Describing Succession of Tradition/Knowledge
Text 22: Aristotle, Sophistical Refutations *34.27-35. Sophistical Refutations* is a study of arguments, particularly of why bad arguments fail. In Aristotle's conclusion, he repeats earlier material and comments on the methods used in the work. He specifically remarks on how such studies take the results of the work of those who have gone before and advance them further, and refers to this phenomenon in succession terms:

> When the first beginning has been discovered, it is easier to add to it and develop the rest... Those who discovered the beginnings of rhetoric carried them forward quite a little way, whereas the famous modern professors of the art, entering into the heritage...of a long series of predecessors (πολλῶν οἷον ἐκ διαδοχῆς) who have gradually advanced it, have brought it to its present perfection—Tisias following the first inventors, Thrasymachus following Tisias, Theodorus following Thrasymachus... (Aristotle, *Soph. Refut.* 34.27-35 §183b.28-32 [Forster, LCL])

The exchanges Aristotle refers to are mapped in Fig. 25 (next page).

The focus in this passage is on the object of succession, and how succession ensures continued vitality for that object. Succession makes the advancement or improvement of an art possible. Artists, whatever their field, take the innovations of artists who preceded them and on that foundation build new innovations. When they do so, they are successors of the original artist. Thus succession here ensures continued institutional vitality—there is no mention of any intent on the artist's part for his/her work to be taken up later, so there is no agenda to be realized.

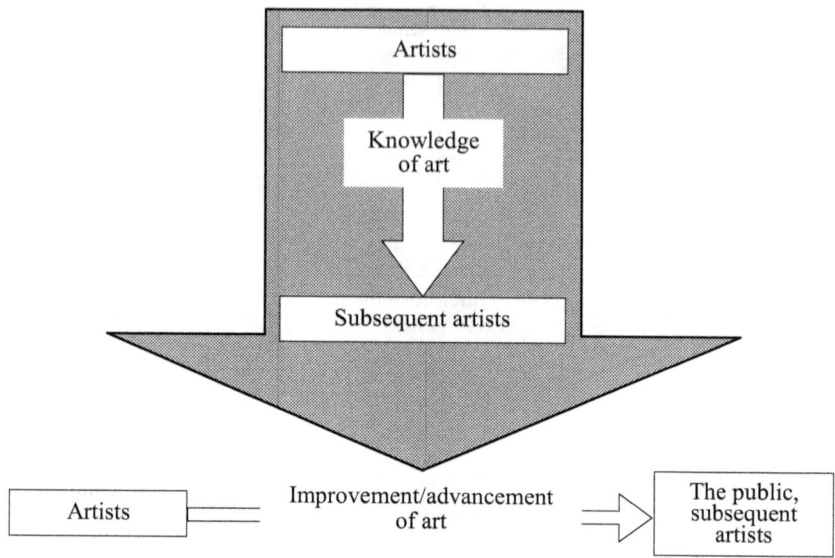

Figure 25. *The Function of Succession in Aristotle,* Sophistical Refutations *34.27-35*

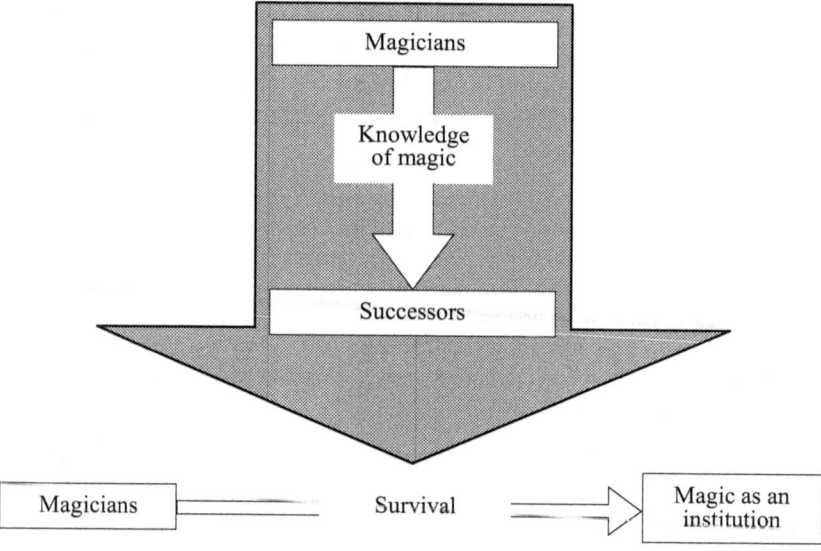

Figure 26. *The Function of Succession in Pliny the Elder,* Natural History *30.2.4-5*

Text 23: Pliny the Elder, Natural History *30.2.4-5.* Pliny the Elder was a Roman soldier and writer of the first century CE. In his *Natural History*, he culled information from the important (and unimportant) works of his day on the topics of medicine, physics, and so on, with a less-than-critical eye (so the *OCD*). In discussing the origins of magic, Pliny first notes its antiquity. He asserts that the survival of magic over such a period is surprising because it lacks an established line of successors for the keeping of its traditions:

> What is especially surprising is the survival, through so long a period, of the craft and its tradition; treatises are wanting, and besides there is no line of distinguished or continuous successors to keep live their memory (*nec continuis successionibus custoditam*). For how few know anything, even hearsay, of those who alone have left their names but without any other memorial? (Pliny, *Natural History* 30.2.4-5 [Jones, LCL])[30]

Figure 26 (opposite) maps the contemplated exchanges.

Again, the focus is on the object of succession, here the institution of magic. As Pliny states it, if magic as an institution was to survive it would need an established line of succession of knowledge or succession of tradition. In that institution, there has been no clear line of succession. If there is no clear succession of knowledge from one possessor to another, the discipline related to that knowledge generally dies out—thus Pliny's surprise at the survival of magic.

Text 24: Tacitus, Annals *15.62.* Tacitus was a Roman orator and writer of the first and second centuries CE. He wrote two works outlining the history of Rome after the death of Augustus: *Histories*, in which he covered the period from the death of Augustus to the assassination of Domitian, 14–96 CE, and *Annals*, in which he specifically surveys the failings of Rome's leadership. In *Annals* 15.48-71, Tacitus recounts the events of the Pisonian conspiracy against Nero.

Nero discovered the plot against him, and began executing all those he suspected of involvement. One whom Nero suspected—apparently more from personal dislike than from any real likelihood that he was involved in the conspiracy—was Nero's old teacher, Seneca. Nero sent word to Seneca that he was to be put to death—ironically, this message came to Seneca through one of the actual conspirators, Gavius Silvanus, whom Nero had not yet discovered. On receiving this sentence, Seneca asked for an opportunity to show his will to his friends so that they could see their places in it. His request was denied. Seneca then said that he would bequeath to them:

---

30. For commentary, see Marie Theresa Bergmann, 'Magic in Pliny's *Natural History*' (MA thesis, Washington University, 1940).

...his sole but fairest possession—the image of his life (*imagineum vitae*). If they bore it in mind, they would reap the reward of their loyal friendship in the credit accorded to virtuous accomplishments. (Tacitus, *Annals* 15.62 [Jackson, LCL])[31]

Here, the focus is on both the object of succession and the effect of succession. The passing on of Seneca's 'image' (his teaching and influence) ensures that his influence continues to be effective and powerful in the lives of his heirs, thus succession here ensures institutional vitality. But also: if Seneca's friends are truly his heirs, they will not only receive what he bequeaths to them, they will also grow into the kind of lives that the bequest sought to produce, something as yet unfinished. Thus succession here also ensures the realization of an effect.

The following figure maps the exchanges in this text:

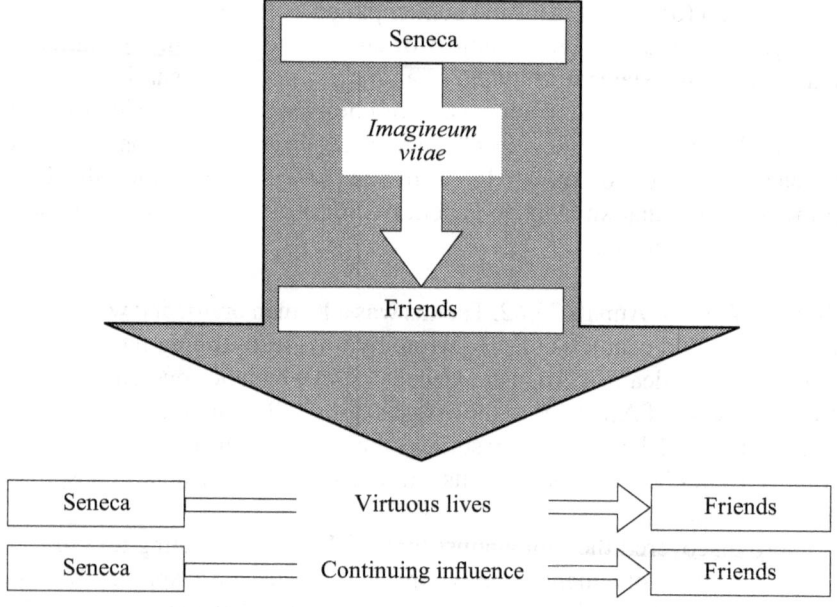

Figure 27. *The Functions of Succession in Tacitus,* Annals *15.62*

---

31. For commentary, see Edward Rosen, 'How the Shackles Were Forged and Later Loosened', *Journal of the History of Ideas* 38 (1977), pp. 109-17; Lawrence Joseph Simms, 'Tacitus on Seneca: An Interpretation' (MA thesis, University of North Carolina, 1969); Roger Boesche, 'The Politics of Pretence: Tacitus and the Political Theory of Despotism', *History of Political Thought* 8 (1987), pp. 189-210.

Note again, the predecessor and successors do not occupy the same station in life or society, they are not equals. And again, as with Text 20: Lysias, *Pension* 6, it is a difference in kind, not in degree—the successors need not take Seneca's place as a teacher, for example, for succession to have taken place.

Texts Describing the Passing on of Possessions
Text 25: Demosthenes, Aphobus *2.19*. Demosthenes was an Athenian orator of the third century BCE. His father (also named Demosthenes) died when he was seven, and left behind a considerable estate. By the time Demosthenes reached the age of eighteen (thus making him eligible to inherit), the executors of his father's will had squandered almost all of the fortune. There was no money for his sister's dowry, and one of the executors (Aphobus, commanded in the will to marry the widow) had taken his mother's dowry but refused to marry her.

Demosthenes took the three executors of his father's will to court, and won a famous (if incomplete) victory. In this speech, he brings his suit against Aphobus, his erstwhile guardian.[32] Here he describes how the instructions of his father's will were to have benefited not only himself and his family, but also Athens: his succession to his father's place, damaged as it was by the executors, could only benefit Athens if his inheritance was restored by the court:

> It was not to prospects such as these that my father left us. Nay, my sister was to be the wife of Demophon with a dowry of two talents, my mother the wife of this most ruthless of all men with a dowry of eighty minae, and I as my father's successor (διάδοχον) was to perform state services (λητουργιῶν) as he had done. Succor us, then, succor us for the sake of justice, *for your own sakes*, for ours, and for my dead father's sake. (Demosthenes, *Aphobus* 2.19 [Murray, LCL] [emphasis added])

Succession here has a complex object—both inheritance and agenda are passed on: Demosthenes notes that, in his fathers' plans, he (the son) 'was to perform state services…as he had done'. The text focuses on two functions. The succession/inheritance, as planned by the elder Demosthenes, would first ensure that his property was preserved and maintained by and for the benefit of his family—thus ensuring continuity of possession. Second, this succession would also have ensured a benefit (continued public service) to Athens from Demosthenes' family—thus ensuring continuity of effect.

The exchanges in this contemplated succession are mapped in Fig. 28 (next page).

---

32. George Kennedy, *The Art of Persuasion in Greece* (Princeton, NJ: Princeton University Press, 1963), pp. 209-11.

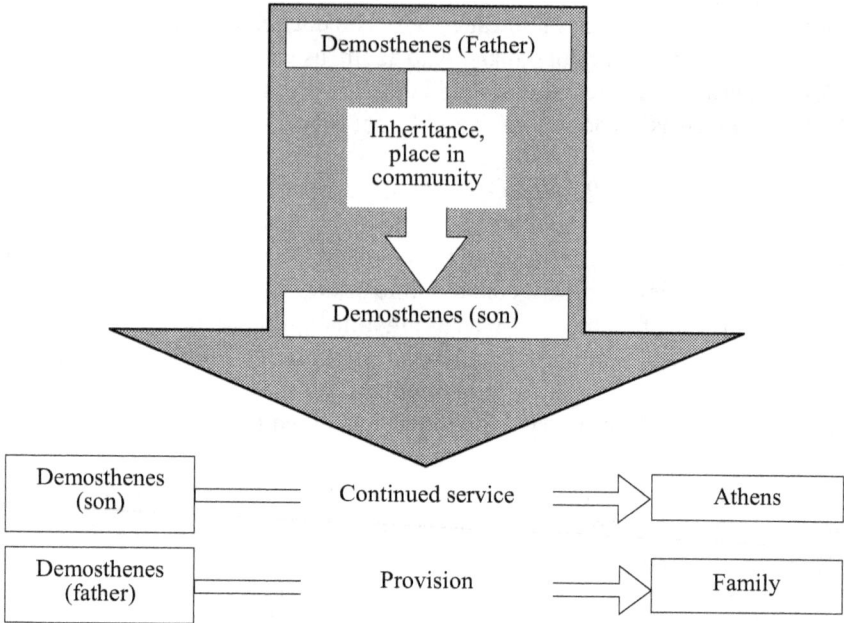

Figure 28. *The Functions of Succession in Demosthenes,* Aphobus 2.19

Text 26: Plato, Laws *5.740b.* One of the Athenian's concerns in *Laws* is that citizenship should not be taken lightly—those involved must always consider that involvement a privilege. One way of keeping the community stabile, and thus keeping the value of citizenship at a maximum, is by limiting the number of households:

> Let the possessor of a lot leave the one of his children who is best beloved, and one only, to be the heir of his dwelling, and his successor (διάδοχον) in the duty of ministering to the gods, the state, and the family, as well the living members of it as those who are departed when he comes into the inheritance; but of his other children, if he have more than one, he shall give the females in marriage according to the law hereafter enacted, and the males he shall distribute as sons to those citizens who have no children, and are disposed to receive them. (Plato, *Laws* 5.740b [Jowett])

Figure 29 (opposite) maps the exchanges in the narrative.

This text focuses on two functions. First, by passing on his property *in toto* to a single heir, the predecessor preserves the value of his citizenship (an institution). Thus succession here ensures continued institutional vitality. Second, having a limited number of landholders promotes stability, and succession of possessions conducted according to this model maintains that stability. Therefore, stability is an effect of proper succession, a benefit the community derives from it. Thus succession here ensures continuity of effect.

2. *Background and Graeco-Roman Texts* 53

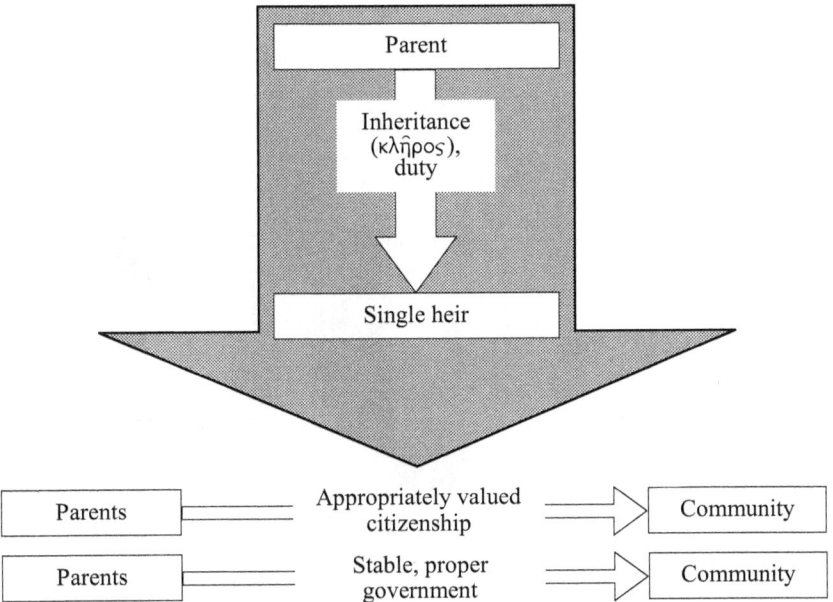

Figure 29. *The Functions of Succession in Plato,* Laws *5.740b*

Text 27: Diodorus Siculus 10.30.1-2. In 10.30.1-2, as part of a narrative describing prominent ancient Athenians, Diodorus tells of Cimon the son of Miltiades. Miltiades died in debtor's prison, being unable to pay the fine that Athens levied against him for his part in a failed military expedition. Cimon, 'who was ambitious to take part in the conduct of the state' (φιλότιμος ὢν εἰς τὴν τῶν κοινῶν διοίκησιν) took his father's place in prison on his father's death, and thus worked off the debt (διεδέξατο τὸ ὄφλημα, Diodorus Siculus 10.30.1-2 [Oldfather, LCL]). Cimon regained political viability by taking on his father's debt (thus erasing his father's shame and earning honor) and went on to serve Athens very successfully as a general.

The transactions described here are mapped in Fig. 30 (next page).

Note that the successor here serves as the sender in the axis of function. I have shown this before, the best comparison is with Text 16. Diogenes Laertius 4.67, where Clitomachus succeeds Carneades as head of a philosophical school and becomes the sender who by his philosophical activity propagates Carneades' teachings for future Academics.

The focus in this passage is on the effect of succession, unrealized in the predecessor's life but completed in the successor's. Thus succession ensures the realization of effect. The successor inherits two things: his predecessor's debt/shame and his predecessor's station in the community/opportunities for honor. By succeeding his father in his shame, and by handling the shame properly, Cimon is also able to succeed his father in honor, by giving Athens a career of distinguished military service (which perhaps they should have received from his father).

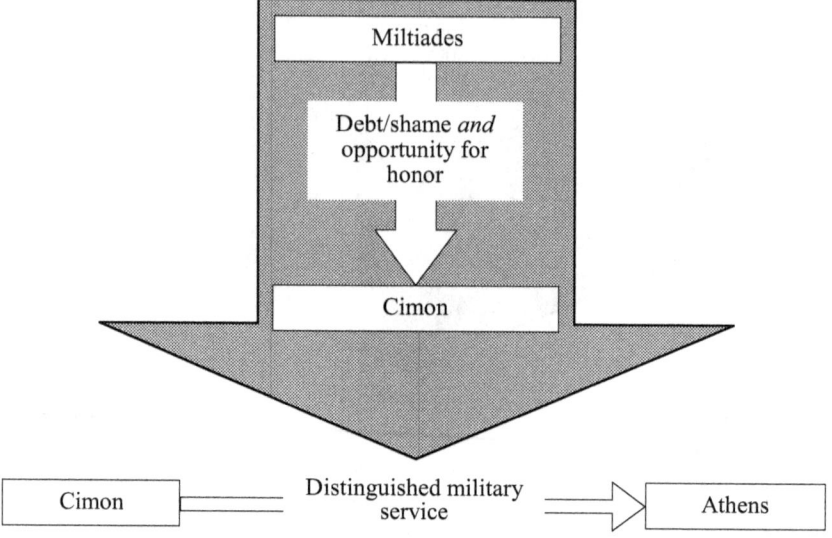

Figure 30. *The Function of Succession in Diodorus Siculus 10.30.1-2*

Text 28: Lucian, Alexander the False Prophet *5*. Lucian was a satirist and essayist of the second century CE. *Alexander* is his short biography of Alexander of Abonoteichus, a self-styled oracle and priest of Asclepius who flourished 150–170 CE.

In this cutting βίος, Lucian goes to great pains to describe Alexander's essential falseness. When Alexander was young he was very handsome, with long curly hair (which some people thought was fake) and 'sold his company' as a means of supporting himself. One of his lovers/benefactors was a man whom Lucian refers to only as 'the Tyanean'. Lucian describes him as a 'quack' (γόης) who sold cures and love potions, a former acolyte of Apollonius of Tyana. This man, recognizing in Alexander a kindred soul (and being quite enamored of the boy), took Alexander as his protégé, thoroughly schooling Alexander in schemes, frauds, and deceptions. When the Tyanean died, Alexander 'inherited and took over' (κληρονόμος καὶ διάδοχος οὗτος ἐγένετο) his schemes. Alexander then set himself up as a fraudulent prophet and oracle of Asclepius (Lucian, *Alexander* 5 [Kilburn, LCL]).

The text focuses on how Alexander and his predecessor shared characteristic attitudes/activities. Thus, succession here preserves continuity of manner. Alexander not only inherited the Tyanean's business, he also inherited and continued the man's fraudulent manner of living.

I can plot the exchanges thus:

2. Background and Graeco-Roman Texts

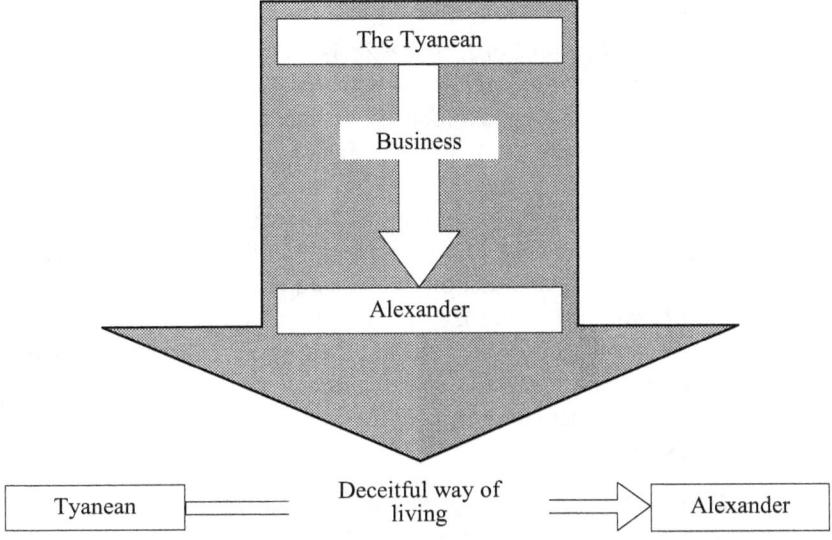

Figure 31. *The Function of Succession in Lucian,* Alexander the False Prophet *5*

3. Summary of Graeco-Roman Texts Describing the Function of Succession

Building on my collaboration with Talbert, I have shown the following:

First, I have shown that references to succession in Graeco-Roman literature sometimes contain not one but two exchanges. The first exchange is the succession itself. The second, when it occurs, is a reference to the function of that succession, what it achieved or might have achieved, why it was necessary or desired.

Second, I have shown that these two exchanges can be described graphically, and that the second exchange can profitably be described in relational terms borrowed from structuralism, namely Sender → Object → Receiver.

Third, I have shown that the functions of succession in this literature tend to fall into five categories, and that these categories separate along lines determined by the focus of succession in the text. If the text focuses on how succession affects property, for example, then the function seems to be different than if the text focuses on characteristic actions shared by predecessor and successor. To this point, we have seen succession function to ensure:

1. *Continuity of possession*, where the text focuses on *property* and how ownership is maintained through succession (Text 1: Herodotus 3.53; Text 4: Aristotle, *Politics* 1293a.13-30, etc.);
2. *Continuity of manner*, where the text focuses on a *characteristic attitude or action* that the predecessor and the successor share (Text 2:

Herodotus 5.90-92; Text 4: Aristotle, *Politics* 1293a.13-30; Text 5: Aristotle, *Athenian Constitution* 28.1-4, etc.);
3. *Continuity of institutional vitality*, where the object of succession is an institution, and the text focuses on that *object* and how succession causes it to remain vital and effective (Text 3: Plato, *Laws* 6.769c, etc.);
4. *Realization of an effect*, where the text focuses on an *effect* that is *succession-dependent*, one which began under the predecessor and was finally realized under the successor (Text 5: Aristotle, *Athenian Constitution* 28.1-4, etc.);
5. Continuity of effect, where the text focuses on an *effect/result* which is *shared by the predecessor and the successor* but the realization of which is not dependent upon the succession (Text 6: Diodorus Siculus 15.8-11, etc.).

Fourth, I have shown that the categories outlined above are not 'watertight'. Sometimes they overlap. Sometimes the delineations between categories seem to blur—for example, sometimes it is difficult to determine what is manner and what is agenda.

Fifth, I have shown that succession seems to function the same way whether the contemplated succession is realized or thwarted (e.g. Text 1: Herodotus 3.53; Text 17: Diogenes Laertius 9.115).

Sixth, I have shown that succession seems to operate apart from what the reader is told of the predecessors' and successors' intentions. Sometimes the predecessor intends for certain things to take place because of the succession (e.g. Text 1: Herodotus 3.53). Sometimes succession achieves what it achieves in spite of an actant's intention (e.g. Text 6: Diodorus Siculus 15.8-11) or without regard to intention (e.g. Text 13: Dio Chrysostom 64).

Seventh, I have shown that, in a single text, multiple succession stories can be grouped together so as to have one function (e.g. Text 3: Plato, *Laws* 6.769). Likewise, I have shown that in a single text, a single succession story can have multiple functions (e.g. Text 4: Aristotle, *Politics* 1293a.13-30; Text 5: Aristotle, *Athenian Constitution*, 28.1-4; Text 24: Tacitus, *Annals* 15.62; Text 25: Demosthenes, *Aphobus* 2.19).

Eighth, I have shown that the comparative greatness of the predecessor over the successor (Alexander's pre-eminence over his Διάδοχοι, Aristotle's pre-eminence over Theophrastus, Augustus's pre-eminence over Agrippa, Artaxerxes' pre-eminence over Ochus) does not invalidate or delegitimize the succession. In fact, the successor does not need to hold equal station in life with the predecessor for succession to have been inferred. A slave can remain a slave and yet be his master's successor in a task. A pupil can remain a pupil—or at least not become a teacher—and yet be his teacher's successor in the handing on of tradition. Thus succession includes differences between the predecessor and the successors in both degree and kind. The predecessor can be far greater than the successor (thus a difference in degree), and succession still have been inferred. Likewise, the predecessor can hold a different office or station in life than the successor (a difference in kind) and succession would still have been inferred.[33]

Therefore: succession is not invalidated by the predecessor having greater glory than the successor. I have *not* shown the converse, however. If the successor is greater than the predecessor, can he be spoken of as a successor? Would it be an insult to Alexander's glory to speak of him as Philip's successor, since he surpassed his father in glory? The closest example I have surveyed so far is Text 25: Demosthenes, *Aphobus* 2.19, where the orator Demosthenes is regarded as his father's successor and heir—but that is not really analogous to regarding Alexander as Philip's successor.

I have also not shown that a successor's legitimacy was a major concern in any of these texts. The closest any has come to questioning whether potential successor A was more legitimate than potential successor B is Text 14: Dio Cassius 53, detailing Augustus's choice of Agrippa over Marcellus. But even there, the focus is not 'Which is legitimate?' but rather 'Why did Augustus choose *this* successor?' I began this study expecting to see the successor's legitimacy figure prominently, and have not to this point. However, if I find in milieus other than Graeco-Roman texts in which succession primarily serves to legitimate a successor—and I do—then it stands to reason that succession can also function that way in Graeco-Roman texts, I simply had not discovered those examples at the time I finalized my textbase.

On the following two pages, sorted by the object of succession as above, are charts listing the texts surveyed to this point and the function of succession in each.

Note how some of the objects of succession tend to fit a predominant category. For example, in the passing on of headship of a philosophical school or the passing-on of knowledge/tradition, continuity of institutional vitality seems to be a logical function. References to succession involving other objects tend to have more varied functions.

Based on these findings, I can begin reconstructing the expectations an ancient audience would have had when hearing/reading texts which utilized succession. Because of the presence of certain terms commonly used in reference to succession, and the presence of certain phenomena commonly thought of in reference to succession, the ancient audience of texts from this milieu

---

33. One way to represent this phenomenon is through envisioning succession as covering points on a continuum of replacement: at one end, the successor is a complete replacement for the predecessor, completely taking the forerunner's place. At the other end, the 'weak' end of succession, the successor is more of a delegate or an agent, not a replacement, and there is little or no hint of the successor taking the forerunner's place.

would have understood these texts to refer to succession. They would further have understood that succession functioned in a certain way in each case, that it could achieve specific things in certain situations.

In the next chapter, I examine texts from Jewish and Christian milieus according to the pattern set forth in this chapter.

Table 1. *Graeco-Roman Texts Describing the Passing-On of Leadership/Rule*

	Text	Function
1.	Herodotus 3.53	Continuity of possession
2.	Herodotus 5.90-92	Continuity of manner
3.	Plato, *Laws* 6.769c	Continuity of effect Continuity of manner Continuity of institutional vitality
4.	Aristotle, *Politics* 1293a.13-30	Continuity of possession Continuity of manner Continuity of effect
5.	Aristotle, *Athenian Constitution* 28.1-4	Continuity of manner Realization of effect
6.	Diodorus Siculus 15.8-11	Continuity of effect
7.	Diodorus Siculus 15.93.1	Continuity of manner
8.	Diodorus Siculus 17–18	Realization of effect
9.	Strabo, *Geography* 11.13.9	Continuity of manner
10.	Strabo, *Geography* 13.1.3	Realization of effect
11.	Livy 23.27.9-12	Continuity of effect
12.	Pausanius, *Description of Greece* 7.12	Continuity of manner
13.	Dio Chrysostom 64.20-22	Continuity of effect Continuity of manner
14.	Dio Cassius 53	Continuity of effect Continuity of manner

Table 2. *Graeco-Roman Texts Describing the Passing-On of the Headship of a Philosophical School*

	Text	Function
15.	Aulus Gellius, *Attic Nights* 13.5	Realization of effect Continuity of manner
16.	Diogenes Laertius 4.67	Continuity of institutional vitality
17.	Diogenes Laertius 9.115	Continuity of institutional vitality Continuity of manner
18.	Diogenes Laertius 10.9	Continuity of institutional vitality
19.	Iamblichus, *On the Pythagorean Way of Life* 36	Continuity of institutional vitality

2. Background and Graeco-Roman Texts

Table 3. *Graeco-Roman Texts Describing the Passing-On of a Task*

	Text	Function
20.	Lysias, *Pension* 6	Continuity of effect
21.	Xenophon, *Anabasis* 1.5.2	Realization of effect

Table 4. *Graeco-Roman Texts Describing the Passing-On of Knowledge or Tradition*

	Text	Function
22.	Aristotle, *Sophistical Refutations* 34.27-35	Continuity of institutional vitality
23.	Pliny the Elder, *Natural History* 30.2.4-5	Continuity of institutional vitality
24.	Tacitus, *Annals* 15.62	Continuity of institutional vitality Realization of effect

Table 5. *Graeco-Roman Texts Describing the Passing-On of Possessions*

	Text	Function
25.	Demosthenes, *Aphobus* 2.19	Continuity of possession Continuity of effect
26.	Plato, *Laws* 5.740b	Continuity of effect Continuity of institutional vitality
27.	Diodorus Siculus 10.30.1-2	Realization of effect
28.	Lucian, *Alexander the False Prophet* 5	Continuity of manner

3

THE ANCIENT UNDERSTANDING OF SUCCESSION, PART 2: SUCCESSION IN JEWISH AND CHRISTIAN TEXTS

In the previous chapter, I did two things. First, I briefly surveyed the field of Graeco-Roman texts in which I found succession to be prominent. I summarized the general contours and features of how these texts described succession. In that summary, I noted certain commonalities, among them a fairly fixed terminology referring to succession.

Second, I examined 28 Graeco-Roman texts in which I found an interest in the function of succession. In that examination, I noted certain commonalities, chief among them the fact that the descriptions of function gravitated into a small cluster of functional emphases—succession ensures continuity of manner, continuity of effect, continued institutional vitality, and so on.

In this chapter, I will do the following. First, I will survey the general features of Jewish references to succession. Second, I will examine 19 Jewish texts that describe the function of succession, and compare/contrast my findings regarding these texts with my findings regarding the Graeco-Roman texts in Chapter 2 above. Third, I will survey 13 Christian texts, excluding the Pastoral Epistles, which describe the function of succession, and compare/contrast my findings regarding these texts with my findings regarding the Graeco-Roman texts in Chapter 2 above and the Jewish texts earlier in Chapter 3. All texts surveyed in this chapter are contemporaneous with the Graeco-Roman materials surveyed in Chapter 2 (i.e. from the period roughly antedating 200 CE). As noted in the previous chapter (p. 20), I have numbered each text sequentially across the chapters so as to facilitate comparisons within the textbase.

1. *Succession in Jewish Texts*

Turning to Jewish texts contemporaneous to the Graeco-Roman texts of Chapter 2, I note at the outset that these also show a strong interest in succession. Note, for example, how the plot of Genesis turns in several places on the issues of legitimacy and succession: for example, will the covenant be handed on through Ishmael or Isaac, Jacob or Esau? Note also the way that Isaac's succession of Abraham is confirmed through the parallel events in

3. Succession in Jewish and Christian Texts 61

their lives: for example, note the parallel between Isaac's sin and lack of faith in Genesis 26 and Abraham's sin and lack of faith in Genesis 12 and 20. Another example: notice the intrigue and references to succession surrounding Solomon's ascendance to David's throne (1 Kgs 1–2), where Adonijah plots against Solomon by requesting to have David's former concubine given to him. Solomon clearly understands this in terms of Adonijah claiming some kind of succession to David's kingdom—Adonijah takes David's concubine, Adonijah stakes a claim on David's throne. These features are similar enough to those noted in the Graeco-Roman texts above to warrant further comparison.

Formally, these Jewish texts are themselves much like the Graeco-Roman texts surveyed above. Beginning with my reading of the Old Testament, I have found in ancient Jewish literature several stories in which succession plays a major role. I have found two succession lists (the list of Edomite kings in Gen. 36.33-39, which is repeated in 1 Chron. 1.44-50; the list of David's officers in 1 Chron. 27.7, 34). I have found major stories in which succession is prominent (e.g. Solomon's succession to David's throne, Elisha's succession of Elijah). I have also found succession anecdotes of a comparatively minor character (e.g. the story of Aaron passing on the office of priest to his son, Eleazar, in Num. 20.25-28). I have also found mentions of succession that do not seem to be related to any succession story.

In terms of the language used—the semantic domain of succession—the Hebrew texts and their translations tend to differ in character from the Greek texts. There appears to be no single consistent counterpart to the Greek διάδοχος, although there are Hebrew terms that I suggest below serve as functional equivalents in context. The Hebrew texts and their translations in the Septuagint (LXX) are more likely to describe the relationship between predecessor and successor with prepositions—'the one after', 'the one who followed'—rather than by any particular technical term.

The LXX uses διάδοχος and διαδέχομαι seven and thirteen times respectively. Occasionally, their use reflects the Graeco-Roman patterns noted above: 'Joshua...was the successor (διάδοχος) of Moses' (Sir. 46.1); Elijah 'anointed...prophets to succeed (διαδόχους) [himself]' (Sir. 48.8); Antiochus Epiphanes 'succeeded to the throne' (διαδέχεται τὴν ἀρχήν) of his father, Seleucus (*4 Macc.* 4.15).

Most of the uses of διάδοχος in the LXX differ from the Graeco-Roman patterns seen above, however. Most frequently, διάδοχος in the LXX refers to a person to whom a leader delegated authority with no hint of replacement—see LXX 1 Chron. 18.17; 2 Chron. 26.11; 28.7; 31.12; Est. 10.3; 2 Macc. 4.29; 4.31; 14.26. Most of these uses are from texts which inarguably existed first in a Semitic original. I do not currently have an explanation for this phenomenon, it will require exploration beyond this study.

As an introduction to my survey of Jewish succession texts, I will here quickly describe the succession list of Edomite kings, which I mentioned above. This text (Gen. 36.33-39, repeated in 1 Chron. 1.44-50) is not covered in the discussion below, because it shows no prominent concern for function. It does, however, illustrate clearly the language the Old Testament used to convey succession. The passage uses the formula 'וימת (successor's name) תחתיו וימלך (predecessor's name)', which roughly translated reads 'and (predecessor) died, and (successor) ruled in his place'. This formula occurs seven times, and the LXX consistently translates the phrase with ἀπέθανεν δὲ...καὶ ἐβασίλευσεν ἀντ' αὐτοῦ. Notice the use of the Hebrew preposition תחת ('after' or 'in the place of'). I will show below that Old Testament texts where succession is prominent frequently use this term.

2. Jewish Texts Describing the Function of Succession

Below are the Jewish texts I have found that describe the function of succession. I gathered these texts by the same process and according to the same criteria used to collect the sample in Chapter 2. Some of these texts, such as the one immediately below, exist in both the LXX and the Hebrew text. In those cases, I have compared the two and noted the semantic and conceptual features of each, making particular note of any differences between them. I have grouped the texts according to the object of succession (here leadership/ rule, tradition/knowledge, or possessions), and have arranged the texts in roughly chronological order within these categories.

Texts Describing Succession of Leadership/Rule
Text 29: Numbers 27.12-23 and Joshua 1.2-9. In Num. 27.12-23, Moses appoints Joshua his successor.[1] The story opens with God telling Moses that he is about to die. Moses responds by asking God to appoint a leader over the people after him, someone to guide the people so that they do not become 'like sheep without a shepherd' (27.17). God responds:

> Take Joshua..., a man in whom is the spirit, and lay your hand upon him; have him stand before Eleazar the priest and all the congregation, and commission (LXX συνίστημι) him in their sight. You shall give him some of your authority (הוד, LXX δόξα, 'glory') so that all the congregation of the Israelites may obey. (27.18-20)

---

1. For discussion and bibliography, see E. Talstra, 'Deuteronomy 31: Confusion or Conclusion? The Story of Moses' Threefold Succession', in Marc Vervenne and Johan Lust (eds.), *Deuteronomy and Deuteronomic Literature: Festschrift for C.H.W. Brekelmans* (Leuven: Peeters, 1997), pp. 87-110; J.R. Porter, 'The Succession of Joshua', in J.R. Porter and John I. Durham (eds.), *Proclamation and Presence: Old Testament Essays in Honour of Gwynne Henton Davies* (Richmond, VA: John Knox Press, 1970), pp. 102-32.

Moses does what God commands, commissioning Joshua in the sight of the people.

This storyline picks up again in the opening verses of the book of Joshua. After Moses' death, God speaks to Joshua and tells him that Moses has died, and that he (Joshua) must now lead the people across the Jordan and into the Promised Land:

> Every place that the sole of your foot will tread upon I have given to you... No one shall be able to stand against you all the days of your life. *As I was with Moses, so shall I be with you.* (1.3, 5 [emphasis mine])

First, note that, as with several of the Graeco-Roman texts above, the object passed on in succession is a complex object, involving both leadership/rule and an implicit agenda. Unlike the Graeco-Roman texts, however, the agenda is not the predecessor's, or not primarily the predecessor's—it is God's (see Josh. 1.3). Second, note that Josh. 1.1 describes Joshua as Moses' 'servant' (משרת, LXX ὑπουργός).[2] As the survey progresses, I will show that משרת is a term frequently used in Old Testament succession texts to refer to the successor. Third, note that Moses is not the one who chooses his successor—God makes the choice. Fourth, note that Joshua does not become a prophet or a lawgiver in the same sense as Moses. This difference in kind does not negate the existence of succession, however—as with the Graeco-Roman examples noted above, succession does not require that the successor becomes the predecessor's equal in every way, or even in most ways. Fifth, note the presence of the standard typological features of a succession narrative, as outlined by Talbert and myself:[3] the naming of what is to be passed on (leadership of the people, as described in Num. 27.16-17); the symbolic succession act (the commissioning speech, the laying-on of hands, the transference of authority/glory/essence); and confirmation that succession has taken place (God's statement that he would be with Joshua as he had been with Moses, a statement echoed in Josh. 1.17; 3.7; 4.14; Joshua parting the Jordan River as Moses had earlier parted the Red Sea [Josh. 3; cf. Exod. 14]).

---

2. I found other uses of משרת to refer to Joshua and Moses in Exod. 24.13; 33.11. An interesting parallel phenomenon appears in the Ugaritic Legend of Keret (trans. H.L. Ginsburg; *ANET*, 142-49, see A.1.23, B.2.25, and C.6.39). This text refers to Keret's son as 'Yassib the lad'. In n. 21, Ginsburg mentions that the term translated 'lad' refers to 'the lad who ministers personally to his father', and—as the rest of the story shows—will succeed him as king.

Josephus and Philo both use Greek succession language in reference to the Moses–Joshua relationship: Moses appointed Joshua as his successor (διάδοχον ἑαυτοῦ 'Ιησοῦν καθίστησιν, Josephus, *Ant.* 4.165), Moses' relationship with his successor (διάδοχος) is an example for 'all future rulers' as an 'archetype and model' (ἀρχέτυπον παράδειγμα) for how they should relate to their successors (διαδόχοις) (Philo, *Virtues* 68-70).

3. See pp. 15-16, above. Also Talbert and Stepp, 'Succession: Part 1', p. 163.

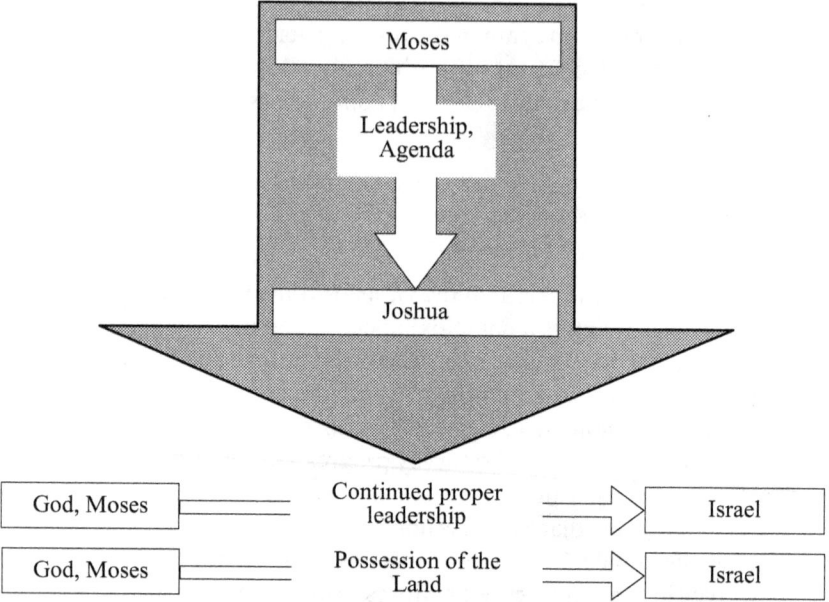

Figure 32. *The Functions of Succession in Numbers 27.12-23 and Joshua 1.2-9*

Note the centrality of God to this succession. God chooses the successor, God sets the agenda for the successor's leadership. God is also the primary sender in the function of the succession.

What is the function of succession in this story? The transference of leadership is clear, as is Moses' desire that Israel should not be left without a leader. In this story, two functions are in play. First, succession serves to ensure continuity of effect (the predecessor and successor achieve the same results, the sheep are not left without a shepherd). Second, succession serves to ensure the realization of an effect (something started under the predecessor—Israel's return to the land promised to them—is completed under the successor).

Text 30: 1 Samuel 9–18 (LXX 1 Kingdoms 9–18). Another long and complex Old Testament succession story is that of David's relationship with Samuel, Saul, and Jonathan.[4] The story opens with the people of Israel living in fear of the Philistines: as long as Samuel, their judge, was ruling, the Philistines were kept at bay (1 Sam. 7.7-14). But as Samuel neared the end of his life,

---

4. For discussion and bibliography, see Robert B. Lawton, 'Saul, Jonathan, and the "Son of Jesse"', *JSOT* 58 (1993), pp. 35-46.

the people once again feared them. Further, they were angry with Samuel because he had placed his sons as judges over Israel after him, and they were wicked and corrupt (1 Sam. 8). The people demanded that Samuel (and God) give them a king, so that they could be like other nations and have a king to 'go out before us and fight our battles' (8.20).

Samuel relented. Soon God spoke to him: he would reveal to Samuel the man whom Samuel would anoint as king, the one who would save Israel from the Philistines (9.16). That man turned out to be Saul: Samuel anointed him, and after the anointing 'the spirit of God possessed him [Saul]' and he prophesied (10.1-10). As king, Saul had initial victories over the Ammonites (ch. 11) and Philistines (ch. 13), but final victory over the Philistines eluded him.[5] Instead, his son Jonathan, received great glory for victory over the Philistines (1 Sam. 14.45, referring back to the victory of 14.1-15).

Then, in 15.1-33, God rejects Saul as king. In 16.1-13, Samuel anoints David to be king: the spirit of the Lord comes upon him (16.13) but departs from Saul (16.14). In 1 Samuel 17, David defeats the Philistines in battle by defeating Goliath: he does so under Saul's authority, but refuses to wear Saul's armor (17.38-39). Then David makes a covenant with Jonathan (Philistine-slayer), the making of which included David accepting Jonathan's clothing and armor (18.1-4). As David and the army were returning home after the battle with the Philistines, the women of the towns they passed through sang 'Saul has killed his thousands/and David his ten thousands' (18.6-7).

Next, David shows that he has inherited Jonathan's role as Philistine-slayer. Saul, being jealous of David, wanted to kill David. He promised his daughter, Michal, in marriage to David, but only if David brought him one hundred Philistine foreskins (Saul thought David would be killed while attempting this mass circumcision). Instead, David kills the Philistines, and brings the foreskins to Saul (18.27). After that time, David is consistently victorious over the Philistines—1 Sam. 19.8; 23; 2 Samuel 5, 8, etc. Once David enters, Saul and Jonathan are never again victorious over the Philistines again.

This story does not contain any of the succession terms I have noticed elsewhere. However, notice in this story the features common to succession narratives: the naming of what is to be passed on (the role of deliverer from the Philistines, 9.16); the symbolic succession act (the anointings in 1 Sam. 10.1-8 and 16.1-13, the Holy Spirit coming on David and leaving Saul, 16.13-14; the exchanges/non-exchanges of armor/clothing, 18.1-4; 17.38-39); and the confirmation that succession has taken place (David's acclaim over

---

5. 1 Sam. 14.47 ('Saul...fought against his enemies on every side...and against the Philistines; wherever he turned he routed them') implies that Saul was decisively victorious over the Philistines, but this impression is qualified by 14.52 ('There was hard fighting against the Philistines all the days of Saul').

Saul, particularly 18.6-7; the absence of any further victories over the Philistines by Saul/Jonathan and the presence of multiple such victories by David).

Thus this story would have been heard and understood as referring to succession, even without the use of succession language. Succession would clearly have been understood because of the presence of types and phenomena from the conceptual field.

Note the imagery used to convey the idea of succession: Saul's victories over the Philistines are fleeting, limited, and ultimately accrue to the glory of others (Jonathan, David). The victories of David and Jonathan over the Philistines are bigger than Saul's victories. David does not accept Saul's armor, but he does accept and wear Jonathan's. In a sense, David functions as a replacement for Jonathan.[6] Notice the complexity: succession from Saul to David takes place (i.e. David becomes king of Israel after Saul). At the same time, succession does *not* take place (the historian refuses to paint David as Saul's heir in any way). In the same terms, succession from Jonathan to David does not occur, but it *does*—David is a replacement for Jonathan.

What of Samuel as David's predecessor? As long as Samuel judged, the Philistines were kept at bay, but during Saul's reign they were a constant thorn in Israel's side. Under David, however, the Philistines were defeated, paid tribute to Israel, and were never again a threat. In essence, Samuel is David's truest predecessor. In that case, we find here an abortive succession from Samuel to Saul, then a realized succession from Samuel to David. The narrative threads are incredibly tangled here.

Figure 33 (opposite) sets out the exchanges involved.

Notice again the sovereignty theme at work here, which also played out in the selection of Joshua as Moses' successor. In the Old Testament stories so far, God chooses the successor, the predecessor does not. God sets the agenda (1 Sam. 9.16), which again is passed on along with the exchange of leadership as a complex object in the primary act of succession.

How does succession function here? The object that is passed on is both the kingship and leadership in the war with the Philistines, which began before Samuel and—in essence if not totally in fact—is completed under David. David made the Philistines pay tribute to him, and they are not portrayed in the rest of Israel's history after David as major antagonists. At the same time, David clearly inherits Jonathan's role as Philistine-slayer. After David's initial victories, Jonathan is not shown fighting (or killing) Philistines until the scene where he is killed by the Philistines and Saul his father takes his own life rather than being captured by them (31.2, 4-6).

---

6. This idea is accented by Saul telling Jonathan in 1 Sam. 20.31, 'As long as the son of Jesse lives upon the earth, neither you nor your kingdom shall be established'. It is further heightened by David's reception of the heir to Jonathan's line, Mephibosheth, whom David treats like one of his own children (2 Sam. 9; cf. 20.15, 42).

3. *Succession in Jewish and Christian Texts* 67

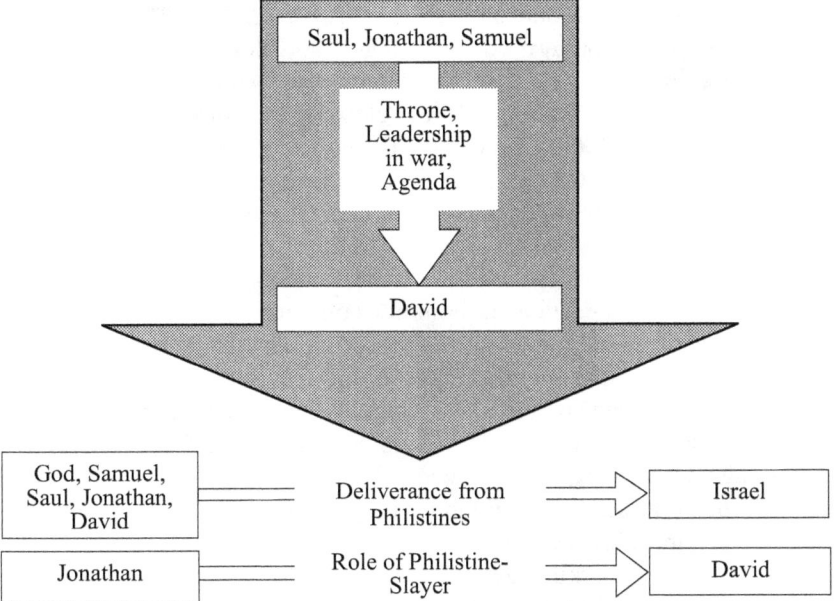

Figure 33. *The Functions of Succession in 1 Samuel 9–18 (LXX 1 Kingdoms 9–18)*

Thus succession of leadership/rule here ensures two things. It first ensures the realization of an effect—the deliverance of Israel from the Philistines, begun under Samuel, continued under Saul and Jonathan, is completed under David. It also ensures continuity of manner (characteristic activity)—David continues Jonathan's work as Philistine-slayer.

Text 31: 1 Kings 1–2 (LXX 3 Kingdoms 1–2). In 2 Samuel 7, David—having solidified his rule as king over all Israel—plans to build a temple for Yahweh, so that the ark of the covenant can have a permanent dwelling. In response to David's plan, God speaks through the prophet Nathan: God does not want David to build a house (temple) for him. Rather, God said:

> The Lord declares to you that the Lord will make you a house... I will raise up your offspring after (אחרי, LXX μετὰ σέ) you, who shall come forth from your body, and I will establish his kingdom. He shall build a house for my name... Your house and your kingdom shall be made sure forever before me; your throne shall be established forever. (2 Sam. 7.11-16)

In 1 Kings 1–2, David is in failing health. His eldest surviving son, Adonijah, lays claim on the throne. This action was in contradiction of the promise that David had made to Bathsheba, whom he had told that Solomon (David's son by her) would inherit the throne from him. Bathsheba and Nathan prompt David to declare Solomon his successor: David promises Bathsheba, 'Your son Solomon shall succeed me as king (ימלך אחרי, LXX βασιλεύσει μετ' ἐμέ), and he shall sit on my throne in my place (ישב על־כסאי תחתי, LXX καθήσεται ἐπὶ τοῦ θρόνου μου ἀντ' ἐμοῦ)' (1 Kgs 1.30). Solomon goes to Gihon, riding on David's mule, and is anointed king there by the priest Zadok. He is then placed on David's throne. At the close of the episode, David prays: 'Blessed be the Lord, the God of Israel, who has today granted one of my offspring to sit on my throne and permitted me to witness it' (1 Kgs 1.48).[7] Solomon later refers to himself as having been placed (LXX τίθημι) by God on his father's throne (2.24).

This story would clearly have been understood in terms of succession. In addition to the language, note the common components of an ancient succession story: the naming of what is to be passed on (David's throne, 1.13, etc.); the symbolic succession act (Solomon riding David's mule and sitting on David's throne while David still lives);[8] and the confirmation that succession has taken place (the people acclaim Solomon as king, 1.40).

Note also what may qualify as succession terminology: תחת, which I also pointed out in the list of the Edomite kings; and אחרי, which is also frequently used in references to succession.[9] Notice also that David sees the succession as the working out of God's promise, even if the text never explicitly refers to that promise (but see Adonijah's words in 2.15).

The exchanges involved are presented in Fig. 34.

How does succession function in this passage? The primary emphasis is on which of the two will succeed David—Adonijah or Solomon. The succession acts serve to legitimate Solomon as David's successor. Thus here I find, for the first time in this study, a text in which succession primarily serves to legitimate a particular successor. I find another function present here also. The succession also fulfills God's promises to David—the promise that David's son would build God a house, and the promise that God would build David a house. Thus succession of leadership/rule here ensures the realization of two effects—benefits that began under the predecessor (the building of the two houses: the Temple and the house of David) are realized under the successor.

---

7. For the suggestion that this narrative (2 Sam. 7–1 Kgs 2) is from a separate 'Davidic succession narrative', see David M. Gunn, *The Story of King David: Genre and Interpretation* (JSOTSup, 6; Sheffield: JSOT Press, 1978); Stephen L. McKenzie, 'The So-Called Succession Narrative in the Deuteronomistic History', in Albert de Pury and Thomas Römer (eds.), *Die sogenannte Thronfolgegeschichte Davids* (Göttingen: Vandenhoeck & Ruprecht, 2000), pp. 123-35.

8. This idea is also at the heart of the conflict between Solomon and Adonijah in 1 Kgs 2: when Adonijah asks for Abishag to be made his wife, a request that costs Adonijah his life. Solomon understands that by taking one of David's concubines, Adonijah is maintaining a claim on David's throne—this is also borne out by Adonijah's words in 2.15.

9. In texts not otherwise mentioned in this study, אחרי is used in the story of Eleazar's succession of Aaron (Exod. 29.29, LXX μετ' αὐτόν), a succession list of David's officers (1 Chron. 27.7, 34; LXX of 27.34 uses μετὰ τοῦτον), and in 'Solomon's' reference to himself as David's successor (Eccl. 2.12).

3. Succession in Jewish and Christian Texts 69

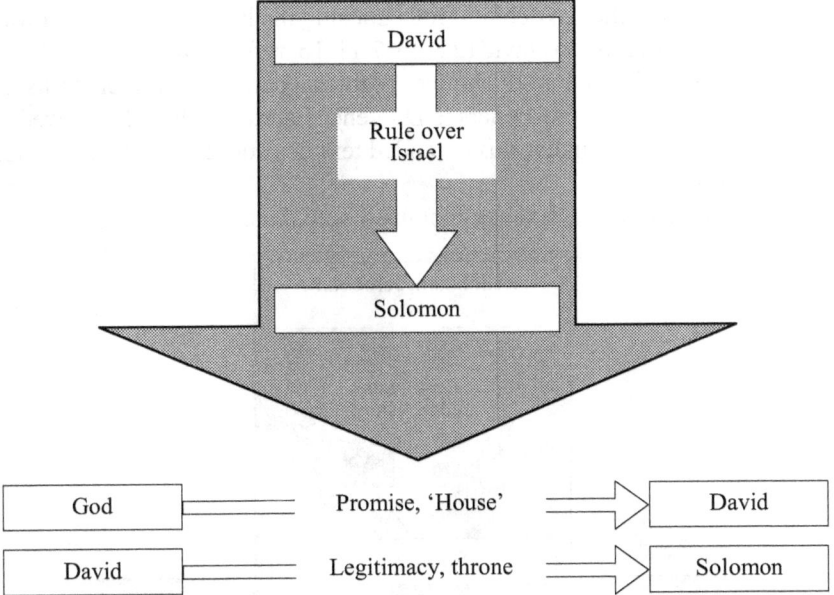

Figure 34. *The Functions of Succession in 1 Kings 1–2 (LXX 3 Kingdoms 1–2)*

Text 32: 1 Kings 11.43, etc. (LXX 3 Kingdoms 11.44, etc.). The succession list of kings of Judah and Israel is contained in a series of passages, beginning with 1 Kgs 11.43 and continuing into 2 Kings (and repeated in 2 Chronicles). The list uses the succession formula בנו תחתיו (*name*) וימלך ('and X his son succeeded him as king' [lit. 'became king in his place']) 38 times, and the usage is consistent and uniform. The LXX references are also uniform. For example, 3 Kgdms 11.43, 'Rehoboam his son ruled after him', is translated ἐβασίλευσε ἀντ' αὐτοῦ. Other LXX references here use the same pattern, with the only variation being the occasional use of the present βασιλεύει instead of the aorist ἐβασίλευσε.[10]

---

10. Uses of the formula בנו תחתיו (name) וימלך in other succession references include: Deut. 10.6 (Aaron succeeded by Eleazar); 2 Sam. 10.1 (Ammonite king [Nahash] succeeded by Hanun, also 1 Chron. 19.1); 2 Kgs 13.24 (Hazael of Aram succeeded by Benhadad); 2 Kgs 19.37 (Sennacherib succeeded by Esar-haddon).

The entire list of references for Text 32 is: 1 Kgs 11.43 (para. 2 Chron. 9.31); 14.20, 31 (para. 2 Chron. 12.16); 15.8 (para. 2 Chron. 14.1); 15.24 (para. 2 Chron. 17.1); 16.6, 28; 22.40, 50 (para. 2 Chron. 21.1); 2 Kgs 8.24; 10.35; 12.21 (para. 2 Chron. 24.27); 13.9; 14.6, 29; 15.7, 22, 38 (para. 2 Chron. 27.9); 16.20 (para. 2 Chron. 28.27); 20.21 (para. 2 Chron. 32.33); 21.18 (para. 2 Chron. 33.20); 21.24 (para. 2 Chron. 33.25); 21.26; 24.6 (para. 2 Chron. 36.8). Two occurrences in 1–2 Chronicles are not paralleled in Kings: 1 Chron. 29.28 (David succeeded by Solomon); and 2 Chron. 26.23 (Uzziah succeeded by Jotham).

Also, note how the list depicts God choosing the kings of Judah as a way of keeping his promise to David (2 Sam. 7.11-16, referred to in 1 Kgs 15.4; 2 Kgs 8.19; 19.34; 20.6). Finally, notice the formal parallels between the list of kings and the lists of philosophers in Diogenes Laertius, which I surveyed in Chapter 2 above. Formally, this extended text is a succession list expanded with anecdotes.

I can illustrate the exchanges contained here thus:

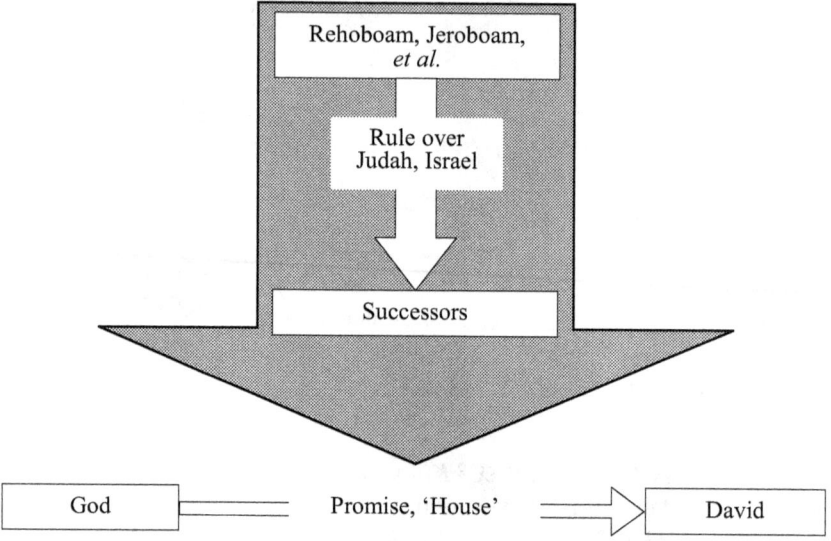

Figure 35. *The Function of Succession in 1 Kings 11.43, etc.*
(LXX *3 Kingdoms 11.44, etc.*)

Here succession of leadership/rule functions in two ways. First, it ensures continuity of possession—David's throne stays in the family. But second, and primarily, succession here (again) functions to ensure the fulfillment of God's promise. David's throne began under his rule, but it continues through his heirs. Thus succession here serves to ensure the ongoing realization of effect. There is really no other prominent consistent theme in the list of kings of Judah—some ruled well, others ruled badly, but God kept his promise by maintaining David's throne, punish David's heirs though he might.

Text 33: 1 Kings 19–2 Kings 2 (LXX 3 Kingdoms 19–4 Kingdoms 2). In 1 Kings 19, Elijah—having just defeated and slaughtered the priests of Baal at Carmel—flees for his life. He travels to Mt Horeb, and God addresses him there. God tells him to anoint new kings over Israel and Aram, and to 'anoint Elisha...as prophet in your place' (תחתיך, 1 Kgs 19.16; LXX ἀντὶ σοῦ). God tells Elijah what his plans are—God is going to judge Omri through Jehu, and punish Ben-hadad (and Israel, it turns out—see 2 Kgs 8.12; 10.32; 13.7)

3. *Succession in Jewish and Christian Texts*

through Hazael. Elijah obeys, and finds Elisha plowing a field. He throws his cloak over Elisha (1 Kgs 19.19). Elisha follows after (אחרי) him and becomes Elijah's servant (וישרתהו, the verb from which משרת derives; 1 Kgs 19.21; LXX καὶ ἐλειτούργει αὐτῷ).

In 2 Kings 2, Elijah is taken up to heaven while Elisha watches. The two walk together and come to the Jordan River, which Elijah parts by striking it with his cloak. The two walk across on dry ground (2 Kgs 2.8). Then, as Elijah is about to ascend, he asks Elisha to make a request of him. Elisha asks for a double share of Elijah's spirit. Elijah tells his apprentice that this request will only be fulfilled if Elisha sees him being taken away (2 Kgs 2.9-10). Then a chariot and horses of fire come between the two, and Elijah is taken up into heaven while Elisha watches.[11]

Elisha then tears his clothes in mourning (2 Kgs 2.11-12). After that, he picks up Elijah's cloak where it had fallen on the ground.[12] He returns to the edge of the Jordan River. Just as Elijah had done shortly before, Elisha strikes the water with the cloak and parts it, and walks across the river on dry ground. When the other prophets see him, they say, 'The spirit of Elijah rests on Elisha' (2 Kgs 2.13-15).

Again, the object of succession is complex—both leadership (the prophet's office) and agenda (justice against Omri and Ben-hadad). Again, the act symbolizing succession is explicitly shown—Elijah casts his cloak over Elisha when he calls him, Elisha sacrifices his oxen (thereby turning his back on his old way of life), follows after Elijah, and becomes his servant. And again, there is explicit confirmation that succession has taken place—Elisha sees Elijah ascending, Elisha takes Elijah's cloak, Elisha reproduces Elijah's miracle (parting the Jordan), the prophets acclaim Elisha as the repository of Elijah's spirit. Not only that, but Elisha actually fulfills some of the agenda that God entrusted to Elijah in 1 Kgs 19.16: he anoints Jehu (2 Kgs 9) and Hazael (2 Kgs 8). Notice also the presence of the same language I remarked on in other succession scenes. Elisha takes Elijah's place (תחת, 1 Kgs 19.16), he follows after (אחרי) Elijah and becomes his servant (וישרתהו, 1 Kgs 19.21).[13]

What is the function of succession in this story? Two ideas are central. First, succession ensures continuity of manner: Elisha takes Elijah's place, performing the same duties and miracles and possessing the same spirit in

---

11. For discussion and bibliography, see Mark A. O'Brien, 'The Portrayal of Prophets in 2 Kings 2', *Australian Biblical Review* 46 (1998), pp. 1-16.

12. The LXX (4 Kgdms 2.13) heightens the sense of succession by adding a detail to the Hebrew text's account, indicating that Elijah's cloak didn't fall on the ground as Elijah was taken up, but instead fell onto Elisha!

13. Josephus (*Ant.* 8.7+353) closes the story by noting that, 'as long as Elijah was alive he [Elisha] was his disciple and attendant (μαθητὴς καὶ διάκονος)'.

double measure. Second, succession ensures the realization of an effect. God tells Elijah,

> You shall anoint Hazael as king over Aram. Also you shall anoint Jehu son of Nimshi as king over Israel; and you shall anoint Elisha son of Shaphat of Abelmeholah as prophet in your place. Whoever escapes from the sword of Hazael, Jehu shall kill; and whoever escapes from the sword of Jehu, Elisha shall kill. Yet I will leave seven thousand in Israel, all the knees that have not bowed to Baal, and every mouth that has not kissed him. (1 Kgs 19.15-18)

God plans, through Jehu and Hazael and Elisha, to judge and purify Israel and to punish specific evil deeds. Part of this process has begun under Elijah—see 1 Kings 18. But the process is not finished when Elijah abdicates the scene. Thus succession is required for it to be completely realized.

I can set out the exchanges thus:

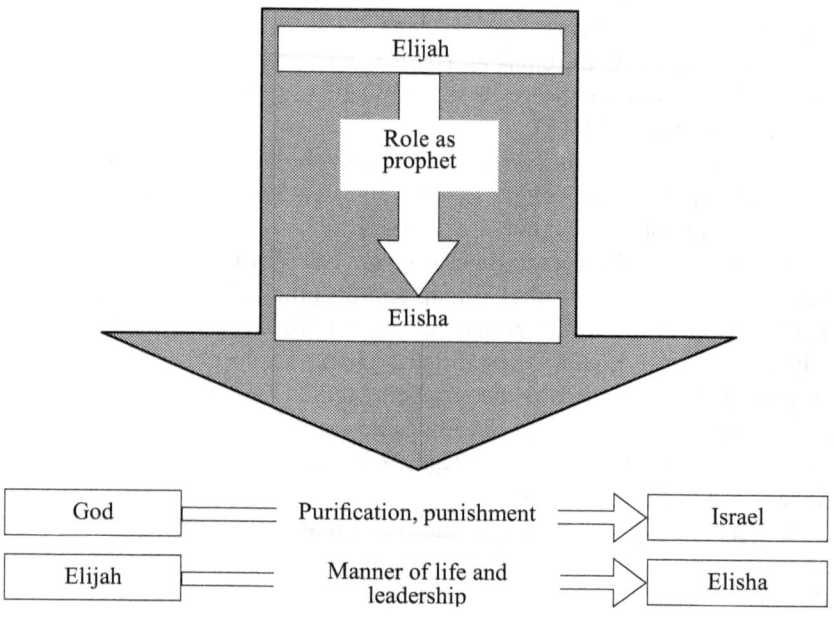

Figure 36. *The Functions of Succession in 1 Kings 19–2 Kings 2*
(LXX *3 Kingdoms 19–4 Kingdoms 2*)

A brief summary is in order. I have noted that these texts *prima facie* evince a concern for succession, and that Old Testament literature includes succession narratives (i.e. narratives where succession is a central concern), mentions of succession in narratives of another nature, and succession lists. Second, these texts show succession involving differences in degree and kind between the predecessor and successor—as with the Graeco-Roman texts above, the successor need not replace the predecessor in every way, but only in one significant way, for the succession to be real. Third, these texts use a fixed terminology to refer to succession, and among these terms are תחת,[14] אחרי,[15] and משרת.[16] Fourth, the features noted by Talbert and me as being standard features of ancient Mediterranean succession narratives are prominent in the Old Testament texts. Fifth, succession in these ancient Jewish texts appears to function much the same way as it functioned in the ancient Graeco-Roman texts surveyed in Chapter 2 above. Sixth, the most striking difference between these Jewish texts and the Graeco-Roman texts is that these texts consistently and emphatically present God as the one who chooses the successor and sets the agenda that succession is to achieve.

This last point bears further mention. Why did God choose Joshua to be successor, or Elisha? Why keep the throne of Judah in the possession of David's family, when there may have been more righteous or capable people available at the time? Or (to go beyond the list of texts I have examined here) why did God choose Jacob and not Esau? Answer: because that is what God decided best fit his purposes. In all these texts, an ancient audience would have understood succession to be a tool of God's sovereignty, something by which he accomplished his will.

Text 34: Sirach 47.11-13. Jesus ben Sirach was a scholar and teacher who flourished in Jerusalem in the early third century BCE.[17] Sirach 44–51 is a long poem covering the history of Israel, devoted to recounting the deeds of Israel's heroes. Sirach 47 covers the careers of Nathan, David, Solomon, and the nation's bifurcation under Jeroboam and Rehoboam. At the end of his section on David, Sirach writes:

> The Lord took away his sins,
>   And exalted his power forever;
> He gave him a covenant of kingship (καὶ ἔδωκεν αὐτῷ διαθήκην βασιλέων)
>   And a glorious throne in Israel. (47.11)

Then the section on Solomon begins:

> After him (David, μετὰ τοῦτον) a wise son rose up
>   Who because of him lived in security;
> Solomon reigned in an age of peace,
>   Because God made all his borders tranquil,
> So that he might build a house in his name
>   And provide a sanctuary to stand forever. (47.12-13)

14. Primarily translated in the LXX with μετά.
15. Primarily translated in the LXX with ἀντί.
16. Translated in the LXX with variations of λειτουργός, ὑπουργός, etc.
17. For discussion and bibliography, see Alexander A. DiLella, 'Wisdom of Ben-Sira', in *ABD*, VI, pp. 931-45; R.A.F. MacKenzie, *Sirach* (Wilmington, DE: Michael Glazier, 1983).

Note the presence of both Greek succession language and Semitic 'translation Greek' succession language—διαθήκην in 47.11 alongside μετὰ τοῦτον in 47.12.

How does succession function in this story? Sirach's reading of God's promise to David is consistent with what I have already shown under Text 34: 1 Kings 1–2 above. Solomon's succession to David's throne was part of God's plan to keep his promise that he would build a house for David and that David's son would build a house for him. Again, succession of leadership is used by God to ensure the realization of an effect—actually, two effects.

The exchanges in this text can be mapped thus:

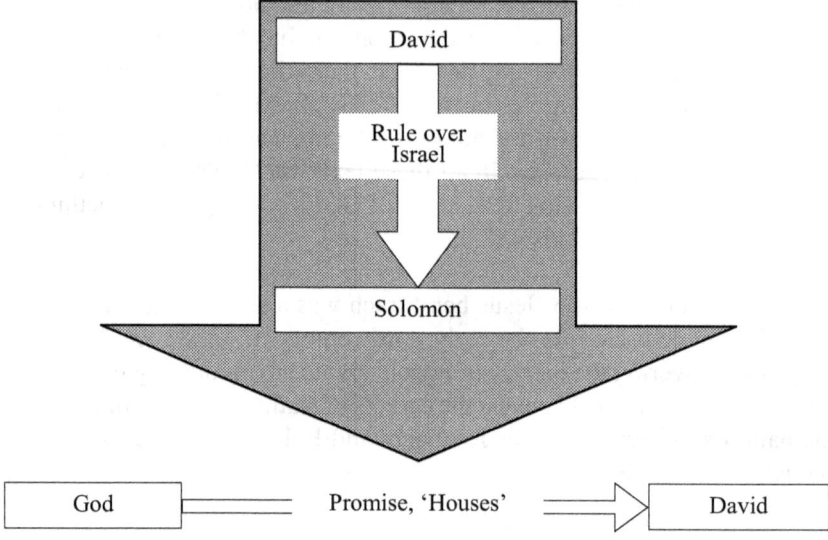

Figure 37. *The Function of Succession in Sirach 47.11-13*

Text 35: Eupolemus (in Alexander Polyhistor, in Eusebius, Preparation for the Gospel *9.30+447c-d).* Eupolemus was a Jewish historian of the second century BCE, here quoted by Eusebius.[18] Eusebius was a bishop and historian of the Church in the early fourth century CE. In his *Ecclesiastical History* he sets forth the orthodox understanding of the history of Christendom to his day.

In *Preparation* (the first part of his *Demonstration of the Gospel*), Eusebius argues for the validity of Christianity and its superiority to other religions of

---

18. For discussion and bibliography, see Carl R. Holladay, 'Eupolemus', in *ABD*, II, pp. 671-72; Ben Zion Wacholder, *Eupolemus: A Study of Judaeo-Greek Literature* (Cincinnati: Hebrew Union College, Jewish Institute of Religion, 1975); John R. Bartlett, *Jews in the Hellenistic World: Josephus, Aristeas, the Sibylline Oracles, Eupolemus* (Cambridge: Cambridge University Press, 1985).

the Graeco-Roman world. In Book 9, he epitomizes material from ancient gentile writers who discuss the Jews. One of the central works quoted here by Eusebius is Alexander Polyhistor's epitome of Eupolemus. In 9.30, Eupolemus writes of how David, when he wanted to build a temple for God, asked God for guidance as to where he should build it. God responded by sending the angel Dianathan, who showed David the spot where the altar was to be placed. Dianathan next told David that he was not the one who would build God's temple. David was instead to gather materials and 'commit the building of the temple to his son'. David died and passed the kingdom (τὴν ἀρχὴν παραδοῦναι) to Solomon, who immediately set out to build the temple as his father had urged.

I can illustrate the exchanges in this text thus:

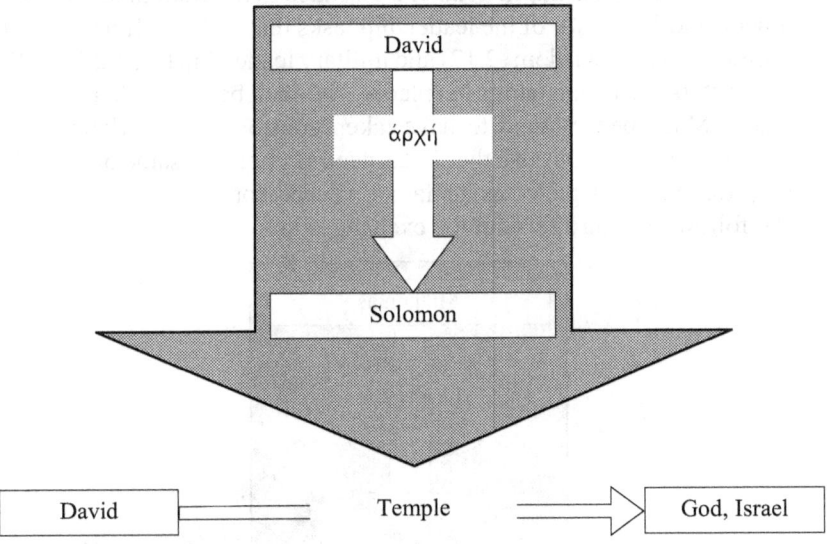

Figure 38. *The Function of Succession in Eupolemus (in Alexander Polyhistor, in Eusebius,* Preparation for the Gospel *9.30+447c-d)*

How does succession function here? It involves the passing on of both succession of leadership/rule and agenda or task (or both). Compare this text with Text 31: 1 Kings 1–2 above: God's role here is similar to his role in that text (he guides the succession, this time through the angel), but in Eupolemus the emphasis is on building the temple rather than on establishing David's throne. Further, the agenda that is passed on here is David's, not God's, therefore David is the sender. Here, as above, succession ensures the realization of an effect: work which David began and prepared for is undertaken in earnest and seen though to completion by his successor.

Text 36: 1 Maccabees 2.65-66; 3.1. In 1 Maccabees 2, the priest Mattathias becomes leader of the Jewish revolt against the Seleucids.[19] He is supported in this work by his sons, most prominent among them Jonathan, Simeon, and Judas Maccabeus. When Mattathias lies near death, he gives a farewell speech to his sons (2.49-68). He reminds them of Old Testament characters who stood up and were faithful under testing, and urges them to likewise stand firm against the oppressors. He then states:

> Here is your brother Simeon who, I know, is wise in counsel; always listen to him; he shall be your father. Judas Maccabeus has been a mighty warrior from his youth; he shall command the army for you and fight the battle against the peoples. (2.65-66)

Note how succession is implied rather than stated here: Mattathias passes on to Simeon and Judas two of the leadership tasks that he himself had filled to that point—counsel/wisdom (2.17) and military leadership (2.24-25, 42-48). He even refers to Simeon taking his place—'he shall be your father'—and in 3.1 Judas Maccabeus is said to have taken control 'in his (Mattathias's) place' (ἀντ' αὐτοῦ). Note also that Judas need not hold the same office as his father (priest) to be depicted as his father's successor.

The following figure sets out the exchanges involved:

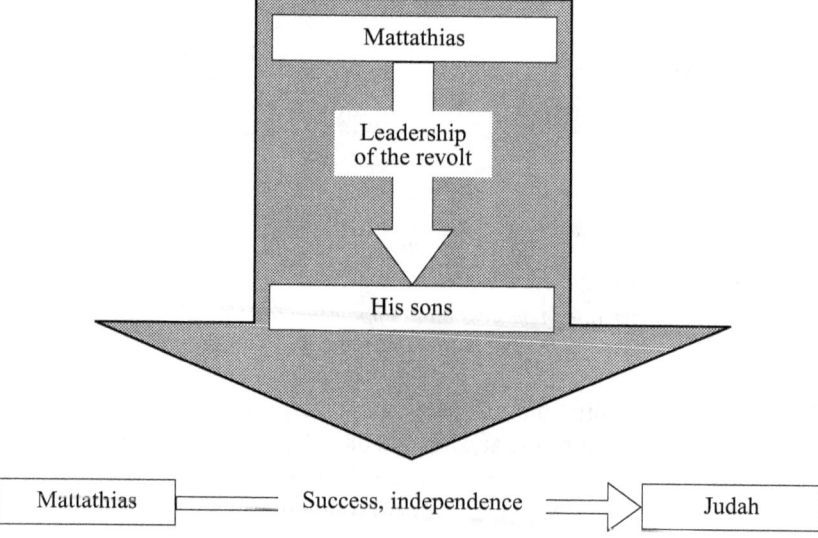

Figure 39. *The Function of Succession in 1 Maccabees 2.65-66; 3.1*

---

19. For discussion and bibliography of 1 and 2 Maccabees, see Thomas Fischer, 'First and Second Maccabees', in *ABD*, IV, pp. 439-50; John J. Collins, *Daniel, First Maccabees, Second Maccabees* (Wilmington, DE: Michael Glazier, 1988).

3. Succession in Jewish and Christian Texts

How does succession function here? Note that there is no mention of God's choosing Mattathias's successors—in that way, the tone differs from the Jewish texts I have surveyed above. The emphasis is on realization of effect. The rebellion, which began under Mattathias's leadership, continues (and ultimately succeeds) under the leadership of his sons, but there is here no explicit comparison of methods or activities between Mattathias and his successors.

Text 37: 1 Maccabees 6.14-15. At the end of the life of Antiochus Epiphanes (Antiochus IV), 1 Maccabees depicts him grieving over his sins in Jerusalem:

> I remember all the wrong I did in Jerusalem. I seized all its vessels of silver and gold, and I sent to destroy the inhabitants of Judah without good reason. I know that it is because of this that these misfortunes (his fatal illness) have come upon me. (6.12-13)

After that, Antiochus sends for his friend, Philip, and makes him his regent:

> He (Antiochus) gave him (Philip) the crown and his robe and the signet, so that he might guide his (Antiochus's) son, Antiochus (Antiochus V, Antiochus Eupator, at this point just a boy) and bring him up to be king. (6.14-15)

Antiochus did this in spite of the fact that he had earlier appointed Lysias to the same position and responsibility (3.33). The resulting rivalry (between Lysias and Philip) led to terms of peace between Lysias and Judas Maccabeus that favored the Jews (6.55-61).

I can illustrate the exchanges involved thus:

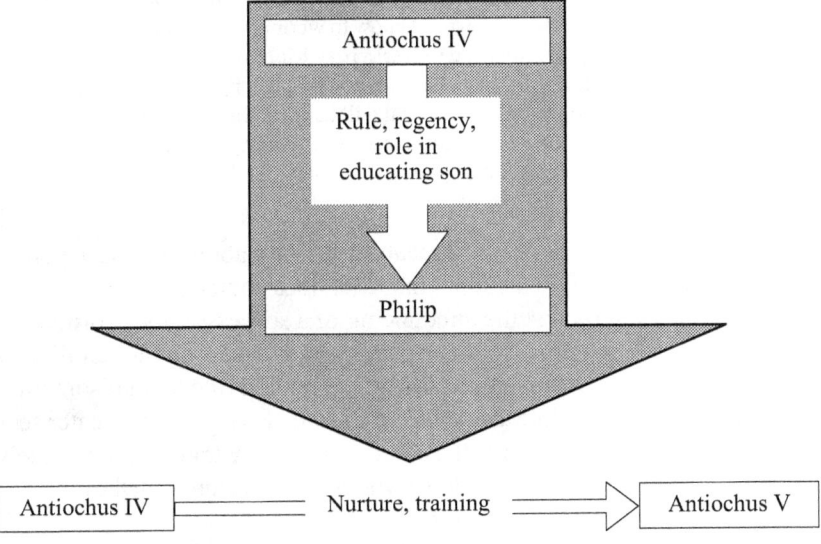

Figure 40. *The Function of Succession in 1 Maccabees 6.14-15*

Note how the presence of succession is more implicit than explicit—although succession *is* clearly present, witness the exchange of clothing and crown. How does succession function in this story? The immediate emphasis is on the education and preparation of Antiochus's son, Antiochus Eupator, to rule. Antiochus will not be able to oversee his son's education, so he chooses a successor who will complete this undertaking. Thus succession here ensures the realization of an effect. At the same time, there is an obvious ironic twist here. While Antiochus IV's immediate goal is achieved by the succession he ordains, the means by which he chooses to achieve it (the double appointment of Lysias and Philip) ends up 'losing' the war with the Jews which he had spent so much to pursue. This is a fatalistic note that echoes some of the Graeco-Roman successions I described earlier—or does it? Would this irony not rather be understood as another example of God's hand at work through succession to bless the Jews?

Text 38: 2 Maccabees 9.22-27. 2 Maccabees retells the story of 1 Maccabees. 2 Maccabees 9 recasts 1 Maccabees 6, emphasizing Antiochus's repentance over his sins against the Jews, repentance that goes unrewarded (2 Macc. 9.13-18). As he nears death, Antiochus writes a letter to the Jews (9.19-27), in which he discloses his illness and announces that he has appointed his son to be his successor. The last half of the letter reads:

> I have good hope of recovering from my illness, but I observed that my father, on the occasions when he made expeditions into the upper country, appointed his successor (ἀνέδειχεν τὸν διαδεχάμενον), so that, if anything unexpected happened or any unwelcome news came, the people throughout the realm would not be troubled, for they would know to whom the government was left (εἰδότες οἱ κατὰ τὴν χώραν ᾧ καταλέλειπται). Moreover, I understand how the princes along the borders and the neighbors of my kingdom keep watching for opportunities and waiting to see what will happen. So I have appointed my son Antiochus to be king (ἀναδέδειχα τὸν υἱὸν Ἀντίοχον βασιλέα)... I am sure that he will follow my policy and treat you with moderation and kindness. (9.22-27)

Unlike the parallel in Text 37: 1 Maccabees 6.14-15 above, this succession is only from Antiochus IV to his son—the letter does not mention a regent. Note how Antiochus asserts that the announcing of a successor, by informing the people of how government would be passed on, would promote stability and keep the people from being anxious over who would rule them if something unexpected happened. Note also that succession also promotes greater security against threats from outside the country. It demonstrated national resolve and unity by publicly informing those who might threaten from the outside as to who the new ruler and leader was.

The exchanges depicted here are illustrated in the following figure:

3. *Succession in Jewish and Christian Texts* 79

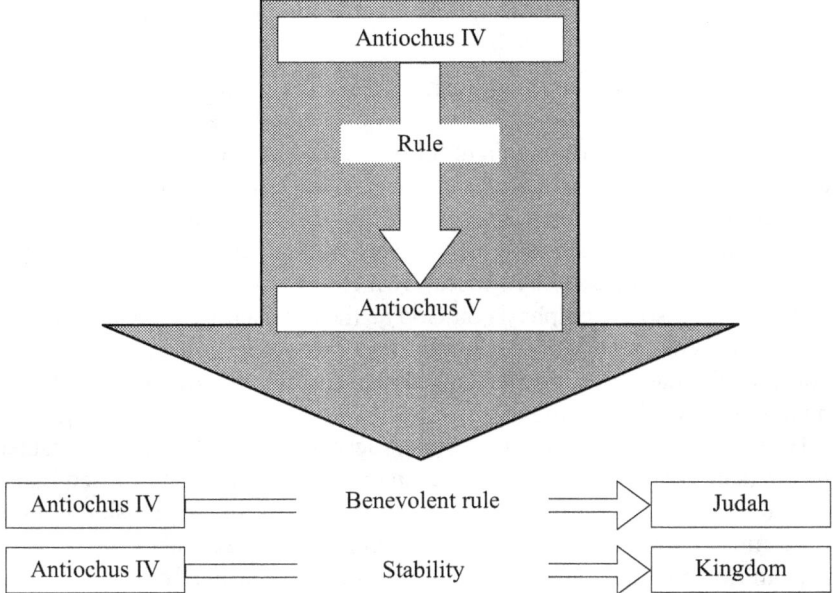

Figure 41. *The Functions of Succession in 2 Maccabees 9.22-27*

Here, succession serves two functions. As Antiochus explains it, it first ensures continuity of manner—however the Jews may have seen him, or however the writers of 1–2 Maccabees and Daniel may depict him, Antiochus here describes himself as a benevolent ruler, and he believes his son will rule in the same manner and according to the same definitions of benevolence. Second, succession here ensures continuity of effect—Antiochus underlines the stability that he hopes this announcement will maintain both within his territory and against threats from without.

Text 39: Pseudo-Philo, Biblical Antiquities. Pseudo-Philo's *Biblical Antiquities* is a retelling of the history of Israel, beginning with Adam and ending with David. It was written in Hebrew or Aramaic, in Palestine, at about the time of Jesus, and 'seems to reflect the milieu of the Palestinian synagogues at the turn of the common era'.[20]

When Pseudo-Philo reaches the story of Moses' death (19.16), he writes of how God spoke to Joshua. God assured Joshua that he had been chosen to lead the people after Moses:

> Take his (Moses') garments of wisdom and clothe yourself, and with his belt of knowledge gird your loins, and you will be changed and become another man. Did I not speak on your behalf to Moses my servant, saying 'This one

20. 'Pseudo-Philo' (trans. D.J. Harrington), in *OTP*, II, pp. 297-377 (300).

will lead my people after you (*post te*), and into his hand I will deliver the kings of the Amorites'? (20.2)[21]

After donning Moses' clothing, Joshua's 'mind was afire and his spirit was moved' (20.3), and he spoke to the people of Israel, warning them against disobedience and ordering them to follow. They responded by accepting his leadership, affirming that it was according to prophecy, and that Moses himself had been glad that Joshua was to be his successor (20.5).

Note the typological act—Joshua takes Moses' clothing and 'becomes another man'—possessed by Moses' own essence (echoes of Elijah–Elisha above). Note also the emphasis on God as the chooser, as the determiner of succession. God told Moses (directly and through prophecy) that Joshua would lead Israel after his (Moses') death. In this regard, Pseudo-Philo is much like Texts 29–33 above.

How does succession function? Here, succession of leadership/rule ensures the realization of an effect. Moses began to lead Israel to the Promised Land, as God had directed. Moses also began to lead Israel in the punishing of the Canaanites. Now that journey and quest continue under Joshua.

I can illustrate the exchanges wrapped up in this scene thus:

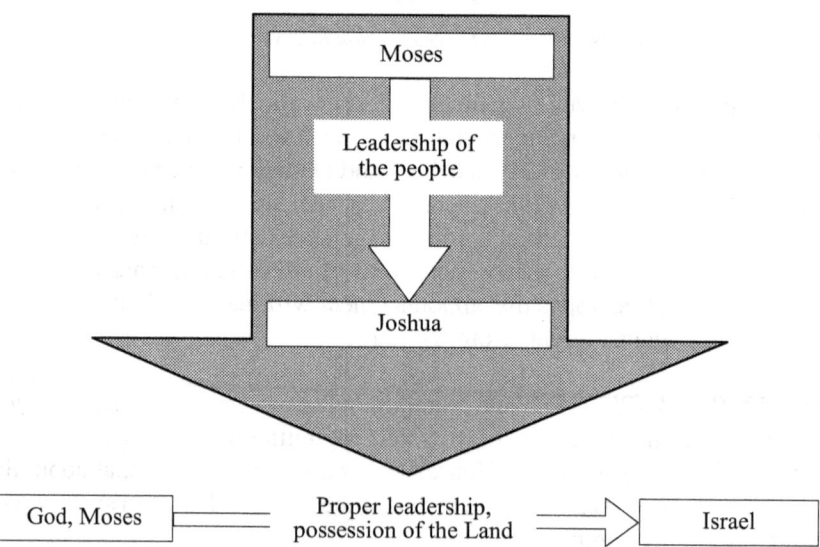

Figure 42. *The Function of Succession in Pseudo-Philo*, Biblical Antiquities

21. Latin text from Howard Jacobson, *A Commentary on Pseudo-Philo's* Liber Antiquitatum Biblicarum *with Latin Text and English Translation* (2 vols.; Leiden: E.J. Brill, 1996). Also note the 'translation Latin' in 25.3, where Pseudo-Philo refers to Moses and 'Joshua, who was ruler after him (*qui post eum fuit princeps*)'. Commenting on 20.2, Jacobson refers to an installation ceremony created by later rabbis 'in which Moses has a crown, robe, and throne brought in and he then proceeds to dress Joshua and seat him on the throne' (II, p. 660).

Text 40: Testament of Moses *1.6-10; 10.15.* The *Testament of Moses* is a Jewish document, apparently from first-century CE Palestine. The document seems to have been written in Hebrew, then translated into Greek, and then into Latin, the language of the surviving text. It is known for its deterministic theology: the past was ordained by God, the future is in his hands and is therefore certain.[22]

In the testament, Moses is shown giving his farewell address to Joshua, his successor. Prior to the address, the author says that Moses called for Joshua so that he (Joshua) might 'become the minister[23] (Lat. *successor*) in the tent of testimony...[and] lead the people into the land which had been promised to their fathers'. At the end of the address, Moses urges Joshua to 'be strong, for God has chosen you to be my successor (Lat. *successor*) in the same covenant' (*T. Mos.* 10.15).

The following figure illustrates the exchanges wrapped up in this scene:

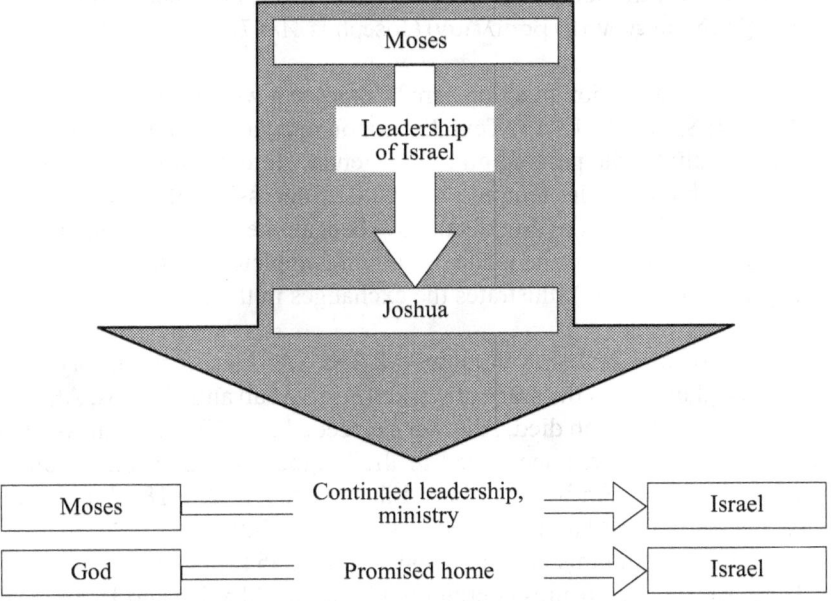

Figure 43. *The Functions of Succession in* Testament of Moses *1.6-10; 10.15*

22. *The Testament of Moses* 1.919-34. For additional discussion and bibliography, see John F. Priest, 'Moses, Testament of', in *ABD*, IV, pp. 920-22; Johannes Tromp, *The Assumption of Moses: A Critical Edition with Commentary* (Leiden: E.J. Brill, 1993).

23. 'Minister' seems at first to reflect the Old Testament usage of משרת which I have pointed out previously, where successors are sometimes deemed the predecessor's servant—see above regarding Joshua in Text 29: Num. 27.12-23–Josh. 1.2-9, and Elisha in Text 33: 1 Kgs 19–2 Kgs 2 (LXX 3 Kgdms 19–4 Kgdms 2). Here, however, it may instead refer to Joshua's service in the tabernacle, in Moses' place, rather than to Joshua's being a משרת to Moses.

How does succession function in this story? Note that, in 1.6-10, Joshua will fill a function that had been previously filled by Moses—ministering in the tabernacle. Thus succession here ensures continuity of manner—Joshua will perform a characteristic activity that his predecessor had performed. It also ensures the realization of an effect—the journey to the land God had promised Abraham was begun under Moses, but it would be completed under his successor.

Text 41: Josephus, Jewish Antiquities *7.14.2+337*. Josephus was a Jewish soldier of the first century CE, who was captured by Roman forces and spent the rest of his life writing histories as a Roman subject. In his retelling of the history of the Jews, Josephus tells the story of how David, when near death, commissioned Solomon to build the temple that he (David) had wanted to build and for which he had prepared. David 'called his son Solomon and bade him build the temple to God after he should have succeeded to the throne (διαδεξάμενον τὴν βασιλείαν) (Josephus, *Ant* 7.14.2+337 [Thackeray, LCL]).[24]

How does succession function here? Compare it with Text 31: 1 Kings 1–2; Text 34: Sirach 47.11-13; Text 35: Eupolemus; again, the passing on of rule also includes the passing on of an agenda. Here, as in Eupolemus, the agenda for building the temple is David's. Succession of leadership/rule ensures the realization of an effect: David began the building of the temple through the preparations he made, Solomon completed the task.

Figure 44 (opposite) illustrates the exchanges in the text.

Text 42: Josephus, Jewish Antiquities *9.2.2+27-28*. Later in his history of the Jews, Josephus retells the story of wicked King Ahab and his sons, Ahaziah and Joram. When Ahab died, Ahaziah succeeded him. Then, when Ahaziah died childless, he 'was succeeded in the kingdom by his brother Joram' (διαδέχεται δ' αὐτοῦ τὴν βασιλείαν). Like Ahaziah (9.2.1+18), Joram 'was very like his father Ahab in wickedness' (9.2.2+27-28).

The exchanges in this text are mapped in Fig. 45 (opposite).

Here, succession ensures continuity of manner. Ahaziah and Joram were successors to Ahab in two senses: both inherited his throne, and both inherited his manner of life.

---

24. For discussion and bibliography, see Louis H. Feldman, 'Josephus', in *ABD*, III, pp. 981-98; idem, *Josephus and Modern Scholarship* (Berlin: W. de Gruyter, 1984); Per Bilde, *Flavius Josephus between Jerusalem and Rome: His Life, his Works and their Importance* (JSPSup, 2; Sheffield: JSOT Press, 1988); Tessa Rajak, *The Jewish Dialogue with Greece and Rome: Studies in Cultural and Social Interaction* (Leiden: E.J. Brill, 2001).

3. Succession in Jewish and Christian Texts

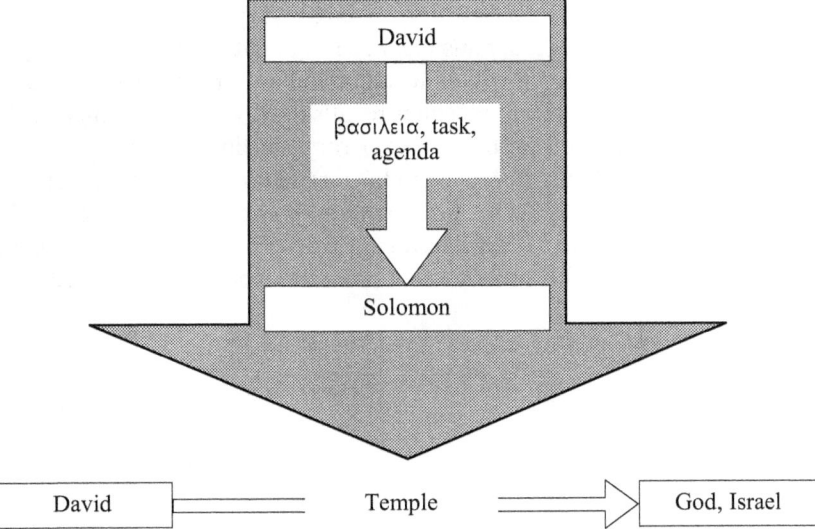

Figure 44. *The Function of Succession in Josephus,*
Jewish Antiquities *7.14.2+337*

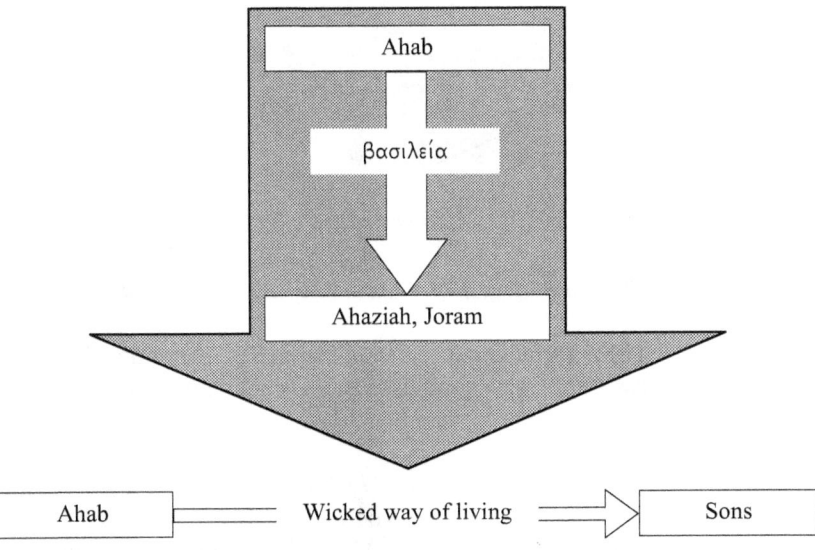

Figure 45. *The Function of Succession in Josephus,*
Jewish Antiquities *9.2.2+27-28*

Text 43: Josephus, Life *1.76+428-29.* When a rival published an account of the Jewish War that cast Josephus in a negative light, he responded by publishing an autobiography in which he attempted to refute his rival's accusations. At the end of this work, Josephus recalls the favorable treatment he has received at the hands of the Roman emperors, starting with Vespasian. At Vespasian's death, Titus succeeded to his throne (τὴν ἀρχὴν διαδεξάμενος) and also succeeded Vespasian as benefactor to Josephus (Josephus, *Life* 1.76+ 428-29 [Thackeray, LCL]). Similarly, Domitian continued treating Josephus well (in the manner of his predecessor) when he (Domitian) ascended to the throne.

The exchanges can be mapped in the following way:

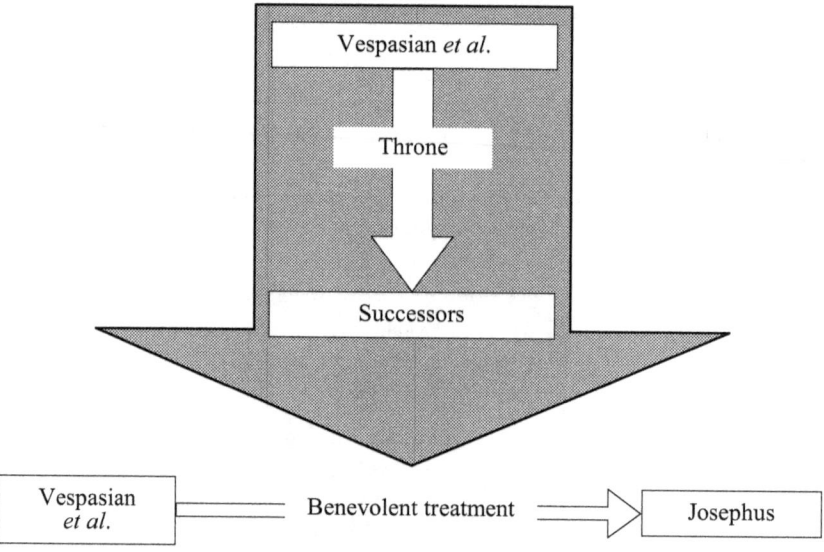

Figure 46. *The Function of Succession in Josephus,* Life *1.76+428-29*

Here, succession of leadership/rule ensures continuity in manner. The members of the succession in view continued their benevolent approach toward Josephus.

Text 44: Josephus, Against Apion *1.17+110.* Josephus wrote a second short apologetic document, *Against Apion,* to defend the Jewish race against Greek polemic, prejudices, and discrimination. Part of his *apologia* is a demonstration of the antiquity and excellence of his Jewish heritage in comparison with the heritage of the Greeks. Some of the anti-Jewish polemicists of Josephus's day made much of the fact that the Greek historians virtually ignored the Jews—see *Apion* 1.1+15. In response, Josephus surveys documents in which ancient Gentile historians mentioned the Jews, including in 1.17+110 comments from Phoenician histories. He notes:

There was a good reason why the erection of our temple should be recorded in their records, for Hiram, King of Tyre, was a friend of our King Solomon, a friendship that he (Solomon) had inherited from his Father (πατρικὴν πρὸς αὐτὸν φιλίαν διαδεδεγμένος. (Josephus, *Apion* 1.17+110)

I can map the exchanges contained here thus:

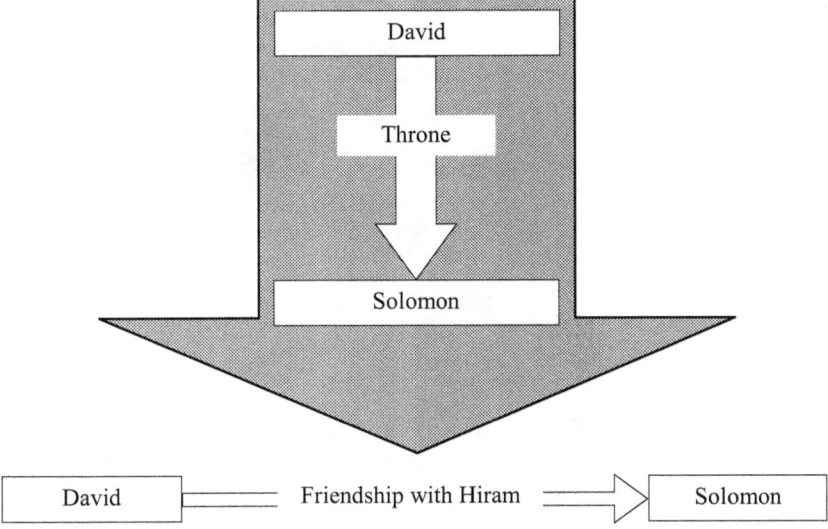

Figure 47. *The Function of Succession in Josephus,* Against Apion *1.17+110*

Here, succession serves to ensure continuity of manner. Solomon both succeeded David as King of Israel and in his manner of acting toward his (David's) friend, Hiram.

Texts Describing Succession of Tradition/Knowledge
Text 45: Josephus, Against Apion *1.8+41.* Elsewhere in his defense of Judaism, Josephus discusses the reliability of Jewish history. He states that the available material from Moses to Artaxerxes is reliable. After Artaxerxes, the history—though complete, and more recent—is less reliable 'because of the failure of the exact succession of the prophets' (διὰ τὸ μὴ γενέσθαι τὴν τῶν προφητῶν ἀκριβῆ διαδοχήν, 1.41).

Here, the succession is a succession of tradition—it is not the leadership of the prophets that is in view, it is their role as tradents. This succession, when active, preserves the tradition and keeps it reliable. When the succession fails, its failure casts doubt on the integrity and reliability of the tradition. Thus succession of tradition here ensures continued institutional vitality.

The following table illustrates the exchanges in the text:

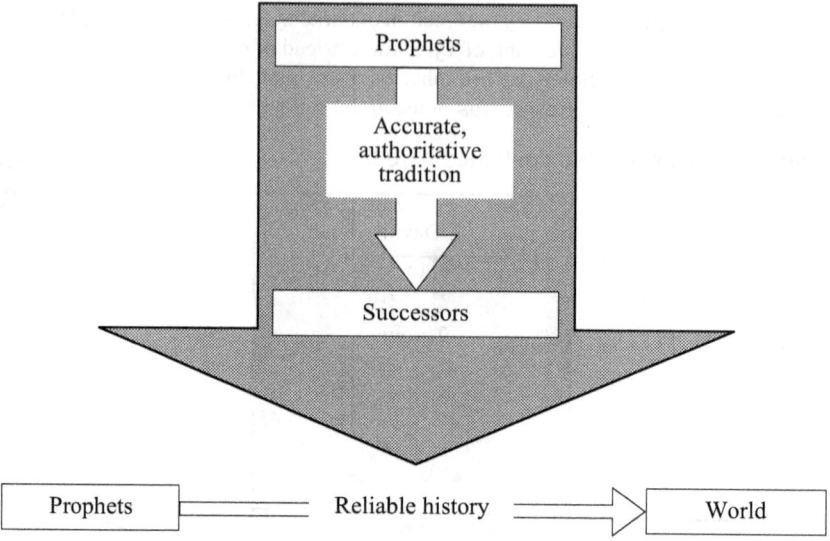

Figure 48. *The Function of Succession in Josephus*, Against Apion *1.8+41*

Text 46: 3 Enoch *48D.6-10*. *3 Enoch* is a Jewish mystical text, redacted into its final form no earlier than the fifth century CE. It is included in this survey because scholars have concluded that much of its material dates to the early second century.[25]

In *3 En.* 48D.6-10, the angel Metatron,

> Prince of the Divine Presence, Prince of the Torah; the angel, Prince of Wisdom; the angel, Prince of Understanding; the angel, Prince of Glory; the angel, Prince of the Palace; the angel, Prince of Kings; the angel, Prince of Rulers; the angel, Prince of the exalted, lofty, great and honored Princes, who are in heaven and earth...

describes what happened when he gave the secret 'by which heaven and earth were created' (the name of God? Torah?) to Moses. The other angels were angry with him for giving such power to humans, until God himself rebuked them and said,

> I ordered it, and entrusted it to Metatron my servant alone, because he is unique among all the denizens of the heights. Metatron...committed it to Moses, and Moses to Joshua, Joshua to the Elders, the Elders to the Prophets, the Prophets to the men of the Great Synagogue, the Men of the Great Synagogue to Ezra the Scribe, Ezra the Scribe to Hillel the Elder, Hillel the Elder to R. Abbahu, R. Abbahu to R. Zira, R. Zira to the Men of Faith, and the Men of Faith to the Faithful—so that they should use it to admonish men and to heal

---

25. '3 (Hebrew Apocalypse of) Enoch' (trans. P. Alexander), in *OTP*, I, pp. 223-315. For discussion and bibliography, see Philip S. Alexander, 'Enoch, Third Book of', in *ABD*, II, pp. 522-26; Hugo Odeberg, *3 Enoch* (New York: Ktav, 1973).

the diseases that befall the world, as it is written, 'Then he said, If you listen carefully to the voice of the Lord your God and do what is right in his eyes, if you pay attention to his commandments, and keep his statutes, I shall inflict on you none of the diseases that I inflicted on the Egyptians, for it is I, the Lord, who gives you healing'. (*3 En.* 48D.6-10)

Note first that this succession is not a succession of leadership but of knowledge, of tradition. Notice also the way that succession serves to keep the object vital and effective: those who are successors in the tradition (i.e. who possess the knowledge) are empowered by it to 'admonish men and to heal'. Thus succession here ensures continued institutional vitality.

I can illustrate the exchanges in the text thus:

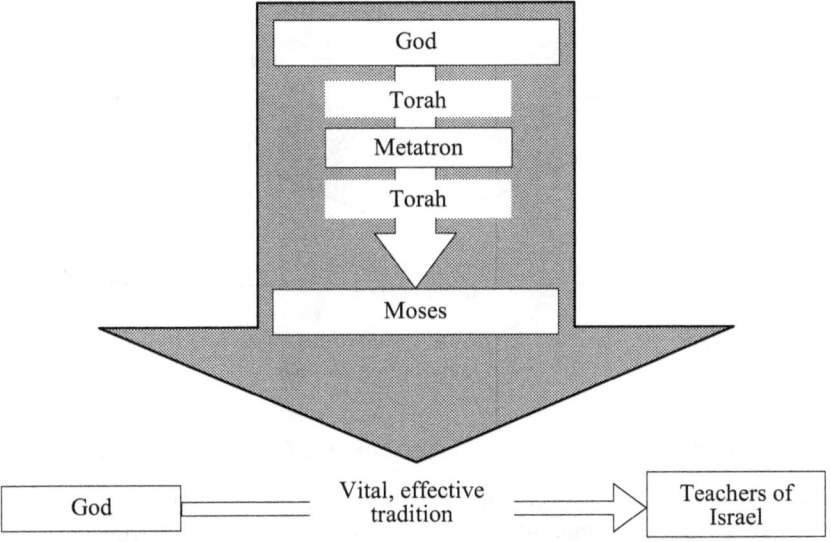

Figure 49. *The Function of Succession in* 3 Enoch *48D.6-10*

Texts Describing Passing on of Possessions
Text 47: Josephus, Life *1.1+3, 6, and* Against Apion *1.7+31*. In the opening paragraphs of his autobiography, Josephus describes his family tree. He is concerned here with showing that he is descended from 'the right kind of people, a descendant of the priestly line not a commoner (οὐκ ἄσημον, ἀλλ' ἐξ ἱερέων ἄνωθεν καταγεγηκός)... With us a connection with the priesthood is the hallmark of an illustrious line' (Josephus, *Life* 1.1+3, 6 [Thackeray, LCL]). Thus Josephus's lineage stands as a character witness on his behalf— no one descended from such a noble line could do the things his enemies accuse him of.

While piecing together his priestly lineage, Josephus twice mentions his διαδοχή (*Life* 1.3, 6; see also *Apion* 1.7+31), which Thackeray translates 'pedigree'. Succession functions here to to fix Josephus's honorable status, which he inherited as part of his lineage. This status is itself the object of succession. This succession of 'possessions' ensures continuity of possession—those born into a noble family share the family's honor.

I can map the exchanges as follows:

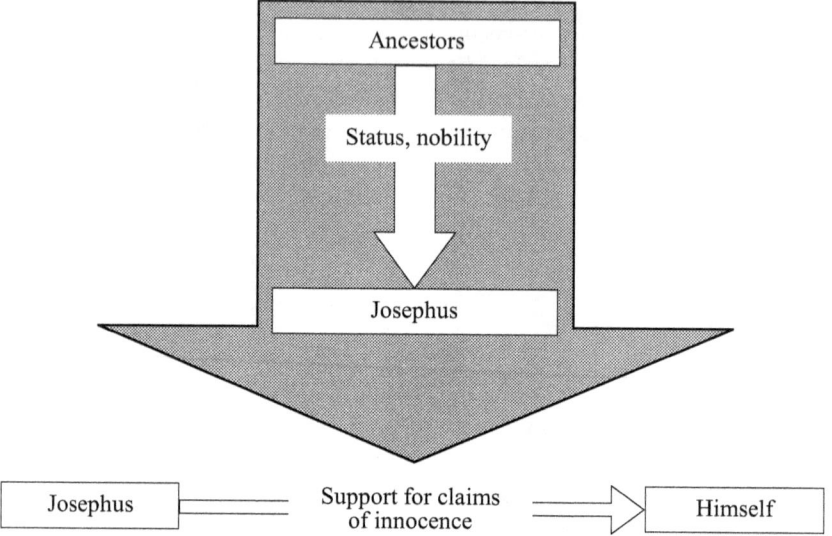

Figure 50. *The Function of Succession in Josephus,* Life *1.1+3, 6,* and Against Apion *1.7+31*

3. *Summary of Jewish Texts Describing the Function of Succession*

Building on the previous chapter, I have shown the following:

First, as with the Graeco-Roman texts, I have shown that references to succession in Jewish literature sometimes contain not one but two exchanges. The first exchange is the succession itself. The second, when it is present, describes the function of that succession, what it achieved or might have achieved, or why it was necessary or desired. And, as with the Graeco-Roman texts, these two exchanges can be described graphically, and the second exchange can profitably be described in terms borrowed from structuralism, namely Sender → Object → Receiver.

Second, as with the Graeco-Roman texts, I have shown that the functions of succession in Jewish literature tend to fall into categories delineated by the focus of succession in the text. If the text focuses on how succession affects property, for example, then the function seems to be different from what it would be if the text focused on characteristic actions shared by predecessor and successor.

The functional categories I generated in my survey of the Graeco-Roman texts are also present in the Jewish texts I surveyed, and they generally

3. Succession in Jewish and Christian Texts 89

function in the same way. In my survey of the Jewish texts, I have generated a new category as well: I found a text in which succession functioned to legitimate one successor over another, or over a potential successor. Thus I now have six functional categories. I have shown that succession functioned to ensure:

1. *continuity of possession* (e.g. Text 47: Josephus, *Life* 1.1+3, 6, and *Against Apion* 1.7+31), where the text focuses on possessions;
2. *continuity of manner* (e.g. Text 30: 1 Sam. 9–18 [LXX 1 Kgdms 9–18]), where the text focuses on characteristic actions/attitudes shared by predecessor and successor;
3. *continued institutional vitality* (e.g. Text 45: Josephus, *Against Apion* 1.8+41), where the object of succession is an institution, and the text focuses on that object and on how succession causes it to remain vital and effective;
4. *realization of an effect* (e.g. Text 33: 1 Kgs 19–2 Kgs 2 [LXX 3 Kgdms 19–4 Kgdms 2]), where the text focuses on an effect which is succession-dependent, which began under the predecessor and was finally realized under the successor;
5. *continuity of effect* (e.g. Text 38: 2 Macc. 9.22-27), where the text focuses on an effect/result which is shared by the predecessor and successor but the realization of which is not dependent upon the succession;
6. *legitimacy of a particular successor* (Text 31: 1 Kgs 1–2 [LXX 3 Kgdms 1–2]), where the text focuses on potential successors to a particular task or office and the dilemma of which is the legitimate (or whether a proposed successor is legitimate) is solved by the actuality/non-actuality of succession itself.

As with the Graeco-Roman texts, the categories outlined above are not 'watertight'. Sometimes they overlap. As with the Graeco-Roman texts, a single succession story can have multiple functions (e.g. Text 29: Num. 27.12-23 and Josh. 1.2-9; Text 30: 1 Sam. 9–18 [LXX 1 Kgdms 9–18]). As with the Graeco-Roman texts, the comparative greatness of the predecessor over the successor (e.g. David's greatness in comparison to the kings of Judah that followed) does not invalidate or delegitimize the succession. And as with the Graeco-Roman texts, the successor does not need to hold equal station in life with the predecessor for succession to have been inferred. David can be Samuel's successor in a particular task without having to fill the same office Samuel filled. Joshua does not need to become a lawgiver to be Moses' successor. Judas Maccabeus does not need to become a priest to succeed his father Mattathias in leadership. Thus succession again includes differences between the predecessor and the successors in both degree and kind. The predecessor can be far greater than the successor, or very different from the successor, and succession would still have been inferred.

Table 6. *Jewish Texts Describing the Passing-On of Leadership/Rule*

	Text	Function
29.	Num. 27.12-23 and Josh. 1.2-9	Continuity of effect Realization of effect
30.	1 Sam. 9–18 (LXX 1 Kgdms 9–18)	Realization of effect Continuity of manner
31.	1 Kgs 1–2 (LXX 3 Kgdms 1–2)	Successor's legitimacy Realization of effect
32.	1 Kgs 11.43 etc. (LXX 3 Kgdms 11.44 etc.)	Continuity of possession Realization of effect
33.	1 Kgs 19–2 Kgs 2 (LXX 3 Kgdms 19–4 Kgdms 2)	Continuity of manner Realization of effect
34.	Sir. 47.11-13	Realization of effect
35.	Eupolemus	Realization of effect
36.	1 Macc. 2.65; 3.1	Realization of effect
37.	1 Macc. 6.14-15	Realization of effect Continuity of manner
38.	2 Macc. 9.22-27	Continuity of manner Continuity of effect
39.	Pseudo-Philo, *Biblical Antiquities*	Realization of effect
40.	*Testament of Moses* 1.6-10; 10.15	Continuity of manner Realization of effect
41.	Josephus, *Ant.* 7.14.2+337	Realization of effect
42.	Josephus, *Ant.* 9.2.2+27-28	Continuity of manner
43.	Josephus, *Life* 1.76+428-29	Continuity of manner
44.	Josephus, *Apion* 1.17+110	Continuity of manner

Table 7. *Jewish Texts Describing the Passing-On of Tradition/Knowledge*

	Text	Function
45.	Josephus, *Apion* 1.8+41	Continuity of institutional vitality
46.	*3 En.* 48D.6-10	Continuity of institutional vitality

Table 8. *Jewish Texts Describing the Passing-On of Possessions*

	Text	Function
47.	Josephus, *Life* 1.1+3, 6, and *Apion* 1.7+31	Continuity of possession

3. Succession in Jewish and Christian Texts

In all these areas, the Jewish texts relating to the function of succession mirror their Graeco-Roman counterparts. I have noted a couple of sharp differences in the Jewish texts' presentation of the function of succession, however. First, there is the overriding presence of God as the one who guides and keeps the succession intact and on the path appropriate to his purposes. The Jewish texts evince none of the Graeco-Roman fatalism I saw in texts like those dealing with Alexander and the failure of his Διάδοχοι. In the Jewish view of succession, I find a particular and ubiquitous confidence in God's sovereignty over history, that God is using succession (as its author) to accomplish his purposes.

Second, as noted above, I found one Jewish text in which showing the successor's legitimacy was a primary functional emphasis: Text 31: 1 Kings 1–2 (LXX 3 Kgdms 1–2). This adds a new category to my list. I am hesitant to categorize any text *sui generis*, but I have also found two texts from the same period (Text 48: Mt. 16.13-20, and Text 54: Apollinarius of Hierapolis, both Christian texts, discussed below) which use succession in the same way. Other texts in which succession functions to legitimate a successor will no doubt surface as my textbase continues to grow.

Opposite, sorted by the object of succession as above, are tables listing the Jewish texts surveyed and the function of succession in each.

To this point in this chapter, I have continued reconstructing the expectations an ancient audience would have had when hearing these Jewish texts utilizing succession. Because of the presence of certain terms commonly used in reference to succession, and the presence of certain phenomena commonly thought of in reference to succession, the ancient audience from this milieu would have understood all these texts to refer to succession. They would further have understood that succession functioned in a certain way in each case, that it achieved a specific thing in each situation. In the next part of this chapter, I examine texts from the Christian milieu according to the same pattern.

4. *Christian Texts Describing the Function of Succession*

Below are the ancient Christian texts I have found that describe the function of succession. I have arranged them according to what is passed on: texts describing succession of leadership/rule, and texts describing the passing on of tradition/knowledge. Each group of texts is addressed in roughly chronological order within its category.

Texts Describing Succession of Leadership/Rule
Text 48: Matthew 16.13-20. One pivotal scene in Matthew's βίος of Jesus is the scene where Peter declares that Jesus is the Messiah. As he travels with his disciples, Jesus asks them, 'Who do the people say that I am?' Their

response indicates that there is much speculation and confusion (and little consensus or understanding) among the people regarding his identity. Jesus then turns the question on his disciples: 'Who do you say that I am?' Peter answers: 'You are the Messiah, the Son of the living God'. In response, Jesus blesses Peter and makes this statement:

> You are Peter (Πέτρος), and on this rock (πέτρα) I will build my church (ἐκκλησίαν)... I will give (δώσω) to you the keys to the kingdom of heaven, and whatever you bind on earth will be bound in heaven, and whatever you loose on earth will be loosed in heaven. (Mt. 16.18-19)

Note first the language of succession (δίδωμι). Note second that the three standard elements of an ancient Mediterranean succession story are present: the naming of what is passed on (the keys to the kingdom), a symbolic act (the name change from Simon to Peter),[26] and the prophesied confirmation of the succession (the decisions of the leaders, personified in Peter, are in accordance with what heaven had decreed).

This scene constitutes a succession of leadership from Jesus to Peter, even though Peter does not 'take the reins' until after Jesus has departed. I take the language, the play on words (Πέτρος, πέτρα) to indicate that the leadership role that is passed on is bigger than any single person, Peter or anyone else. The fact that Peter was the leader of the Church post-Easter, both in Jerusalem and in the Gentile mission, and that this leadership is alluded to here ('I will build my church') is clear.

Succession's object, 'the keys to the kingdom', refers to the authority Jesus gave to his followers (led by Peter) through the Spirit on Pentecost. This authority 'unlocks' (i.e. it teaches and communicates) proper knowledge of who Jesus is and what he is about (thus the association with Peter's confession). David Garland notes, 'This saying divinely legitimates the teaching authority of the church over against that of the church's opponents'.[27]

This succession functions in two ways. First, it serves to ensure continued institutional vitality. When Jesus departs, his church will continue to be led properly and taught because he has passed on that authority to his followers, as led by Peter. Second, succession here serves to legitimate Peter as the leader of the earliest church.

These exchanges are illustrated in the following figure:

---

26. To this point, only the Matthean narrator has referred to Simon as Peter.
27. David E. Garland, *Reading Matthew: A Literary and Theological Commentary on the First Gospel* (Reading the New Testament; New York: Crossroad, 1993), pp. 172-73; see also W.D. Davies and Dale C. Allison, *A Critical and Exegetical Commentary on the Gospel according to Saint Matthew* (ICC; 3 vols.; Edinburgh: T. & T. Clark, 1991), II, pp. 638-39.

3. Succession in Jewish and Christian Texts

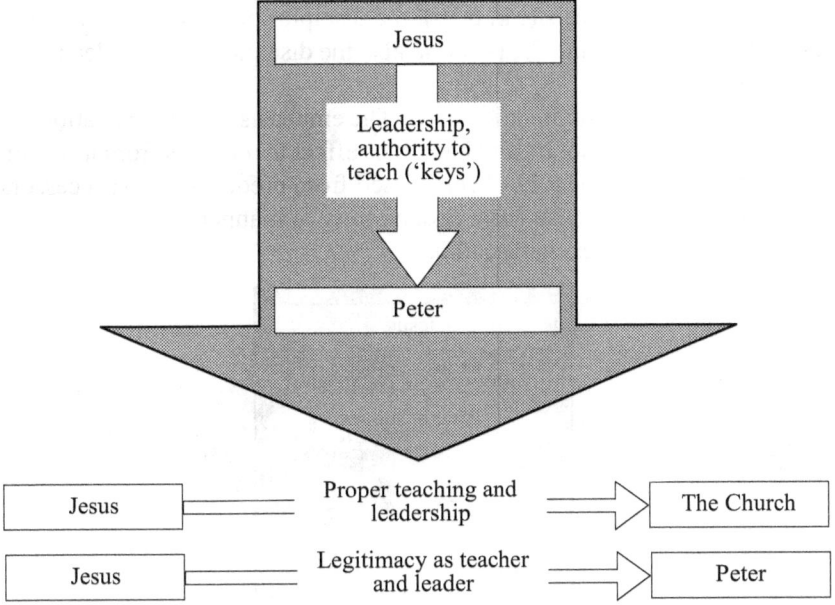

Figure 51. *The Function of Succession in Matthew 16.13-20*

Text 49: Luke 22.28-30. At Luke's version of the Last Supper, Jesus' disciples dispute with one another about greatness. In response, Jesus reminds them that, in *his* kingdom, the king (Jesus himself) is *their* servant. And then Jesus says:

> You are those who have stood by me in my trials; and I confer (διατίθεμαι) on you, just as my Father has conferred (διέθετο) on me, a kingdom (βασιλείαν), so that you may eat and drink at my table in my kingdom (βασιλεία), and you will sit on thrones judging the twelve tribes of Israel. (Lk. 22.28-30)

Here, Jesus promises his disciples that they will have a place of honor in his kingdom after his ascension. They will serve as judges, rendering just and righteous verdicts and decisions over and on behalf of God's people. Here, Jesus 'bequeaths to his apostles a position of honor and authority within his reign and under his authority'. A vital aspect of Jesus' ministry—'rendering God's righteous verdict in Israel'—continues in the actions of Jesus' disciples after he has ascended.[28] And note that Jesus' disciples do not need to become his equals to serve as his successors in this particular task/place.

Note also how this succession/transfer of authority is confirmed by the parallels between the career of the disciples in Acts and the career of Jesus in Luke. Jesus heals a lame man (Lk. 5.17-26), the disciples heal a lame man

---

28. Both quotations are from Talbert and Stepp, 'Succession: Part 2', p. 171.

(Acts 3.1-10). Jesus heals (Lk. 6.19), the disciples heal (Acts 5.15). Just as Jesus raised the dead (Lk. 7.11-17), so also the disciples raise the dead (Acts 9.36-43).

How does succession function here? The emphasis is on the vocation that the disciples receive, not on any benefit or effect that results from it. A vital and characteristic activity has been passed from predecessor to successors. Therefore, succession here ensures continuity of manner.

I can illustrate the exchanges thus:

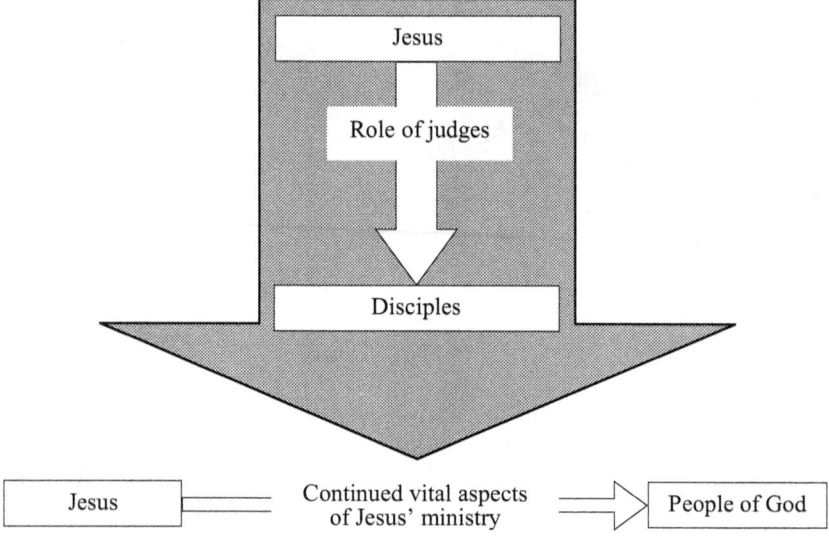

Figure 52. *The Function of Succession in Luke 22.28-30*

Text 50: Acts 6–7. In Acts 6, the Church is growing rapidly, and the new growth is accompanied by growing pains. The Greek-speaking Jewish Christians complain against the Aramaic-speaking Jewish Christians 'because their widows were being neglected in the daily distribution (ἐν τῇ διακονίᾳ τῇ καθημερινῇ) of food' (Acts 6.1). In response, the twelve call the people together, and inform the group that, while this particular ministry is vital and important, it should not fall to them (the twelve) to oversee it. Their reason: to oversee such a ministry would not leave them time for their central tasks, prayer and preaching.[29] They then tell the congregation to choose from among them seven men who could properly carry out that ministry (6.2-4).

The congregation agrees, and chooses seven men for this role. As part of commissioning the seven to this new ministry, the apostles pray over them

---

29. Compare this scene to the exchange between Moses and Jethro in Exod. 18.13-26, which also uses succession language in reference to the authority Moses passes to the judges.

and lay hands on them (6.6). Among the men chosen is Stephen. In the scenes that immediately follow, Stephen is shown preaching and performing miracles—things which, prior to this point in Acts, only the apostles had done. Note the naming of what is passed on—the διακονία. Note the symbolic acts which accompany the succession—prayer and the laying-on of hands. Note also the confirmation that succession has taken place—Stephen, successor to the apostles in one aspect of their ministry, begins to succeed them in other aspects (i.e. preaching and performing miracles).

The succession is partial—Stephen does not become a 'new apostle' nor is he numbered among the twelve, but the succession is still realized. In a sense, here the successor is the predecessor's delegate, given some of the predecessor's authority to accomplish certain tasks—in this case, a list which the Holy Spirit quickly expands, so that the delegate becomes more and more a successor. I have shown a phenomenon like this before, in the LXX's use of διάδοχος (p. 61 above) and in the treatment of Text 20: Lysias, *Pension* 6.

In these texts, regardless of milieu, succession seems to allow for varying degrees of difference between the predecessor and the successor. A way to grasp this phenomenon is by envisioning succession as a continuum of replacement. At the strong end of this continuum, the successor is a complete (or near-complete) replacement for the predecessor. To this point, we have seen several examples of this strong degree of replacement, including Text 29: Num. 27.12-13 and Josh. 1.2-9 (Joshua receives a portion of Moses' glory, and God was with him just as he was with Moses); Text 7: Diodorus Siculus 15.93.1 (the Persians urge Ochus to take his predecessor's name, in hopes he will rule as his predecessor did); and Text 33: 1 Kings 19–2 Kings 2 (Elisha serves as prophet with a double-portion of the spiritual power of his predecessor, Elijah). At the weak end of this continuum, the successor is a delegate or agent of the predecessor, and there is little or no sense of the successor having replaced the predecessor (the LXX's use of διάδοχος, Text 20: Lysias, *Pension* 6; Text 50: Acts 6–7).

Compare Acts 6–7 with the text immediately preceding it in this survey, Text 49: Luke 22.28-30. In that text, the apostles receive authority from Jesus. Luke describes this bequest in succession terms, but the apostles replace Jesus in only a very limited way. Stephen's succession in Acts 6–7 is somewhat stronger than the apostles' succession in Lk. 22.28-30, but it is still not a full replacement since Stephen is not counted among the apostles—although he does precede an apostle (James, son of Zebedee) in martyrdom.

How does succession function in Acts 6–7? The story focuses first on the health of the Church, which was threatened by conflict and by the possibility that some who were truly in need would be overlooked. The twelve dealt with this threat by succession, and kept their priorities in order at the same time, ensuring the Church's continued health. Thus succession of leadership/

rule here functions first to ensure continued institutional vitality. The text also focuses on the shared activities of the predecessors and the successors (Stephen, later Philip), how delegates become replacements or surrogates. Thus, here, succession of leadership/rule also ensures continuity of manner.

The following figure illustrates the exchanges in this text:

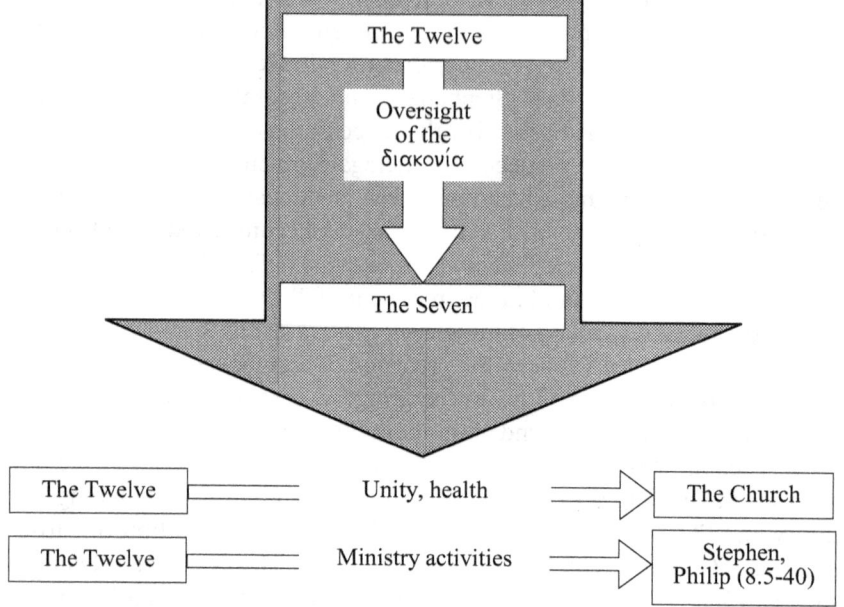

Figure 53. *The Functions of Succession in Acts 6–7*

Text 51: Acts 24.27 and 25.9. After Paul's arrest in Jerusalem in Acts 21, he languishes for two years in the prison of the Roman governor, Felix, in Caesarea. At the end of that period, Felix was succeeded by Porcius Festus (ἔλαβεν διάδοχον ὁ Φῆλιξ, Acts 24.27). Although Felix had it in his power to release Paul, he wanted to curry favor with the Jewish leaders (θέλων χάριτα καταθέσθαι τοῖς Ἰουδαίοις), so he bound Paul over into the custody of his successor.

Paul fared no better under Porcius Festus. The Jewish leaders, renewing their plot to ambush and kill Paul (see 23.12-22), asked Festus to bring Paul to Jerusalem to stand trial. Festus, wanting to do a favor for the Jews (θέλων τοῖς Ἰουδαίοις χάριν καταθέσθαι), pressures Paul to make the trip to Jerusalem and be heard there. Paul responded by appealing to Caesar.

Here, succession of leadership/rule ensures continuity of manner. Festus not only succeeds Felix in office, he also succeeds his predecessor in his disposition toward the Jews and the treatment of Paul that disposition gave rise to.

3. Succession in Jewish and Christian Texts

The following figure sets out the exchanges in this narrative:

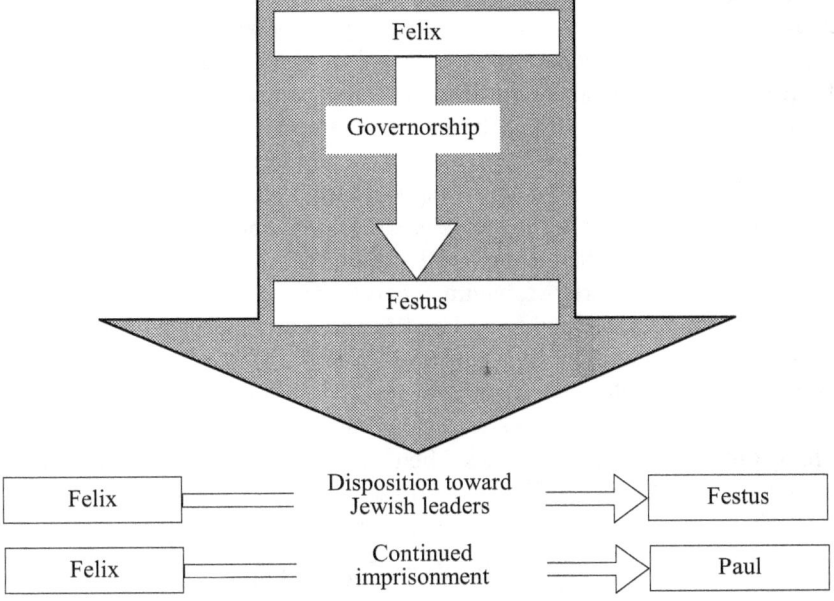

Figure 54. *The Functions of Succession in Acts 24.27 and 25.9*

Text 52: 1 Clement 42–44. 1 Clement is a letter, written c. 95, from Clement and the leaders of the church at Rome to the church at Corinth. This letter was precipitated by a leadership crisis in Corinth, in which the congregation deposed its older, established leaders and set up younger leaders in their place. Clement writes to Corinth to urge them to reinstate the established leaders and to restore peace and harmony to their congregation. The emphasis throughout the letter is on orderliness.[30]

Succession is first mentioned in 1 Clement 42, where Clement remarks on the orderliness of the gospel's entry into the world: 'The apostles received

---

30. Clement of Rome, 'The Letter of the Romans to the Corinthians', in *The Apostolic Fathers* (trans. J.B. Lightfoot and J.R. Harmer; ed. Michael W. Holmes; Grand Rapids: Baker Book House, 1989), pp. 23-64. For discussion and bibliography, see Barbara Ellen Bowe, *A Church in Crisis: Ecclesiology and Paraenesis in Clement of Rome* (Minneapolis: Fortress Press, 1988); James S. Jeffers, *Conflict at Rome: Social Order and Hierarchy in Early Christianity* (Minneapolis: Fortress Press, 1991); Laurence L. Welborn, 'Clement, First Epistle of', in *ABD*, I, pp. 1055-60; David G. Horrell, *The Social Ethos of the Corinthian Correspondence: Interests and Ideology from 1 Corinthians to 1 Clement* (Edinburgh: T. & T. Clark, 1996); Odd Magne Bakke, *'Concord and Peace': A Rhetorical Analysis of the First Letter of Clement with an Emphasis on the Language of Unity and Sedition* (Tübingen: J.C.B. Mohr [Paul Siebeck], 2001).

the gospel for us from the Lord Jesus Christ; Jesus the Christ was sent forth from God... Both, therefore, came of the will of God in good order' (42.1-2). Moreover, the apostles made for an orderly passing on of the gospel: 'Preaching both in the country and in the towns, they appointed (καθίστανον) their firstfruits...to be bishops and deacons for the future believers' (42.4). In 43.1–44.1, Clement describes the apostles' rationale for this system of leadership: just as Moses knew there would be jealousy over the priesthood, and so caused a miraculous demonstration of God's choice of Aaron (and the tribe of Levi) to rule over it (ch. 43), so also the apostles knew 'that there would be strife over the bishop's office' (44.1).

For this reason, therefore, having received complete foreknowledge, they appointed the officials mentioned earlier and afterwards gave the offices a permanent character; that is, if they (the appointed leaders) should die, other approved men should succeed to their ministry (διαδέχωνται τὴν λειτουργίαν αὐτῶν). Those, therefore, who were appointed (καθίστημι) by them, or, later on, by other reputable men—these men we consider to be unjustly removed from their ministry (44.2-3).

I can set out the exchanges in this text thus:

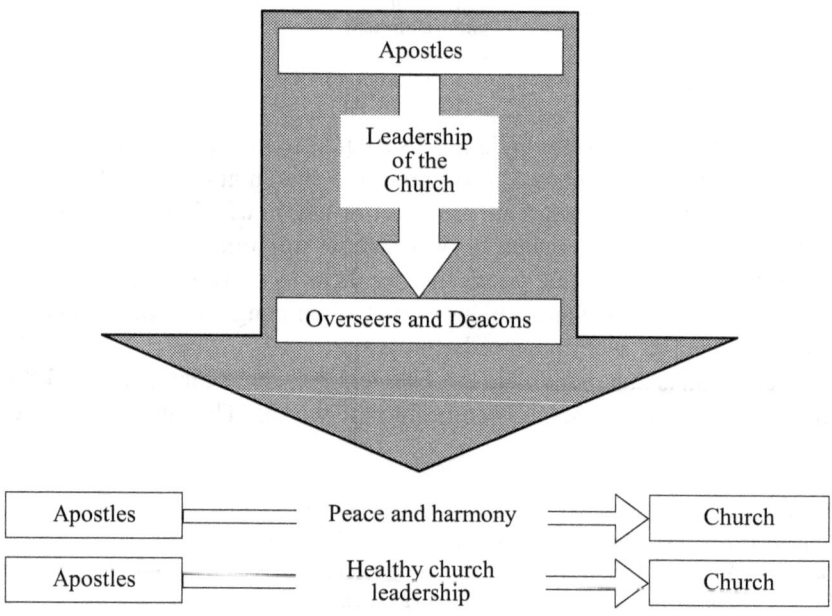

Figure 55. *The Functions of Succession in 1 Clement 42–44*

How does succession function in this text? First, succession here ensures continuity of effect: the apostles led the Church well. One of the effects of their leadership was harmony in the Church. This harmony continues (or should continue) because the apostles provided for succession in the leadership they established. And note how Clement does not speak of the successors in leadership attaining the apostolic office themselves—they do not have to acquire the predecessors' office for the succession to be legitimate, in spite of how this text has been misconstrued over the centuries.

Second, succession here also promotes the health of the institution of church leadership itself. Healthy church leadership—and therefore a healthy church—depends on propriety and orderliness. Therefore, proper and orderly succession of leadership is of the essence. Thus succession here ensures continued institutional vitality. Note also how God motivated this succession (by giving the apostles foreknowledge), even though he is not shown directly choosing the successors.

Text 53: Athenagoras, Legatio *37.* Legatio is an apology for Christianity addressed to the M. Aurelius and Commodius, co-rulers in 176–80 CE.[31] It is an open letter written to rebut accusations that were publicly being made against Christians. Throughout, Athenagoras emphasizes Christians' loyalty to the empire and their desire for irenic coexistence with those around them: 'Athenagoras finds no fundamental conflict between the Church and the Empire. The suggestion that the Church could play a role in securing the stability of the Empire is not far from his mind.'[32] At the letter's close, Athenagoras prays for the emperors to be blessed by orderly succession and continued prosperity:

> [We] pray...that the succession to the kingdom (βασιλείαν) may proceed from father to son, as is most just, and that your reign may grow and increase as all men become subject to you... This is also to our advantage, that we may lead a quiet and peaceable life (ἤρεμον καὶ ἡσύχιον βίον διάγοιμεν). (37.2-3)

The exchanges in this prayer for orderly succession are set out in Fig. 56 (next page).

Succession of leadership/rule here ensures both continuity of manner and continuity of effect. Athenagoras optimistically views the emperors' rule as benevolent, and prays for succession that will keep the empire stable. If the rule is benevolent, such succession will also grant a peaceful life for subjects of that rule.

---

31. Athenagoras, *Legatio and De resurrectione* (trans. and ed. William R. Schoedel; Oxford: Clarendon Press, 1972). For discussion and bibliography, see P. Lorraine Buck, 'Athenagoras's Embassy: A Literary Fiction', *HTR* 89 (1996), pp. 209-26; Leslie W. Barnard, *Athenagoras: A Study in Second Century Christian Apologetic* (Paris: Beauchesne, 1972); Henry A. Lucks, *The Philosophy of Athenagoras: Its Sources and Value* (Washington, DC: Catholic University of America Press, 1936).

32. William R. Schoedel, 'Introduction', in Athenagoras, *Legatio and De resurrectione*, pp. ix-xxxvi (xxiii).

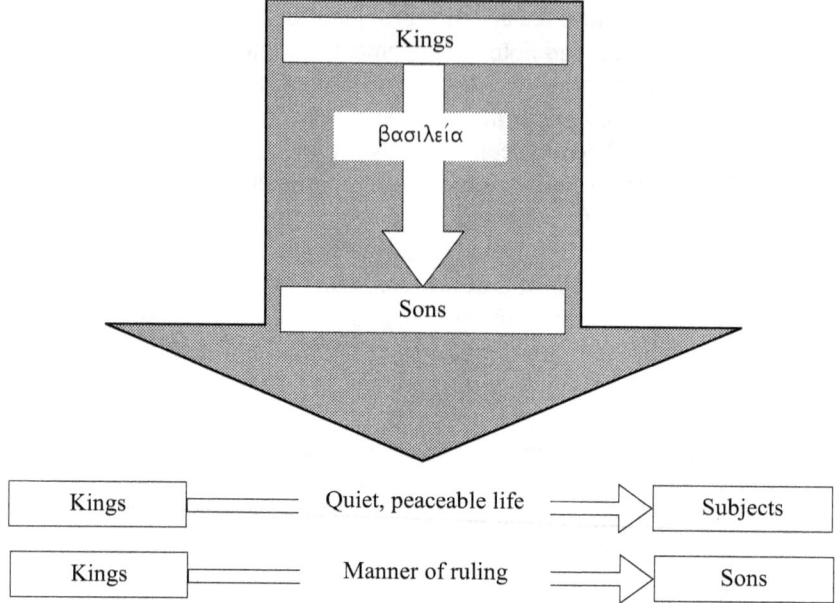

Figure 56. *The Functions of Succession in Athenagoras,* Legatio *37*

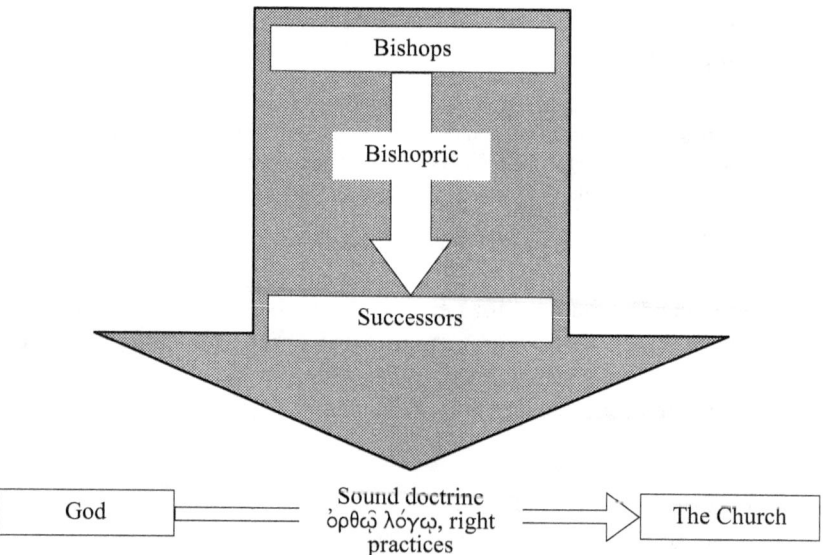

Figure 57. *The Function of Succession in Hegesippus
(in Eusebius,* Ecclesiastical History *4.21-22)*

3. Succession in Jewish and Christian Texts

Text 54: Hegesippus (in Eusebius, Ecclesiastical History *4.21-22).* In 4.21-22, Eusebius discusses the work of Hegesippus, a second-century Christian writer who was known for his 'correct opinions on the sound faith of the apostolic tradition' (Eusebius, *Ecclesiastical History* 4.21.1 [Lake, LCL]).[33] Eusebius tells how Hegesippus, when writing about other Christian leaders, was centrally concerned with their uniform adherence to apostolic faith and doctrine. As an example, he notes that Hegesippus wrote about 1 Clement:

> The church of the Corinthians remained in the true doctrine until Primus was the bishop of Corinth, and I...spent some days with the Corinthians during which we were refreshed by the true word (ὀρθῷ λόγῳ, cf. 2 Tim 2.15). When I was in Rome I recovered the list of the succession (διαδοχήν) until Anicetus, whose deacon was Eleutherus; Soter succeeded (διαδέχεται) Anicetus, and after him came Eleutherus. *In each list* (διαδοχῇ) *and in each city things are as the law, the prophets, and the Lord preach.* (4.22.3 [emphasis mine])

Figure 57 (opposite) maps the exchanges involved here.

In this passage, succession ensures the efficacy ('I was refreshed'), soundness, and integrity of doctrine and practice. Thus, here succession of leadership/rule ensures continued institutional vitality.

Text 55: Clement of Alexandria, Stromateis. Clement of Alexandria was a Christian teacher of the late second century CE. In his *Stromateis* ('Miscellanies'), he makes a broad survey of the intersection between the Christian faith and non-Christian philosophies and religions.

In *Stromateis* 1.21.109, Clement briefly traces the history of Israel after Moses. He writes that Joshua 'took over the leadership of the people', and that he 'held the succession from Moses for 27 years. *Then* the Hebrews fell into sin' (1.21.109.2-4 [emphasis mine]).[34] He continues, telling how the people would fall under foreign domination for several generations. Then the people would repent, and God would hear their prayers for deliverance. As long as the people had strong leaders, such as Deborah, they were faithful. But when the strong leader left the stage, the people rebelled and were unfaithful to God. Clement notes that Gideon, then Abimelech, then Boleas ruled in succession:

---

33. For discussion and bibliography, see Glenn F. Chesnut, 'Hegesippus', in *ABD*, III, pp. 110-11; T. Halton, 'Hegesippus in Eusebius', *StPatr* 17 (1982), pp. 688-93.

34. Clement of Alexandria, *Stromateis* (trans. John Ferguson; Fathers of the Church, 85; 2 vols.; Washington, DC: Catholic University of America Press, 1991). For discussion and bibliography, see Denise Kimber Buell, *Making Christians: Clement of Alexandria and the Rhetoric of Legitimacy* (Princeton, NJ: Princeton University Press, 1999); W.E.G. Floyd, *Clement of Alexandria's Treatment of the Problem of Evil* (London: Oxford University Press, 1971).

([Gideon was] succeeded by his son Abimelech... He was succeeded by Boleas... *After him*, the people fell into sin again.

They repented again and found a leader in Jephtah...; after him, authority passed to Abatthan...; then to Hebron...; then to Eglom...*and after him*, the people fell into sin again and were subject to foreigners. (1.21.110.4–111.2)

How does succession function here? For Clement, succession is part of what made for leadership, and leadership helped the people stay faithful to God. The emphasis here is not on the manner of leading—Clement refers not to strong leadership or devout leadership, although those factors may be found in the Old Testament stories, but simply to leadership *per se*. The focus is rather on the effect. Therefore: here, succession of leadership/rule ensures continuity of effect—as long as the succession is working, the people will be faithful to God. As soon as it fails, they fall away.

I can map the exchanges in this text as follows:

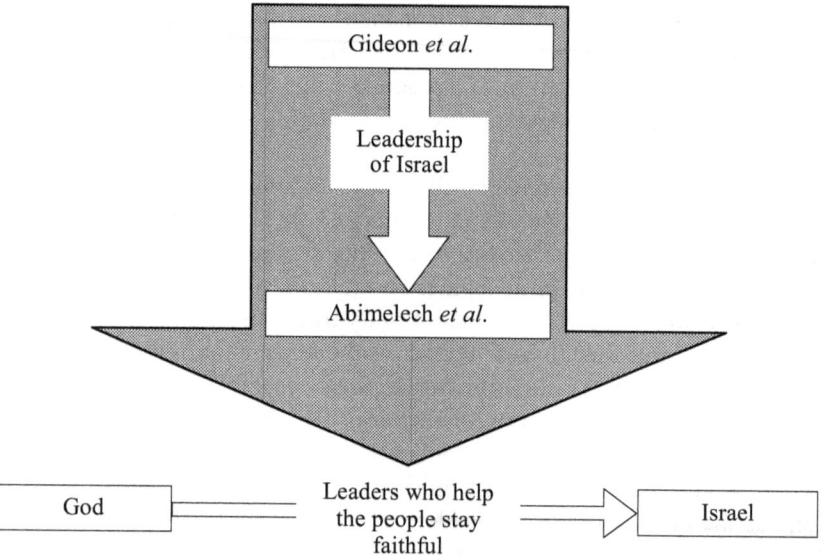

Figure 58. *The Function of Succession in Clement of Alexandria,* Stromateis

Text 56: Apollinarius of Hierapolis (in Eusebius, Ecclesiastical History *5.14-19).* Here, Eusebius recounts the struggle over Montanism. In 5.17, he quotes Apollinarius of Hierapolis, a second-century Christian writer. Apollinarius debated Montanism by comparing its prophetic practices with New Testament prophets and the true Christian prophets that followed (including a certain Ammia and Quadratus):

If the Montanist women succeeded to Quadratus and Ammia in Philadelphia in the prophetic gift (διεδέξαντο...τὸ προφητικὸν χάρισμα), let them show who among them succeeded the followers of Montanus and the women, for

3. *Succession in Jewish and Christian Texts* 103

the apostle grants that the prophetic gift shall be in all the Church until the final coming, but this they could not show, seeing that this is already the fourteenth year from the death of Maximilla. (5.17.4)[35]

I can map the exchanges considered in this passage thus:

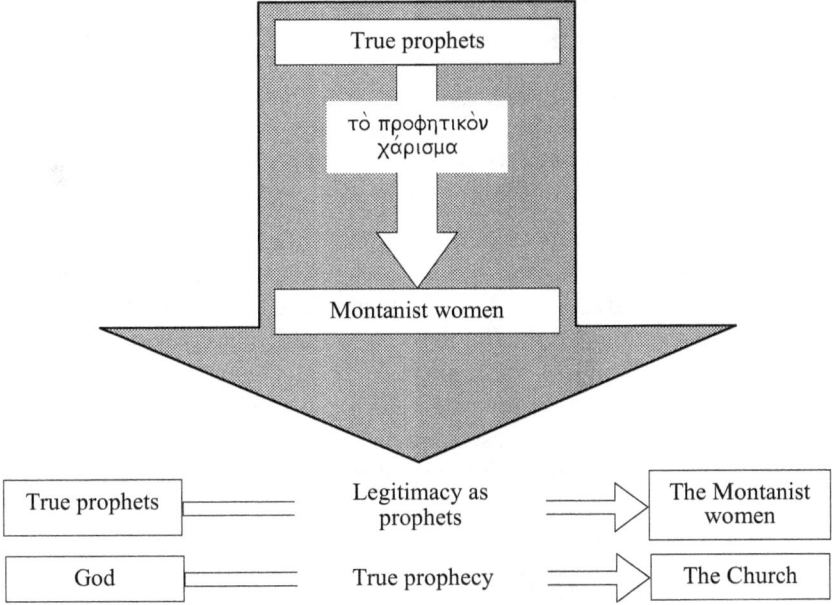

Figure 59. *The Functions of Succession in Apollinarius of Hierapolis (in Eusebius,* Ecclesiastical History *5.14-19)*

How does succession function here? First, it very clearly gives legitimacy to the successor(s). In Apollinarius's (and Eusebius's) mind, legitimacy is inherited through succession. The Montanists lack an established line of succession from their original leader and prophetess. This lacuna makes illegitimate their claim to stand in the line of Christian prophets. If their gift was legitimate, it would always exist in the Church, and there would thus be no gaps in the line of succession. Since gaps exist, their gift cannot be legitimate.

In this passage, succession also serves a second function. It ensures continued institutional vitality—proper succession is vital for a healthy prophetic office. Therefore, succession of leadership/rule here also ensures institutional vitality.

---

35. For discussion and bibliography, see Alistair Stewart-Sykes, 'The Original Condemnation of Asian Montanism', *JEH* 50 (1999), pp. 1-22.

104   *Leadership Succession in the World of the Pauline Circle*

Texts Describing Succession of Tradition/Knowledge
Text 57: Luke 1.1-4. The opening of Luke's Gospel is a beautifully balanced *classical* prologue: in it, Luke shows his reader 'that what he is going to say will be important, essential, personal, [and] useful' (Lucian, *How to Write History* 53 [Kilburn, LCL]). Luke's prologue reads:

> Since many have undertaken to set down an orderly account of the events that have been fulfilled among us, just as they were handed on to us by those who from the beginning were eyewitnesses and servants of the word, I too decided, after investigating everything carefully from the very first, to write an orderly account for you, most excellent Theophilus, so that you may know the truth concerning the things about which you have been instructed. (Lk. 1.1-4)

The succession mentioned here is a succession of tradition, knowledge passed on from eyewitnesses to others. Luke sees himself as occupying a place in this line of tradents—the eyewitnesses and servants of the word who came before have passed the tradition on to Luke and his contemporaries. Luke, being conscious of his role as tradent, and having investigated everything from the beginning, sets out to write a properly–ordered account (καθεξῆς) of the ministry of Jesus and his followers. His stated purpose: to give his reader, Theophilus, certainty of the truth about the things he had learned.

I can set out the exchanges in this text in the following way:

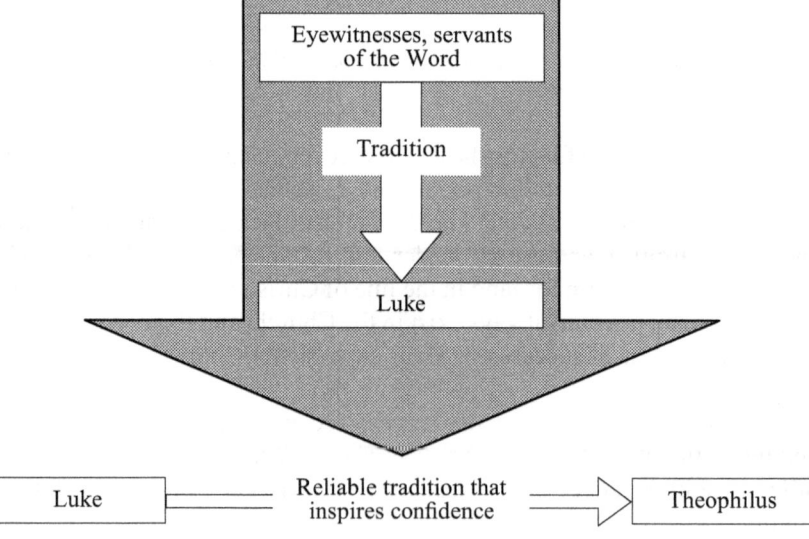

Figure 60. *The Function of Succession in Luke 1.1-4*

How does succession of tradition function in this text? Succession makes the tradition reliable, so that the teaching that flows from the tradition can have its proper effect—so that it can promote the reader's/hearer's certainty (faith) in what he/she had been taught. Thus succession of tradition here ensures continued institutional vitality.

Text 58: Athenagoras, Legatio *28.* In chs. 4–30, Athenagoras defends Christianity against charges of atheism. The second half of this defense is a comparison of Christianity with other religions. Athenagoras specifically addresses why Christians do not worship statues/idols. According to him, the power that idols possess is demonic, not from the gods—he cites various sources and their treatments of the Egyptian origins of the Greek gods in support of this. These stories are reliable because son succeeds father in possession of both the stories and the priesthood:

> When they talk about these things, who should be believed more readily than those who have received in a natural succession from father to son the account of these stories along with the priesthood (οἱ κατὰ διαδοχὴν γένους παῖς παρὰ πατρός, ὡς τὴν ἱερωσύνην καὶ τὴν ἱστορίαν διαδεχόμενοι)? (28.5)

I can map the exchanges envisioned here thus:

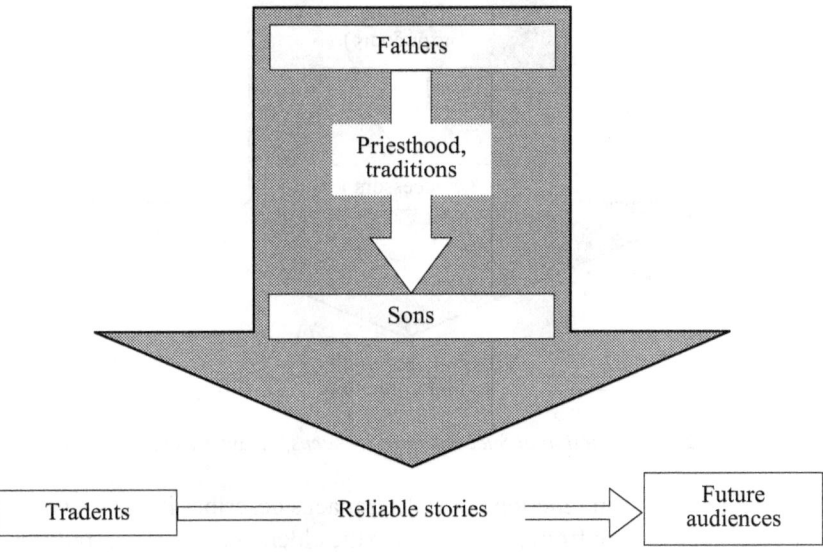

Figure 61. *The Function of Succession in Athenagoras,* Legatio *28*

How does succession function here? Again, the story centers on succession of tradition—the succession in the priesthood (i.e. succession of task or office or leadership/rule) is incidental, the focus is on the stories that are passed down. This succession ensures that the tradition is reliable and trustworthy, thus ensuring continued institutional vitality.

Text 59: Irenaeus, Against Heresies *3.2.1-2.* Irenaeus was a Christian leader who lived near the end of the second century. In *Against Heresies*, he describes the debate between orthodox Christian leaders and the heretics of his day.[36] In describing the arguments of the second-century heretics, he notes that, when confronted with scripture, their normal response was to say that the scripture was being misunderstood or misapplied. This was due, they asserted, to the orthodox debater's lack of the secret knowledge needed properly to understand scripture. The heterodox held that this secret knowledge resided with Valentinus or Marcion or Cerinthus, and so on.

The customary orthodox response was to point 'to that tradition which originates from the apostles [and] which is preserved by means of the succession of presbyters in the Churches' (3.2.2). From the orthodox perspective, this succession gave their interpretations authority.[37]

I can illustrate the exchanges in the text thus:

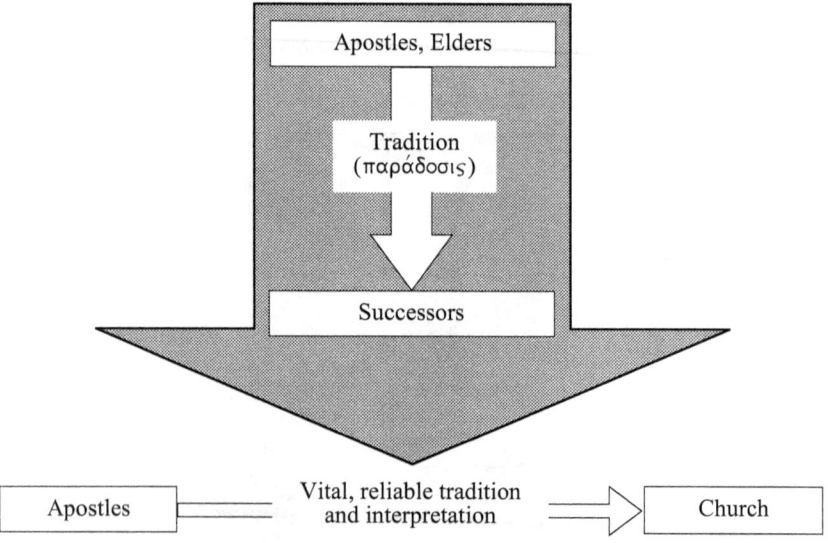

Figure 62. *The Function of Succession in Irenaeus,* Against Heresies *3.2.1-2*

How does succession function here? As Irenaeus describes it, the succession of tradition passed on from the apostles to the elders preserves the tradition's authority. Note that the elders do not have to become apostles themselves for the succession to be legitimate—here again, succession can involve

36. For discussion and bibliography, see Mary Ann Donovan, 'Irenaeus', in *ABD*, III, pp. 457-61; Denis Minns, *Irenaeus* (London: Geoffrey Chapman, 1994); Robert M. Grant, *Irenaeus of Lyons* (New York: Routledge, 1997).

37. Irenaeus, *Against Heresies* 3.2.1-2 (*ANF* 1.415). In response, the heretics sometimes claimed that—due to their secret knowledge—they knew better how to understand the scriptures than even the elders, or apostles, or Jesus himself.

differences in kind between the predecessor and the successors. Therefore, succession here functions to ensure the continued vitality of the tradition. Because of succession, the Church knows how to interpret, apply, and understand the scriptures.

Text 60: Irenaeus, Against Heresies *3.3.1-3*. Irenaeus continues: to contradict the heretics, he points to the succession of overseers in the churches. His assertion is that this succession ensures that there could be no 'secret knowledge'—the so-called 'secret knowledge' is in fact a new invention. His reasoning: the apostles cared enough about the well-being of the Church to establish a succession of leaders, so that the Church would continue to thrive after their death. According to 3.3.1, If they

> had known hidden mysteries, which they were in the habit of imparting to 'the perfect', apart and privily from the rest, they would have delivered them especially to those to whom they were also committing the churches themselves.

Later, in 3.3.3, Irenaeus asserts:

> In this order, and by this succession, the ecclesiastical tradition from the Apostles and the preaching of the truth have come down to us. And this is most abundant proof that there is but one and the same vivifying faith, which has been preserved in the Church from the Apostles until now, and handed down in truth.

Note that the succession from the apostles to the overseers, the overseers do not need to become apostles themselves for the succession to be realized.

I can illustrate the exchanges involved thus:

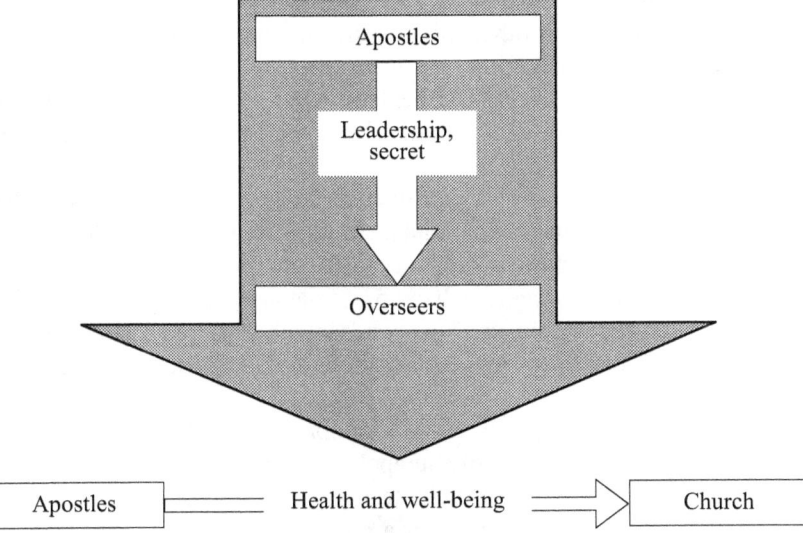

Figure 63. *The Function of Succession in Irenaeus,* Against Heresies *3.3.1-3*

How does succession function here? In the hypothetical exchange Irenaeus proposes (and then discards), the apostles—concerned for the future health of the Church—pass on not only leadership but also secret knowledge to the overseers. Thus succession of tradition/knowledge (and succession of leadership/rule) here ensures continued institutional vitality.

5. *Summary of Christian Texts Describing the Function of Succession*

Building upon the previous chapter and the first section of this chapter, I have shown the following. First, as with the Graeco-Roman and Jewish texts surveyed above, I have shown that references to succession in Christian texts sometimes contain not one but two exchanges. The first exchange is the succession itself. The second, when it is present, describes the function of the first succession, what it achieved or might have achieved, why it was necessary or desired. And again, these two exchanges can be described graphically, and the second exchange can profitably be described in terms from structuralism, Sender → Object → Receiver.

Second, as with the Graeco-Roman and Jewish texts surveyed above, I have shown that the functions of succession in Christian literature tend to fall into categories delineated by the focus of succession in the text. If the text focuses on how succession affects property, for example, then the function seems to be different than if the text focuses on the legitimacy of the successor(s).

Functionally, the Christian texts fell into some of the categories also found in the Graeco-Roman and Jewish texts, and they generally function in the same way as texts from other milieus in said categories. In the Christian texts, I have shown succession function to ensure:

1. *continuity of manner* (e.g. Text 50: Acts 6–7), where the text focuses on characteristic actions/attitudes shared by predecessor and successor;
2. *continued institutional vitality* (e.g. Text 52: 1 Clem. 42–44), where the object of succession is an institution, and the text focuses on that object and on how succession causes it to remain vital and effective;
3. *continuity of effect* (e.g. Text 53: Athenagoras, *Legatio* 37), where the text focuses on an effect/result which is shared by the predecessor and successor but the realization of which is not dependent upon the succession;
4. *legitimacy of a particular successor* (e.g. Text 48: Mt. 16.13-20; Text 56: Apollinarius of Hierapolis), where the text focuses on potential successors to a particular task or office and the dilemma of which is the legitimate (or whether a proposed successor is legitimate) is solved by the actuality/non-actuality of succession itself.

I did not find any Christian texts that fit some of the functional categories, however. In my admittedly limited textbase, I found no Christian examples of succession serving to ensure continuity of possession or the realization of an effect. Perhaps this is merely due to the limited size of my textbase, or perhaps a different Christian conception of a particular aspect of succession (or a particular aspect of history: an understanding of the tension between the now and the not-yet different from that in Judaism?) is in view. Only further study will tell.

Third, as with the Graeco-Roman and Jewish texts surveyed earlier, I found that the categories were less than 'watertight'. Again, they tended to blur together at times. At other times, in a single story succession could function in multiple ways.

Fourth, as with the Graeco-Roman and Jewish texts surveyed earlier, the comparative greatness of the predecessor over the successor (e.g. Jesus' greatness in comparison to that of his disciples) does not invalidate or delegitimize the succession. And as with the Graeco-Roman and Jewish texts, the successor does not need to hold equal office or equal station in life with the predecessor for succession to have been inferred—overseers/elders can be successors of the apostles without having to become apostles themselves, for example. This phenomenon is best understood in terms of a continuum of replacement, from weak succession (delegation or agency) to strong succession (full replacement, the successor as predecessor *redivivus*).

In contrast with the Graeco-Roman texts and their use of succession (and in keeping with the Jewish texts and their use of succession), the Christian texts are consistently optimistic; they present succession as something that God uses to achieve his purposes. This is true even in secular successions: witness Athenagoras's confidence that God would work benevolently through the succession of Roman rulers. The Christian texts *do* depict God as the hand behind succession, but—in contrast with the Jewish texts on this point—the sense of God directly choosing the successors is not explicit.

Below (see next page), sorted by the object of succession as above, are charts listing the Christian texts surveyed and the function of succession in each.

On the basis of the Graeco-Roman, Jewish, and Christian texts surveyed in this and the previous chapter, I can now reconstruct some of the expectations an ancient audience would have had when hearing a text utilizing succession. The texts which I have surveyed in these two chapters were not 'hidden in a corner' somewhere—these were central texts in the ancient Graeco-Roman, Jewish, and Christian literary milieus. Given the consistency and prominence with which succession appears in these central texts, an ancient audience would know the literary conventions of succession.

Table 9. *Christian Texts Describing the Passing-On of Leadership/Rule*

	Text	Function
48.	Mt. 16.13-20	Continuity of institutional vitality Successor's legitimacy
49.	Lk. 22.28-30	Continuity of manner
50.	Acts 6–7	Continuity of institutional vitality Continuity of manner
51.	Acts 24.27 and 25.9	Continuity of manner
52.	1 Clem. 42–44	Continuity of effect Continuity of institutional vitality
53.	Athenagoras, *Legatio* 37	Continuity of manner Continuity of effect
54.	Hegesippus	Continuity of institutional vitality
55.	Clement of Alexandria, *Stromateis*	Continuity of effect
56.	Apollinarius of Hierapolis	Successor's legitimacy Continuity of institutional vitality

Table 10. *Christian Texts Describing the Passing-On of Knowledge or Tradition*

	Text	Function
57.	Lk. 1.1-4	Continuity of institutional vitality
58.	Athenagoras, *Legatio* 28	Continuity of institutional vitality
59.	Irenaeus, *Against Heresies* 3.2.1-2	Continuity of institutional vitality
60.	Irenaeus, *Against Heresies* 3.3.1-3	Continuity of institutional vitality

Because of the presence of these conventions—terms commonly associated with succession (the semantic domain, different and yet similar across the milieus) and the presence of certain phenomena commonly thought of in reference to succession (the conceptual domain, essentially uniform across the milieus)—an ancient Mediterranean audience would have understood these texts to refer to succession. Further, they would have been prepared to hear that succession achieved something—that it functioned in a particular way to accomplish a particular end.

In the opening chapter of this monograph, I asked how such an audience, conditioned by their texts in this way, would have heard the Pastoral Epistles. Would they have understood these letters, and the relationships between Christian leaders described therein, in terms of succession? If so, what would they have understood as the purpose of succession in the Pastorals? And how would such an understanding/expectation have affected their understanding of what the Pastorals teach regarding church leadership? Having laid the groundwork, I can now attempt to answer these questions.

4

SUCCESSION IN THE PASTORAL EPISTLES, PART 1:
FIRST TIMOTHY

This chapter is the first of three chapters exploring how the authorial audience of the Pastoral Epistles, based on the way succession functioned in the texts of their culture, would have understood the function of succession in the Pastoral Epistles. In this chapter, I examine the function of succession in 1 Timothy. In the next chapter, Chapter 5, I examine the function of succession in 2 Timothy and Titus. In the following chapter (Chapter 6), I offer a brief reading of these letters based on a historically grounded understanding of how succession would have functioned for the authorial audience.

Over the previous two chapters, I have examined several dozen ancient texts from various milieus in which the function of succession is an explicit consideration. I closed the last chapter of that survey by concluding that, because of the presence of terms commonly associated with succession and the presence of phenomena commonly associated with succession (the semantic and conceptual fields of succession, respectively), an ancient Mediterranean audience would have inferred succession when hearing these texts. They would also have been prepared to hear succession function in particular ways to achieve particular ends.

I opened this study by asking how the authorial audience of the Pastorals, conditioned by their knowledge of literary conventions pertaining to succession and other knowledge that they brought with them to the text, would have understood the Pastoral Epistles. Having laid the foundation, I can now address these questions. First, would they have understood these letters, and the relationships between Christian leaders described therein, in terms of succession? Second, if they would have understood these letters in terms of succession, what would they have understood as the function of succession in the Pastorals? And how would such an understanding/expectation have affected their understanding of what the Pastorals teach regarding church leadership? In this chapter, I ask these questions of 1 Timothy. In the next chapter, I ask the same questions of 2 Timothy and Titus.

Evidence of succession. In this study, I have seen three types of evidence which would have led the authorial audience to infer succession. First, I find the presence of terms already seen in other succession-specific contexts, terms from the semantic field of succession. Alongside these, I also find related/ cognate terms and synonyms, which, in the context established by the terms from the semantic field and the other evidence, also serve as succession terms. Second, I find the presence of phenomena already seen in other succession-specific contexts, phenomena from the conceptual field of succession. In my survey of texts in Chapters 2 and 3, I frequently saw the same actions or types of actions repeated in stories of succession. These phenomena serve alongside the terms from the semantic field as cues to infer succession. Third, I find that the standard elements of an ancient Mediterranean succession story (see p. 15 above)[1] are present in several cases.

How shall I weigh and consider this evidence? The Pastoral Epistles present nine different relationships that the authorial audience might perceive in terms of succession—for example, Timothy's relationship to Paul in 1 Timothy, Timothy's relationship to Paul in 2 Timothy. There is some evidence of succession with regard to each of the nine relationships, but it is not apportioned equally. One relationship might be described with all three types of evidence—terms, phenomena, and the standard elements of a Mediterranean succession story. Other relationships may have only a single word or phenomenon attached to them.

In order to determine the likelihood that the authorial audience would infer succession in a given relationship, I will consider each relationship separately. I will rate the prominence of each type of evidence for each relationship on a scale from *total absence* to *presence* to *prominence*. I will then consider the three types of evidence for succession in a given relationship as a whole, so as to determine their overall prominence.

I set the following standard so as not to place the threshold too low. If two (or more) of the three types of evidence are prominent in the description of a given relationship, I consider it certain that the authorial audience would have inferred succession. If one type of evidence is prominent and others are at least present, I consider it likely that the authorial audience would have inferred succession. If one type of evidence is prominent but the others are completely absent, or if two types are present but not prominent, I consider it possible that the audience would have inferred succession.[2]

When considered *in toto*, this evidence will indicate that the authorial audience would have understood four of the relationships described in 1 Timothy

---

1. Talbert and Stepp, 'Succession: Part 1', pp. 160-67.
2. This matches the overall standards applied to the evidence in Chapters 2 and 3, above.

to involve succession. Paul's succession from Christ is the foundational succession relationship—the other succession relationships in the letter are built upon it. I will thus consider this foundational succession relationship first, followed by three other relationships: Timothy's succession from Paul, Timothy's succession from the elders, and other leaders' succession from Paul and/or Timothy.

1. *Paul's Succession from Christ*

Evidence of Succession from Christ to Paul
Terms from the semantic field of succession. First Timothy describes Paul's relationship to Christ in terms of succession: 'The law is laid down not for the innocent but for…[those who do whatever] is contrary to the sound teaching that conforms to the glorious gospel of the blessed God, which he entrusted to me (ὃ ἐπιστεύθην ἐγώ, lit. "with which I was entrusted")' (1.9, 11). Πιστεύω is a known succession term (e.g. Dio Cassius 53.31.3). Note also a second succession term, τίθημι:

> I am grateful to Christ Jesus our Lord, who has strengthened me, because he judged me faithful and appointed (θέμενος) me to his service. (1.12)

> For this I was appointed (εἰς ὃ ἐτέθην ἐγώ) a herald and an apostle…, a teacher of the Gentiles. (2.7)

Although not included on Talbert and Stepp's list,[3] τίθημι is another known succession term (e.g. see Solomon's statement regarding his succession to his father's throne in 1 Kgs 2.24 [LXX 3 Kgdms 2.24]).[4]

In the light of these succession terms, two other terms in close proximity would have been read/heard in reference to succession as well:

> Paul, an apostle (ἀπόστολος) of Christ Jesus by the command (κατ' ἐπιταγήν) of God our Savior… (1.1)

I am here treating ἀπόστολος as a synonym for succession terms: should I instead treat it as a succession term proper? The basic force of the term—one sent, those sent by Jesus to be his witnesses—is certainly in harmony with the idea of succession. However, insufficient evidence from outside the New Testament leads me to regard it for the time being as a synonym rather than a succession term proper.

In the light of these passages, I consider the semantic evidence of succession from Christ to Paul to be prominent.

---

3. See above, p. 16.
4. See above, p. 68.

Phenomena from the conceptual field of succession. I find no phenomena from the conceptual field used in 1 Timothy to describe this relationship.

Standard Elements of a Mediterranean succession story. Two of the three standard elements of an ancient Mediterranean succession story are present. Note the naming of what is being passed on—the gospel (1.11). Note also the confirmation that succession has taken place, via parallel characteristic actions—God makes commands (ἐπιταγή, 1.1) and Paul makes authoritative commands regarding the gospel (*passim*, especially 1.3, παραγγέλλω). These constitute two of the three standard features in the conventional form of ancient Mediterranean succession stories. The only exception to the conventional form is the absence in 1 Tim. 1.1-11 of some kind of symbolic act. This symbolic act, which Talbert and I show can include a speech of commissioning,[5] is supplied to the audience by their knowledge of Paul's commissioning to be Jesus' apostle to the Gentiles. The author of 1 Timothy clearly presupposed this knowledge on the part of his audience: note the allusions to Paul's conversion/commissioning in 1.1, 11, 12-15, and 2.7. Unless the authorial audience possessed knowledge of Paul's life and career external to the text of 1 Timothy, these allusions would have been indecipherable. In their reading/hearing of the Pastorals, the authorial audience would have filled this particular gap with their knowledge of Paul's commissioning as apostle to the Gentiles. Thus, for the authorial audience, all the standard components of an ancient Mediterranean succession story are present. I consider this evidence to be prominent.

Summary. In the light of the prominence of the terms from the semantic field of succession, and in the light of the fact that the three standard components of an ancient Mediterranean succession story are present and prominent, I conclude that the authorial audience would have understood Paul to be Jesus' successor in the keeping of the gospel.

2. *The Function of the Succession from Christ to Paul*

As described in 1 Timothy, Paul's calling to ministry *is* a succession from Christ to Paul. Christ, the predecessor, entrusts tradition (gospel) to Paul, his successor. The authority and vocation that Paul pursues because of his calling, which he claims and works out through this letter, are the results of this succession.

Some commentators have noted (correctly) that succession from Paul to Timothy is at the heart of 1 Timothy—although without having a historical

---

5. Talbert and Stepp, 'Succession: Part 2', p. 171.

understanding of the concept of succession.⁶ None of the commentators I have surveyed, however, sees that the succession from Christ to Paul serves as the letter's central warrant and the starting place for what is passed from Paul to Timothy.

Note that, as with the Jewish and Christian succession references in Chapter 3 above, God initiates and guides this succession:

> Paul, an apostle of Christ Jesus by the command (ἐπιταγήν) of God our Savior and of Christ Jesus our hope. (1.1)

Here, Paul describes his calling to apostleship as being due to a direct command of God. The authorial audience would have understood this description to refer to Paul's encounter with Jesus on the road to Damascus.⁷ The direct commission from Jesus Christ sets Paul and the others who wear the proper appellation 'apostle' apart from other believers and leaders in the first-century Church—they are unique because Jesus personally called them to serve as witnesses to his resurrection (Acts 1.7-8, etc.).⁸

Succession from Christ defines Paul's vocation, prescribing the actions he takes: as Christ's successor in care of the gospel, he does whatever is

---

6. In the terms of this study, one of the more perceptive comments is that of Thomas Scott Caulley, 'Fighting the Good Fight: The Pastoral Epistles in Canonical-Critical Perspective', in *Society of Biblical Literature Seminar Papers, 1987* (SBLSP, 26; Atlanta: Scholars Press, 1987), pp. 550-64. Caulley writes, 'In the Pastorals the figure of Timothy is presented as the primary Pauline successor in a conscious analogy to Moses and Joshua' (p. 561). Jerome D. Quinn and William Wacker, *The First and Second Letters to Timothy* (Eerdmans Critical Commentary; Grand Rapids: Eerdmans, 1999), p. 78, see the succession, but misread it because they do not work from an historical understanding of the phenomenon. They assert that the opening of 1 Timothy contains 'a chain of command that transmits the will and orders of the commander...from God the Father and Jesus Christ through Paul the Apostle to Timothy...and thence to particular congregations of believers'. See also William Mounce, *The Pastoral Epistles* (WBC; Nashville: Thomas Nelson, 2000), p. 43. Ernst Käsemann, 'Paul and Early Catholicism', in *idem, New Testament Questions of Today* (trans. Wilfred F. Bunge; London: SCM Press, 1969), pp. 236-51 (247), likewise asserts that the Pastorals show the monarchical bishop, the presbytery, and the deacons, organized in an official system centering on apostolic succession.

7. Marshall notes: 'the point at which this decisive event occurred is almost certainly to be understood as the Damascus revelation to Saul' (I. Howard Marshall, with Philip H. Towner, *A Critical and Exegetical Commentary on the Pastoral Epistles* [ICC; Edinburgh: T. & T. Clark, 1999]), p. 389.

8. For the view that the Pastorals present Paul as the one and only apostle, see Raymond Collins, *1 & 2 Timothy and Titus: A Commentary* (NTL; Louisville, KY: Westminster/John Knox Press, 2002), p. 8; Jurgen Roloff, *Der erste Brief an Timotheus* (Zurich: Benziger, 1988), p. 56. Michael Wolter, *Die Pastoralbriefe als Paulustradition* (Göttingen: Vandenhoeck & Ruprecht, 1988), pp. 91, 95, asserts that for the Pastorals, Paul is the only link to Christ, and thus the only guarantor of salvation for those who follow him. See Marshall, *Pastoral Epistles*, p. 354, however.

consistent with the purpose of that succession (i.e. whatever ensures the continued vitality of the gospel). Succession also gives him the authority by which he performs these actions. Paul's actions and Paul's authority are woven together in his vocation as successor to Christ in the keeping of the gospel.

First Timothy's statements regarding Paul's vocation as it results from this succession can be grouped under three headings. Below I analyze what each group says about Paul's actions and authority. The headings are: Paul fights for orthodoxy, Paul promotes orthopraxy, and Paul oversees the work of other church leaders.

Paul Fights for Orthodoxy (i.e. 'Fights the Good Fight')
In Paul's struggle to maintain the purity and efficacy of the gospel, succession accomplishes three things. First, it separates him from the false teachers and authorizes him for the task. Second, it gives him authority over the content of teaching. Third, it gives him authority over who is and is not authorized to teach.

Succession separates Paul from the false teachers.[9] Immediately after opening the letter, Paul claims authority over what is being taught in his churches:

> I urge you, as I did when I was on my way to Macedonia, to remain in Ephesus so that you may instruct (παραγγέλλω, 'command') certain people not to teach any different doctrine... (1.3)

Paul next contrasts his calling by direct command of God to the calling of the false teachers: 'They (the "certain people" from 1.3 who are teaching doctrines different from those that Paul teaches) want to be teachers of the law' (1.7a). These people have no calling or commission other than their own desires—they have essentially called themselves to be teachers, whereas Paul was called to that function (and others) by direct command of God.

Notice further the contrast between the result of the false teachers' self-appointment and the result of Paul's having been appointed by God. The false teachers want to be teachers 'without understanding either what they are saying or the things about which they make assertions' (1.7b).[10] Paul and those who follow him, on the other hand, *do* understand the law and its use:

> Now we know that the law is good if one uses it legitimately. This means understanding that the law is laid down not for the innocent but for the lawless and disobedient, ...and whatever else is contrary to the sound teaching that conforms to the glorious gospel of the blessed God, which he entrusted (ἐπιστεύθην) to me. (1.8-11)

---

9. On the contrast between Paul and the false teachers, see E. Schlarb, *Die gesunde Lehre: Häresie und Wahrheit im Spiegel der Pastoralbriefe* (Marburg: Elwert, 1990), pp. 83-93, 179.
10. Schlarb, *Lehre*, p. 91; Roloff, *Brief*, p. 71.

4. First Timothy

How does Paul know how the gospel is to be used? How does he possess the authority to tell people in his churches how they can and cannot use it? He possesses this knowledge and authority because he stands in a line of succession of tradition from Christ! Christ bequeathed the gospel and its care to him. This succession enables and legitimates Paul. Therefore, the authorial audience would have understood Paul's authority over teaching to be a result of his succession from Christ.

Paul's description of himself as Christ's successor is of a piece with the apostles being Jesus' successors as judges over restored Israel in Lk. 22.28-30.[11] In Paul, a vital aspect of Jesus' earthly ministry—authoritative care of the gospel and its teaching—continues in Jesus' absence.[12] It continues because Jesus has passed that responsibility on to a successor, Paul. And because Paul is Jesus' successor in care of the gospel, he can speak authoritatively regarding it. Indeed, when Paul as Christ's successor speaks regarding matters that Christ has entrusted to him, he does not speak with his own voice or rest on his own authority—he speaks with the authority of the one who bequeathed the gospel to him, the voice and authority of Christ himself.

Paul further describes the results of this authority, and of the proper application of the Law, in 1.3-5:

> I urge you...to remain in Ephesus so that you may instruct ('command') certain people not to teach any different doctrine, and not to occupy themselves with myths and endless genealogies that promote speculations rather than the divine training (οἰκονομίαν θεοῦ, 'God's stewardship') that is known by faith. But the aim of such instruction ('the command') is love that comes from a pure heart, a good conscience, and sincere faith.

Here, the audience would hear Paul compare the results of false teaching ('speculations' or 'controversies') with the results of true teaching. True teaching[13] promotes the οἰκονομίαν θεοῦ, that is, God's church/household is properly administered, good stewardship over God's household is practiced.[14]

---

11. Talbert and Stepp, 'Succession: Part 2', pp. 169-72.

12. Marshall, *Pastoral Epistles*, p. 390, notes that Paul's task here is 'the proclamation and preservation of the gospel'.

13. True teaching, in this immediate context, refers to the Pauline understanding of the Old Testament and its application to Christians: see Quinn and Wacker, *First and Second Letters to Timothy*, pp. 102-103.

14. I am taking οἰκονομίαν θεοῦ to be the opposite of ἐκζητήσεις. It is also possible to take οἰκονομίαν θεοῦ as the opposite of μύθοις καὶ γενεαλογίαις and take ἐκζητήσεις as the opposite of ἀγάπη ἐκ καθαρᾶς καρδίας καὶ συνειδήσεως ἀγαθῆς καὶ πίστεως ἀνυποκρίτου, as the NRSV appears to do—but that translation forces an unnatural meaning on οἰκονομίαν. Commentators suggest three basic understandings of οἰκονομίαν: first, that it refers to the household duties of the stewards of God's house (Marshall, *Pastoral Epistles*, pp. 367-68; Ceslas Spicq, *Saint Paul: Les Epîtres pastorales* [Ebib; Paris: J. Gabalda, 4th edn, 1969], p. 324; Roloff, *Brief*, p. 66; Quinn and Wacker, *First and Second Letters to*

False teaching, on the other hand, damages the Church by bringing about division.[15]

Succession gives Paul authority over the content of teaching. Consider next the passages that point to Paul's authority over the content that he allowed to be taught in his churches. Two passages address the steps Paul takes to safeguard the teaching of the true gospel:

> I urge you, as I did when I was on my way to Macedonia, to remain in Ephesus so that you may instruct (παραγγέλλω, 'command') certain people not to teach any different doctrine... (1.3)

> Teach and urge these duties.[16] Whoever teaches otherwise and does not agree with the sound words of our Lord Jesus Christ and the teaching that is in accordance with godliness is conceited, understanding nothing... (6.2b-4)

Notice the near-absolute authority that Paul claims for himself and Timothy in these verses. How can they order people to teach or not to teach according to what they endorse? How can they say that those who disagree with them disagree with God? Paul has this authority because he is an apostle, called by direct command of God (1.1). He has this authority because he is Christ's successor as keeper of the gospel (1.11).[17] As a result of this succession, he is able to pass on this authority and these responsibilities to *his* successor who will safeguard true teaching in his place.

Second, several passages show how Paul endorses the proper content for teaching. In this category are some of the traditional materials Paul includes/ endorses. These supply some of the doctrinal content of Paul's teaching as 1 Timothy describes it:

Timothy, pp. 74-77; H. von Lips, *Glaube–Gemeinde–Amt: Zum Verständnis der Ordination in den Pastoralbriefen* [Göttingen: Vandenhoeck & Ruprecht, 1979], pp. 145-47; Luke Timothy Johnson, *The First and Second Letters to Timothy* [AB, 35A; New York: Doubleday, 2001], p. 164); second, that it refers to God's plan (usually of salvation); third, that it refers to a combination of the two (George W. Knight, *The Pastoral Epistles: A Commentary on the Greek Text* [New International Greek Testament Commentary; Grand Rapids: Eerdmans, 1992], pp. 75-76).

15. Mounce, *Pastoral Epistles*, p. 22, asserts that the false teachers should also be understood in terms of οἰκονομίαν: they were leaders, entrusted with stewardship over the Church, who had pursued mysticism ('speculations and myths') instead of faithfully discharging their offices in the best interests of the Church.

16. The immediate antecedent to 'these duties' is the list of duties for slaves, elders, and widows in 1 Tim. 5.3–6.2a.

17. Again, the fact that Paul claims this authority does not mean that he is pictured as the only true apostle—just the only apostle that matters for the particular purposes of the Pastorals (see n. 8 above). See Marshall, *Pastoral Epistles*, p. 435, who notes that Paul is not the only legitimate source of the gospel and its implications for the readers of the Pastorals, but he *is* the source for material for refuting the false teachers.

> The saying is sure and worthy of full acceptance, that Christ Jesus came into the world to save sinners. (1.15)

> There is one God;
>   There is also one mediator between God and humankind,
> Christ Jesus, himself human,
>   Who gave himself a ransom for all. (2.5-6a)

> He was revealed in the flesh,
>   vindicated in spirit,
>   seen by angels,
> proclaimed among Gentiles,
>   believed in throughout the world,
>   taken up in glory. (3.16)

Other passages contain material of a more explicitly doctrinal nature:

> [In response to the pseudo-pious asceticism of the false teachers] For everything created by God is good, and nothing is to be rejected, provided it is received with thanksgiving; for it is sanctified by God's word and by prayer. If you put these instructions before the brothers and sisters, you will be a good servant of Christ Jesus... (4.4-6)

> Have nothing to do with profane myths and old wives' tales. Train yourself in godliness...godliness is valuable in every way, holding promise for both the present life and the life to come...to this end we toil and struggle, because we have set our hope on the living God, who is the Savior of all people, especially of those who believe. These are the things you must insist on and teach. (4.7-11)[18]

> [Referring back to the descriptions of propriety in 5.1–6.2a] Teach and urge these duties. (6.2b)

These passages center on the content of what Timothy and those under his authority must teach: proper Christology, the goodness of creation, the priority of everyday godliness over speculative *gnosis* (whatever the historical referent) (see also 1.4). Most prominently, Timothy must hold to and promote the pure tradition he received from Paul, and the resulting propriety with which God wants his people to live.

Third, several passages show how Paul refutes false teaching. Under this heading belong those passages where Paul describes or refutes particular areas/brands of false teaching:

---

18. Roloff, *Brief*, p. 240, pointing to the parallel with Col. 1.29, argues that here πιστὸς ὁ λόγος refers forward (to 4.10, 'to this end we toil and struggle, because we have set our hope on the living God'; so also Mounce, *Pastoral Epistles*, p. 254, who limits it to 4.10b) rather than backward (to 4.8, 'godliness is valuable in every way, holding promise for both the present life and the life to come'). Lorenz Oberlinner, *Die Pastoralbriefe: Kommentar zum ersten Timotheusbrief* (HTKNT, XI/1; Freiburg: Herder, 1994), p. 196, suggests that the whole of 4.8, 10 is the faithful saying, with πιστὸς ὁ λόγος in the middle of the λόγος.

I urge you...to remain in Ephesus so that you may instruct (παραγγέλλω, 'command') certain people not to teach any different doctrine, and not to occupy themselves with myths and endless genealogies that promote speculations rather than the divine training ('stewardship') that is known by faith. (1.3-4)

Now the Spirit expressly says that in later times some will renounce the faith by paying attention to deceitful spirits and teachings of demons, through the hypocrisy of liars whose consciences are seared with a hot iron. They forbid marriage and demand abstinence from foods, which God created to be received with thanksgiving by those who believe and know the truth. For everything created by God is good, and nothing is to be rejected, provided it is received with thanksgiving; for it is sanctified by God's word and by prayer. (4.1-5)

In exercising his authority over the content of teaching, Paul describes the falsehoods that are being taught and warns his people away from them. He does not debate or refute the false doctrines themselves, but instead polemically attacks the teachers who promulgate them.[19] Here, Paul characterizes the false teachings as 'endless', useless, promoting division, demonic in origin, and superficial.[20] They enslave those who follow, and that without doing anything to produce God's will in their lives.

Paul's rationale for rebuking false teaching is further outlined in 4.7-10. He is concerned that nothing hinder the spread of the gospel, and is worried that the disorder that results from false teachings will keep the gospel from gaining a hearing:

---

19. See Abraham Malherbe, *Paul and the Popular Philosophers* (Minneapolis: Fortress Press, 1989), pp. 121-36, 136-45; Luke Timothy Johnson, '2 Timothy and the Polemic against False Teachers: A Re-examination', *Ohio Journal of Religious Studies* 6/7 (1978–79), pp. 1-26; Robert L. Karris, 'The Background and Significance of the Polemic of the Pastoral Epistles', *JBL* 93 (1973), pp. 549-64. For discussion of the contours of the false teaching 1 Timothy was written to combat, see Marshall, *Pastoral Epistles*, pp. 532-35; R. Collins, *1 & 2 Timothy and Titus*, pp. 12, 116-19; Schlarb, *Lehre*, pp. 91-93; Spicq, *Epitres*, p. 114; Johnson, *First and Second Letters to Timothy*, pp. 244-48; Martin Dibelius and Hans Conzelmann, *The Pastoral Epistles* (Hermeneia; Philadelphia: Fortress Press, 1972), pp. 65-67; Jouette M. Bassler, *1 Timothy, 2 Timothy, Titus* (Abingdon New Testament Commentaries; Nashville: Abingdon Press, 1996), pp. 25-31; Norbert Brox, *Die Pastoralbriefe* (RNT; Regensburg: Friedrich Pustet, 1963), pp. 31-42; Philip H. Towner, 'Gnosis and Realized Eschatology in Ephesus (of the Pastoral Epistles) and the Corinthian Enthusiasm', *JSNT* 31 (1987), pp. 95-124; idem, *The Goal of our Instruction* (JSNTSup, 34; Sheffield: JSOT Press, 1989), pp. 33-42. It is difficult to know how far to push the effects of false teachings as a motivation in this letter—were the false teachings affecting conduct in worship, thus motivating 2.8-15? Perhaps, as has been suggested, Paul's prohibition against women teaching (2.12) was motivated by false teaching proceeding from female teachers. Are the christological statements less an affirmation of aspects of Paul's gospel and more a direct refutation of bad Christology that was being taught? It is probably possible to see false teaching behind every problem mentioned in the letter—but would that be accurate?

20. Marshall, *Pastoral Epistles*, p. 365.

> Have nothing to do with profane myths and old wives' tales. Train yourself in godliness, for, while physical training is of some value, godliness is valuable in every way, holding promise for both the present life and the life to come. The saying is sure and worthy of full acceptance. For to this end we toil and struggle, because we have our hope set on the living God, who is the Savior of all people, especially (μάλιστα) of those who believe. (4.7-10)[21]

False teaching, Paul says, has no value. In contrast, training in godliness has *great* value because it holds benefits not only for this life but also for eternity. And for this purpose (i.e. because of the life that is to come), Paul and those who are with him work and struggle, because their hope is in God who is the Savior of all people. Because of the audience's awareness of Paul's commission as missionary to the Gentiles (alluded to in 1.1, 11, 12-15; 2.7), they would have heard in this passage a reference to the priority of evangelism for the Church and how false teaching endangered that priority.

Succession gives Paul authority over who is and is not authorized to teach. Paul first required those whom he authorized to teach to submit to his authority regarding the content of teaching. In some passages, Paul gives direct orders regarding what is and is not to be taught in his churches:

> I urge you…to remain in Ephesus so that you may instruct (παραγγέλλω, 'command') certain people not to teach any different doctrine… (1.3)

> Have nothing to do with profane myths and old wives' tales. Train yourself in godliness…godliness is valuable in every way, holding promise for both the present life and the life to come…to this end we toil and struggle, because we have set our hope on the living God, who is the Savior of all people, especially of those who believe. These are the things you must insist on and teach (παράγγελλε ταῦτα καὶ δίδασκε). (4.7-11)

The authorial audience would have understood from these passages that Paul fought for the true teaching by entrusting the responsibility of teaching to those who would fulfill it under his authority and with approved content. Paul's standard for measuring all teaching was his gospel and the teachings that flowed from it, bequeathed to him by Christ. Any teaching that did not measure up to that standard, or that went beyond it into speculation, Paul ordered discarded. And he expected his people to follow that order.

Paul can authorize or withhold authorization to teach as he sees fit. Note how he entrusts the role to one group and not to another:

---

21. T.C. Skeat, ' "Especially the Parchments": A Note on 2 Timothy IV.3', *JTS* 30 (1979), pp. 173-77, argues that μάλιστα here should be translated 'namely' rather than 'especially'. Marshall, *Pastoral Epistles*, p. 556; Roloff, *Brief*, p. 248; and Knight, *Pastoral Epistles*, p. 203, follow Skeat in this.

> I permit no woman to teach or to have authority over a man; she is to keep silent. (2.12)
>
> Now a bishop must be...an apt teacher. (3.2)

Paul here claims authority to refuse to allow women (or other people) to teach, for reasons of propriety or if the situation otherwise warrants. He can make this determination regardless of whatever gifts or desire to teach they might have (2.12). He can command other people to be capable of (and prepared for) teaching (3.2).

Notice also how Paul commissions Timothy and entrusts authority to him. Consider how Paul charges him for his task, and what these passages indicate about Paul's authority over teaching. We see an initial outworking of this commissioning in 1.3: 'As I urged you when I was going to Macedonia, remain at Ephesus that *you may charge* certain persons not to teach any different doctrine'. Because Christ entrusted Paul with the gospel, Paul not only has authority to command people as to what they should and should not teach. He also has the authority to delegate that command to others (his successors) so that they can carry it out in his absence.

The authorial audience would also have understood Paul's commissioning of Timothy (and other authorized teachers) to be an implication of 1.8-11:

> Now we know that the law is good, if one uses it legitimately. This means understanding that the law is laid down not for the innocent but for the lawless and disobedient, for the godless and sinful, for the unholy and profane, for those who kill their father or mother, for murderers, fornicators, sodomites, slave traders, liars, perjurers, and whatever else is contrary to the sound teaching that conforms to the glorious gospel of the blessed God, which he entrusted to me.

From this text, the audience understands that Paul not only knows how the gospel is to be used and that he uses it properly. He also has taught Timothy (and, by extension, those teachers whom he authorizes) how they will use the gospel properly as well (not 'I know' but '*We* know').[22] By using the first-person plural indirect address, Paul authorizes and gives special endorsement to Timothy and to those among the audience who are authorized to teach.

Note also the following:

> I am giving you (παρατίθεμαι) these instructions (παραγγελίαν, literally 'this commandment'), Timothy, my child, in accordance with the prophecies made earlier about you, so that by following them you may fight the good fight (στρατεύῃ...τὴν καλὴν στρατείαν), having faith and a good conscience. (1.18-19)

---

22. So also Marshall, *Pastoral Epistles*, pp. 374-75; Quinn and Wacker, *First and Second Letters to Timothy*, p. 91, broaden the application to all who 'overhear' 1 Timothy.

But as for you, man of God, shun all this; pursue righteousness, godliness, faith, love, endurance, gentleness. Fight the good fight (ἀγωνίζου τὸν καλὸν ἀγῶνα) of the faith; take hold of the eternal life, to which you were called and for which you made the good confession in the presence of many witnesses. In the presence of God, who gives life to all things, and of Christ Jesus, who in his testimony before Pontius Pilate made the good confession, I charge (παραγγέλλω) you to keep the commandment (ἐντολήν) without spot or blame until the manifestation of our Lord Jesus Christ, which he will bring about at the right time. (6.11-15)

Timothy, guard what has been entrusted to you (τὴν παραθήκην φύλαξον). (6.20)

In these passages, Paul gives further authority over the teaching in these churches to Timothy. This includes authority over who is and who is not to be entrusted with the teaching role. These passages indicate that Paul protects the teaching of the true gospel by entrusting it to his duly commissioned successor, someone singled out for the task by prophecies and trained in the work by Paul himself. He entrusts his gospel to Timothy only after solemnly charging him as to how he is to keep it pure and use it properly.

Several other things are interesting here. First, note the repeated references to command and commandment. In 1.5 and 1.18 παραγγέλλω/παραγγελία have the same referent, Paul's command through Timothy in 1.3 that those who are teaching other doctrines must stop doing so.[23] This command is the heart of what is passed on to Timothy in 6.14, even though ἐντολή is used there: the command of 6.14 is broader than the command to fight false teaching in 1.3, 5, 18, but it centers on that charge, as does the letter.[24] In 6.14, Paul changes the term in the interest of variety—instead of writing παραγγέλλω τηρῆσαί σε τὴν παραγγελίαν, Paul uses the synonym ἐντολή. Further, this command is the heart of what is entrusted to Timothy in 6.20— the command of 1.3 and its implications as outlined in the rest of the letter are entrusted as a deposit into Timothy's care. He must guard this deposit by keeping it pure and unadulterated, and by using it properly.

---

23. Knight, *Pastoral Epistles*, p. 107; Mounce, *Pastoral Epistles*, p. 107; Marshall, *Pastoral Epistles*, pp. 368-69, 406-407. In the latter reference, Marshall asserts that 1.18 resumes a thought begun in 1.3. Quinn and Wacker, *First and Second Letters to Timothy*, p. 79, see 1.5 as referring back not only to 1.3 but also to the Shema and the greatest commandment (Mt. 22.37); so also Knight, *Pastoral Epistles*, p. 76. But see R. Collins, *1 & 2 Timothy and Titus*, pp. 47-48; and Dibelius and Conzelmann, *Pastoral Epistles*, p. 32.

24. Contra Knight, *Pastoral Epistles*, pp. 266-68, R. Collins, *1 & 2 Timothy and Titus*, pp. 166-67; Quinn and Wacker, *First and Second Letters to Timothy*, p. 533. Marshall, *Pastoral Epistles*, p. 665; and Johnson, *First and Second Letters to Timothy*, p. 308, see ἐντολή as referring to everything that is entrusted to Timothy in the letter.

Second, note the repeated instruction for Timothy to 'fight the good fight'. In this context, the imperatives would have been understood in terms of 'fight for the true teaching', 'fight for sound doctrine', in spite of the differences in language.[25] There is only one primary struggle in view here, the fight for the true teaching and against false teaching. Note also that πίστις is articular in 6.12: in the Pastoral Epistles, ἡ πίστις is used to refer to the body of teaching, not to faith as a gift or a virtue but to *the* faith, the content of what is believed.[26]

Third, notice the *inclusio* formed by the succession language in 1.18-19a and 6.20. Paul entrusts (παρατίθημι) the commandment to Timothy, just as the gospel was entrusted to him. Paul has bequeathed the commandment and its implications to Timothy by making them a deposit (παραθήκη) and giving them into Timothy's care.[27] The authorial audience would have heard this language as an indication of succession between Paul and Timothy, a topic about which I will have more to say below.

Summary. In 1 Timothy, succession of tradition from Christ to Paul empowers Paul to 'fight the good fight'. It separates him from the self-appointed false teachers by giving him understanding of how to use properly the scriptures. It gives him authority over the content of teaching, and over who is and who is not authorized to teach. This last authority also includes the authority to pass Paul's own task and authority on to his own successor.

---

25. *Contra* Marshall, *Pastoral Epistles*, p. 659, Knight, *Pastoral Epistles*, p. 263; and Mounce, *Pastoral Epistles*, p. 355, all of whom read 6.12 as Timothy's struggle for righteousness or faith in a more general sense. Paul will refer to himself as having fought the good fight in 2 Tim. 4.7. Marshall, *Pastoral Epistles*, p. 408, does read 1.18 in terms of fighting heresy: this is a charge for Timothy to 'directly engage the heretics' (p. 410). R. Collins, *1 & 2 Timothy and Titus*, p. 49; and Knight, *Pastoral Epistles*, pp. 108-109, interpret even 1.19 more broadly.

26. Of the 35 times that πίστις occurs in the Pastorals, thirteen are articular. Of these thirteen occurrences, only 2 Tim. 3.10 does not supply a reference to the body of teaching/ doctrine/praxis associated with Paul's gospel—and that occurrence is in a list, and the use of the article can be explained in terms of assimilation to the other items in the list. The articular uses of πίστις are: 1 Tim. 1.19; 3.9; 4.1, 6; 5.8; 6.10, 21; 2 Tim. 3.8, 10; 4.7; Tit. 1.13; 2.2.

27. Gordon D. Fee, *1 and 2 Timothy, Titus* (New International Biblical Commentary on the New Testament; Peabody, MA: Hendrickson, rev. edn, 1988), p. 161, *contra* Marshall, *Pastoral Epistles*, p. 675; R. Collins, *1 & 2 Timothy and Titus*, p. 175; and Johnson, *First and Second Letters to Timothy*, p. 311. Quinn and Wacker, *First and Second Letters to Timothy*, pp. 558-59, also note the *inclusio* formed by 1.18 and 6.20, and from it argue that the παραθήκη is the whole letter (so also Mounce, *Pastoral Epistles*, p. 371). Knight, *Pastoral Epistles*, p. 276, argues for the apostolic teaching; Dibelius and Conzelmann, *Pastoral Epistles*, p. 92, assert that it is the apostolic tradition.

Paul Promotes Orthopraxy
By his example. In 1.12-16, Paul describes one of the reasons for which Christ saved and called him to his task: his very life is an illustration of God's grace, of the gospel at work:

> I am grateful to Christ Jesus our Lord, who has strengthened me, because he judged me faithful and appointed me to his service, even though I was formerly a blasphemer, a persecutor, and a man of violence. But I received mercy because I had acted ignorantly in unbelief, and the grace of our Lord overflowed for me with the faith and love that are in Christ Jesus. The saying is sure and worthy of full acceptance, that Christ Jesus came into the world to save sinners—of whom I am the foremost. But for that very reason I received mercy, so that in me, as the foremost, Jesus Christ might display the utmost patience, making me an example (ὑποτύπωσιν) to those who would come to believe in him for eternal life. (1.12-16)

Here the audience would have heard Paul describe himself and his conversion as examples from which others could learn. This is both like and unlike the way in which Seneca bequeathed to his friends the *imagineum vitae* in Text 24: Tacitus, *Annals* 15.62 (see pp. 52-54). The center here seems to be less on how Paul is a moral example for people to imitate, although that idea may have been present. But the primary point of Paul's example is the way God's grace can overwhelm and change the sinner.[28] In essence, 'If God can save and transform and use someone who is as bad as Paul was, then perhaps *no one* is a lost cause'.[29]

By calling his people to propriety. Paul repeatedly states his concern that members of his churches should conduct themselves with propriety. Witness:

---

28. Martinus C. de Boer, 'Images of Paul in the Post-Apostolic Period', *CBQ* 42 (1980), pp. 359-80 (370-71), notes that Paul's past status as a persecutor of the Church in juxtaposition with the radical transformation his life underwent serve as a foundation for his authority.

29. Johnson, *First and Second Letters to Timothy*, p. 186; Mounce, *Pastoral Epistles*, p. 47. Those who hold that Paul is presented in the Pastorals as the only apostle tend to see Paul in 1.16 as more than an example, as a prototype. Since Paul is the only apostle, and his gospel the only source of salvation, he is an embodiment of conversion. See, among others, Dibelius and Conzelmann, *Pastoral Epistles*, pp. 29-30, who state that this is why Paul is called the 'first of sinners' here: he 'is the typical representative of those who have received the mercy which the sinner can experience': see also Roloff, *Brief*, p. 97; R. Collins, *1 & 2 Timothy and Titus*, p. 58; Lewis R. Donelson, *Pseudepigraphy and Ethical Argument in the Pastoral Epistles* (Hermeneutische Untersuchungen zur Theologie, 22; Tübingen: J.C.B. Mohr [Paul Siebeck], 1986), p. 103; Wolter, *Pastoralbriefe*, p. 57. Against this position, see Marshall, *Pastoral Epistles*, pp. 403-404. Regarding the paraenetic function of personalia in pseudepigraphical moral instruction, see Benjamin Fiore, *The Function of Personal Example in the Socratic and Pastoral Epistles* (AnBib, 105; Rome: Biblical Institute Press, 1986), pp. 227-29.

> I urge you, [to] instruct certain people not to teach any different doctrine, and not to occupy themselves with myths and endless genealogies that promote speculations rather than the divine training (οἰκονομία) that is known by faith. (1.3-4)

οἰκονομία is usually understood as 'stewardship/management' or 'plan'. In the context of 1 Timothy, where the Church is referred to as the household of God (οἴκῳ θεοῦ, 3.15), οἰκονομία would have been understood in terms of 'leadership/teaching that produces actions and lifestyle appropriate to the household of God'. Thus we find Paul's concern for propriety set alongside his concern for correct teaching from the beginning of the letter.

Other passages reinforce this concern:

> I am giving you these instructions, Timothy, my child, in accordance with the prophecies made earlier about you, so that by following them you may fight the good fight, having faith and a good conscience. (1.18-19)[30]

> First of all, then, I urge that supplications, prayers, intercessions, and thanksgivings be made for everyone, for kings and all who are in high positions, so that we may lead a quiet and peaceable life in all godliness and dignity. (2.1-2)

> I desire, then, that in every place the men should pray, lifting up holy hands without anger or argument; also that the women should dress themselves modestly and decently in suitable clothing, not with their hair braided, or with gold, pearls, or expensive clothes, but with good works, as is proper for women who profess reverence for God. Let a woman learn in silence with full submission. I permit no woman to teach or to have authority over a man; she is to keep silent. For Adam was formed first, then Eve; and Adam was not deceived, but the woman was deceived and became a transgressor. Yet she will be saved through childbearing, provided they continue in faith and love and holiness, with modesty (σωφροσύνη). (2.8-15)

> I am writing these instructions to you so that, if I am delayed, you may know how one ought to behave in the household of God. (3.14-15)

These passages speak of appropriateness in the household of God. The goal as Paul expresses it is to live peaceably, maintaining a good reputation with outsiders.

One reason for the emphasis on propriety is that it effects the hearing of the gospel. There are admittedly no explicit calls to evangelistic action in 1 Timothy. The authorial audience, however, by virtue of their external knowledge of Paul's commissioning and missionary activity, would need no great degree of explicitness to infer those convictions and priorities when they heard or read the text. Consider again 2.1-7:

---

30. On conscience, see Marshall, *Pastoral Epistles*, pp. 217-27. R. Collins, *1 & 2 Timothy and Titus*, p. 28, points out parallels in Hellenistic moral philosophy to the use of conscience in the Pastoral Epistles. See also Margaret Thrall, 'The Pauline Uses of ΣΥΝΕΔΗΣΙΣ', *NTS* 14 (1967–68), pp. 118-25.

> First of all, then, I urge that supplications, prayers, intercessions, and thanksgivings be made for everyone, for kings and all who are in high positions, so that we may lead a quiet and peaceable life in all godliness and dignity. This is right and is acceptable in the sight of God our Savior, who desires everyone to be saved and to come to the knowledge of the truth.
> For there is one God;
> there is also one mediator between God and humankind,
> Christ Jesus, himself human,
> who gave himself a ransom for all—
> this was attested at the right time. For this (εἰς ὅ)³¹ I was appointed a herald and an apostle (I am telling the truth, I am not lying), a teacher of the Gentiles in faith and truth.

At the outset, the authorial audience would hear this passage as a call to appropriate behavior. The purpose of this call is not accommodation but propriety and good citizenship in the interest of winning a hearing for the gospel.³² This priority is first expressed at the end of 2.2 ('so that we may lead a quiet and peaceable life'),³³ and then further unpacked in terms of God's desire for all to be saved (2.4). The audience would have heard two things here: first, something about *their* vocation, that the purpose of propriety was to assist in the spreading of the gospel. Second, they would have heard a further description of Paul's vocation: because God desired for all to be saved, Jesus Christ became the μεσίτης between God and humanity, and gave himself as a ransom for all.³⁴ In his time, God sent witnesses to testify to these actions (2.6b), and Paul was himself appointed to be κῆρυξ καὶ ἀπόστολος [καὶ] διδάσκαλος ('preacher and apostle and teacher') in service of this testimony. The implication would have been clear. Part of Paul's vocation, the vocation he received as Christ's successor when he was called to apostleship, was his call to testify to and spread the gospel. Paul urges his audience to propriety (and away from behavior that might cause scandal) in the service of this calling.

Similarly, this passage (particularly 2.1-4) is one of several that hint at the presence of anti-Christian polemic in the communities around the authorial

---

31. An accusative of result pointing back to μαρτύριον from the previous verse.
32. Marshall, *Pastoral Epistles*, p. 424: 'Here (and throughout the PE [Pastoral Epistles]) it [propriety] was aimed at communicating the Gospel in a way that would ensure its relevance for the culture'. The contrary position is articulated by Dibelius and Conzelmann, *Pastoral Epistles*, pp. 39-41.
33. Marshall, *Pastoral Epistles*, p. 422, notes that ἵνα ἤρεμον...βίον is Hellenistic, and gives parallels; so also Johnson, *First and Second Letters to Timothy*, p. 190.
34. See Marshall, *Pastoral Epistles*, pp. 425-33, regarding the universality of the offer of salvation in the Pastoral Epistles. Marshall argues that this universal emphasis is underlined as polemic against elitist false teaching—'there is *one* God, *one* mediator for all'. See also R. Collins, *1 & 2 Timothy and Titus*, p. 61. Dibelius and Conzelmann, *Pastoral Epistles*, p. 41, note that ἐπίγνωσις ἀληθείας is a technical term for salvation.

audience.[35] Here, Paul endorses good citizenship in language later echoed by Christian leaders and apologists like 1 Clement (20.10; 60.4) and Athenagoras (37.2-3).[36] Good citizenship and propriety lead to peace and harmony with society, a cardinal virtue in the Roman Empire. If the Church does things that promote peace and harmony with those around her, it will gain a hearing for the gospel. If it does not behave with propriety and do what promotes peace and harmony, then opportunities to share the gospel will be lost and persecution will increase:

> I desire, then, that in every place the men should pray, lifting up holy hands without anger or argument; also that the women should dress themselves modestly and decently in suitable clothing, not with their hair braided, or with gold, pearls, or expensive clothes, but with good works, as is proper for women who profess reverence for God. Let a woman learn in silence with full submission. I permit no woman to teach or to have authority over a man; she is to keep silent. For Adam was formed first, then Eve; and Adam was not deceived, but the woman was deceived and became a transgressor. Yet she will be saved through childbearing, provided they continue in faith and love and holiness, with modesty. (2.8-15)

This passage also seems to reflect the presence of anti-Christian polemic, an awareness of the potential for damaging scandal around the Church, although they may also have been motivated by particular aspects of the false teaching. Whatever the situation that gave rise to these verses, particularly the

---

35. R. Collins, *1 & 2 Timothy and Titus*, p. 65: 'Christians were coming under attack as being disturbers of the social order'. The false teachers were headed in directions (denigrating marriage, the emancipation of women from roles traditional in Roman society) that made further disruption—thus further attacks—likely. Similarly, David L. Balch, *Let Wives Be Submissive: The Domestic Code in 1 Peter* (SBLMS 26; Chico, CA: Scholars Press, 1981), p. 106, notes that the 'accomodationist' approach is not due to a lessened expectation of the Parousia but due to real or potential attacks from outside the Church. See also Edwin A. Judge, *The Social Pattern of Christian Groups in the First Century: Some Prolegomena to the Study of New Testament Ideas of Social Obligation* (London: Tyndale Press, 1960), pp. 73, 76: David C. Verner, *The Household of God: The Social World of the Pastoral Epistles* (SBLDS, 71; Chico, CA: Scholars Press, 1983), p. 186. For the traditional view, see Käsemann, 'Catholicism', pp. 242, 247, and the more contemporary articulation of the same view by J.C. Beker, *Heirs of Paul* (Philadelphia: Fortress Press, 1991), p. 44.

36. Marshall, *Pastoral Epistles*, p. 423: 'Effective leadership of the State will maintain an environment conducive to witness'. R. Collins, *1 & 2 Timothy and Titus*, pp. 51-53, notes that these prayers are '*for* the emperor, not *to* the emperor' (p. 53). The audience would have understood that, while idol worship and emperor worship are wrong, prayers for God to bless those in authority are right and beneficial. See also Johnson, *First and Second Letters to Timothy*, pp. 194-96. Mounce, *Pastoral Epistles*, pp. 94-149, offers an *incredibly* detailed discussion of the prohibitions and restrictions of 2.8-15 and their purpose. See also Marshall, *Pastoral Epistles*, pp. 437-43.

prohibition of 2.12, the general emphasis would have been clear. Paul here endorses appropriateness in conduct, shunning extravagance and ostentation. The last word in the paragraph is σωφροσύνη: hearing this virtue at the end of the paragraph would have reinforced this point ('PRACTICE PROPRIETY!') even more clearly to the audience:[37]

> Do not speak harshly to an older man, but speak to him as to a father, to younger men as brothers, to older women as mothers, to younger women as sisters—with absolute purity. (5.1-2)

> Let all who are under the yoke of slavery regard their masters as worthy of all honor, so that the name of God and the teaching may not be blasphemed. Those who have believing masters must not be disrespectful to them on the ground that they are members of the church; rather they must serve them all the more, since those who benefit by their service are believers and beloved. (6.1-2a)[38]

In these passages, the audience would have continued to hear about propriety in relationships in the household of God. These instructions call the audience to treat each other with respect, chaste affection, and great care. If they practice these behaviors, Paul's people will keep their enemies from having any grounds for accusing them of improper, impious, immoral behavior:

> Honor widows who are really widows (i.e. truly destitute). If a widow has children or grandchildren, they should first learn their religious duty to their own family and make some repayment to their parents...
> Let a widow be put on the list if she is not less than sixty years old and has been married only once; she must be well attested for her good works... But refuse to put younger widows on the list; for when their sensual desires alienate them from Christ, they want to marry, and so they incur condemnation for having violated their first pledge. Besides that, they learn to be idle, gadding about from house to house; and they are not merely idle, but also gossips and busybodies, saying what they should not say. So I would have younger widows marry, bear children, and manage their households, so as to give the adversary no occasion to revile us. For some have already turned away to follow Satan. If any believing woman has relatives who are really widows, let her assist them; let the church not be burdened, so that it can assist those who are real widows. (5.3-16)

> As for those who in the present age are rich, command them not to be haughty, or to set their hopes on the uncertainty of riches, but rather on God who richly provides us with everything for our enjoyment. They are to do good, to be rich in good works, generous, and ready to share, thus storing up for themselves the treasure of a good foundation for the future, so that they may take hold of the life that really is life. (6.17-19)

37. Towner, *Instruction*, pp. 221, 257.
38. Regarding slaves in the Pastoral Epistles, see Reggie Kidd, *Wealth and Beneficence in the Pastoral Epistles* (SBLDS, 122; Atlanta: Scholars Press, 1990), pp. 140-54; Verner, *Household*, pp. 140-45.

Paul's concerns here are pastoral. He wants to be sure that Christian families do not shirk their responsibilities (by not taking care of their own), and that the household of God does not shirk its responsibility (by not providing for the widows who are truly in need).[39] He is further concerned to warn the wealthy in the church away from materialism and toward benefaction and proper honor (as opposed to shameful and scandalous pride, which might prove divisive). This is all motivated, at least in part, by his desire that the Church's reputation with outsiders does not suffer, thus hindering the hearing of the gospel.[40]

These passages clearly illustrate the authority over the daily lives of the members of the οἶκος that Paul claimed for himself as Christ's successor in care of the gospel.[41] They also illustrate his continuing concern for propriety, by which he hoped to maintain holiness, to aid in keeping the gospel pure, and to avoid scandal. This task—keeping the gospel pure and scandal free—is part of the vocation which Paul received as Christ's successor in the care of the gospel, as is the authority by which he completes out this task.

Paul Oversees the Work of Other Church Leaders
He instructs Timothy on what he should do and how he should act. Contrary to his example elsewhere (e.g. Phlmn 8–9), where Paul preferred for his people to 'do the right thing' for reasons other than simply because he ordered them to do so, Paul in 1 Timothy shows no qualms about using his apostolic authority. Throughout the letter, he presumes to have authority to tell Timothy his successor how to lead (3.14-15; 4.12), what his character and behavior should be (4.12, 16; 5.22b-25), how he should carry out Paul's orders (4.11; 5.20), and how he passes on ministry and authority to others (5.21). These statements show the authority that Paul held over his delegates' activities. And he can delegate similar authority over church leaders to Timothy as well—witness 1 Tim. 3.1-13 and 5.20, treated below.

He exercises church discipline. Paul presumes to have authority to exercise church discipline, even over those who are (apparently) leaders. Witness:

---

39. For the issues, mostly legal, surrounding the status of widows, see Bruce Winter, 'Providentia for the Widows of 1 Timothy 5.3-16', *TynBul* 39 (1988), pp. 83-99.

40. Johnson, *First and Second Letters to Timothy*, pp. 275-76, notes the potential for scandal if the public learned that 'a board of elderly men' was supporting 'a group of younger women [the younger widows] who lived in public idleness and self-indulgence'. For the Roman view of women as being predisposed for sexual impropriety and scandal, see Balch, *Domestic*, p. 106; David L. Balch and Carolyn Osiek, *Families in the New Testament World: Households and House Churches* (Louisville, KY: John Knox Press, 1997), p. 39.

41. John M.G. Barclay, 'The Family as the Bearer of Religion', in Halvor Moxnes (ed.), *Constructing Early Christian Families: Family as Social Reality and Metaphor* (London: Routledge, 1997), pp. 66-80, particularly 72-78.

> By rejecting conscience, certain persons have suffered shipwreck in the faith; among them are Hymenaeus and Alexander, whom I have turned over to Satan, so that they may learn not to blaspheme. (1.19b-20)

The statement 'I have turned over to Satan' is not quite so harsh as it may first appear.[42] The ancient audience would have understood 'turning over to Satan' to have redemptive purposes, thus softening the statement somewhat.[43] Further, notice how the language Paul uses to describe Hymenaeus and Alexander parallels the language Paul uses to describe himself:[44]

> I was formerly a blasphemer (βλάσφημον), a persecutor, and a man of violence. But I received mercy because I had acted ignorantly in unbelief (ἐν ἀπιστίᾳ)... (1.13)

Compare Paul's description of himself with his description of Hymenaeus and Alexander as people who had 'suffered shipwreck in the faith' and who needed to 'learn not to blaspheme'. The point of Paul's example in 1.12-16 would have come through clearly with regard to Hymenaeus and Alexander: if God can redeem, save, and use a man like Paul, he can redeem, save, and use anyone—no one is forever disqualified.

He dictates the qualifications, character, and task of other church leaders. The lists of qualifications for overseers and deacons further demonstrate Paul's authority over church leaders:

> Whoever aspires to the office of bishop desires a noble task. Now a bishop must be above reproach, married only once, temperate, sensible, respectable, hospitable, an apt teacher, not a drunkard, not violent but gentle, not quarrelsome, and not a lover of money. He must manage his own household well, keeping his children submissive and respectful in every way—for if someone does not know how to manage his own household, how can he take care of God's church? He must not be a recent convert, or he may be puffed up with conceit and fall into the condemnation of the devil. Moreover, he must be well thought of by outsiders, so that he may not fall into disgrace and the snare of the devil.
> Deacons likewise must be serious, not double-tongued, not indulging in much wine, not greedy for money; they must hold fast to the mystery of the faith with a clear conscience. And let them first be tested; then, if they prove themselves blameless, let them serve as deacons. Women likewise must be serious, not slanderers, but temperate, faithful in all things. Let deacons be

---

42. Quinn and Wacker, *First and Second Letters to Timothy*, pp. 158-59, list Hellenistic parallels to the phrase.
43. So Knight, *Pastoral Epistles*, pp. 111-12; R. Collins, *1 & 2 Timothy and Titus*, p. 51. Marshall, *Pastoral Epistles*, p. 414, guardedly asserts that the discipline in view does not have redemptive purpose.
44. Johnson, *First and Second Letters to Timothy*, p. 187.

married only once, and let them manage their children and their households well; for those who serve well as deacons gain a good standing for themselves and great boldness in the faith that is in Christ Jesus. (3.1-13)

In these passages, Paul claims to have authority to set the standards of conduct for leaders in the church—'They must measure up with regard to these virtues, they must have this kind of character. Here is the standard by which you will monitor them.'[45]

He acts through his successor toward other church leaders. I find four passages where Paul acts through Timothy with regard to other church leaders. I discuss these passages elsewhere, so I will mention them here only briefly. The first passage is 3.1-13 (discussed above), regarding the qualifications and tasks of overseers and deacons, and Timothy's responsibilities toward them. The second passage is 5.19-25 (discussed below, under Timothy's succession from Paul), regarding the handling of accusations of sin against an elder. There Paul warns Timothy to stay away from the sins of others, and to not be caught unaware by the hidden sins of some who might appear to qualify for leadership (5.24). Also in this second passage, note 5.22 (also discussed below, under Timothy's succession from Paul), where Paul instructs Timothy to be careful and deliberate in the way he chooses and ordains his successors/delegates. In these passages (3.1-13 and 5.19-25), Paul carries out his vocation by providing safeguards to protect his churches both against the human failings of even good leaders and particularly against the corrupt character of fraudulent leaders.

The third passage is 1.18-19, where Paul bequeaths the command to Timothy, enabling him to fight the good fight. The fourth is 3.14-15, where Paul writes to tell Timothy how people should conduct themselves as part of the church. These passages describe how Paul provided for his church an empowered, enabled successor to continue his (Paul's) ministry by watching over the church in his absence.

Summary. These tasks—exercising church discipline, instructing (and otherwise acting toward) church leaders through Timothy, setting standards for other leaders—and the authority to perform them belong to Paul because he is Christ's successor in the care of the gospel.

---

45. Marshall, *Pastoral Epistles*, pp. 472-73, notes that 3.1-13 contains both practical instructions for appointing new leaders *and* ethical instructions for those already in leadership. R. Collins, *1 & 2 Timothy and Titus*, p. 79, notes the importance of the church's reputation as a consideration when choosing new leaders: 'Unless the community's leadership enjoys a good reputation among the outsiders who can observe it, not only will its leadership fall into disrepute, so too will the community itself'. Johnson, *First and Second Letters to Timothy*, pp. 224, 286-87, suggests that such a scandal has already occurred, and that this passage is essentially damage control.

4. First Timothy

Paul as Christ's Successor in 1 Timothy

As Christ's successor in the care of the gospel, Paul received a broad set of responsibilities and a broad authority to carry them out. I have shown the following:

1. That the authorial audience would have inferred that Paul was Christ's successor as keeper of the gospel and the Church founded thereon.
2. That because of this succession, Paul has a particular vocation:
   a. He fights for orthodoxy.
      i. Because of succession, Paul (and his followers) know how the law is to be used, and in their hands it produces the proper fruit. This is in contrast with the false teachers, who have no succession, do not know how the law is to be used, and therefore produce bad fruit (1.1-11).
      ii. Because of succession, Paul has authority over the teaching in his churches.
         (a) He acts with Christ's authority to safeguard it (1.3; 6.2b-4).
         (b) He endorses the proper content (1.15; 2.5-6a; 3.16; 4.4-6, 7-11; 6.2b).
         (c) He refutes false teaching (1.3-4; 4.1-5, 7-10).
      iii. Because of succession, Paul can entrust the teaching role to the 'right' people.
         (a) Those who will teach in accordance with Paul's authority (1.3; 4.7-11).
         (b) Those who can appropriately be entrusted with the role, so that propriety and other priorities are not flouted (1.3; 2.12; 3.2).
         (c) Paul commissions Timothy to carry out these responsibilities (1.3, 18-19; 6.12-15, 20).
   b. He promotes orthopraxy.
      i. By his example (1.12-16).
      ii. By calling his people to propriety (1.3-4, 18-19; 2.1-7, 8-15; 3.14-15; 5.1-2, 3-16; 6.1-2a, 17-18).
   c. He oversees the work of other church leaders.
      i. He instructs Timothy on what to do and how to carry out his instructions (3.14-15; 4.11, 12, 16; 5.20, 21, 22b-25).
      ii. He exercises church discipline (1.19b-20).
      iii. He dictates the qualifications, character, and task of other church leaders (3.1-7, 8-15).
      iv. He acts through his successor toward other leaders (1.18-19; 3.1-13, 14-15; 5.19-25).

How does this succession of tradition (and the resulting tasks) from Christ to Paul function? Remember that the primary object is the gospel (1.11)—not office or agenda or task, though these are wrapped up in the object. The focus is on this object, which Jesus passed on to Paul so that it would fulfill its purpose among the Gentiles, and so that it would be effective and pure. Thus the first function of the succession from Christ to Paul in 1 Timothy is to ensure continued institutional vitality.

Second, when Paul received the gospel he also received the task of keeping the gospel pure and effective, and the authority to perform that task. His vocation is a result of this succession, the commissioning he received at his conversion (2.7). Thus succession of tradition legitimates Paul. Third, Paul as a result of this succession fills a role that Jesus himself filled while he was on earth—he is the authoritative keeper of the true gospel. Thus, from the perspective of the gospel, this succession ensures continuity of effect—the gospel continues to be cared for and preserved and appropriately used in Jesus' absence because Jesus appointed Paul his apostle and successor in that task.

I can illustrate the exchanges between Jesus and Paul thus:

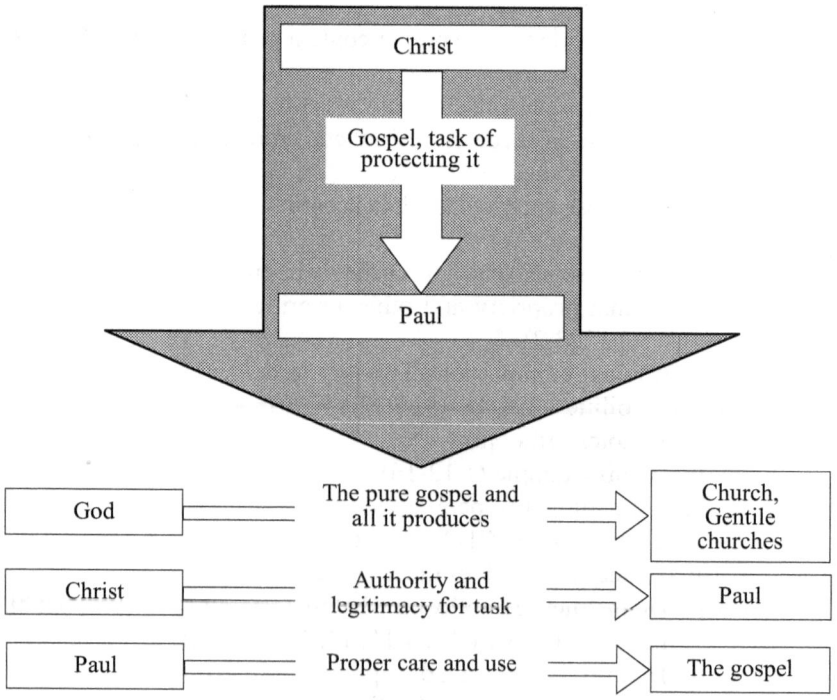

Figure 64. *The Functions of the Succession from Christ to Paul in 1 Timothy*

3. *Timothy's Succession from Paul and from the Elders*

Above, I showed that the succession from Christ to Paul is foundational for understanding 1 Timothy. I also showed that Paul's vocation as Christ's successor involves authority to pass task and authority on to his own successor, Timothy. This second succession (from Paul to Timothy) is itself preceded and woven together with a third succession, the succession from the elders to Timothy. This third succession is less prominent than the first two, and is less central to the letter. I treat it together with the succession from Paul here because of the way the two are interwoven. Timothy's succession from the elders is treated almost as a preparatory step to his succession from Paul: indeed, his succession from Paul subsumes the earlier succession.

Evidence of Succession from Paul to Timothy
Terms from the semantic field of succession. Timothy's relationship to Paul is described in terms of succession. Note:

> I am giving you these instructions (ταύτην τὴν παραγγελίαν παρατίθεμαί σοι, lit. 'I am entrusting this command to you'), Timothy... (1.18)

> Timothy, guard what has been entrusted (τὴν παραθήκην φύλαξον) to you. (6.20)

In the light of this succession terminology, three other terms in the letter would have been heard in terms of succession. Note:

> I urge you (παρεκάλεσά σε)...to remain in Ephesus so that you may instruct certain people not to teach any different doctrine. (1.3)

> In the presence of God and of Christ Jesus and of the elect angels, I warn you (διαμαρτύρομαι) to keep these instructions without prejudice... (5.21)

> In the presence of God...and of Christ Jesus...I charge you (παραγγέλλω) to keep the commandment without spot or blame. (6.13-14)

On the basis of this evidence, I consider the semantic evidence of succession from Paul to Timothy to be prominent.

Phenomena from the conceptual field of succession. First under this heading, I find that the letter itself—as an 'epistolary speech of commissioning'— serves as an act symbolic of succession.[46] Through this letter, Paul commissions Timothy to a particular ministry.

---

46. So Oberlinner, *Pastoralbriefe*, p. 293 (in reference to 6.12), but he offers no parallels from the primary texts. The ancient epistolary theorists did not list this as a type of letter: see A.J. Malherbe, *Ancient Epistolary Theorists* (SBLRBS, 19; Atlanta: Scholars Press, 1988), pp. 30-57, 66-81.

Second, note the parallel actions shared by Paul and Timothy. Both teach and preach (Paul in 2.7, Timothy in 4.13).⁴⁷ Both serve as examples for their followers (Paul in 1.16, Timothy in 4.12). Both exercise church discipline (Paul in 1.19-20, Timothy in 5.19-20). Both have successors in their tasks (Paul in 1.18 and 6.14-20, Timothy in 5.22). And Timothy acts with Paul's authority due to the commission he has received from Paul (*passim*). In the light of these parallels, I consider the conceptual evidence of succession from Paul to Timothy to be prominent.

Standard elements of an ancient Mediterranean succession story. The three standard elements of an ancient Mediterranean succession story are present. In Paul's command regarding what is and is not to be taught in his churches in Ephesus (1.3, 5, 18; 6.14, 20), I find the naming of what is passed on. The letter of 1 Timothy itself serves as a commissioning speech, particularly the bequeathing statement in 1.18-19 and the charge in 6.12-20: here I find the symbolic act accompanying the succession. And in the abovementioned parallels between Paul and Timothy, I find confirmation that succession has taken place. In the light of these elements, all the components of a standard ancient Mediterranean succession story are present. I regard this evidence as prominent.

Summary. Due to these three prominent bodies of evidence, it is clear that the ancient audience would have understood the relationship between Paul and Timothy in terms of succession.

Evidence of Succession from the Elders to Timothy
Terms from the semantic field of succession. I find no terms from the semantic field used 1 Timothy to describe this relationship.

Phenomena from the conceptual field of succession. 1 Timothy mentions the elders laying hands on Timothy in 4.14. In 4.11-14, Paul instructs Timothy as to the things he should pay attention to—teaching, preaching—and that he should not allow anyone to ignore his authority because of his youth. As part of this encouragement/admonition, Paul reminds Timothy of his gift: 'Do not neglect the gift that is in you, which was given to you through (διά) prophecy with (μετά) the laying on of hands by the council of elders' (4.14).⁴⁸ This

---

47. Marshall, *Pastoral Epistles*, p. 563: παράκλησις likely refers to 'the exposition of scripture, leading to commandments or encouragements'. See also Roloff, *Brief*, p. 254, Knight, *Pastoral Epistles*, pp. 207-208.

48. The gift Timothy received is not the Holy Spirit, nor an office, but a special spiritual enablement to ministry, allowing him to accomplish specific tasks: so also Marshall, *Pastoral Epistles*, pp. 564-65; Johnson, *First and Second Letters to Timothy*, p. 253;

is likely the same 'ordination' referred to in 2 Tim. 1.6,[49] although the language is different: there the gift is given through (διά) the laying-on of Paul's hands, here the agency is less clear (διά and μετά here are apparently synonyms),[50] and it is the whole body of elders involved in the laying-on of hands.

Also related to the elders' relationship to Timothy are the parallel actions between them. The elders lead, preach, and teach (5.17), Timothy leads, preaches, and teaches (4.11-16). In the light of these elements, particularly the strong symbolic action of the laying-on of hands, I regard the conceptual evidence as prominent.

Elements of a standard Mediterranean succession story. Are the three standard elements of an ancient Mediterranean succession story present? The first element (the naming of the tasks that are passed on from the elders to Timothy) is not explicit but rather implied in the tasks and responsibilities that Timothy inherits from the elders. The other elements are prominent, however: the symbolic act that accompanies the succession is explicitly described in the laying-on of hands (4.14), and the succession is confirmed explicitly by the prophecies (1.18; 4.14) and implied by the parallel actions. Thus the standard elements of an ancient Mediterranean succession story are not present.

Summary. From this survey, I conclude that succession from the ordaining elders to Timothy would possibly have been inferred by the authorial audience. Even if inferred, however, it does not carry nearly the same prominence as the successions from Christ to Paul or Paul to Timothy.

4. *The Function of the Successions to Timothy*

I showed above that Paul's calling to ministry in 1 Timothy *is* a succession. So also with Timothy's call to ministry. Note:

Quinn and Wacker, *First and Second Letters to Timothy*, p. 391. Roloff, *Brief*, p. 255; and Oberlinner, *Pastoralbriefe*, pp. 208, 211, hold that the gift is the office of Timothy's ministry. Knight, *Pastoral Epistles*, p. 108, holds that the call foretold by the prophecies was a 'general call to ministry'. David Daube, *The New Testament and Rabbinic Judaism* (London: Athlone Press, 1956), pp. 244-46, describes ordination in terms of a possible background from Jewish mysticism: see Quinn and Wacker, *First and Second Letters to Timothy*, pp. 392-402, for a reading based on Daube's suggestion; see Marshall, *Pastoral Epistles*, p. 569, for a far less sympathetic treatment.

49. So Marshall, *Pastoral Epistles*, pp. 568-69; R. Collins, *1 & 2 Timothy and Titus*, p. 133; Knight, *Pastoral Epistles*, p. 209; Quinn and Wacker, *First and Second Letters to Timothy*, p. 402.

50. Marshall, *Pastoral Epistles*, pp. 566-67, asserts that the gift should be understood to have passed through the hands of the elders, as foretold by prophecy.

> I urge (παρακαλέω) you, as I did when I was on my way to Macedonia, to remain in Ephesus so that you may instruct (παραγγέλλω, 'command') certain people not to teach any different doctrine. (1.3)

> I am giving you (παρατίθεμαι) these instructions (παραγγελίαν, literally 'this commandment'), Timothy, my child, in accordance with the prophecies made earlier about you, so that by following them you may fight the good fight, having faith and a good conscience. (1.18-19)

In these, the letter's initial references to Timothy's task, his calling to this ministry is described as a succession from Paul,[51] but this succession differs from Paul's calling to ministry in two ways. First, whereas the succession that marked Paul's call to ministry was a succession of tradition (the gospel was entrusted to him, 1.11), the succession that marks Timothy's call to ministry is a succession of task. Second, Timothy's calling from God is indirect (through the work of prophets) rather than by direct command of God (as Paul's was). Timothy is instead called to ministry by Paul himself—part of Paul's authority as Christ's successor. His ministry is thus initiated by both Paul (see also 1.3) and God ('in accordance with the prophecies made earlier about you'). As with the example of Paul and the examples from the Old Testament in the preceding chapter, God (through the prophecies) initiates and guides the succession.

Note, third, that Timothy's calling involves a much more limited (though not unimportant) task than Paul's. As described in 1.3, Timothy is to confront a group of people in the Ephesian church—apparently leaders, apparently influential—who are teaching things that Paul does not endorse. Timothy must stop them from teaching these unauthorized doctrines, this is his task as Paul's successor. And as Paul's successor, he receives not only the task but also the authority to carry it through.

The description of this succession continues in 6.11-15, 20:

> But as for you, man of God, shun all this; pursue righteousness, godliness, faith, love, endurance, gentleness. Fight the good fight of the faith; take hold of the eternal life, to which you were called and for which you made the good

---

51. When Dibelius and Conzelmann, *Pastoral Epistles*, p. 57, assert, 'There is no concept of succession, no extension of the position of the addressee into the present', they misread the evidence because they are operating with a political (rather than an historical) understanding of succession. They are correct in what they assert—that there is no succession from Paul to Timothy in the terms as they apparently intend them (apostolic succession, as defined in the modern debates—there is no passing on of the apostolic office from Paul to Timothy). But because of a lack of historical perspective, they do not see that the succession allows for differences in degree and kind (as outlined above, pp. 56-57, 89, 109). Paul can make Timothy his successor in a task, and the succession be real and effective, without Paul having to pass on his apostolic office to Timothy. Likewise (although for different reasons), Spicq, *Épitres*, I, pp. 65-66.

confession in the presence of many witnesses. In the presence of God, who gives life to all things, and of Christ Jesus, who in his testimony before Pontius Pilate made the good confession, I charge (παραγγέλλω) you to keep the commandment (ἐντολήν) without spot or blame until the manifestation of our Lord Jesus Christ, which he will bring about at the right time... Timothy, guard what has been entrusted to you (τὴν παραθήκην φύλαξον).

This charge refers back to παραγγελίαν in 1.18 (and παραγγέλλω in 1.3), returning to the command that Paul is delivering into Timothy's care. In this limited and specific circumstance, something of great value and power has been delivered into Timothy's custody—care and administration of the gospel and all that it produces (the οἰκονομία of 1.4). Timothy must guard this precious deposit by using it properly and carefully.

A fourth passage describes a second succession that Timothy also belongs to, his succession from the elders:

> Until I arrive, give attention to the public reading of scripture, to exhorting, to teaching. Do not neglect the gift that is in you, which was given to you through prophecy with the laying on of hands by the council of elders. Put these things into practice, devote yourself to them, so that all may see your progress. Pay close attention to yourself and to your teaching; continue in these things, for in doing this you will save both yourself and your hearers. (4.13-15)

Timothy's 'ordination' by the elders involves several things.[52] First, it calls him to specific tasks—reading scripture (ἀνάγνωσις), exhortation (παράκλησις), and teaching (διδασκαλία). Second, it involves a spiritual gift that was given to him through prophecy *accompanied by* the laying-on of hands. The laying-on of hands does not seem to be the means of the gifting here, rather it *accompanied* the special gift from the Spirit.[53] Third, note the description of elders' work in 5.17: 'ruling' (προΐστημι) and 'laboring in preaching and teaching' (κοπιῶντες ἐν λόγῳ καὶ διδασκαλίᾳ). These actions are synonymous with the actions to which Paul calls Timothy, even if the terms are not identical.

These successions define Timothy's vocation, the things he must do and the authority by which he must do them. The areas of his vocation are the same as those described above for Paul: Timothy fights for orthodoxy, he promotes orthopraxy, and he oversees the work of other church leaders.

---

52. Roloff, *Brief*, p. 102, asserts that this passage refers to a structured, institutionalized ordination ceremony. Lips, *Glaube*, pp. 232-40, argues against such a structured ceremony.

53. This is different from the description in 2 Tim. 1.6, where Paul tells Timothy to 'rekindle the gift of God that is within you through the laying on of my hands' (ὅ ἐστιν ἐν σοὶ διὰ τῆς ἐπιθέσεως [genitive of agency] τῶν χειρῶν μου). In 2 Tim. 1.6, the laying-on of hands is clearly the agency by which the gift is given.

Timothy Fights for Orthodoxy

The initial statement of Timothy's succession from Paul describes his call to fight for the orthodox Pauline gospel:

> I am giving you (παρατίθεμαι) these instructions (παραγγελίαν, 'this commandment')...so that by following them you may fight the good fight, having faith and a good conscience. (1.18-19)

As noted above, 'fighting the good fight' means 'fighting for the pure Pauline gospel'. Just as the authorial audience would have heard Paul's succession defining his vocation (keeping the gospel and all it produces pure and healthy), so also they would have heard Timothy's succession defining his vocation and giving him authority to carry it through. The bequest from Paul to Timothy enables or empowers Timothy to fight the good fight. As Paul's successor in this fight, Timothy receives from Paul both the task and the authority to carry it out. He becomes Paul's agent in guarding the gospel and the Church founded thereon. Note also 6.12-15, 20:

> Fight the good fight of the faith; take hold of the eternal life, to which you were called and for which you made the good confession in the presence of many witnesses. In the presence of God, who gives life to all things, and of Christ Jesus, who in his testimony before Pontius Pilate made the good confession, I charge (παραγγέλλω) you to keep the commandment (ἐντολήν) without spot or blame... Timothy, guard what has been entrusted to you (τὴν παραθήκην φύλαξον).

This description of Timothy's vocation carries the idea that something of great power and value (Paul's gospel and the teaching that flows from it)[54] has been entrusted into Timothy's care, and that Timothy must guard its integrity and keep it safe by using it properly. Note the parallel Paul outlines between Timothy and Christ. Timothy has made the good confession in the presence of many witnesses. Christ made the good confession in the presence of Pilate. The point of the parallel would be that, as Jesus stood for the truth when under pressure and persecution, so also Timothy has and will stand for the truth when facing the same.[55]

In a way, the entire letter describes the outworking of the authority over teaching which Paul has passed on to Timothy. The idea comes through more explicitly in a couple of other passages, however:

> I urge you...to remain in Ephesus so that you may instruct ('command') certain people not to teach any different doctrine. (1.3)

> We know that the law is good, if one uses it legitimately. (1.8)

---

54. See p. 124 n. 27 above.
55. So Marshall, *Pastoral Epistles*, p. 662; Mounce, *Pastoral Epistles*, p. 357.

From these statements, the audience would have understood Timothy to be one who was fighting on Paul's behalf to keep the teaching in their churches in line with what Paul taught, and thus keeping it effective and right and beneficial. His job is to confront false teachers and false teaching, to guard the flock against the ravenous wolves that threatened the Church from within (cf. Acts 20.29-31). Note also 4.6-11, which follows the refutation of pseudo-pious asceticism in 4.1-5:

> If you put these instructions before the brothers and sisters, you will be a good servant of Christ Jesus, nourished on the words of the faith and of the sound teaching that you have followed. Have nothing to do with profane myths and old wives' tales. Train yourself in godliness, for, while physical training is of some value, godliness is valuable in every way, holding promise for both the present life and the life to come. The saying is sure and worthy of full acceptance. For to this end we toil and struggle, because we have our hope set on the living God, who is the Savior of all people, especially of those who believe. These are the things you must insist on and teach (παράγγελλε ταῦτα καὶ δίδασκε). (4.6-11)

The audience would have understood this statement in the light of the description of the false teaching that immediately precedes it (regarding the demonic origin and pseudo-pious ascetic nature of the false teaching) and Paul's refutation ('Everything God created is good and for our enjoyment, if we properly give thanks'). Timothy's job is to keep on teaching and promoting the healthy teachings that flow from Paul's gospel, and he has the authority necessary for teaching and refuting false teaching. As Paul's successor in this task, Timothy serves as Paul's voice. He is the one who, in Paul's absence, keeps Paul's people from falling prey to deceptive philosophies.

Timothy Promotes Orthopraxy
By actualizing Paul's commands. I noted above Paul's ongoing concern with appropriate conduct in his churches. As with Timothy's authority over teaching, the audience would have assumed that Paul both expected Timothy to carry out these instructions had given him the authority required to do so. Some of the commands Timothy was actualizing would have been unpopular (or worse) with influential people in the Church (e.g. 2.12, regarding withholding the teaching office from women; 5.3-16, regarding how the Church was to provide [or not provide] for those who were in need). How is Timothy understood to have authority to carry them out? He has this authority because he is Paul's successor in this particular task. When Timothy speaks to the things Paul has bequeathed to him, he speaks with the voice and authority of Paul. If Timothy's authority over teaching (which Paul entrusted to him) and other issues that flow from teaching (authority over the daily lives of members of his churches, authority over church leaders) were questioned or opposed, Timothy did not need to rely on his own authority. As long as he was faithful

with that which was entrusted to him, he spoke with the voice and authority of the one who made that bequest.[56]

By promoting proper and orderly behavior. Four passages show Timothy promoting good behavior. Three of these I discuss above, and will only mention here. In the first, 1.3-5, Timothy fights false teachings, which produce controversies, and supports the true teaching, which promotes the οἰκονομίαν θεοῦ). In the second, 5.3-16, Timothy makes sure that the church takes care of those widows who are truly in need, so that the church's compassion does not become license for the needy to be irresponsible or for their families to shirk their duties. In the third, 6.17-19, Timothy warns wealthy Christians that they must be benevolent and do good rather than being caught up in their own extravagances).[57]

The fourth passage is 4.11-16:

> These are the things you must insist on and teach. Let no one despise your youth, but set the believers an example in speech and conduct, in love, in faith, in purity. Until I arrive, give attention to the public reading of scripture, to exhorting, to teaching. Do not neglect the gift that is in you, which was given to you through prophecy with the laying on of hands by the council of elders. Put these things into practice, devote yourself to them, so that all may see your progress. Pay close attention to yourself and to your teaching; continue in these things, for in doing this you will save both yourself and your hearers.

---

56. This provides the best way to read 3.14-15. The passage could be read to indicate that Timothy was lacking in some sort of knowledge—and (apparently) fairly elementary knowledge at that: 'I hope to come to you soon, but I am writing these instructions to you so that, if I am delayed, you may know how one ought to behave in the household of God'. But the point of the passage is not that Timothy did not know how people should act in the household of God. It is instead that Timothy (who had to be admonished not to allow people to look down on him because of his youth [see 4.12]) might be lacking in confidence to face controversial issues. Paul reminds Timothy (and the authorial audience, which is overhearing the letter) that when he (Timothy) spoke on these issues he spoke with Paul's authority. See Mounce, *Pastoral Epistles*, p. 219; Marshall, *Pastoral Epistles*, pp. 74-75, 559-60.

57. L. William Countryman, *The Rich Christian in the Church of the Early Empire: Contradictions and Accommodations* (New York: Edwin Mellen Press, 1980), p. 33, notes that the early Church was an economic cross-section of society, with both wealthy and poor. In a reciprocity-based culture, where public benefaction was expected to purchase public honor (p. 118), such a mixture made insubordination (e.g. rich women insisting on being given the office of teaching in disregard for propriety) a constant threat. See also Fredrick W. Danker, *Benefactor: Epigraphic Study of a Graeco-Roman and New Testament Semantic Field* (St Louis: Clayton, 1982), pp. 317-493. Kidd, *Wealth and Beneficence*, p. 159, argues that the Pastorals both represent and undercut bourgeois values, by enforcing hierarchy on the one hand and calling for humility and servant attitudes from leaders on the other.

As part of Timothy's struggle in support of true teaching and proper conduct, he must guard against allowing people to take him lightly because of his apparent youth. He is instead to win their respect by his example (τύπος).[58] As he fights for the pure Pauline gospel and displays right conduct in his life, Timothy saves himself and those he is leading. Further, he is to devote himself to reading scripture, exhorting (παράκλησις) and teaching (διδασκαλία), and he must attend to the gift and ministry he received when the elders 'ordained' him.

By guarding the church's reputation and standing. I find eight passages where Timothy is to urge his people toward propriety, possibly in response to anti-Christian polemic in the community around them.[59] Seven of these simply involve Timothy actualizing Paul's instructions regarding appropriate behavior, and need little discussion here: 2.1-4 (good citizenship gains a hearing for the gospel); 2.8-15 (appropriateness vs. ostentation, proper role for women); 5.1-2 (propriety in relationships); 5.3-16 (taking care of the truly needy); 5.14-15 (counsel for younger widows); 6.1-2 (propriety for Christian slaves); and 6.17-19 (how the wealthy in the church should conduct themselves). The other passage to consider here is 3.14-15:

> I am writing these instructions to you so that...you may know how one ought to behave in the household of God (οἴκῳ θεοῦ), which is the church.

The audience would have heard this passage in the light of οἰκονομίαν in 1.4, and would have understood that part of Timothy's vocation was properly administering the church, making sure that her people maintained the behavior and deportment appropriate for the οἴκῳ θεοῦ.

Summary. Timothy has the authority to promote proper and orderly behavior (behavior in keeping with the gospel) in Paul's churches. He has this authority because Paul passed it on to him in the task he bequeathed to Timothy when he made Timothy his successor.

Timothy Oversees the Work of Other Leaders
As with the above two areas, the text assumes this authority for Timothy wherever Paul gives instruction (i.e. the text assumes that Timothy would

---

58. R. Collins, *1 & 2 Timothy and Titus*, p. 130, maintains that Paul not only preached, he also provided an example for those to whom he preached. Timothy is to do likewise'. Johnson, *First and Second Letters to Timothy*, p. 255, suggests that the idea of 'example' in the Pastorals be understood against the background of Hellenistic moral philosophy, since the philosophers understood that virtue is learned initially (and best) by imitation of the teacher.

59. Marshall, *Pastoral Epistles*, pp. 572-73, notes parallels between these instructions on household propriety and Hellenistic moral philosophy.

have had the authority to actualize Paul's direct instructions). I can add at least four additional aspects to our picture of Timothy's authority under this heading, however.

Timothy has authority over overseers. Note first the authority that Timothy has over overseers:

> Now a bishop must be above reproach, married only once, temperate, sensible, respectable, hospitable, an apt teacher, not a drunkard, not violent but gentle, not quarrelsome, and not a lover of money. He must manage his own household well, keeping his children submissive and respectful in every way—for if someone does not know how to manage his own household, how can he take care (ἐπιμελήσεται) of God's church? He must not be a recent convert, or he may be puffed up with conceit and fall into the condemnation of the devil. Moreover, he must be well thought of by outsiders, so that he may not fall into disgrace and the snare of the devil. (3.2-7)

Note a couple of things. First, Paul here gives Timothy authority to monitor the qualifications and character of the overseers, and to monitor their work as well. In an established Church, Timothy is able to set the standards by which the overseers will be measured. He is not one of the overseers, but stands apart from and over them. This weighs against those who read Timothy and Titus as ciphers for second-century bishops. Second, note that the description of the overseers' authority (when divorced from the second-century baggage that is too often read back into the text[60]) is nothing like the office of monarchical bishop that evolved later. The overseers needed to have good reputations, be men of solid character. They needed to be able to teach and able to manage (προϊστάμενον, the same word as used for how the elders rule the church in 5.17) their *families* well—if they could not, they would not be able to care for (ἐπιμελέομαι) the church properly. There is no indication in 1 Timothy (or Titus, for that matter) that the office of overseer was a more powerful office in the Pauline church than elder.[61]

---

60. See, for instance, Campenhausen, *Ecclesiastical Authority*, p. 107: 'In the Pastoral Epistles the "bishop" is always spoken of in the singular. The simplest explanation for this is that monarchical episcopacy is by now the prevailing system, and that the one bishop has already become the head of the presybterate, even if his supreme position is not nearly so strongly emphasised as it is in the Epistles of Ignatius'. Thus Campenhausen asserts that Timothy and Titus are 'codes' for the early second-century bishops—ignoring the fact that texts keep them separate from the leadership of the congregations. See also p. 118: 'Canon law has arrived… The bishop is responsible for the whole sphere of the faith and the moral life of the congregation'. Käsemann, 'Catholicism', p. 247, likewise asserts that the Pastorals show the monarchical bishop, the presybterate, and the deacons, all official functionaries, under the aegis of leadership 'placed in apostolic succession'.

61. Mounce, *Pastoral Epistles*, pp. 162-63, argues that overseer and elder are interchangeable terms in the Pastorals; so also James T. Burtchaell, *From Synagogue to*

4. First Timothy

Timothy has authority over deacons. Not only did Timothy possess the authority to monitor the character and work of overseers, he had a similar authority over deacons:

> Deacons likewise must be serious, not double-tongued, not indulging in much wine, not greedy for money; they must hold fast to the mystery of the faith with a clear conscience. And let them first be tested; then, if they prove themselves blameless, let them serve as deacons. Women likewise must be serious, not slanderers, but temperate, faithful in all things. Let deacons be married only once, and let them manage their children and their households well; for those who serve well as deacons gain a good standing for themselves and great boldness in the faith that is in Christ Jesus. (3.8-13)

Here Paul describes the authority that Timothy had over male and female deacons,[62] and the character qualifications for that office, which are very similar to the qualifications for overseer. Not only is Timothy to monitor and oversee the deacons' work, he is to test the candidates for that office to see if they are qualified. Among the qualifications Paul mentions is that deacons must 'hold fast to the mystery of the faith' (i.e. be committed to what Paul teaches rather than what the false teachers promote). If they pass the test, Timothy will allow them to serve as deacons; if they fail, Timothy will not allow them to serve. This is not the only qualification, and the test is not described: apparently it involves a time during which the candidates would be measured against the standards set forth.[63]

In the two preceding sections, Timothy has authority over church leaders

---

Church: Public Services and Offices in the Earliest Christian Communities (Cambridge: Cambridge University Press, 1992), pp. 296-97, 344-45. See also Frances Young, *The Theology of the Pastoral Epistles* (Cambridge: Cambridge University Press, 1994), pp. 99-111. Campenhausen, *Ecclesiastical Authority*, p. 107, insists that elders and overseers are leaders from two streams of the Church, the former Jewish and the latter Hellenistic, and that the Pastorals are part of the fusion of the two systems of leadership into one. On the other hand, R. Alastair Campbell, *The Elders: Seniority within Earliest Christianity* (Edinburgh: T. & T. Clark, 1994), pp. 196-204, argues that the overseer is a new office at the time of the Pastorals, and that they were written 'not to effect an amalgamation of overseers and elders, but to legitimate the authority' of the new office (p. 196).

62. Marshall, *Pastoral Epistles*, pp. 492-94, concludes that 3.11 refers to female deacons. See also Quinn and Wacker, *First and Second Letters to Timothy*, pp. 285-86; R. Collins, *1 & 2 Timothy and Titus*, pp. 90-92. See also Jennifer H. Stiefel, 'Women Deacons in 1 Timothy: A Linguistic and Literary Look at "Women Likewise..." (1 Tim. 3.11)', *NTS* 41 (1995), pp. 442-57. Knight, *Pastoral Epistles*, p. 171, argues that the reference is to the wives or female assistants of male deacons.

63. Marshall, *Pastoral Epistles*, p. 492; but see Quinn and Wacker, *First and Second Letters to Timothy*, p. 284, who assert that the test would go beyond the standard in 3.2-12: 'The qualifications do not offer in themselves sufficient warrant for accepting a person into the diaconal ministry. Additional testing is needed.'

because of succession. He has authority to monitor the work and character of overseers, and to set the standards aspiring overseers must meet. He has authority to test and approve of deacons before they begin to serve. He does not have this authority because of his own merits, but because he is Paul's successor.

Timothy has authority over elders. Paul describes the authority that Timothy holds over elders:

> Let the elders who rule well be considered worthy of double honor, especially those who labor in preaching and teaching; for the scripture says, 'You shall not muzzle an ox while it is treading out the grain', and, 'The laborer deserves to be paid'. Never accept any accusation against an elder except on the evidence of two or three witnesses. As for those who persist in sin, rebuke them in the presence of all, so that the rest also may stand in fear. (5.17-20)

Timothy is to monitor the relationship between the elders and the church, making certain that they are properly respected and recompensed. Paul does not describe Timothy as monitoring the character of elders, but he does describe the authority Timothy has if an elder is accused of falling into sin. In such a case, Timothy is to act as judge over the elder, by adjudicating whether the accusation has basis in fact and publicly rebuking the elder if it does. The point of this rebuke before the entire congregation is to show all how serious a thing it is when a leader of God's Church persists in sin. Thus the authorial audience would have understood that Timothy, as Paul's successor, shares his predecessor's authority to exercise church discipline.[64]

Timothy has authority to pass his task and authority on to successors. The final passage that describes Timothy's authority over church leaders is 5.22a, which says, 'Do not ordain anyone hastily, and do not participate in the sins of others; keep yourself pure'. Timothy here would be understood as having the authority to pass on some of his tasks and authority to other leaders, to perpetuate the succession of task from Paul to himself then on to other leaders.[65] Paul instructs Timothy to choose his successors/delegates well, in keeping with the seriousness of the task: the verses surrounding the instruction of 5.22a focus on sin, particularly the sin of leaders, and this is no accident:[66]

---

64. R. Collins, *1 & 2 Timothy and Titus*, p. 148, does not connect 5.20 with what precedes: he takes 5.20 to be a general reference to those in the congregation who persist in sin. Quinn and Wacker, *First and Second Letters to Timothy*, p. 465, critique of this view.

65. For the view that this refers to reinstating a fallen leader, see Dibelius and Conzelmann, *Pastoral Epistles*, p. 80. Against, see Marshall, *Pastoral Epistles*, pp. 620-22; Lips, *Glaube*, pp. 174-77; Brox, *Pastoralbriefe*, p. 201; Roloff, *Brief*, p. 313.

66. Knight, *Pastoral Epistles*, pp. 239-41; Johnson, *First and Second Letters to Timothy*, p. 282; Mounce, *Pastoral Epistles*, pp. 319-21. Quinn and Wacker, *First and Second*

4. First Timothy

> [Regarding elders] As for those who persist in sin, rebuke them in the presence of all, so that the rest also may stand in fear. In the presence of God and of Christ Jesus and of the elect angels, I warn you to keep these instructions without prejudice, doing nothing on the basis of partiality. Do not ordain anyone hastily, and do not participate in the sins of others; keep yourself pure... (5.20-22).

> The sins of some people are conspicuous and precede them to judgment, while the sins of others follow them there. So also good works are conspicuous; and even when they are not, they cannot remain hidden. (5.24-25)

Again, note the similarity in authority between Paul and Timothy: as Paul had authority to pass on tasks and authority to delegates/successors, so also Timothy. This authority was passed on to him as part of his succession from Paul.

Four other passages require brief mention here. I have discussed 2.12 (not allowing women to teach), 3.1-13 (character and tasks of overseers and deacons), and 5.17-20 (Timothy judges elders) above. Here, let me simply note again the huge responsibility that Paul gave to his protégé when he gave him these instructions. The audience again would have understood that it was Timothy's task to realize Paul's wishes on these matters, and that Paul had given to Timothy the authority to carry out these instructions.

I have also discussed 5.22 ('Do not ordain anyone hastily') above, but its import requires me to repeat the point here briefly. From 5.22, the audience would have understood that Timothy had the authority to pass on to others the tasks that Paul had delegated to him. They would have understood that Timothy's stay in Ephesus was of limited duration. What would happen when Timothy left? Who would protect and care for the church then? Those whom Timothy had ordained to that particular task, those to whom Timothy had passed those aspects of his authority and vocation, would then lead the church.

5. Timothy as Paul's Successor and the Elders' Successor in 1 Timothy

In this second section, I have shown the following:
1. That the authorial audience would have inferred that Timothy was Paul's successor in the tasks outlined below (1.3, 18-19; 6.12-15, 20;). He was also the elders' successor in general ministry (4.13-15).
2. That because of this succession, Timothy has a particular vocation:

Letters to Timothy, p. 477, state: 'The involvement in "the sins of others" in verse 22 referred to the perils of hasty ordination, and now verse 24 returns to that subject'.

a. He fights for orthodoxy (1.3, 8, 18-19; 4.6-11; 6.12-15, 20).
   b. He promotes orthopraxy:
      i. By actualizing Paul's commands (2.12; 3.14-15; 5.3-16).
      ii. By promoting good behavior (1.3-5; 4.11-16; 5.3-16; 6.17, 19).
      iii. By guarding the church's reputation and standing with outsiders (2.1-4, 8-15; 3.14-15; 5.1-2, 3-16, 14-15; 6.1-2, 17-19).
   c. He oversees the work of other church leaders:
      i. He has authority over overseers (3.2-7).
      ii. He has authority over deacons (3.8-13).
      iii. He has authority over elders (5.17-19).
      iv. He has authority to pass *his* task and authority on to his own successors (5.22).

The above outline shows that Timothy's task mirrors his predecessor's. The ancient audience would have understood all of this in terms of the central function of that succession: Paul passed on a particular task, and the authority to perform it, to Timothy. This succession of task first legitimates Timothy, giving him the authority he needs to carry on the task. He is not self-appointed, therefore he does not work from his own authority but from the authority of the one who appointed him. Thus succession here primarily functions to legitimate and empower Timothy as Paul's successor.

Note also that Timothy is acting in Paul's place. Paul expects Timothy to be his agent, to do the things in Paul's absence that Paul would do if he were there. Thus succession of task also ensures continuity of manner: because Timothy is Paul's true successor in this task, he acts in the way that Paul would have acted, with Paul's authority, to face the crisis. Timothy leads as Paul would have led.

Third, Paul made Timothy his successor so as to keep the gospel pure and effective. Thus, in this aspect, the succession of task from Paul to Timothy thus functions like the succession of tradition from Christ to Paul—to ensure continued institutional vitality.

Figure 65 (opposite) illustrates the exchanges involved.

The succession from Paul to Timothy is built on the succession from the elders to Timothy. The succession from the elders introduced Timothy into ministry, and is subsumed by his succession from Paul. The prior succession appears also to have been primarily a passing on of tasks—Timothy shares characteristic tasks with his predecessors, leading and preaching and teaching. Thus this succession, if inferred, would function for the authorial audience to ensure continuity of manner.

The exchanges are set out in Fig. 66 (opposite).

4. *First Timothy*

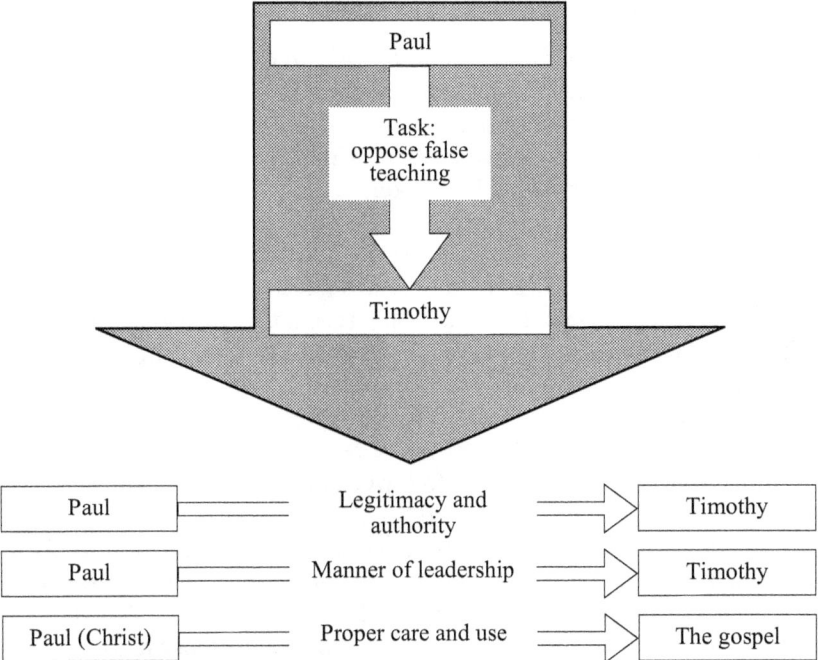

Figure 65. *The Functions of the Succession from Paul to Timothy in 1 Timothy*

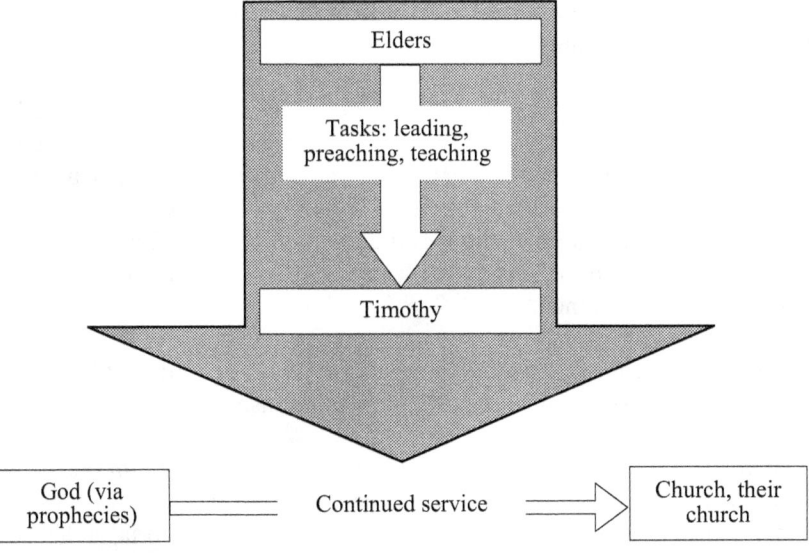

Figure 66. *The Function of the Succession from the Elders to Timothy in 1 Timothy*

6. Other Leaders' Succession from Paul or Timothy

Evidence of Succession from Paul or Timothy to Other Leaders
Under this rubric, I will consider as one all the different relationships between Paul/Timothy and other church leaders mentioned in 1 Timothy. I realize that if these relationships were considered individually instead of as a group, the evidence of succession would be weaker.

Terms from the semantic field of succession. Two terms, one specifically from the semantic field of succession that I have already outlined and one synonym, come into play here. The term from the semantic field as outlined above is in 4.16: 'Pay close attention to yourself and to your teaching; continue in these things, for in doing this you will save both yourself and your hearers (τοὺς ἀκούοντάς σου)'. As I showed in Chapter 2 above, τοὺς ἀκούοντάς σου is language often used in ancient Graeco-Roman texts referring to a philosopher or teacher and his/her followers, those who 'listened' to him/her. Such force could have been inferred here.

The synonym is in 2.12: 'I permit (ἐπιτρέπω) no woman to teach'. In classical use, ἐπιτρέπω carries the sense of *entrusting* something to someone (*LSJ*), and Johnson does in fact translate 2.12 in that way—'I do not entrust teaching to a woman'.[67] By New Testament times, this sense had been taken over by the sense of *allowing* someone to do something, but it is at least plausible that ancient readers/hearers would have heard 2.12 in terms of succession, the contemplated entrusting of a particular task to a successor/delegate.

Thus I judge that for this relationship, there is semantic evidence present but certainly not prominent.

Phenomena from the conceptual field of succession. In 5.22, Paul writes: 'Do not ordain (lit. "place hands on", χεῖρας...ἐπιτίθει) anyone hastily, and do not participate in the sins of others...' As noted above, the ancient audience would have heard this verse in terms of Timothy having successors (as yet unnamed) in his tasks. In the light of the function of the placing on of hands discussed earlier (in the succession from the elders to Timothy), I find this evidence to be prominent.

Standard elements of a Mediterranean succession story. I do not find any of these elements present with regard to this relationship.

Summary. In view of the evidence, particularly the laying-on of hands, and in view of the way the successions from Christ to Paul and from Paul to Timothy permeate the letter, I consider it likely that the authorial audience of the Pastorals would see succession in this relationship.

---

67. Johnson, *First and Second Letters to Timothy*, p. 201.

7. The Function of Succession from Paul or Timothy to Other Leaders

While much less prominent in 1 Timothy than the succession from Christ to Paul, or the two successions that Timothy is recipient of, the idea of succession from Paul or Timothy to other church leaders could have played some role in the authorial audience's hearing of 1 Timothy. The letter *does* mention the vocations, the task and authority, of church leaders other than Timothy and Paul.

First, they would have assumed that Paul was calling all the church leaders who heard/read the letter (witness the second-person plural pronoun in the closing, 'Grace be with you' [μεθ' ὑμῶν], 6.21) to obey his instructions in passages such as 1.3 (command the false teachers to stop teaching things that do not fit with the gospel) and 2.12 (women are not allowed to teach or usurp authority).

Second, the letter does mention/prescribe several specific tasks for different groups. The overseers must be able to teach and to care for (ἐπιμελέομαι) the church (3.2, 5). The elders ordain other leaders and pass their tasks on to them (4.14). The elders rule the church (προΐστημι) and should also teach and labor in the word (κοπιῶντες ἐν λόγῳ καὶ διδασκαλίᾳ, 5.17). Finally, with Tit. 2.3-5 in mind, it is possible to read the virtue list applying to widows as including a couple of tasks that would be expected of those who were on the official list: 'supplications and prayers' (5.5) and ministering through good deeds, such as 'show[ing] hospitality, wash[ing] the saint's feet, help[ing] the afflicted, and devot[ing] herself to doing good in every way' (5.10).[68]

In each of these cases, the leaders/workers had task and authority that were passed on to them by a supervisor/predecessor, someone whom they followed in these tasks and to whom they answered for them. In the context of 1 Timothy, in which succession plays such a prominent role, and in the light of the scant but still present evidence of succession thinking (outlined above) in reference to Paul's/Timothy's relationships with other leaders, it is likely that the audience would have understood these tasks and the authority required to carry them out to be the result of succession from Paul, Timothy, or other

---

68. For discussions of the office of widows, see Marshall, *Pastoral Epistles*, pp. 574-81; G. Stählin, 'χήρα', in *TDNT*, IX, pp. 440-65; Mounce, *Pastoral Epistles*, pp. 273-77; Bonnie B. Thurston, *The Widows: A Women's Ministry in the Early Church* (Philadelphia: Fortress Press, 1989), pp. 53-55. Quinn and Wacker, *First and Second Letters to Timothy*, p. 426, allude to a pre-existing source setting up an 'ecclesiastical order of widows' behind 5.3-16. For the possibility that the order included older virgin women who had never been married (thus technically not widows), see Marshall, *Pastoral Epistles*, p. 578. Sarah B. Pomeroy, *Goddesses, Whores, Wives, and Slaves: Women in Classical Antiquity* (New York: Schocken Books, 1995), p. 161, notes that Roman law encouraged widows to remarry; see also Winter, 'Providentia', p. 85.

unnamed leaders—and ultimately, these successions go back to Christ himself. I find no function explicitly attached to this relationship, other than a general sense of such succession giving continued good health to the institution, the Church.

8. Summary: The Function of Succession in 1 Timothy

In this chapter, I have shown that the observations made earlier regarding succession in Graeco-Roman, Jewish, and Christian texts generally apply to 1 Timothy. In the relationships in 1 Timothy in which succession is prominent, I find at least two exchanges. I find some of the same terminology and kinds of phenomena, the same standard components making up the succession story. I see the same differences in kind and degree: Paul does not become Jesus' equal, yet he is Jesus' successor. Timothy does not become an apostle, but he is Paul's successor. Further, succession here has objects like those seen above—succession of tradition, succession of task. These successions fit the same functional categories as seen above, ensuring legitimacy, and continuity of institutional vitality and manner and effect. Further, these categories seem to function in much the same ways as in the texts surveyed above, although I have examined the functions in 1 Timothy at much greater depth. Particularly notable is the similarity 1 Timothy shares with many of the Jewish and Christian texts regarding God's role in succession. In the Pastorals as in these earlier texts, God initiates and guides the pivotal lines of succession, he is in control. The text is consistently optimistic about God using succession to achieve his purposes. In the following table I illustrate the relationships and the functions of succession in 1 Timothy:

Table 11. *The Functions of Succession in 1 Timothy*

Text	Function
Succession of tradition from Christ to Paul	Continued institutional vitality Legitimates successor Continuity of effect
Succession of task from Paul to Timothy	Legitimates successor Continuity of manner Continued institutional vitality
Succession of task from the elders to Timothy	Continuity of manner

In this chapter, I have explored how the authorial audience would have understood succession to function in 1 Timothy. In the next chapter, I examine 2 Timothy and Titus according to the same framework. In Chapter 6, I synthesize these findings and offer a brief reading of the Pastoral Epistles from the perspective of the authorial audience.

5

SUCCESSION IN THE PASTORAL EPISTLES, PART 2: SECOND TIMOTHY AND TITUS

This chapter is the second of three chapters exploring how the authorial audience would have understood the function of succession in the Pastoral Epistles, based on the way succession functioned in the texts of their culture. In the last chapter, I examined 1 Timothy against the backdrop provided by my survey of ancient Mediterranean texts in which the function of succession played a significant role. Against that backdrop, I explored two questions regarding 1 Timothy: first, would the authorial audience have inferred succession in this text? Second, having inferred succession, how would the authorial audience have understood succession to function? Here, I ask the same questions of the remaining Pastoral Epistles, 2 Timothy and Titus, following the same basic approach.

1. *Evidence of Succession from Christ to Paul in 2 Timothy*

Terms from the semantic field of succession. Like 1 Timothy, 2 Timothy uses succession terminology to describe Paul's relationship to Christ. In 1.11-12, Paul describes his calling to ministry in known succession language:

> For this gospel I was appointed (τίθημι) a preacher and apostle and teacher, and therefore I suffer as I do. But I am not ashamed, for I know whom I have believed, and I am sure that he is able to guard until that Day what has been entrusted to me (δυνατός ἐστιν τὴν παραθήκην μου φυλάξαι). (RSV translation)

The first succession term (τίθημι, 'appoint') is unambiguous. It is used in a similar way in 1 Tim. 1.12 and 2.7 (see p. 113 above), and 2 Kgs 2.24. The second phrase (δυνατός ἐστιν τὴν παραθήκην μου φυλάξαι) presents more difficulty. In this phrase, μου has traditionally been read as a subjective genitive with God as its object: thus 'I am persuaded that he (God) is able to guard until that day what I have entrusted to him'.[1] I take παραθήκη μου as

---

1. So Johnson, *First and Second Letters to Timothy*; Fee, *1 and 2 Timothy, Titus*; Knight, *Pastoral Epistles*; Mounce, *Pastoral Epistles*; NRSV, NIV, ASV, KJV, NKJV, NLT. But

an objective genitive, however: 'he (God) is able to guard/keep what has been entrusted (divine passive, God is the one who entrusts) to me'. In favor of this reading, note that παραθήκη is used two other times in the Pastorals (and only here in the New Testament), 1 Tim. 6.20 and 2 Tim. 1.14. In those cases, it unambiguously refers to the body of Paul's teaching, bequeathed to him by Christ (1 Tim. 1.11) and passed on to Timothy (1 Tim. 6.20; 2 Tim. 1.14). Note second that the context demands that παραθήκη has the same referent in 1.12 that it has in 1.14 (i.e. the body of Paul's teaching and all that entails, bequeathed to Timothy). Thus I take τὴν παραθήκην μου to be an objective genitive (so also Collins, Spicq, RSV, NCV, CEV). I consider this evidence from the semantic field of succession to be prominent.

Phenomena from the conceptual field of succession. I find no phenomena from the conceptual field used in 2 Timothy to describe this relationship. This absence is itself interesting: in a letter that makes so much of Paul's suffering on behalf of the gospel, on behalf of the cause of Christ, one might expect to hear Paul's sufferings seen in allusion to Jesus' sufferings (e.g. something like Col. 1.24). Yet the letter never draws such parallels.[2]

Standard elements of a Mediterranean succession story. Are the three standard elements of an ancient Mediterranean succession story present? I find the naming of what is passed on (the παραθήκη, the roles of κῆρυξ, ἀπόστολος, and διδάσκαλος), the first component. As in 1 Timothy, the text alludes to Paul's calling to be an apostle (in 1.11). Thus the authorial audience's knowledge of Paul's calling to be an apostle would provide the second component, the symbolic act. It is important to note, however, that Paul in 2 Timothy never appeals to his apostolic authority as a warrant (a consistent

---

consider an intriguing alternative: τὴν παραθήκην μου could also be a subjective genitive referring to that which Paul has entrusted to another person (rather than God): 'he [God] is able to guard...what I have deposited *with you* [i.e. with Timothy]'. In this reading, Paul would be telling Timothy something like, 'God has maintained the power of the gospel during my ministry, he will continue to do so even after I am gone'. In the end, I think the objective genitive, as outlined above, is the best choice. Paul is the focus of 1.11-12, Timothy does not become the focus until the imperatives of 1.13-14. But see Marshall, *Pastoral Epistles*, p. 711, who favors a reference to what Paul is entrusting to his successors, and Wolter, *Paulustradition*, pp. 116-18, who insists that that μου must here be subjective and not objective. See also I. Howard Marshall, *Kept by the Power of God: A Study of Perseverance and Falling Away* (Carlisle: Paternoster Press, 3rd edn, 1995), p. 247 n. 21.

2. The only passage that might be read as drawing a parallel between Paul's suffering and Christ's suffering is 2.11, 'if we endure, we shall also reign with him'. But even here the emphasis is not on co-suffering with Christ. Most of the verbs in the hymn (2.11-12) feature συν- prefixes, which do arguably refer to activity in or with Christ. The verb translated 'endure' (ὑπομένομεν), however, lacks the prefix.

motif in 1 Timothy)—he instead depends on his personal relationship with Timothy to provide authority for his instructions. The third standard component of an ancient Mediterranean succession story does not appear to be present, however: 2 Timothy draws no parallels (in suffering or otherwise) between Paul and Christ.

Summary. In the light of the succession terminology of 2 Tim. 1.11-12, I conclude that the ancient Mediterranean audience might have understood Paul to have been Jesus' successor in the keeping of the gospel, but that the evidence is not prominent enough to say with certainty. They would reach this conclusion if they read/heard 2 Timothy in the light of 1 Timothy. They could reach this conclusion *even if* the only text they had was 2 Timothy.

In the following analysis, I proceed on the assumption that the authorial audience would have read Paul's relationship to Christ in 2 Timothy as one of succession. Two assumptions, if changed, would change this analysis. First, if one assumes (and I do not) that the Pastorals were written and received as a unit (rather than discrete documents), then one should assume that the authorial audience would read/hear Paul's relationship to Christ in 2 Timothy in the light of his relationship to Christ in 1 Timothy and indeed Titus.³ In that case, the authorial audience would have inferred succession because of the influence of the other letters. Second, one can read the genitive in 1.12 differently, as do many of the commentators surveyed above. If one does not read that phrase as an objective genitive, then the case for Paul's succession from Christ is much weaker.

2. *The Function of the Succession from Christ to Paul in 2 Timothy*

If the authorial audience understood παραθήκη μου in 1.12 as an objective genitive, then they likely would have understood the phrase to refer to the gospel that Paul received from Christ. As with 1 Timothy, this is a succession of tradition, the gospel passed from Christ to Paul (and then a verse later passed from Paul to Timothy). However, this succession from Christ to Paul, even if inferred, does not have the same prominence in 2 Timothy as in 1 Timothy. There, the succession from Christ to Paul was foundational, Paul played two central roles in the succession narrative of the letter—Christ's successor in the passing on of tradition, Timothy's predecessor in the passing on of task. Here in 2 Timothy, however, Paul plays only one prominent role —predecessor to Timothy. This succession (from Paul to Timothy), examined below, is the center and foundation of 2 Timothy. The first succession (from Christ to Paul) in 2 Timothy is more like the succession from the elders

3. In taking the Pastorals as discrete documents, I am following Johnson, *First and Second Letters to Timothy*, p. 15; Richards, *Difference and Distance*, pp. 20-24.

to Timothy in 1 Timothy: it sets the stage for the major act of succession on which the letter centers.

If the authorial audience of 2 Timothy would have inferred succession in this relationship, how would they have understood it to function? In 1 Timothy, succession of tradition from Christ to Paul was the foundation of Paul's authority and of the vocation which he was actively pursuing. In 2 Timothy, succession from Christ still defines Paul's vocation. Here, however, the vocation is not that of an active missionary but that of one preparing for martyrdom, suffering and dying for the gospel. Paul's job now is to finish preparations to pass the care of the gospel—the very institution he received as a bequest from Christ, not just a handful of related specific contextualized tasks—to his successor, Timothy.

As was the case in 1 Timothy, the ancient audience would have understood Paul's calling to ministry in 2 Timothy to be a succession from Christ to Paul. Christ, the predecessor, entrusts tradition (gospel) to Paul, his successor. As with 1 Timothy, they would have understood that Paul received his vocation as a result of this succession. Also as with 1 Timothy, God is the initiator of this succession.[4] Note: 'Paul, an apostle of Christ Jesus *by the will of God* according to the promise of the life which is in Christ Jesus...' (1.1).[5]

Thus, God calls Paul to be an apostle ('to the gentiles', the audience would have understood [4.17]) (1.1). His calling involves empowerment by the Spirit (1.7) to act according to God's purpose (1.9). His task is preserving, furthering, and perpetuating the work of the gospel (1.11-12). Here, as with 1 Timothy, succession defines Paul's vocation. It prescribes his responsibilities, the actions Paul performs as he carries out these responsibilities, and the authority by which he performs them.

Second Timothy's statements regarding Paul's vocation as it results from this succession can be grouped under two general headings. Below I analyze what each says about Paul's actions and authority. The headings are: Paul fights for orthodoxy, and Paul suffers for the benefit of the gospel.

---

4. This description differs from the opening of 1 Timothy: there, Paul's apostleship was by God's *command* (as fits the emphasis of that letter, the command and authority that Paul bequeathed to Timothy for his [Timothy's] fight against false teaching in Ephesus [1 Tim. 1.3, 18]). Here, Paul's apostleship is by God's *will*. Marshall, *Pastoral Epistles*, p. 685, observes that in 2 Timothy, the center is 'the person of Paul, whose call to apostleship is part of God's plan'. In 1 Timothy and Titus, which focus on apostleship by God's command, the focus is on the task which Paul received and passed on in those letters. See also Wolter, *Paulustradition*, pp. 149-52.

5. Regarding 'according to the promise of life', both Marshall, *Pastoral Epistles*, p. 685, and Lorenz Oberlinner, *Die Pastoralbriefe: Kommentar zum zweiten Timotheusbrief* (HTKNT, XI/2; Freiburg: Herder, 1995), p. 8, refer to God's promise of salvation in Christ, the message for which Paul was sent by God.

Paul Fights for Orthodoxy (i.e. 'Fights the Good Fight')
By his own teaching activity. In 1.11, Paul describes the task/role to which he was appointed: 'For this gospel I was appointed a herald and an apostle and a teacher (κῆρυξ καὶ ἀπόστολος καὶ διδάσκαλος)…' Note that the nouns are anarthrous, Paul is not appointed the apostle, the teacher, and so on. Again, the Pauline exclusivity of the Pastorals can be overstated. And in 4.6-7, pointing back to his career as an apostle and teacher and preacher, Paul characterizes his ministry: 'I have fought the good fight…I have kept the faith'. In the context of 2 Timothy, even if read on its own terms, 'fighting the good fight' and 'keeping the faith' likely refer to Paul's struggle to keep the gospel pure and true to what he received.[6] The focus of Paul's service is the gospel and its purity and vitality.

Also, in two passages, Paul refers to how his life provides for his followers an example of sound teaching and appropriate conduct. He expects them to follow this example:

> Hold to the standard of sound teaching that you have heard from me, in the faith and love that are in Christ Jesus. (1.13)

> Now you have observed my teaching, my conduct, my aim in life, my faith, my patience, my love, my steadfastness, my persecutions and suffering the things that happened to me in Antioch, Iconium, and Lystra. (3.10-11)

This theme—the teacher/predecessor as τύπος, an example to be emulated —would be familiar to the audience from Hellenistic moral philosophy.[7] Notice that Paul's example functions differently here than in 1 Timothy. In 1 Timothy, Paul served as an example to all people of how God's grace could overwhelm, save, and change a sinner. In 2 Timothy, Paul's example is something given for imitation, and his example seems to be aimed at a more restricted audience. Part of the reason for this difference is the difference in the authorial audience between 1 Timothy and 2 Timothy, a difference marked by the different epistolary types used. In 1 Timothy, Richards points to the 'I–thou–they' triangle, and classifies that letter as a Deliberative (paraenetic) Letter-Essay, which contains instruction and admonishment for both the recipient and the larger audience (the community) behind the

---

6. So Johnson, *First and Second Letters to Timothy*, pp. 431-32, R. Collins, *1 & 2 Timothy and Titus*, p. 276. Marshall, *Pastoral Epistles*, p. 808, reads the phrases in a more general way. Note that πίστις is articular.

7. See Johnson, *First and Second Letters to Timothy*, p. 255, for a note regarding how the moral philosophers utilized imitation as a didactic tool. For the idea that ὑποτύπωσιν is a reference to an outline of Paul's teaching, a skeleton to be used and improvised on in Timothy's teaching, see Donald Guthrie, *The Pastoral Epistles* (TNTC; Downers Grove, IL: Intervarsity Press), p. 145, and J.N.D. Kelly, *A Commentary on the Pastoral Epistles* (BNTC; A. & C. Black, 1963), p. 166. Marshall, *Pastoral Epistles*, p. 712, argues against this reading.

recipient.[8] The audience of a literary deliberative letter such as 2 Timothy, while still larger than just a single recipient, is more narrowly focused than the audience of 1 Timothy: here, the paraenesis is aimed at those in the community who 'can put [themselves] in the recipient's place', that is, those serving and leading in the community or aspiring to do so.[9] The authorial audience of 2 Timothy thus is a group of people who are overhearing the letter and putting themselves in Timothy's place, called to imitate Paul's conduct and manner as teacher and leader.

By endorsing specific content. In two passages, Paul makes bare (i.e. non-descriptive) references to the content of teaching that Timothy (and others of his followers) had heard from his lips. This content, which they had heard from Paul, was part of the example they were to follow. The statements themselves do not describe this content, but simply state the maxim, 'Be faithful to what you heard':

> What you have heard from me through many witnesses entrust to faithful people who will be able to teach others as well. (2.2)
>
> Now you have observed my teaching...my persecutions and suffering... (3.10-11)

Paul also endorses preformed or traditional materials which were part of his teaching:

> Remember Jesus Christ, raised from the dead, a descendant of David—that is my gospel... (2.8)
>
> The saying is sure:
> If we have died with him, we will also live with him;
>   if we endure, we will also reign with him;
> if we deny him, he will also deny us;
>   if we are faithless, he remains faithful
> —for he cannot deny himself. (2.11-13)

And other passages contain material of a more doctrinal nature:

> This grace was given to us in Christ Jesus before the ages began, but it has now been revealed through the appearing of our Savior Christ Jesus, who abolished death and brought life and immortality to light through the gospel. (1.9b-10)
>
> All scripture is inspired by God and is useful for teaching, for reproof, for correction, and for training in righteousness, so that everyone who belongs to God may be proficient, equipped for every good work. (3.16-17)[10]

8. Richards, *Difference and Distance*, pp. 179-82.
9. Richards, *Difference and Distance*, p. 133.
10. One might also place the warnings of apostasy in the last days (3.1-9; 4.3-4) in this category.

5. Second Timothy and Titus

Compared to 1 Timothy, 2 Timothy has less specifically doctrinal material. In 1 Timothy, where the central concern was false teaching vs. the true gospel, such passages dealt with the content of teaching that Timothy was to deliver and endorse. In 2 Timothy, the purpose is different—the concern is not with refuting false teaching but with how Paul's gospel will continue with an authorized successor after Paul's death—a successor who will himself suffer for the gospel. Thus these passages focus not on what Timothy will teach but on how Timothy will face suffering. When *in extremis*, he must remember Paul's teaching and the example Paul presents of how to face suffering. He must pass the παραθήκη on to others, so that it continues past his own death/martyrdom just as (through him) it continues past Paul's.

By establishing a successor. Paul fought for the true gospel by establishing an empowered, equipped, faithful successor, someone who would carry on the banner of Paul's pure gospel in Paul's absence. The first reference to this act is 1.6-7, which I will deal with extensively below, under Timothy's succession from Paul. Here I will simply note that in 1.6-7 Paul reveals that he has authority to establish a successor, someone to whom he can pass on his gospel and the tasks that come with it. He not only designates his successor through a symbolic succession act ('laying on of hands', 1.6), he also empowers him ('the gift...that is within you through[11] the laying on of my hands'). Furthermore, as Christ's successor, Paul has authority to dictate the parameters of his bequest to Timothy. Below, I show four of these parameters that Paul has dictated: he dictates his successor's attitude toward and handling of the gospel, he prescribes the character required of his successor, he calls his successor to share in his sufferings, and he warns his successor of incipient dangers to the Church.

First, Paul dictates his successor's attitude toward and handling of the gospel. Four passages indicate that Timothy must handle the gospel faithfully. This includes sharing Paul's attitude toward the gospel, including having the same goals and priorities (as Paul) for his use of the gospel:

> Hold to the standard of sound teaching that you have heard from me, in the faith and love that are in Christ Jesus. Guard the good treasure entrusted to you, with the help of the Holy Spirit living in us. (1.13-14)

> Remember Jesus Christ, raised from the dead, a descendant of David—that is my gospel... (2.8)

> Do your best to present yourself to God as one approved by him, a worker who has no need to be ashamed, rightly explaining the word of truth. (2.15)

---

11. The structure is διά + genitive, a genitive of means/agency: thus the gift comes *through* the laying on of hands (cf. 1 Tim. 4.14, where the gift is given *through* [διά] prophecy *accompanied by* [μετά] the laying on of hands by the elders).

> But as for you, continue in what you have learned and firmly believed, knowing from whom you learned it, and how from childhood you have known the sacred writings that are able to instruct you for salvation through faith in Christ Jesus. All scripture is inspired by God and is useful for teaching, for reproof, for correction, and for training in righteousness, so that everyone who belongs to God may be proficient, equipped for every good work. (3.14-17)

This fourth passage requires some comment. 'Knowing from whom you learned (ἔμαθες) it' refers to Paul (among others), making ἔμαθες a succession term for Timothy's relationship to Paul.[12] Paul here relates his gospel to the Old Testament ('the sacred writings', 'all scripture') and ties them together in the same way as in 1 Tim. 1.8-11. For Timothy properly to handle the gospel, he must also properly view and use the law (again, cf. 1 Tim. 1.8-11). This means holding to the gospel Paul taught him and committed to him,[13] which is the realization of the Old Testament truths he learned from childhood. It also means viewing and using and depending on scripture and gospel in the same ways Paul views and uses and depends on them: they are 'useful for teaching, for reproof, for correction, and for training in righteousness, so that everyone who belongs to God may be proficient, equipped for every good work'. This passage should be taken as a direct response to misuse of the scriptures by the false teachers.[14] Timothy knows from whom he heard these things—the integrity of the message and the integrity of the messenger are inextricably linked.

Timothy's faithful handling of the gospel also includes passing it on to others who will handle it faithfully, and then themselves pass it on. Note:

> What you have heard from me through many witnesses entrust to faithful people who will be able to teach others as well. (2.2)

This passage refers to a multi-generational succession of tradition. In the context of the whole letter, I find here a reference to a sequence of four exchanges in a succession of tradition: Christ to Paul, Paul to Timothy, Timothy to the faithful men, and the faithful men to others. Thus the gospel is perpetuated. Note also 2.14:

---

12. Johnson, *First and Second Letters to Timothy*, p. 419, notes how scribes changed the plural τίνων to the singular τίνος, emphasizing the reference to Paul.
13. Marshall, *Pastoral Epistles*, p. 787, asserts that ἐν οἷς (translated in the NRSV as 'in what') refers to the παραθήκη, which 'has not only been taught to Timothy, it has also been committed to him as a sacred trust, so that he can then pass it on to others unchanged'. Dibelius and Conzelmann, *Pastoral Epistles*, p. 119, and Johnson, *First and Second Letters to Timothy*, p. 419, also see this verse as a command to be faithful to the Pauline tradition, as opposed to those who are 'progressing'.
14. Marshall, *Pastoral Epistles*, pp. 789-90; Johnson, *First and Second Letters to Timothy*, pp. 419-20.

5. Second Timothy and Titus

> Remind them of this, and warn them before God that they are to avoid wrangling over words, which does no good but only ruins those who are listening.

To whom is Timothy to deliver the warning of 2.14? At first glance, it might appear that Paul is calling Timothy to admonish officially ('before God') the false teachers, but they do not appear in the passage until 2.17. In context, the warning must be aimed at Timothy's church, particularly his own successors (2.2).[15] Thus, part of Timothy's passing the gospel on to them is him warning them about their own demeanor/conduct/character, and how it will affect their hearers.[16]

Second, Paul prescribes the character required of his successor. As in 1 Timothy, Paul exercises great authority over Timothy's conduct. I discuss several such passages below, under Timothy's vocation, and so I will only briefly mention them here.

In 2.4-7, Paul calls Timothy to live by the rules endemic to his vocation: just as soldiers do not involve themselves in civilian affairs, so ministers of the gospel must separate themselves from everyday concerns and priorities so as to serve their calling. In 2.15-18 and 2.20-26 (see also 4.5), Paul warns Timothy away from careless talk and ignoble conduct, noting the dangers they present to the Church (rather than to Timothy personally).

In three passages, Paul bequeaths specific tasks to Timothy. The first two, 2.2 and 2.14, are mentioned above. The third is 4.1-2, 5, which outlines both Timothy's tasks *and* character:

> In the presence of God and of Christ Jesus, who is to judge the living and the dead, and in view of his appearing and his kingdom, I solemnly urge you: proclaim the message; be persistent whether the time is favorable or unfavorable; convince, rebuke, and encourage, with the utmost patience in teaching...
> As for you, always be sober, endure suffering, do the work of an evangelist, carry out your ministry fully. (4.1-2, 5)

With regard to this passage, note first the solemn tone of this charge, which echoes the tone and weight and force of 1 Tim. 6.13-15. Note second the

---

15. So Knight, *Pastoral Epistles*, pp. 409-10. R. Collins, *1 & 2 Timothy and Titus*, p. 232; Marshall, *Pastoral Epistles*, pp. 745-46; and Dibelius and Conzelmann, *Pastoral Epistles*, p. 110, see this as a general warning to Timothy's church. Michael Prior, *Paul the Letter-Writer and the Second Letter to Timothy* (JSNTSup, 23; Sheffield: JSOT Press, 1989), pp. 158-60, and Johnson, *First and Second Letters to Timothy*, p. 383, read this verse as an instruction for Timothy to keep the instructions always in his *own* mind—thus 'Keep these instructions foremost in your mind as you bear witness (διαμαρτυρόμενος) in the presence of God', rather than 'Remind them of this, and warn them (διαμαρτυρόμενος) before God'.

16. Thus, in comparing 1 Timothy with 2 Timothy, I note that in 2 Timothy there is no mention of confronting or commanding false teachers, whereas such confronting/commanding was central to 1 Timothy.

parallels between Paul's description of his own tasks in 1.11 and Timothy's tasks here. Paul here calls Timothy to reproduce important parts of his (i.e. Paul's) own ministry.

Third, Paul calls his successor to share in his sufferings. I will discuss this more fully below, under Timothy's vocation. Suffice it here to note that in 1.8; 2.3, 12; 3.12, and 4.5, Paul makes it clear that succeeding him in ministry means joining/succeeding him in his sufferings.

Fourth, Paul warns his successor of incipient dangers to the Church. In 3.1-9, 12-13, and 4.3-4, Paul warns Timothy of dangers that await the Church, threats both from within (from false teachers) and from without (persecution). Again, I will discuss these passages more fully below, under Timothy's vocation.

Paul Suffers for the Gospel

Several passages note the fact of Paul's suffering on behalf of/in service of the gospel. Witness:

> Do not be ashamed, then, of the testimony about our Lord or of me his prisoner, but join with me in suffering for the gospel (συγκακοπάθησον τῷ εὐαγγελίῳ)[17]... (1.8)

> You are aware that all who are in Asia have turned away from me... (1.15)

> Do your best to come to me soon, for Demas, in love with this present world, has deserted me and gone to Thessalonica. (4.9-10)

> Alexander the coppersmith did me great harm; the Lord will pay him back for his deeds. You also must beware of him, for he strongly opposed our message. (4.14-15)

Other passages build on the fact of Paul's suffering by noting that, in spite of the hardship, God is achieving his purposes for the Church through Paul in the midst of the suffering:

> For this gospel (εἰς ὅ) I was appointed a preacher and apostle and teacher, and therefore I suffer as I do. But I am not ashamed, for I know whom I have believed, and I am sure that he is able to guard until that Day what has been entrusted (παραθήκη) to me. (1.11-12 [RSV translation])

> Remember Jesus Christ, raised from the dead, a descendant of David—that is my gospel, for which (ἐν ᾧ)[18] I suffer hardship, even to the point of being chained like a criminal. But the word of God is not chained. Therefore I endure everything for the sake of the elect (διὰ τοὺς ἐκλεκτούς), so that they may also obtain the salvation that is in Christ Jesus, with eternal glory. (2.8-10)

---

17. Dative of advantage without a preposition, 'for the benefit of/in service of the gospel'.

18. Another dative of advantage.

In both passages, Paul links his suffering to his service of the gospel. In the second, he even notes that he suffers for the benefit of the elect (i.e. the elect gentiles who will hear the gospel through his ministry, of which suffering persecution plays a significant part). Paul states that he is not ashamed (of the gospel? or of his sufferings?) because God will guard/keep effective and vital the παραθήκη which was entrusted to Paul. Further: even though he is chained, the word of God is not—it continues to work salvation for the hearers and have its effect, in spite of (or even because of) his chains.[19] Paul need not be ashamed of his persecution, because even the persecution serves only to further the cause of Christ. Paul may be suffering, but there is no indication that God has let him down.[20]

Paul's attitude toward persecution is also at the center of passages that focus on the personal outcome of his sufferings. Note:

> If we endure, we will also reign with him... (2.12)

> Now you have observed my teaching, my conduct, my aim in life, my faith, my patience, my love, my steadfastness, my persecutions and suffering the things that happened to me in Antioch, Iconium, and Lystra. What persecutions I endured! Yet the Lord rescued me from all of them. Indeed, all who want to live a godly life in Christ Jesus will be persecuted. (3.10-12)

> As for me, I am already being poured out as a libation, and the time of my departure has come. I have fought the good fight, I have finished the race, I have kept the faith. From now on there is reserved for me the crown of righteousness, which the Lord, the righteous judge, will give me on that day, and not only to me but also to all who have longed for his appearing. (4.6-8)

> At my first defense no one came to my support, but all deserted me. May it not be counted against them! But the Lord stood by me and gave me strength, so that through me the message might be fully proclaimed and all the Gentiles might hear it. So I was rescued from the lion's mouth. The Lord will rescue me from every evil attack and save me for his heavenly kingdom. (4.16-18)

In these verses, note first how Paul's life in the face of persecution is held up as ongoing demonstration of how God delivers his people when they face suffering. Paul is himself an example of personal faithfulness under persecution. All who are faithful will be persecuted—such suffering is a badge of authenticity for a minister of the gospel. Note second that Paul's life has shown that God can further the gospel by delivering his people *from* suffering (3.10-12; 4.16-18). Paul's life will now show that God can further the gospel by delivering his people *through* suffering (i.e. through righteous death) (2.12; 4.6-8). Thus Paul is here shown in terms of the righteous one

---

19. Brox, *Pastoralbriefe*, p. 243.
20. Marshall, *Pastoral Epistles*, p. 709.

who suffers on behalf of others (cf. Col. 1.24).[21] Note third how Paul looks forward, through the suffering, to an eternal crown/reward which makes the suffering he faces pale in comparison.

Paul as Christ's Successor in 2 Timothy
In this first section, I have shown the following:
1. That the authorial audience would have inferred that Paul was Christ's successor as keeper of the gospel (1.11-12).
2. That because of this succession, Paul has a particular vocation:
   a. He fights for orthodoxy. Because of succession, Paul has authority over the teaching in his churches.
      i. His life and teaching activity serve as an example for his followers to emulate (1.11, 13; 3.10-11; 4.6-7).
      ii. He endorses the proper content of teaching (1.9b-10; 2.2, 8, 11-13; 3.10, 16-17).
      iii. He establishes an empowered, equipped, faithful successor, who will carry on the banner of his (i.e. Paul's) teaching in his absence (1.6-7). As part of establishing this successor:
         (a) Paul dictates his successor's attitude toward and handling of the gospel (1.13-14; 2.2, 8, 14, 15; 3.14-17).
         (b) Paul prescribes the character required of his successor (2.4-7; 4.1-5).
         (c) Paul calls his successor to share in his sufferings (1.8; 2.3, 12; 3.12; 4.5).
         (d) Paul warns his successor of incipient dangers to the Church (3.1-9, 12-13; 4.3-4).
   b. Paul suffers on behalf of the gospel (1.8, 15; 4.9-10, 14-15).
      i. In spite of the suffering, God achieves his purposes for the Church through Paul (1.11-12; 2.8-10).
      ii. Paul knows that his sufferings are not the end of the story—a great reward awaits him if he is faithful (2.12; 3.10-12; 4.6-8, 16-18).

Compare the above outline with the similar outline of Paul's vocation in 1 Timothy (p. 133 above). There are similarities: Christ bequeaths the gospel into Paul's care so that it will be preserved and perpetuated. This bequest is again the starting point for the letter—all that Paul does, all that he wants to

---

21. Marshall, *Pastoral Epistles*, p. 785, notes that Paul here alludes to himself as 'the righteous sufferer who is preserved by God, although paradoxically he also knows that death will come'. See also R. Collins, *1 & 2 Timothy and Titus*, p. 260. Prior, *Letter-Writer*, pp. 93-94, argues that 4.6 is *not* a reference to Paul's impending death: see Marshall's response, *Pastoral Epistles*, pp. 805-806.

pass on, is predicated on the fact that he received this bequest from Christ, though here it is much less prominent, not as central. Paul's care of the gospel requires him to pass authority and task on to Timothy.

At the same time, the description of Paul's succession from Christ and his resulting vocation in 2 Timothy is much more narrow in focus. The description centers on Paul's sufferings (thus his approaching death) and his interactions with Timothy, specifically the succession that is taking place between Paul and Timothy (which will itself lead Timothy to his own sufferings—see 3.12; cf. Heb. 13.23). As with 1 Timothy, Paul is acting to keep the gospel pure and effective, but here these actions center on passing authority on to his successor. Everything Paul says and does in this letter is said/done with an eye toward passing it on to Timothy. Paul's career is not an independent thing, functioning on its own as in 1 Timothy. Here, Paul's career is at an end, and the letter centers on Paul passing this παραθήκη on to his successor.

How would the authorial audience have understood this succession from Christ to Paul to function? This succession, as with the succession between Christ and Paul in 1 Timothy, is a succession of tradition. Any tasks involved are secondary, the outgrowth of that bequest.

I can illustrate the exchanges thus:

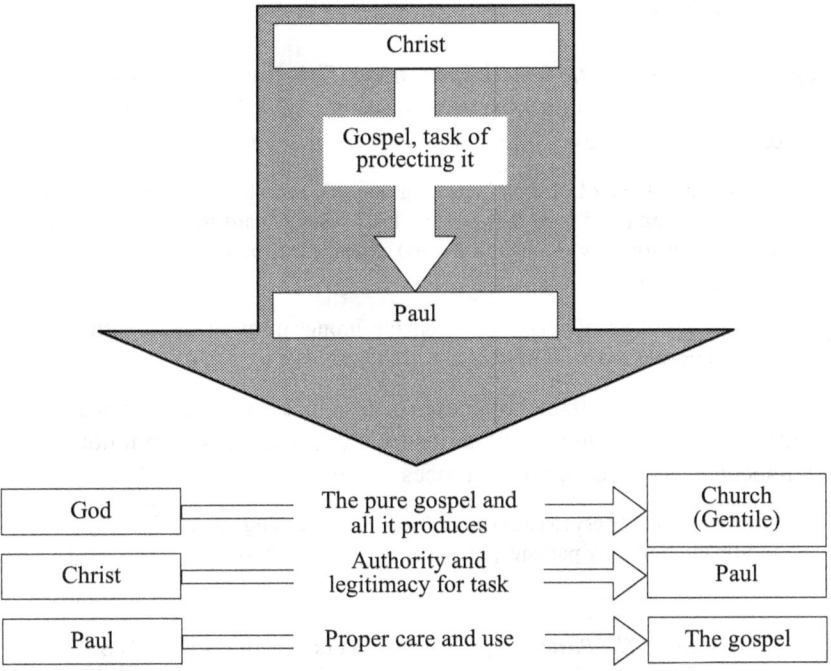

Figure 67. *The Functions of the Succession from Christ to Paul in 2 Timothy*

What does this succession achieve? First, as with Paul's succession from Christ in 1 Timothy, this succession legitimates Paul, insofar as it enables him to prepare a successor and pass the care of the tradition (not just a limited set of tasks) on to him. Thus the succession from Christ to Paul in 2 Timothy (as in 1 Timothy) legitimates Paul as the keeper of the gospel in Christ's absence.

Second, the gospel is passed from Christ to Paul so that it will continue to be vital and pure and effective. Paul's work and example, and now even his sufferings and preparation for his successor, all serve to advance the cause of the true gospel. Because of the succession, the gospel continues to be used properly and cared for in Christ's absence. Thus succession of tradition here ensures continued institutional vitality.

3. Evidence of Succession from Paul to Timothy (and on to the Faithful) in 2 Timothy

Above, I showed that the succession from Christ to Paul is foundational for understanding 2 Timothy. As with 1 Timothy, 2 Timothy begins with succession from Paul to Christ but centers on a second exchange, succession from Paul to Timothy.

Terms from the semantic field of succession. Timothy's relationship to Paul is described as a succession in several passages in 2 Timothy, using known succession terminology. Note:

> Hold to the standard of sound teaching that you have heard (ἤκουσας) from me, in the faith and love that are in Christ Jesus. Guard the good treasure entrusted to you (τὴν καλὴν παραθήκην), with the help of the Holy Spirit living in us. (1.13-14)

> What you have heard (ἃ ἤκουσας) from me through many witnesses entrust to faithful people who will be able to teach others as well. (2.2)

In the context established by these succession terms, the ancient audience would have heard synonymous terms (related to succession but not succession-specific) as succession references. Note:

> Now you have observed (παρηκολούθησας) my teaching, my conduct, my aim in life, my faith, my patience, my love, my steadfastness... (3.10)[22]

---

22. B.S. Easton, *The Pastoral Epistles* (New York: Charles Scribner's Sons, 1947), p. 66, asserts that παρακολουθέω refers to Timothy imitating Paul. Marshall, *Pastoral Epistles*, p. 783, sees the verb in a more general way, in the sense of 'observing' (so also R. Collins, *1 & 2 Timothy and Titus*, p. 257). Johnson, *First and Second Letters to Timothy*, p. 416, says that 'the motif of imitation lies just below the surface'.

> But as for you, continue in what you have learned (ἔμαθες) and firmly believed,[23] knowing from whom you learned (ἔμαθες) it. (3.14)

> In the presence of God and of Christ Jesus, who is to judge the living and the dead, and in view of his appearing and his kingdom, I solemnly urge you (διαμαρτύρομαι): proclaim the message; be persistent whether the time is favorable or unfavorable; convince, rebuke, and encourage, with the utmost patience in teaching. (4.1-2)[24]

I consider the semantic evidence of succession between Paul and Timothy to be prominent.

Phenomena from the conceptual field of succession. I find two types of conceptual evidence that would have led the ancient audience to conclude that Timothy was Paul's successor. They would have concluded this first on the basis of the parallels between Paul and Timothy which the letter explicitly draws, and second on the basis of the narrative of Paul and Timothy's relationship that the letter sketches.

In regard to the parallels explicitly drawn between Paul and Timothy, note that both share a heritage of faith (Paul's Jewish heritage in 1.2-3, Timothy's Jewish heritage in 1.5); both have/will have successors (Paul's in 1.6, 14; Timothy's in 2.2, etc.); both are empowered by God (1.7); both are saved and called to a common calling (1.9); both are indwelt by the same Spirit (1.14); both have the same vocations (Paul's in 1.11, Timothy's in 4.2-5); both will share in suffering for a common gospel (1.8; 2.3; 3.12; 4.5); both will be rewarded for enduring the suffering (2.12; 4.6-8); and both will face the same opponents (4.14).

In regard to the narrative of the relationship, note first that in 1.6-7, Paul describes himself personally 'ordaining' Timothy:

> I remind you to rekindle the gift of God that is within you through the laying on of my hands; for God did not give us a spirit of cowardice, but rather a spirit of power and of love and of self-discipline.

---

23. Might ἐπιστώθης (from πιστόω, not πιστεύω) also function as a succession term, as does ἐπιστεύθην (also an aorist passive indicative) in 1 Tim. 1.11? Rudolf Bultmann, 'πιστόω', in *TDNT*, VI, pp. 178-79, asserts that πιστόω carries the force of making someone reliable, binding someone 'by an oath, contract, pledge', so that they can be trusted. Further study of this term is needed.

24. Marshall, *Pastoral Epistles*, p. 797, sees 4.1-5 as an ordination charge to Timothy: see also Spicq, *Epîtres*, p. 798. R. Collins, *1 & 2 Timothy and Titus*, pp. 267-68, refers here to Timothy's succession to Paul's 'ministry of evangelization and teaching', and notes that Timothy is to imitate Paul, 'preach as Paul preached...expect suffering as Paul suffered'. R. Collins, *1 & 2 Timothy and Titus*, p. 274, refers to succession in the tasks of ministry, '"fulfill the ministry" connotes the idea of succession of ministry'. See also Marshall, *Pastoral Epistles*, p. 804; Johnson, *First and Second Letters to Timothy*, p. 433.

This ordination differs from the one mentioned in 1 Tim. 4.14. In 2 Timothy, the ordination is personal and private, and the spiritual gift in question comes through the laying-on of Paul's hands. Further, Timothy's power and σωφροσύνη depend on the gift—Paul is an agent of the Spirit's empowering Timothy for ministry. The two letters may refer to different ordination ceremonies, or they may refer to differing aspects of a single ceremony.[25]

Note second the allusion to Paul in 2.4: 'No one serving in the army gets entangled in everyday affairs; the soldier's aim is to please the enlisting officer'. Paul is the one who enlists Timothy, Timothy is beholden to him.

Note third how Paul describes his and Timothy's relationship when calling Timothy faithfully to handle what has been bequeathed to him:

> What you have heard from me through many witnesses entrust to faithful people who will be able to teach others as well. (2.2)

> Continue in what you have learned and firmly believed, knowing from whom you learned it. (3.14)

Paul in these passages describes his relationship with Timothy in terms of a teacher and a close disciple. In the ancient audience's milieu, succession was a prominent feature of this type of relationship, the language given to succession references and inferences.

Fourth, notice how Paul's closing remarks imply a deep personal relationship between Timothy and himself:

> Do your best to come to me soon, for Demas, in love with this present world, has deserted me and gone to Thessalonica; Crescens has gone to Galatia, Titus to Dalmatia. Only Luke is with me. Get Mark and bring him with you, for he is useful in my ministry. I have sent Tychicus to Ephesus. When you come, bring the cloak that I left with Carpus at Troas, also the books, and above all the parchments. (4.9-13)

In this passage, Paul describes Timothy in terms of his personal משרת, his personal servant. Just as Joshua ministered personally to Moses and served his personal needs, just as Elisha ministered to Elijah and served his personal needs, so also Timothy to Paul.[26]

---

25. Gordon D. Fee, *God's Empowering Presence: The Holy Spirit in the Letters of Paul* (Peabody, MA: Hendrickson, 1994), pp. 785-89, sees two separate events. Marshall, *Pastoral Epistles*, pp. 697-98 (after discussing the differences), and R. Collins, *1 & 2 Timothy and Titus*, p. 199, see a single event; Johnson, *First and Second Letters to Timothy*, p. 345, wavers. Whether a single event or two events are in view, the differences in the description in 2 Timothy point to the heightened sense of succession here, in which more than limited authority for a single task passes from Paul to Timothy. See also Wolter, *Paulustradition*, pp. 218-22, and M. Warkentin, *Ordination—A Biblical-Historical View* (Grand Rapids: Eerdmans, 1982), pp. 136-52.

26. See above, pp. 62-64, regarding Joshua and Moses, and pp. 70-72, regarding Elisha and Elijah. See Marshall, *Pastoral Epistles*, pp. 812-13, *contra* V. Hasler, *Die Briefe an*

I consider the conceptual evidence of succession between Paul and Timothy in 2 Timothy to be prominent.

Standard elements of a Mediterranean succession story. Are the three standard elements of a Mediterranean succession story present? Note first the naming of what is passed on—the παραθήκη (1.14). Second, the symbolic act accompanying the succession is present in the letter itself (i.e. the letter serves the purpose of a commissioning speech, particularly the solemn charge in 4.1) and the laying-on of hands in 1.6. Third, the aforementioned parallels between Paul and Timothy and the succession-laden narrative description of Timothy's relationship to Paul that the ancient audience would have heard behind the letter confirm that succession has taken place. Thus I consider all three standard elements of a Mediterranean succession story to be present, and the evidence of succession between Paul and Timothy to be prominent.

Summary. In the light of the conceptual evidence, the terms from the semantic field of succession, and the presence of all three standard components of an ancient Mediterranean succession story, I conclude that the ancient audience would clearly have understood Timothy to be Paul's successor.

4. *The Function of the Succession from Paul to Timothy (and on to the Faithful)*

I have already shown that both Paul and Timothy's callings to ministry in 1 Timothy would have been understood by the ancient audience in terms of succession. Above, I also showed the same for Paul's calling to ministry in 2 Timothy. So also for Timothy's calling in 2 Timothy—the ancient audience would have understood Timothy's call to ministry, as described here, to be a succession from Paul. Note:

> For this reason I remind you to rekindle the gift of God that is within you through the laying on of my hands; for God did not give us a spirit of cowardice, but rather a spirit of power and of love and of self-discipline.
> Do not be ashamed, then, of the testimony about our Lord or of me his prisoner, but join with me in suffering for the gospel, relying on the power of God, who saved us and called us with a holy calling, not according to our works but according to his own purpose and grace. (1.6-9)

The letter's first mention of Timothy's ministry is in terms of his succession from Paul—he is set apart by Paul through personal 'ordination'. And as

---

Timotheus und Titus (Zürich: Theologischer Verlag, 1978), pp. 78-79, who suggests that 4.9-13 was invented by the pseudepigrapher to develop a succession between Paul and Timothy.

noted above, the ordination imparted spiritual gifting, and a spirit 'of power and love and self-discipline' to Timothy. Thus Timothy is empowered for his task through his succession from Paul.[27] Further, Timothy suffers together with Paul, and together with Paul is called to a holy calling according to God's 'purpose and grace'. Thus I see that Timothy's ministry is inextricably interwoven with Paul's. Paul's ministry in 1 Timothy may have stood on its own, but in 2 Timothy Paul's ministry and Timothy's ministry are interdependent. Paul faces death, and must have a successor if his ministry is to continue. Timothy must have this bequest from Paul, for it is as Paul's successor that he has a call to preserve, promote, and perpetuate the work of the gospel—a calling which he inherited from his predecessor. Again, this succession of tradition (and the tasks that accompany the bequest) defines Timothy's vocation in 2 Timothy, dictating his actions and giving him authority to perform them.

Second Timothy's statements regarding Timothy's vocation can be grouped under four general headings. Below I analyze what each says about his actions and authority. The headings are: Timothy conducts himself as a proper successor to Paul's ministry, Timothy safeguards his churches, Timothy suffers for the gospel, and Timothy fights for orthodoxy.

Timothy Conducts Himself as a Proper Successor to Paul's Ministry
Several passages refer to Timothy's conduct in a general way, 1.8 ('Do not be ashamed then of testifying to our Lord' [RSV translation]) and 2.1 ('Be strong in the grace that is in Christ Jesus') among them. In the same vein, note also:

> Share in suffering like a good soldier of Christ Jesus. No one serving in the army gets entangled in everyday affairs; the soldier's aim is to please the enlisting officer. And in the case of an athlete, no one is crowned without competing according to the rules. It is the farmer who does the work who ought to have the first share of the crops. Think over what I say, for the Lord will give you understanding in all things. (2.4-7)

The common theme running through these verses is that Timothy, while living out his vocation, must live by the rules endemic to that vocation. Ministry is a high calling. Just as soldiers do not involve themselves in civilian affairs but separate themselves from civilian concerns because of their calling, so also the minister of the gospel. Part of the calling of the gospel is suffering. Ministers who accept/embrace this calling (instead of running from it)

---

27. So Kelly, *A Commentary*, p. 159; Oberlinner, *Pastoralbriefe*, pp. 31-32; R. Collins, *1 & 2 Timothy and Titus*, p. 200. Marshall, *Pastoral Epistles*, p. 699 takes the reference to be to the general gifting of spiritual power, made available to all believers—but compare p. 697. Johnson, *First and Second Letters to Timothy*, p. 344, takes χάρισμα τοῦ θεοῦ to be a subjective genitive, 'the gift that God gave you through the laying on of my hands'.

will be rewarded. Paul has embraced the cost of his high calling, and expects Timothy to do the same.[28]

Other passages focus on the goal of appropriate conduct in Timothy's ministry:

> Remind them of this, and warn them before God that they are to avoid wrangling over words, which does no good but only ruins those who are listening. Do your best to present yourself to God as one approved by him, a worker who has no need to be ashamed, rightly explaining the word of truth. Avoid profane chatter, for it will lead people into more and more impiety, and their talk will spread like gangrene. (2.14-17a)

Here, appropriate conduct includes the proper passing on/explanation of the gospel. It also includes avoiding empty, foolish talk, because such chattering has effects detrimental to the Church. The point of v. 14 ('avoid wrangling over words') is not that Timothy cannot discuss or try to persuade others of the truth of the Pauline gospel, but rather that he can never '[descend] to their level':[29]

> In a large house there are utensils not only of gold and silver but also of wood and clay, some for special use, some for ordinary. All who cleanse themselves of the things I have mentioned will become special utensils, dedicated and useful to the owner of the house, ready for every good work. Shun youthful passions and pursue righteousness, faith, love, and peace, along with those who call on the Lord from a pure heart. Have nothing to do with stupid and senseless controversies; you know that they breed quarrels. And the Lord's servant must not be quarrelsome but kindly to everyone, an apt teacher, patient, correcting opponents with gentleness. God may perhaps grant that they will repent and come to know the truth, and that they may escape from the snare of the devil, having been held captive by him to do his will. (2.20-26)

Here, appropriateness means purifying oneself from ignoble things (or impure people, the false teachers),[30] whatever is not in keeping with the calling and purpose of ministry. This includes the manner in which Timothy responds to his opponents: rather than with anger or harshness, he is to correct them with gentleness, patience, and kindness. He is to respond in this way in hopes that his winsome conduct will gain a hearing for the true gospel when they see their error, so that even they can be restored (cf. 1 Tim. 1.20).[31] Noble

---

28. Marshall, *Pastoral Epistles*, p. 722, asserts that the common thread is 'singlemindedness and devotion to duty'. Johnson, *First and Second Letters to Timothy*, pp. 368-69, draws parallels between this passage and passages from Philippians.

29. Marshall, *Pastoral Epistles*, p. 746.

30. Johnson, *First and Second Letters to Timothy*, p. 388, and Marshall, *Pastoral Epistles*, p. 762, see reference to the false teachers here—Timothy is to avoid them and separate himself from them.

31. Marshall, *Pastoral Epistles*, p. 767; R. Collins, *1 & 2 Timothy and Titus*, p. 244.

purposes—and the purpose of the gospel is the most noble of all—require noble character and spotless conduct.

Timothy Safeguards his Churches

As Paul's successor in care of the gospel, Timothy must safeguard his churches (which are founded on and depend upon that gospel) from great dangers from outside the church and greater dangers from inside. Note:

> You must understand this, that in the last days distressing times will come. For people will be lovers of themselves, lovers of money, boasters, arrogant, abusive, disobedient to their parents, ungrateful, unholy, inhuman, implacable, slanderers, profligates, brutes, haters of good, treacherous, reckless, swollen with conceit, lovers of pleasure rather than lovers of God, holding to the outward form of godliness but denying its power. Avoid them! For among them are those who make their way into households and captivate silly women, overwhelmed by their sins and swayed by all kinds of desires, who are always being instructed and can never arrive at a knowledge of the truth. As Jannes and Jambres opposed Moses, so these people, of corrupt mind and counterfeit faith, also oppose the truth. But they will not make much progress, because, as in the case of those two men, their folly will become plain to everyone...
>
> ...all who want to live a godly life in Christ Jesus will be persecuted. But wicked people and impostors will go from bad to worse, deceiving others and being deceived. (3.1-9, 12b-13)

Paul warns Timothy that dangerous people (cf. the 'savage wolves' of Acts 20.29) are coming to attack the church from within. Such people are corrupt; they have the outward appearance of faith and piety but not the inward reality.[32] Timothy must be discerning, mark such people and watch out for them and avoid being associated with them. Even worse: as these dangerous and deceptive people slash and burn their way through the Church, persecution from the outside will come against the true ministers of Christ. Such persecution is a badge of the authenticity of their faith and ministry.

Another danger Timothy must face is the possibility that the faithful will drift into apostasy:

> For the time is coming when people will not put up with sound doctrine, but having itching ears, they will accumulate for themselves teachers to suit their own desires, and will turn away from listening to the truth and wander away to myths. (4.3-4)

---

32. For the possibility that μόρφωσιν in 3.5 refers to training or education (i.e. 'they possess the form [i.e. they have been trained in] godliness, but they do not know its power'), see W. Pöhlmann, 'μορφόω', in *EDNT*, II, pp. 443-44. Pöhlmann follows Adolf Schlatter, *Romans: The Righteousness of God* (trans. Siegfried Schatzmann; Peabody, MA: Hendrickson, 1995), pp. 69-75, on μορφόω in Rom. 2.20, and extends that understanding to μορφόω here. By his hypothesis, the point would not be any contrast between internal reality and external appearance.

5. Second Timothy and Titus

In the face of the persecution and internal division of 3.1-13, weak and immature believers (and even some believers who should not be weak or immature) will be tempted to take the path of least resistance. They will find the true Pauline gospel and the life of faith for which it calls too difficult. As a result, they will reject the truth and its teaching[33] and will look for and find teachers (from among the imposters of 3.13) who will tell them what they want to hear, weakening and adulterating the gospel that Christ gave to Paul and Paul now gives to Timothy.[34] Timothy must be on guard against this weakening tendency, and encourage and protect his churches both from weariness with truth and from deceptive teachers. He must also keep preaching the true gospel: 'Proclamation of the truth is all the more necessary when it is being rejected and the temptation is to fall in with the prevailing mood'.[35]

Timothy Suffers for the Gospel
In addition to the general applicability of some of Paul's statements about suffering dealt with above, note the following:

> Share in suffering like a good soldier of Christ Jesus. (2.3)

> If we endure, we will also reign with him… (2.12)

These passages indicate that, as with Paul's ministry, Timothy's ministry will involve suffering on behalf of the gospel.[36] Further, since Timothy is Paul's successor, he will share Paul's sufferings and enemies. Note:

> Do not be ashamed, then, of the testimony about our Lord or of me his prisoner, but join with me in suffering for the gospel, relying on the power of God. (1.8)

> As for you, always be sober, endure suffering… (4.5)

> Alexander the coppersmith did me great harm; the Lord will pay him back for his deeds. You also must beware of him, for he strongly opposed our message. (4.14-15)

But Timothy will not only share in Paul's sufferings—he and Paul will also receive the same reward when their sufferings have run their course:

> I have fought the good fight, I have finished the race, I have kept the faith. From now on there is reserved for me the crown of righteousness, which the Lord, the righteous judge, will give me on that day, and not only to me but also to all who have longed for his appearing. (4.7-8)

---

33. Marshall, *Pastoral Epistles*, p. 802, sees ὑγιαίνουσα διδασκαλία as a reference to the teachers of the true gospel, who in this text are being rejected in favor of false teaching.

34. Easton, *Epistles*, p. 69, notes that here those who are 'already corrupted [see 3.6] seek out teachers who will encourage them in evil'.

35. Marshall, *Pastoral Epistles*, p. 801.

36. Marshall, *Pastoral Epistles*, p. 804.

Note the parallels between Paul's sufferings and Timothy's sufferings as his successor. Both suffer for the sake of the gospel (1.8; 2.3). They face the same enemies (4.14-15). And they receive the same reward at the end of their labors (4.7-8).

Timothy Fights for Orthodoxy
Timothy fights for orthodoxy by carrying out his assigned tasks. Timothy's vocation centers around the gospel that Paul has passed onto him and the tasks that come with this bequest:

> Guard the good treasure (παραθήκη) entrusted to you, with the help of the Holy Spirit living in us. (1.14)

As noted above, this παραθήκη is to be identified with the παραθήκη that Paul received as a bequest in his succession from Christ (1.12). Timothy's ministry revolves around his use of and care of this deposit/bequest:

> In the presence of God and of Christ Jesus, who is to judge the living and the dead, and in view of his appearing and his kingdom, I solemnly urge you: proclaim the message; be persistent whether the time is favorable or unfavorable; convince, rebuke, and encourage, with the utmost patience in teaching... As for you, always be sober, endure suffering, do the work of an evangelist, carry out your ministry fully. (4.1-2, 5)

This charge closes the *inclusio* that began with Timothy's 'ordination' at Paul's hands in 1.6, just as the charge to Timothy in 1 Tim. 6.13-21 closed the *inclusio* that began with Paul's commissioning of Timothy in 1 Tim. 1.3. Timothy is to finish the work that Paul gave him: preaching, teaching, suffering for Christ. By these activities, Timothy preserves and protects and perpetuates the gospel that Paul bequeathed to him. (Note also the discussion of 2.14 above, p. 161.)

Timothy fights for orthodoxy by his dependence on and use of Paul's gospel. Note first that Timothy imitates the content/methods of Paul's teaching. In his ministry, Timothy must follow Paul's example as a teacher:

> Hold to the standard of sound teaching that you have heard from me, in the faith and love that are in Christ Jesus. (1.13)

> Remember Jesus Christ, raised from the dead, a descendant of David—that is my gospel. (2.8)

Second, Timothy must pass Paul's gospel on to his (Timothy's) successors without changing it. Note:

> You then, my child, be strong in the grace that is in Christ Jesus; and what you have heard from me through many witnesses entrust to faithful people who will be able to teach others as well. (2.1-2)

As already noted, this passage outlines a multi-generational succession of tradition: Paul receives the παραθήκη from Christ, then passes it on to Timothy, then Timothy passes it on (παράθου—cognate of παραθήκη, and the same word as used in 1 Tim. 1.18 to refer to Paul's bequeathing the command to Timothy there) to the 'faithful people' who, in turn, teach it to others. Note that this is not a succession of office,[37] but of tradition, and thus *not* parallel to 1 Clement 42, which does refer to the passing on of offices. Here, the focus is on the vitality of the tradition, making sure that the proper teaching of the true gospel continues and is ubiquitous.[38]

In this regard, note also 2.15: 'Do your best to present yourself to God as one approved by him, a worker who has no need to be ashamed, rightly explaining (ὀρθοτομοῦντα) the word of truth'. In context, BDAG translates the phrase ὀρθοτομοῦντα τὸν λόγον τῆς ἀληθείας as 'guide the word of truth along a straight path without being turned aside by wordy debates or impious talk'.[39] Thus here, with reference to the παραθήκη, the force is 'teach and hand on Paul's gospel without deviation or alteration'. Timothy is to teach Paul's gospel as Paul taught it, rather than modifying it or introducing his own interpretations of scripture into it.[40] In the light of 2.2 and 2.15, note how Paul elsewhere in the letter defends the continuing efficacy and power of his gospel and interpretation of scripture:

> Hold to the standard of sound teaching that you have heard from me, in the faith and love that are in Christ Jesus. Guard the good treasure entrusted to you, with the help of the Holy Spirit living in us. (1.13-14)[41]
>
> Remember Jesus Christ, raised from the dead, a descendant of David—that is my gospel. (2.8)
>
> Continue in what you have learned and firmly believed, knowing from whom you learned it, and how from childhood you have known the sacred writings that are able to instruct you for salvation through faith in Christ Jesus. All

---

37. *Contra* Brox, *Pastoralbriefe*, p. 241.

38. Johnson, *First and Second Letters to Timothy*, pp. 370-71, notes that in this text Paul is imprisoned, false teachers abound, and people from Pauline churches are abandoning the true gospel. In the face of these problems, Timothy must establish a group of teachers who will be faithful to the true gospel.

39. 'ὀρθοτομέω', in BDAG, *s.v.*

40. Guthrie, *The Pastoral Epistles*, p. 160. See also Oberlinner, *Pastoralbriefe*, p. 95; R. Collins, *1 & 2 Timothy and Titus*, p. 233; and Marshall, *Pastoral Epistles*, p. 748, who all focus on the teaching aspect.

41. R. Collins, *1 & 2 Timothy and Titus*, p. 215, reads 1.14 ('Guard the good treasure') to refer to 'the proper transmission of the treasure for safekeeping from one generation to the next. Marshall, *Pastoral Epistles*, p. 714, notes the parallel between 1.14 and 1 Tim. 6.20, and concludes that the παραθήκη must be 'the content of the gospel which Paul has committed to Timothy and which he is to pass on faithfully to other teachers'.

scripture is inspired by God and is useful for teaching, for reproof, for correction, and for training in righteousness, so that everyone who belongs to God may be proficient, equipped for every good work. (3.14-17)

Because of the succession of tradition that began with Christ and continues through Paul and Timothy and their successors (and their successors' successors), the tradition remains reliable, powerful, and effective. Paul's gospel (with its use of the Old Testament) has not lost its power or effectiveness, it has not become outdated. It requires no improvements from upstarts. Timothy (and his successors) should keep using it, viewing it, and relying on it in the same way that Paul did.

Timothy as Paul's Successor in 2 Timothy
In this second section, I have shown the following:
1. That the authorial audience would have inferred that Timothy was Paul's successor as keeper of the gospel and the Church founded thereon. This inference would be based on terms and synonyms used in the letter (1.13-14; 2.2; 3.10, 14; 4.1-2) and other conceptual evidence in the letter (1.6-7; 2.2, 4; 3.14; 4.9-11). Of particular note would be the parallels between Paul and Timothy: 1.3 (Paul's heritage of faith) and 1.4 (Timothy's heritage of faith); 1.11-12 (Paul entrusted with the deposit) and 1.14 (Timothy entrusted with the deposit); 1.11 (Paul's appointed tasks) and 4.2-5 (Timothy's appointed tasks); 4.5 (Timothy endures suffering) and 4.6-8 (Paul endures suffering); see also further parallels in 1.7, 8, 9; 2.2, 3; 3.12.
2. That because of this succession, Timothy has a particular vocation (1.6-9).
    a. He conducts himself as a proper successor to Paul's ministry. This includes:
        i. Timothy's general conduct (1.8; 2.1, 4-7).
        ii. The goal of Timothy's conduct—by propriety, to restore the errant and to gain a hearing for the gospel (2.15-17a, 20-26).
    b. He safeguards his churches against dangers from within and without (3.1-9, 12b-13; 4.3-4).
    c. He suffers for the gospel (2.3, 12). As Paul's successor, he shares Paul's sufferings *and* enemies (1.8; 4.5, 7-8).
    d. He fights for orthodoxy.
        i. He fights for orthodoxy by carrying out his assigned tasks (1.14; 4.1-2, 5).
        ii. He fights for orthodoxy by his dependence on/use of Paul's gospel.

(a) Timothy imitates the content and method of Paul's teaching (1.13; 2.8).
(b) Timothy must pass Paul's gospel on to his (Timothy's) successors without making changes to it (1.13-14; 2.1-2, 8, 15; 3.14-17).

Again, comparison with Timothy's vocation as Paul's successor outlined in 1 Timothy reveals similarities and differences. The most significant difference is that, in 1 Timothy, Paul's bequest to Timothy was limited and temporary, a mixture of delegation and succession. The succession was necessitated by a specific problem (false teaching and its effects) facing a specific group of churches. In 2 Timothy, the succession is necessitated by Paul's impending martyrdom. Here we see Paul ordaining and commissioning the one who will replace him as keeper of the pure gospel for the Gentiles. These are the actions of an apostle about to leave the scene, not (as in 1 Timothy) the actions of an apostle who is confident in his ongoing apostolic authority to safeguard his churches.

First, I must again note that the object of the succession has changed. In 1 Timothy, Paul passed on to Timothy a limited set of tasks and the authority required to carry out those tasks. In 2 Timothy, Paul is about to leave the scene, and passes on to Timothy his παραθήκη, the very gospel with which Christ entrusted Paul at his conversion and commissioning. Paul must pass this on to Timothy because his career is at its end.

Paul's career is at an end. If the gospel which was bequeathed to Paul is to continue to be kept pure and effective, Paul must prepare a successor and bequeath to him that gospel. Thus Paul's bequest to Timothy first serves to ensure continued institutional vitality or of effect (the two overlap here), and the gospel continues to properly be cared for. This succession continues past Timothy through the faithful ones to whom Timothy will entrust the gospel, and who will in turn teach others.

Second, by holding up his example as something for Timothy to emulate, Paul attempts by this succession to ensure continuity of manner. Timothy must approach the gospel in a way faithful to his predecessor, and expect his own successors to take the same attitude.

Third, this succession legitimates Timothy as Paul's replacement—no mere delegate or agent this time. This succession, as with the succession between Christ and Paul in 1 Timothy, is a succession of tradition. Any tasks involved are secondary, the outgrowth of that bequest.

I can illustrate the exchanges between Paul and Timothy (and the faithful) thus:

178   *Leadership Succession in the World of the Pauline Circle*

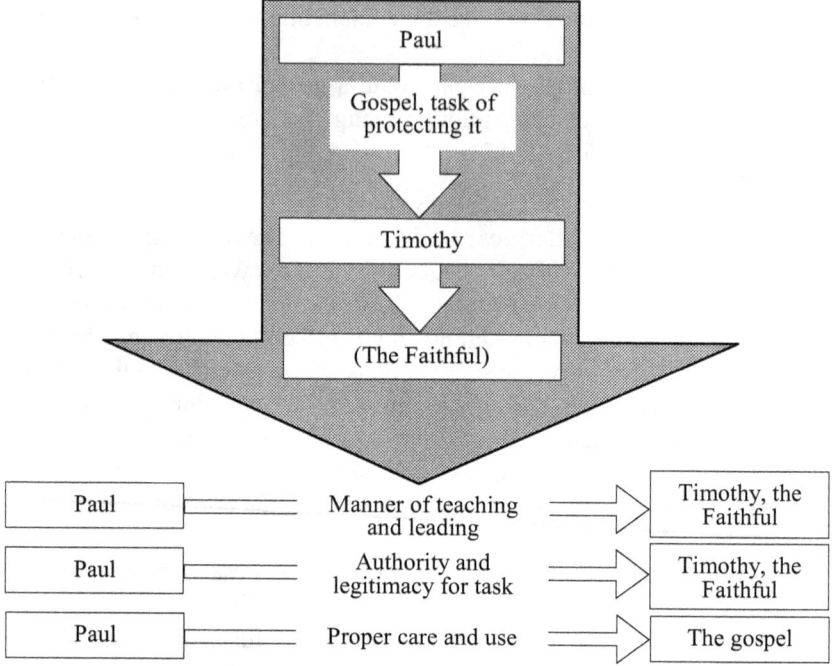

Figure 68. *The Functions of the Succession from Paul to Timothy in 2 Timothy*

Summary: The Functions of Succession in 2 Timothy
In this treatment of succession in 2 Timothy, I have shown that the observations made earlier regarding succession in Graeco-Roman, Jewish, and Christian texts generally apply. I have also shown that the observations made earlier regarding succession in 1 Timothy generally apply. In the relationships in 2 Timothy in which succession is prominent, I find not one but at least two exchanges. I find some of the same terminology, conceptual phenomena, and story components as found in earlier texts. I see the same kinds of differences in degree and kind between the predecessor and the successor as remarked on earlier: Timothy does not need to inherit Paul's apostolic office for him to be Paul's successor and (in a very strong sense) replacement. Further, succession in 2 Timothy involves the same objects as those seen earlier, and fits into the same functional categories as seen in earlier texts. These categories seem to function in much the same way as in the Graeco-Roman, Jewish, and Christian texts seen earlier.

Also in harmony with what is shown earlier in the Jewish and Christian texts, and in harmony with 1 Timothy, is the view of God's role in succession. God chooses the successor and initiates and guides the pivotal lines of succession. Here again, God uses succession as a tool to achieve his purposes.

In the table below, I have illustrated the relationships and the function of succession in 2 Timothy.

Table 12. *The Functions of Succession in 2 Timothy*

Text	Function
Succession of tradition from Christ to Paul	Continued institutional vitality Legitimates successor
Succession of tradition from Paul to Timothy (and the Faithful)	Legitimates successor Continuity of manner Continued institutional vitality Continuity of effect

In this section, I have explored the function of succession in 2 Timothy. In the remainder of this chapter, I examine Titus according to the same framework.

5. *Evidence of Succession from Christ to Paul in Titus*

Terms from the Semantic Field of Succession
In Titus's opening description of Paul's ministry, I find one clear succession term (πιστεύω) and one synonym which, in context, would have been understood as relating to succession (ἐπιταγή):

> Paul, a servant of God and an apostle of Jesus Christ, for the sake of the faith of God's elect and the knowledge of the truth that is in accordance with godliness, in the hope of eternal life that God, who never lies, promised before the ages began—in due time he revealed his word through the proclamation with which I have been entrusted (ἐπιστεύθην) by the command (ἐπιταγήν) of God our Savior. (1.1-3)

Here, Paul uses this language in describing his call to ministry in much the same way he uses the same terms in the opening of 1 Timothy.[42] Although the succession term is solitary, I regard the semantic evidence as prominent.

Phenomena from the Conceptual Field of Succession, Standard Elements of an Ancient Mediterranean Succession Story
I find none of these present in regards to Paul's place as Christ's successor in Titus.

Summary
In light of the prominent succession term, it is possible that the authorial audience would have inferred succession from Christ to Paul. I am left

---

42. R. Collins, *1 & 2 Timothy and Titus*, p. 309, likens the language in 1.3 to the official screening of a candidate for a dangerous assignment before the mission is entrusted to him.

without any evidence to back up this single term, however. In the letters to Timothy, Paul's authority comes from the fact that his apostleship is seen in terms of a succession of tradition from Christ. Whatever the nature of his authority in Titus, it does not appear to depend on succession. Where does his authority come from? Investigation into that question is beyond the scope of this study.

6. *Evidence of Succession from Paul to Titus in Titus*

Above, I pointed to strong evidence in 1 Timothy and 2 Timothy that the ancient audience would have understood Timothy to be Paul's successor, indeed Paul's replacement. There is less such evidence for the relationship between Titus and Paul. I find no succession terms used to describe Titus's relationship with Paul,[43] nor do I find any of the standard elements of an ancient Mediterranean succession story. I do, however, find conceptual evidence of succession between Paul and Titus.

Note first that Paul assigns tasks to Titus, and bequeaths some of his (Paul's) own authority to complete the tasks:

> I left you behind in Crete for this reason, so that you should put in order what remained to be done, and should appoint elders in every town, as I directed you. (1.5)

> Declare these things; exhort and reprove with all authority. Let no one look down on you. (2.15)

Note also that Titus and Paul will have common enemies because of their service to a common gospel (one which Paul received as Christ's successor, 1.1-3):

> Show yourself in all respects a model of good works, and in your teaching show integrity, gravity, and sound speech that cannot be censured; then any opponent will be put to shame, having nothing evil to say of us. (2.7-8)

Note third that Titus, like Timothy before him, ministers personally to Paul and acts as Paul's personal representative in his (Paul's) dealings with the congregation and with other leaders:

> When I send Artemas to you, or Tychicus, do your best to come to me at Nicopolis, for I have decided to spend the winter there. Make every effort to send Zenas the lawyer and Apollos on their way, and see that they lack

---

43. Wolter, *Paulustradition*, pp. 183-84, suggests that ἀπολείπω (used of Paul's leaving Titus in Crete in Tit. 1.5) is used in contexts of official transfers of authority. The term is indeed seen in succession contexts (see the list of terms from Talbert and Stepp, p. 16 above). Here, however, the idea is not that Paul has left a task to Titus but rather that Paul has left Titus to a task.

nothing. And let people learn to devote themselves to good works in order to meet urgent needs, so that they may not be unproductive. All who are with me send greetings to you. Greet those who love us in the faith. (3.12-15)

Summary

From this brief survey, I see that succession in Titus is not as prominent as in the letters to Timothy. Neither the succession from Christ to Paul nor the succession from Paul to Titus, although both do appear to be present, is central to the letter. Neither succession is prominent enough to shape our understanding of the letter.

Nevertheless, succession is present in Titus. As I have noted above, succession literature contains parallels to Titus's relationship with Paul, the *successor as delegate* rather than the *successor as partial replacement*. For example: Text 20: Lysias, *Pension* 6 uses succession language to describe a slave who takes over his master's work (i.e. the slave was the master's successor in a particular task). This slave was his master's delegate for the task and did not replace his master in any other way. The parallels to Paul's relationship to Titus are clear. Further, I have also shown texts where differences in both kind and degree exist between the predecessor and the successor. If Titus was understood as a successor, his succession would have been understood in this way. Third, I have also noted the way that the LXX used διάδοχος to refer to a delegate rather than a successor (LXX 1 Chron. 18.17; 2 Chron. 26.11; 28.7; 31.12; Est. 10.3; 2 Macc. 4.29, 31; 14.26).

As I have suggested above, the clearest way of describing the differences between succession from Paul to Titus and succession from Paul to Timothy is in terms of a continuum of replacement. At the weak end of the continuum, the predecessor delegates limited authority to a successor, so that the successor can carry out a limited task. Here there is no hint of the successor replacing the predecessor. On the strong end of the continuum, the successor becomes the predecessor's replacement—see, for example, Ochus's name change in Text 7: Diodorus Siculus 15.93.1, where the people of Persia renamed their ruler in hopes that he would rule in the benevolent and competent manner of his predecessor. In the survey of ancient literature, situations from all across this continuum were described in succession language, and fit into the same functional categories.

On this continuum, Titus sits too far to the weak side of succession. He is represented as Paul's delegate, not Paul's replacement. His work had limited scope and required limited authority. Timothy in 2 Timothy sits near the other end of the continuum—he is Paul's replacement in practically every way *except* the apostolic office. Timothy in 1 Timothy would sit somewhere in the middle, receiving more of Paul's authority than Titus but not as much as Timothy does in 2 Timothy.

7. Conclusions

In this and the preceding chapter, I have examined from the perspective of the authorial audience the function of succession in the Pastoral Epistles. I have shown how, for the authorial audience, succession defined Paul's and Timothy's vocations in 1 Timothy and 2 Timothy. Succession defined their tasks. It determined the shape of their 'job descriptions'. It also gave them the authority and resources they needed to carry out these tasks. I have also pointed to a fundamental difference between the way Paul and Titus are presented in Titus and the ways Paul and Timothy are presented in 1 Timothy and 2 Timothy.

In the next chapter, I offer a brief, cogent reading of the Pastoral Epistles from the perspective of the authorial audience. How would this audience, based on their understanding of the functions of succession, have read these letters? This reading will provide a solid foundation for more detailed readings and interpretations of the Pastorals, which I plan to pursue in future projects. In the final chapter of this study (Chapter 7) I summarize my findings and their implications, and suggest avenues for further research.

6

SUCCESSION IN THE PASTORAL EPISTLES, PART 3: READING THE PASTORAL EPISTLES FROM THE PERSPECTIVE OF THE AUTHORIAL AUDIENCE

This chapter is the last of three chapters exploring how the authorial audience of the Pastoral Epistles would have understood the function of succession in those letters. Here I offer a brief, cogent reading of the Pastorals from the perspective of the authorial audience, a reading which I believe will provide a foundation for future, more detailed readings and interpretations of these letters.

How would the authorial audience of the Pastoral Epistles have read the letters in the light of their knowledge of succession?

These letters, by the different settings from which each purports to come, demand to be read in the light of a historically grounded understanding of succession. The theme common to their settings is *Paul's departure*,[1] which by its nature raises concerns with authority and stability. Succession addresses these issues.

Succession is present in Titus, even though the letter does not contain prominent enough evidence of succession to shape our understanding of the phenomenon, and thus was not primary to this study. Nevertheless, succession literature contains parallels to Titus's role in the letter, quiet though the parallels may be: witness my discussion of Text 20: Lysias, *Pension 6*; Text 50: Acts 6–7, and the uses of διάδοχος in the LXX (discussed pp. 45, 61, and 95 above). Further, most critics would argue that the authorial audience of Titus has knowledge of the other Pastorals (i.e. most critics assume that the Pastorals were originally conceived of, executed, and received as a unit). If that is the case, the influence of the depictions of succession in the letters to Timothy would have influenced the audience of Titus to see Paul as Christ's successor and Titus as Paul's successor.

In 1 and 2 Timothy, succession is prominent. It acts and functions much like it did in the Graeco-Roman, Jewish, and Christian texts surveyed in

---

1. Robert A. Wild, 'The Image of Paul in the Pastoral Letters', *Bible Today* 23 (1985), pp. 239-45.

Chapters 2–3 above. In both letters, I found the same two exchanges, the same terminology and the same kinds of phenomena, same objects, the same standard components of the succession story, the same differences in kind and in degree between predecessor and successor. These successions further fit some of the same functional categories as seen in Chapters 2 and 3, and these categories appear to work in much the same way as the categories worked in the Graeco-Roman, Jewish, and Christian texts surveyed. In particular, the letters to Timothy are consistently optimistic about how God uses succession to achieve his purposes, as are most of the Jewish and Christian texts. God initiates and guides the pivotal lines of succession; they are tools in his hands.

How does succession function in these letters to Titus and Timothy? As I said above, the common theme is departure. This theme raises issues that Paul addresses through succession. How does this work out in each of the letters?

1. *Titus*[2]

In Titus, Paul departs from new church work on Crete and leaves Titus behind to organize leadership for the new churches. Paul delegates to Titus the authority he needs to accomplish this work. The authorial audience would have seen this relationship in terms of succession.

For Titus, the most pressing concern is church order: the new Cretan Christians do not know how to behave. As a result, the church's reputation suffers and the gospel is not being heard. Paul gives Titus the task of establishing indigenous leadership for the churches, and instructing these leaders and their people on how they should live. He instructs Titus to choose leaders on the basis of certain qualifications. These qualifications center on the potential leader's character and maturity, rather than on talents or skills. Paul's instructions contain little information about the tasks a leader will perform or the abilities a leader needs to possess, and much information about the kind of person a leader needs to be.

Titus's authority and commission are limited, as is his stay in Crete. In the terms discussed above (p. 181), Titus is Paul's agent or delegate rather than Paul's replacement. As I have observed, succession allows for varying degrees of difference between the predecessor and the successor. The easiest way to categorize these degrees of difference is to see succession in terms of a continuum of replacement. On the weak end of the continuum sits the idea

---

2. When reading the Pastorals together, I read them in the order Titus → 1 Timothy → 2 Timothy. Among modern scholars who propose a particular order—and most do not, most simply assume that the letters can be harmonized and treated as a unit without considering order—this is the order most favored, beginning with Jerome Quinn, 'The Pastoral Epistles', *Bible Today* 23 (1985), pp. 228-38.

of delegation, where a leader/predecessor gives a limited amount of authority to the successor, so that the successor can serve as the predecessor's delegate/agent. In this case, there is little or no hint of the successor replacing the predecessor. On the strong end of the continuum sits the predecessor redivivus, where the successor is essentially seen as the reincarnation of the predecessor (see, e.g., Ochus's name change in Text 7: Diodorus Siculus 15.93.1 and the constant reminders that God was with Joshua just as he was with Moses in Text 29: Num. 27.12-23 and Josh. 1.2-9, pp. 30-31 and 62-64 above).

On this continuum, Titus sits far to the weak side of succession. He is represented as Paul's delegate, not as Paul's replacement. There is no hint of a Mosaic 'transfer of glory', no mention of the laying-on of hands. His work had limited scope, and requires limited authority—but enough to get the job done. To meet this need, Paul commissions Titus to put a Pauline leadership structure in place and endorses the practical instructions Titus will give. He does this by sending to (and through) Titus an open letter to Titus's community, written to authorize Titus for the work entrusted to him.[3]

2. *First Timothy*

In 1 Timothy, Paul departs from his work with established churches, leaving Timothy behind in Ephesus to face false teaching and recalcitrant church leaders. Paul uses succession to give Timothy the authority he needs to carry out this task.

For Timothy, the most pressing concern is false teaching and the disorder that follows it.[4] Timothy's task is to face and correct these troublemakers, who are established church leaders and teachers. To accomplish this task, he needs a different kind of authority and commission than that received by Titus on Crete. Paul gives Timothy the standing needed to correct false teachers and false teaching and to discipline apostate church leaders by making Timothy his successor through this letter. The letter contains instruction for Timothy and strong (though indirect) admonition for the larger audience behind Timothy.

The succession involved is a succession of task (namely the command from 1.3, 'command those who are teaching other things to STOP!') from Paul to Timothy. This succession is limited geographically (Timothy has task

---

3. According to Richards, *Difference and Distance*, p. 95, the letter to Titus is an 'official communication in which a superior authorizes a subordinate for work entrusted to him or her... [which] "paves the way" for the agent acting on the letter-writer's behalf'.

4. Here is both a parallel and a contrast between Titus and 1 Timothy: in both situations disorder is addressed, but the disorder in Titus springs from a different source than does the disorder in 1 Timothy.

and authority in Ephesus, not elsewhere) and vocationally (he does not have any task or authority not given him in the letter). But his stay in Ephesus is of indefinite duration, whereas Titus's stay in Crete was not. And because of the nature of the opposition, Timothy's task itself is larger than Titus's task—although it is still limited, he does not completely become Paul's replacement.

I found three relationships in 1 Timothy which the authorial audience would have understood in terms of succession. The first was Paul's succession from Christ, which involved the passing on of tradition (gospel). I illustrated this exchange thus:

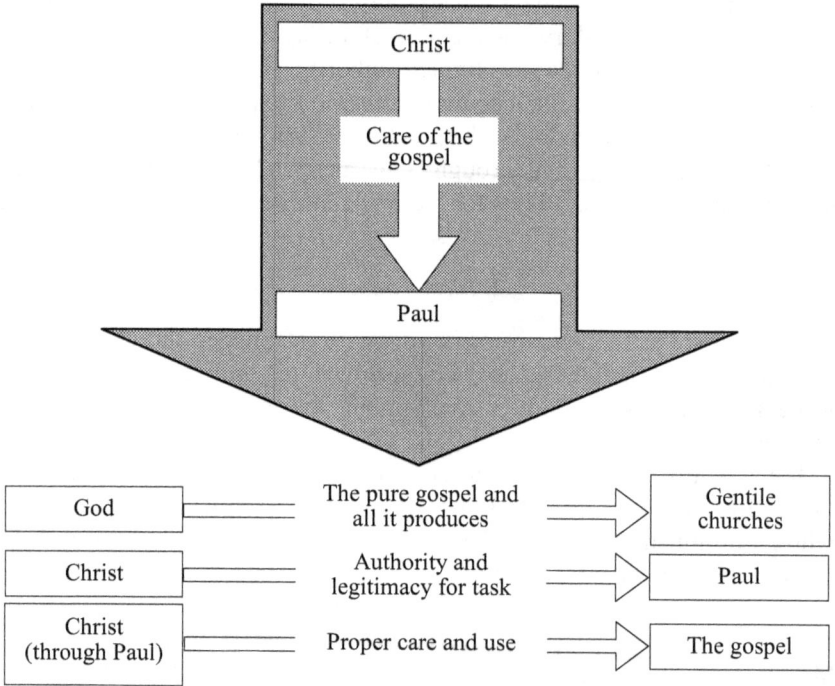

Figure 69. *The Functions of the Succession from Christ to Paul in 1 Timothy*

This succession of tradition (and the resulting tasks) from Christ to Paul functioned first to ensure institutional vitality: Jesus passed care of the gospel on to Paul so that it would fulfill its purpose among the Gentiles, and so that it would be effective and pure. It functioned second to legitimate Paul: when Christ passed the gospel and the tasks attached to it into Paul's keeping, he also gave to Paul the authority necessary to carrying out those tasks. Paul here, especially in 1.3-11, describes his ministry as something entrusted to him by Jesus Christ. This bequest gives Paul the gifting and authority required to care for the gospel properly.

Third, succession functioned to ensure continuity of manner. While Jesus was on earth, he was the keeper (as well as the source) of the true gospel. Now Jesus is working through his successors. Paul, by succession, becomes an authoritative keeper of the true gospel. He thus fills a role that Jesus himself filled while on earth.

The second relationship in 1 Timothy which the authorial audience would have understood in terms of succession was the succession of task between Paul and Timothy. Paul passed on to Timothy a particular task and the authority to perform it.

I illustrated the exchanges involved thus:

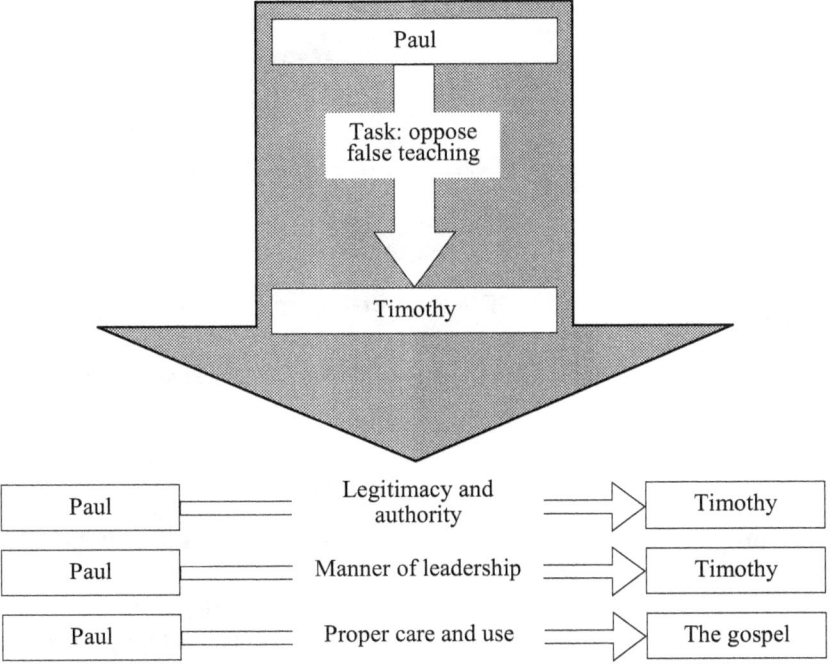

Figure 70. *The Functions of the Succession from Paul to Timothy in 1 Timothy*

This succession of task first legitimates Timothy, giving him the authority he needs to carry on the task. Second, this succession of task also ensures continuity of manner: because of the task, Timothy is acting in Paul's place, doing the things in Paul's absence that Paul would do if he were there. As Paul's true successor, Timothy acts in the way that Paul would have acted, with Paul's authority, to complete the task. Third, this succession ensures continued institutional vitality: Paul made Timothy his successor so as to keep the gospel pure and effective.

The succession from Paul to Timothy is built on a succession of task from the elders to Timothy. The succession from the elders introduced Timothy into ministry, and is subsumed by his succession from Paul. This succession functioned to ensure continuity of manner: Timothy took on the same tasks as the elders, doing the things that his predecessors had done.

I illustrated the exchanges thus:

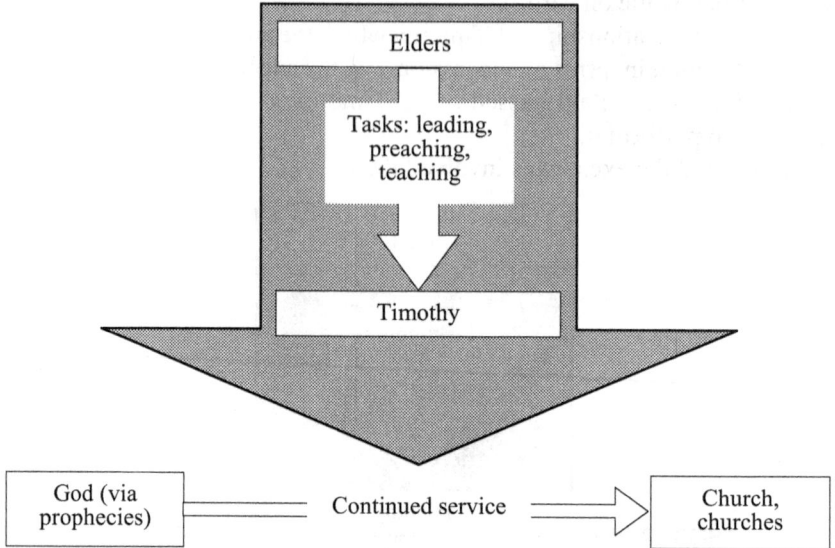

Figure 71. *The Function of the Succession from the Elders to Timothy in 1 Timothy*

3. Second Timothy

In 2 Timothy, Paul—about to depart from this life—writes to Timothy from Rome, calling him to be faithful to his (Paul's) message and ministry and example. This calling is wrapped up in a succession of tradition from Paul to Timothy, by which Paul gives Timothy the authority and example he needs to carry it out.

For Paul, the most pressing concern is what will happen to his gospel and churches after his death.[5] Timothy's task, passed on to him by succession from Paul, is to care for the gospel. This succession differs from the central successions in 1 Timothy and the implied successions in Titus, both of which involved single (albeit difficult and important) tasks. In 2 Timothy, Paul is not passing on a single task. Instead, he passes on to Timothy the care of his gospel itself, which involves multiple tasks (suffering, teaching faithfully, passing the gospel on to others) under its rubric. This is a succession of tradition, *not* task, built on the succession between Jesus and Paul.

---

5. It is interesting that, in 2 Timothy (unlike 1 Timothy and Titus), the primary concerns do not belong to the recipient but to Paul himself.

So: Paul, knowing that he is facing death, acts so that his gospel will continue to be taught and followed faithfully. He entrusts the care of his gospel to his successor, Timothy, and authorizes Timothy to pass on to others this message and all that is attached to it. Timothy's authority and commission are again limited: he does not inherit Paul's apostolic office, for example. But, in terms of the continuum of succession, this succession is stronger than the succession in 1 Timothy (and much stronger than that in Titus). Here Timothy becomes the caretaker of Paul's message, able to apply and teach it authoritatively. He becomes the official repository of Paul's gospel, voice, teaching, and example.

I found two relationships in 2 Timothy which the authorial audience would have understood in terms of succession. The first is Paul's succession from Christ. This succession, like the succession between Christ and Paul in 1 Timothy, is a succession of tradition: the tasks that are involved are secondary, the outgrowth of that bequest. This succession functions first to legitimate Paul: it enables him to prepare a successor (Timothy) and pass the care of the gospel (not just a limited set of tasks, as in the bequest from Paul to Timothy in 1 Timothy) on to him. Second, this succession ensures continued institutional vitality: the gospel is passed from Christ to Paul so that it will continue to be vital and pure and effective.

I illustrated the exchanges thus:

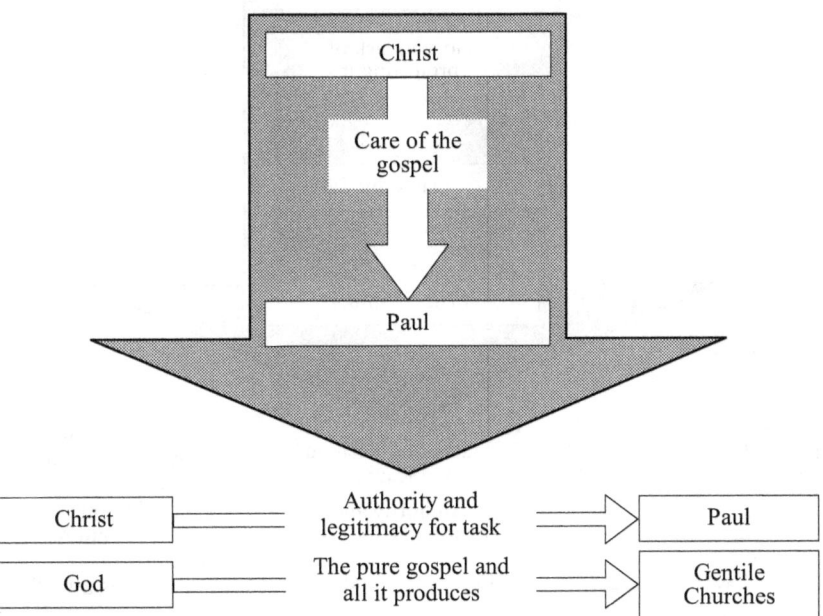

Figure 72. *The Functions of the Succession from Christ to Paul in 2 Timothy*

The tasks that Paul receives in his succession from Christ are narrower in 2 Timothy than in 1 Timothy because of the way the letters differ in how they situate Paul. In 1 Timothy, Paul is a mature apostle at the peak of his career, overseeing the work of his successor while he attends to other matters. In 2 Timothy, Paul is in prison and waiting to die. The entire description of his vocation in 2 Timothy aims at what is being passed on to Timothy, and there is no hint of Paul's work continuing through any means other than succession through Timothy ('All have left me').

This relationship between Paul and Timothy is the second relationship in 2 Timothy which the authorial audience would have understood in terms of succession. In 1 Timothy, this relationship is depicted in terms of a succession of task. There, Paul addresses a specific problem by sending Timothy to a specific set of churches and giving him a specific set of tasks, along with limited authority to carry them out. In 2 Timothy, however, this relationship is depicted in terms of a succession of tradition. Paul, who is about to leave the scene, passes the παραθήκη which he received from Christ into Timothy's care so that Timothy can take his (Paul's) place.

I illustrated the exchanges between Paul and Timothy (and the faithful) thus:

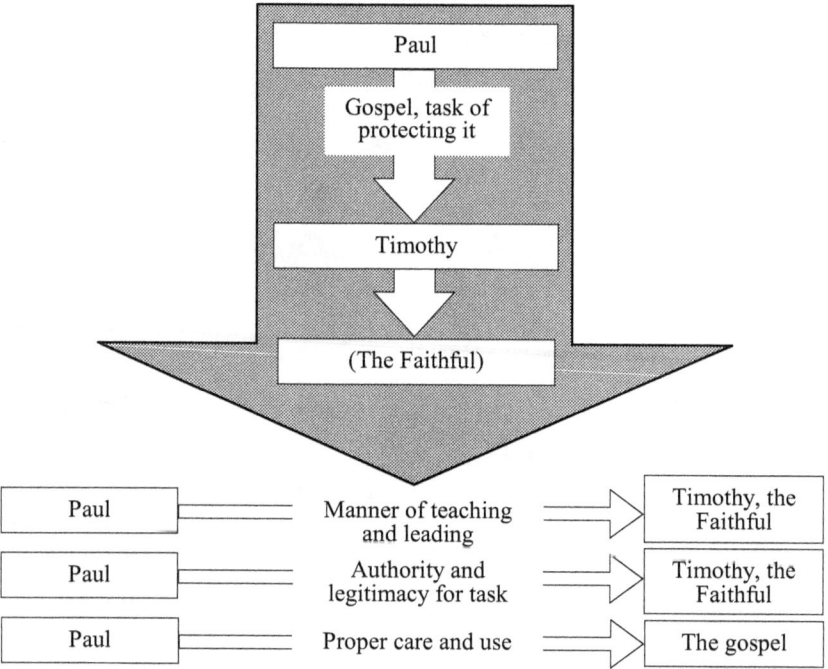

Figure 73. *The Functions of the Succession from Paul to Timothy (and on to the Faithful) in 2 Timothy*

How would the authorial audience have understood this succession to function? This succession functions first to ensure continued institutional vitality and continuity of effect (there is much overlap between the two here): because Paul has passed the gospel on to a qualified and commissioned successor, it continues to be cared for properly. And because Timothy will pass the gospel on to qualified and commissioned successors, the chain of proper care will continue. Second, succession functions to ensure continuity of manner: Paul holds up his example as something for Timothy to emulate, so that Timothy will approach the care and use of the gospel in a way faithful to his predecessor—as will Timothy's successors. Third, this succession legitimates Timothy as Paul's replacement.

4. *Summary and Conclusion*

In the Pastoral Epistles, Paul addresses the needs of three different situations. He uses the language and imagery of succession, terms and concepts familiar to his audience, to address these problems. From these terms and phenomena, the audience would have understood that Paul was giving different types of tasks and authority to his agents, with different levels of authority and empowerment necessary to carry out those tasks.

In this chapter, I have offered a brief reading of the Pastoral Epistles from the perspective of the authorial audience, as conditioned by their knowledge of succession. On many different levels—literary, historical, and theological—this reading will provide a solid, historically grounded foundation for future, more detailed work in the Pastoral Epistles.

In the next chapter, I summarize my findings in this study, explore some of the implications of the study for our understanding of the Pastoral Epistles and of Christian ministry itself, and suggest avenues for further research.

7

Conclusion

Here I do three things. First, I summarize the evidence presented in this study. Second, I examine this study's implications for reading the Pastorals, for our understanding of apostolic succession, and for our understanding of the nature of Christian ministry in general. Third, I suggest avenues for future research.

1. *Summary of the Evidence*

In the Chapters 2 and 3 of this study, I surveyed 60 ancient Mediterranean texts that gave prominent attention to the function of succession. These texts came from across the literary milieu of the Mediterranean world before 200 CE, Graeco-Roman, Jewish, and Christian. I began the survey by outlining the semantic and conceptual phenomena usually attached to accounts of succession in Mediterranean antiquity. I then introduced the idea of function, how in at least these texts, if not many more, stories of succession included not one but at least *two* exchanges. The first exchange is the simple passing on of office or task or property from predecessor to successor. The second exchange is functional: here, succession is seen to achieve something beyond the primary exchange. I showed that these multiple exchanges could be profitably described with a graphic, and that the functional exchanges could be described in language borrowed from structuralism, Sender → Object → Receiver. I showed that succession seems to function in the same way, whether the function was hoped for or not, and whether the succession is actual, hypothetical, or thwarted. Succession also seems to function in spite of differences in kind and degree between the predecessors and the successors: for example, a slave can be described as a king's successor in a particular task without the slave becoming a king.

These functions tended to fall into a set of six categories, which separated along lines determined by the focus of succession in the text. If the text focuses on how succession affects property, for example, then the function differs from the function in texts that focus on characteristic actions shared

7. Conclusion

by predecessor and successor. These categories are not watertight. In some texts, the distinction between categories blurs. In other texts, several different functions can be included in a single succession story.

I did notice one significant difference between the presentation of succession in the Graeco-Roman texts and the presentation of succession in the Jewish and Christian texts. In the latter, God was consistently seen as the initiator and guide of succession. God chose the successors, the predecessors (or fate, or providence) did not. God used the succession as a tool to achieve his purposes. This theistic view of succession tended to be much more optimistic than the Graeco-Roman view of succession, which tended toward ironic fatalism. This is true even with regard to the Christian view of secular successions—witness Athenagoras's faith in the succession of Roman rulers. The Christian texts *do* differ slightly from the Jewish texts in their depiction of God as the hand behind succession, in that the sense of God directly choosing the successors is not as explicit.

In Chapters 4 and 5 of this study, I surveyed the Pastoral Epistles against this background. In 1 and 2 Timothy, which I have designated Text 61 and Text 62 in my textbase, I found that succession functioned in much the same way as in the Graeco-Roman and Jewish and Christian materials of Chapters 2 and 3. I found the same phenomena accompanying succession, the same sense that succession achieved a particular function, and the same functional categories.

As for the functional categories themselves, I saw succession function to do the following:

1. *Ensure continuity of possession*: here the text focuses on *property* and how ownership is maintained through succession (Text 1: Herodotus 3.53; Text 4: Aristotle, *Politics* 1923a.13-30; Text 47: Josephus, *Life* 1.1+3, 6, and *Apion* 1.7+31, etc.);
2. *Ensure continuity of manner*: here the text focuses on a *characteristic attitude or action* that the predecessor and the successor share (Text 2: Herodotus 5.90-92; Text 4: Aristotle, *Politics* 1923a.13-30; Text 5: Aristotle, *Ath. Cons.* 28.1-4; Text 30: 1 Sam. 9–18 [LXX 1 Kgdms 9–18]; Text 50: Acts 6–7, etc.);
3. *Ensure continuity of institutional vitality*: here the object of succession is an institution, and the text focuses on that *object* and how succession causes it to remain vital and effective (Text 3: Plato, *Laws* 6.769c; Text 45: Josephus, *Apion* 1.8+41; Text 51: 1 Clem. 42–44, etc.);
4. *Ensure realization of an effect*: here the text focuses on an *effect* that is *succession-dependent*, one which began under the predecessor and was finally realized under the successor (Text 5: Aristotle, *Ath. Cons.* 28.1-4; Text 33: 1 Kgs 19–2 Kgs 2 [LXX 3 Kgdms 19–4 Kgdms 2], etc.);

5. *Ensure continuity of effect*: here the text focuses on an *effect/result* which is *shared by the predecessor and the successor* but the realization of which is not dependent upon the succession (Text 6: Diodorus Siculus 15.8-11; Text 38: 2 Macc. 9.22-27; Text 52: Athenagoras, *Legatio* 37, etc.).
6. *Legitimate the successor*: here, the focus is on the authority and legitimacy that the successor receives because of the succession (Text 31: 1 Kgs 1–2 [LXX 3 Kgdms 1–2]; Text 56: Apollinarius of Hierapolis, etc.).

Below, sorted as before by the object of succession, are charts listing all of the texts in this monograph and the function of succession in each.

Table 13. *Texts Describing the Passing-On of Leadership/Rule*

	Text	Function
	(Graeco-Roman Texts)	
1.	Herodotus 3.53	Continuity of possession
2.	Herodotus 5.90-92	Continuity of manner
3.	Plato, *Laws* 6.769c	Continuity of effect Continuity of manner Continuity of institutional vitality
4.	Aristotle, *Politics* 1923a.13-30	Continuity of possession Continuity of manner Continuity of effect
5.	Aristotle, *Athenian Constitution* 28.1-4	Continuity of manner Realization of effect
6.	Diodorus Siculus 15.8-11	Continuity of effect
7.	Diodorus Siculus 15.93.1	Continuity of manner
8.	Diodorus Siculus 17–18	Realization of effect
9.	Strabo, *Geography* 11.13.9	Continuity of manner
10.	Strabo, *Geography* 13.1.3	Realization of effect
11.	Livy 23.27.9-12	Continuity of effect
12.	Pausanius, *Description of Greece* 7.12	Continuity of manner
13.	Dio Chrysostom 64.20-22	Continuity of effect Continuity of manner
14.	Dio Cassius 53	Continuity of effect Continuity of manner
	(Jewish Texts)	
29.	Num. 27.12-23 and Josh. 1.2-9	Continuity of effect Realization of effect
30.	1 Sam. 9–18 (LXX 3 Kgdms 9–10)	Realization of effect Continuity of manner
31.	1 Kgs 1–2 (LXX 3 Kgdms 1–2)	Successor's legitimacy Realization of effect

32.	1 Kgs 11.43, etc. (LXX 3 Kgdms 11.44, etc.)	Continuity of possession Realization of effect
33.	1 Kgs 19–2 Kgs 2 (LXX 3 Kgdms–4 Kgdms 2)	Continuity of manner Realization of effect
34.	Sir. 47.11-13	Realization of effect
35.	Eupolemus	Realization of effect
36.	1 Macc. 2.65; 3.1	Realization of effect
37.	1 Macc. 6.14-15	Realization of effect Continuity of manner
38.	2 Macc. 9.22-27	Continuity of manner Continuity of effect
39.	Pseudo-Philo, *Biblical Antiquities*	Realization of effect
40.	*Testament of Moses* 1.6-10; 10.15	Continuity of manner Realization of effect
41.	Josephus, *Ant.* 7.14.2+337	Realization of effect
42.	Josephus, *Ant.* 9.2.2+27-28	Continuity of manner
43.	Josephus, *Life* 1.76+428-29	Continuity of manner
44.	Josephus, *Apion* 1.17+110	Continuity of manner
(Christian Texts)		
48.	Mt. 16.13-20	Continuity of institutional vitality Successor's legitimacy
49.	Lk. 22.28-30	Continuity of manner
50.	Acts 6–7	Continuity of institutional vitality Continuity of manner
51.	Acts 24.27; 25.9	Continuity of manner
52.	1 Clem. 42–44	Continuity of effect Continuity of institutional vitality
53.	Athenagoras, *Legatio* 37	Continuity of manner Continuity of effect
54.	Hegesippus	Continuity of institutional vitality
55.	Clement of Alexandria, *Stromateis*	Continuity of effect
56.	Apollinarius of Hierapolis	Successor's legitimacy Continuity of institutional vitality

Table 14. *Texts Describing the Passing-On of the Headship of a Philosophical School*

	Text	Function
15.	Aulus Gellius, *Attic Nights* 13.5	Realization of effect Continuity of manner
16.	Diogenes Laertius 4.67	Continuity of institutional vitality
17.	Diogenes Laertius 9.115	Continuity of institutional vitality Continuity of manner
18.	Diogenes Laertius 10.9	Continuity of institutional vitality
19.	Iamblichus, *On the Pythagorean Way of Life* 36	Continuity of institutional vitality

Table 15. *Texts Describing the Passing-On of a Task*

	Text	Function
	(Graeco-Roman Texts)	
20.	Lysias, *Pension* 6	Continuity of effect
21.	Xenophon, *Anabasis*	Realization of effect
	(Christian Texts)	
	1 Timothy (Paul → Timothy)	Legitimates successor Continuity of manner Continued institutional vitality
	1 Timothy (Elders → Timothy)	Continuity of manner

Table 16. *Texts Describing the Passing-On of Knowledge or Tradition*

	Text	Function
	(Graeco-Roman Texts)	
22.	Aristotle, *Sophistical Refutations* 34.27-35	Continuity of institutional vitality
23.	Pliny the Elder, *Natural History* 30.2.4-5	Continuity of institutional vitality
24.	Tacitus, *Annals* 15.62	Continuity of institutional vitality Realization of effect
	(Jewish Texts)	
45.	Josephus, *Apion* 1.8+41	Continuity of institutional vitality
46.	*3 En.* 48D.6-10	Continuity of institutional vitality
	(Christian Texts)	
57.	Lk. 1.1-4	Continuity of institutional vitality
58.	Athenagoras, *Legatio* 28	Continuity of institutional vitality
59.	Irenaeus, *Against History* 3.2.1-2	Continuity of institutional vitality
60.	Irenaeus, *Against History* 3.3.1-3	Continuity of institutional vitality
	1 Timothy (Christ → Paul)	Continuity of institutional vitality Legitimates successor Continuity of effect
	2 Timothy (Christ → Paul)	Continued institutional vitality Legitimates successor
	2 Timothy (Paul → Timothy)	Legitimates successor Continuity of manner Continued institutional vitality Continuity of effect

Table 17. *Texts Describing the Passing-On of Possessions*

	Text	Function
	(Graeco-Roman Texts)	
25.	Demosthenes, *Aphobus* 25	Continuity of possession Continuity of effect
26.	Plato, *Laws* 5.740b	Continuity of effect Continuity of institutional vitality
27.	Diodorus Siculus 10.30.1-2	Realization of effect
28.	Lucian, *Alexander* 5	Continuity of manner
	(Jewish Texts)	
47.	Josephus, *Life* 1.1+3, 6, and *Apion* 1.7+31	Continuity of possession

Above, I noted how some of the objects of succession tend to fit a predominant category: in the passing on of headship of a philosophical school or knowledge/tradition, continuity of institutional vitality is a logical function. References to succession involving other objects tend to have more varied functions.

2. *Conclusions Drawn from this Study*

From this study of succession in the Pastoral Epistles, I draw conclusions in two areas. First, what are the implications of this study for the continued exploration of the Pastoral Epistles? Second, what are the implications of this study for a New Testament understanding of Christian ministry?

Implications of this Study for the Continued Exploration of the Pastoral Epistles
This study has implications for the study of the Pastoral Epistles in four areas. First, I have shown benefits that come from approaching the Pastorals as individual letters rather than as a single work. Second, I have shown that a unifying theme runs through the three letters. This theme can be the basis for synthetic work arising from the Pastorals. Third and fourth, two of the issues ubiquitous to research in the Pastorals today, authorship and dating, are directly impacted by features of the Pastorals that I have uncovered.

Treating the Pastorals as discrete documents. In this study, building on the perspectives of William Richards and Luke Timothy Johnson, I have exposed some of the important differences that exist between the three letters, and I have shown that these differences have theological importance. Because of these differences, the Pastoral Epistles cannot be treated as a homogenous, single work. Any future treatment of the Pastorals must consider and weigh the differences between the letters, differences which include (but are not limited to) the differences in setting and purpose that I have uncovered here.

At the same time, I have demonstrated that a common theme, described below, runs through the letters and pulls the letters together. The existence of this theme demands that studies in the Pastorals *begin* by treating the letters as discrete documents and *finish* by synthesizing the findings. Such a treatment of the Pastorals should be much like the treatment of other units within the Pauline corpus. For example, Galatians and Romans cannot legitimately be treated as a single work. But the interplay of theology and theme between the two letters demands that, when one is exploring Paul's theology, the findings in one be compared and combined with the findings in the other. In the same way, future treatments of the Pastorals need to take seriously the fact that they come to us not as a unit but as three separate yet deeply interrelated letters. Only then will the significance of the commonalities and distinctives each possesses against the others be fully recognized. Much work remains to be done in this area, on all sorts of levels—rhetorical, theological, historical, and literary.

The unifying theme of the Pastoral Epistles. The theme of the Pastoral Epistles is not church order, emergent Catholicism, bourgeois Christianity, and so on. The theme of the Pastoral Epistles is Paul's departure and absence, and how Paul through succession addresses the problems this absence will cause. This center provides the foundation for a cogent, coherent, unified reading of the Pastoral Epistles.

Authorship. In this study, I have attempted to show that a scholar can set aside his/her conclusions regarding authorship and study how the Pastoral Epistles functioned apart from the author and his specific *Sitz im Leben*. Still, the work I have done raises some specific implications and possibilities in the area of authorship.

First, future work on the Pastorals needs to proceed with an awareness that, whatever the scholar concludes regarding authorship, the ancient historical audience (and the authorial audience as studied in this monograph) would have heard and received these materials as Pauline. Modern critics who treat the letters as pseudonymous in a way that marginalizes their materials must admit that they are not receiving the Pastorals with the same orientation toward the text as the ancient audience or the authorial audience. They have become resistant readers.

Second, regarding the setting of the historical author, the Pastorals seem to come from a setting where there is an acute sense of apostolic absence, impending and/or realized. In 1 Timothy and Titus, the absence is realized but promises to end soon—Paul will send someone to relieve Titus of his duties, so that Titus can rejoin him in Nicopolis (Tit. 3.12). Paul plans to make a visitation to Timothy in Ephesus, although his return may be delayed (1 Tim. 3.14-15).[1] In 2 Timothy, the absence is both realized (Paul and Timothy are separated, Paul is in prison) and impending (Paul is facing death). The absence will apparently be broken temporarily: Paul, in the same language as Tit. 3.12 (σπούδασον), urges Timothy to do everything he can to reach Paul before winter, bringing his master's precious books and cloak.

How does this setting (apostolic absence) work if the Pastorals are Pauline, directly or indirectly? That is, if Paul wrote the letters himself or through an amanuensis, or if one of Paul's disciples in Paul's name wrote/edited the letters together after Paul's death, as Marshall and others envision, then how does this setting of realized and impending absence shape the function of the letters? The setting of impending absence achieves at least three things. First, it heightens the power of the instructions and the necessity of carrying them out. Second, it legitimizes Timothy and Titus, particularly Timothy, as they carry out their ministry in the first post-apostolic generation. And what of Timothy's successors (2 Tim. 2.2)? They also belong to the stream of tradition that came to the Church from Jesus Christ through Paul and Timothy. Thus the letters, especially 2 Timothy, legitimize their ministries. Third, the setting of absence demonizes those who stood against Paul and (in a post-apostolic setting) stand against his legitimate successors.

What if the letters are truly pseudonymous, generated *in toto* more than a decade after Paul's death, through the work of a writer who was not part of Paul's circle? This was a time of great diversity and conflict in the Church. Church leaders would have longed for apostolic authority and homogeneity in such a tumultuous time. Those who stood in a line of tradition from Paul and Timothy, even if their affiliation was in spirit rather than through an unbroken physical pipeline of succession, could use the Pastorals to claim legitimacy over those who were not part of that line. Those who saw themselves as standing for the true Pauline faith could use the Pastorals to demonize their opponents, painting them as insurgents who sought to overturn the received body of Pauline tradition and agitate for doctrinal innovation.

Third, regarding the historical author, once we weigh the motives behind post-Pauline authorship, and the way succession functions in these letters, Timothy had stronger and better motives for writing the letters than any other

---

1. Jeffrey T. Reed, 'To Timothy or Not? A Discourse Analysis of 1 Timothy', in Stanley E. Porter and D.A. Carson (eds.), *Biblical Greek Language and Linguistics: Open Questions in Current Research* (JSNTSup, 80; Sheffield: JSOT Press, 1993), pp. 115-17, shows how the discourse features of 1 Timothy make it unlikely that the promise of Paul's apostolic visit in 3.14-15 is a cipher for Paul's death. Thus, whatever the situation of the historical author, he is likely not using ἐὰν δὲ βραδύνω as a code to indicate a post-apostolic setting. Reed's arguments, though not applied by him to Tit. 1.5 and 3.12-15, seem to suggest a similar conclusion there—the second person pronouns need to be taken seriously, whatever one's conclusions regarding authorship and date.

known figure of his or a later generation.[2] On this hypothesis, by his writing Timothy served as Paul's tradent and successor in somewhat the same way that Plato (by his writing) served as Socrates' tradent and successor.

An objection that might be raised to Timothy's authorship of the Pastorals is that the author of 1 Timothy depicts Timothy in an unflattering way—weak, young, immature, halting. Two points in response to that objection: first, notice the parallel with Plato in his *Phaedo*, where Phaedo, a disciple of Socrates, describes his master's execution to the Pythagorean Echecrates. When listing the members of Socrates' school who were in the chamber at their master's death, Phaedo explains Plato's absence from the scene by saying, 'Plato, I believe, was ill'. Second, I would note how the issue of Timothy's weakness is addressed via succession. In 1 Timothy, where Timothy's weakness is an issue, he has no authority or strength on his own, apart from his calling to minister and the commissioning Paul gives him through succession to carry out his task. In 2 Timothy, Timothy is not weak, there is no mention of any lack on his part. There he is Paul's full successor and replacement, the keeper of Paul's gospel, the official repository of Paul's voice and ministry. And again, Timothy has this status in 2 Timothy due to his succession from Paul.

Fourth, regarding the dating of the letters, the theme of absence and the way succession functions lead me to conclude that the letters are post-Pauline, but by how great an interval? The theme and setting work best if the letters were written/edited into their final form in the first few years after Paul's death. For all the talk about emergent Catholicism and church hierarchy in the Pastorals, there really is not much hierarchy here. True, the offices of deacon and overseer/elder are named.[3] But the fact that the name of a second-century church office is used in the Pastorals does not prove that the letters come from the second century: witness the same names used of church offices in Rom. 16.1 and Phil. 1.1. In the Pastorals, these offices are not described in any hierarchical way. There is nothing in the text of the Pastorals that demands that the offices be understood in terms of the second-century Church, particularly if the influence of synagogue leadership structure is taken into account.

Implications of this Study for our Understanding of Christian Ministry
This study has implications for our understanding of Christian ministry in three areas. First, in this study I have shown that the Pastoral Epistles cannot be appealed to in support of the practice of apostolic succession, at least

---

2. For a tantalizing (and far too brief) discussion of this possibility, see Richard J. Bauckham, 'Pseudo-Apostolic Letters', *JBL* 107 (1988), pp. 469-94.
3. Titus 1.5-7 shows that 'overseer' and 'elder' are interchangeable names for a single office, not two offices.

insofar as it is commonly understood and practiced. Second, I have uncovered important aspects of the nature of Christian ministry. Third and finally, building on what I have show regarding succession in this study, particularly its place in the theology of the Pastorals, I will show in this conclusion the importance of succession for ministry in the Church today. In this final discussion, I will provide a foundation for the proper and beneficial practice of succession in Christian ministry today.

The Pastorals cannot be enlisted in support of Apostolic Succession. In this study, I have shown that the Pastorals cannot be enlisted to support the understanding of Apostolic Succession currently held by churches with an episcopal ministry. The Pastoral Epistles do not show the passing on of an office but rather succession of tradition and task. The establishing or refining of offices that is in view in the Pastorals is functional: office exists in service of task, not vice versa. In other words, the offices exist to make certain that important tasks are completed. Even if the offices in the Pastorals *are* understood in terms of their second-century counterparts, the overseer is removed at least one step (Timothy, Titus) from the apostle.[4]

Further, when 'ordination' is in view in the Pastorals, the emphasis is not on an unbroken pipeline of the laying-on of hands. By treating the letters as discrete documents, I have shown that Timothy serves as Paul's successor in task in 1 Timothy without the benefit of having been ordained by Paul (or conversely, even if his ordination *was* Pauline, I have shown that it was not important for the purpose of succession that the direct physical connection be made explicit in 1 Timothy). The emphasis is not on the physical laying-on of hands, but on God's choice of the successor ('through prophecy') and the successor's continued faithfulness, vigilance, and holiness.

The Pastorals and the nature of Christian ministry. Regarding the nature of Christian ministry as depicted in the Pastorals, I have demonstrated three things.

First, faithful Christian ministry begins with and stands in a stream of succession that begins with the ministry of Jesus Christ. As an apostle, Paul stands in succession from Christ, and part of Jesus' ministry was passed on to him. In 2 Timothy, Paul passes full and official deposit of this ministry on to Timothy, even though he does not give Timothy his apostolic office or title. Timothy is Paul's successor, the official keeper of the gospel which Paul received in succession from Jesus Christ. Timothy will in turn pass Paul's legacy and gospel on to other faithful ministers, and they in turn to others, in perpetuity.

4. Succession functions in this same way in Text 52: 1 Clem. 42–44, so that that document also cannot be enlisted in support of Apostolic Succession; see pp. 97-99 above.

So it is with faithful Christian ministry today. Christian ministers stand in a stream that begins with Jesus Christ and continues through the ages, to the present, and then on into future generations. This stream of succession works on varying levels of continuity. As successors of Jesus Christ in ministry, Christian leaders must imitate their predecessor's attitude of self-sacrifice. In succession terms, this constitutes continuity of manner. Christian leaders must give of themselves so that the gospel continues to be heard and to be effective, and so that the Kingdom of God continues to advance in ways appropriate to it, so that lives are changed and God is glorified through their witness. In succession terms, this constitutes continued institutional vitality. Further, the goal of Christian ministry is to carry out the commission that Jesus gave to the Church in Mt. 28.18-20 and Acts 1.8, to be living witnesses and agents of the Kingdom of God in and throughout the world. In succession terms, this constitutes realization of effect.

Second, the authority for Christian ministry comes from the calling of God to minister, and not from hierarchy or office or title. Notice how Paul in the Pastorals recognizes that Timothy's ministry ultimately comes from God and not from Paul—see 1 Tim. 1.18 and 4.14, and 2 Tim. 1.9. Further, authority and office in the Pastorals are functional. They derive from the task to which God calls the minister and the spiritual gifting God gives the minister to do that task. Task and gifting do not generate from title or office. Notice the qualification lists in Titus 1 and 1 Timothy 3: in these lists, the focus is not on job descriptions or flow charts or hierarchical relationships. The lists instead focus on the leader's maturity and character, evidence of the Holy Spirit in the leader's life. The lists do pay some attention to talents and gifts, but even that is functional in nature. In the Pastorals, authority and office have more to do with the type of person the leader is than the title or office the leader possesses.

Third, by the pattern of the Pastoral Epistles, the focus of ministry is on both the work of the gospel in the life of the minister and the work of the gospel in the life of the Church. In the life of the minister, the gospel produces integrity in teaching and conduct. Teaching that is true to the gospel is healthy for the Church. The minister who teaches τὴν ὑγιαίνουσαν διδασκαλίαν promotes the health of the Church, and is thus faithful to his/her calling (1 Tim. 4.12). This faithfulness robs opponents of the gospel of opportunities to criticize the work of Christ (Tit. 2.7-8), and enables the minister—as is appropriate for one who stands in the stream of succession from Christ through Paul—to say with Paul, 'You have observed my conduct, my teaching...' and 'What you have heard from me, pass on to faithful men and women who will then be able to teach it to others' (2 Tim. 3.10 and 2.2, both paraphrased).

In the life of the Church, the gospel produces integrity of belief and conduct. The faith that grows from the true gospel gives the Church harmony and health, as opposed to the quarrels and disputes that arise when beliefs are based on myths and endless speculations and demonic teaching (1 Tim. 1.4; 4.1). Further, as the Church lives with integrity, humbly and respectfully living out the gospel before the watching world, the Church wins a hearing for the gospel and advances the work of the Kingdom of God (1 Tim. 2.1-4).

The importance of succession for Christian ministry today. Succession is largely neglected in Christian ministry today. This is likely due in part to the individualistic nature of the Western concept of self, the way this individualism shapes the ministries most Christian leaders lead, and the nature (dare I say fallen?) of the pervasive concept of human leadership and power, in and out of Christendom. Transition in leadership often occurs at times *not* of the leader's choosing, and in circumstances less than ideal. Transition points are seldom without stress, conflict, and difficulty. For these reasons and others, Christian leaders often neglect to plan for succession.

Still, transition in leadership is inevitable. The general neglect and apathy that characterize many Christian leaders' attitude toward succession is unfortunate and inexplicable. From my study of succession in the Pastoral Epistles, and drawing on my study of succession in other Jewish and Christian literature in Chapter 3, I offer the following rationale for approaching succession in a deliberate and intentional manner.

Succession in Christian ministry, if approached in a deliberate, prayerful, and intentional way, can benefit the Church. It has this potential because it demonstrates an understanding of the realities of church life and leadership.

First, use of succession shows an awareness of future needs. Many Christian leaders practice leadership by crisis. In contrast, providing for succession is a proactive task. Rather than waiting for transition to be forced upon them, Christian leaders can, from the outset of their ministries, be planning for how emergent leaders will be brought up and prepared to lead. This demonstrates a deliberate and pastoral consideration of future needs. It follows the example of Moses: when his life was nearing its end, Moses approached God and asked for a successor so that Israel would not be left like sheep without a shepherd (see Text 29: Num. 27.12-23 and Josh. 1.2-9, pp. 62-64 above).

Second, use of succession shows an awareness of the necessity of good leadership for the continued institutional vitality of the Church. It is instructive to consider the differences between the depictions of Israel after Moses' death, when they thrived under the leadership of Moses' successor Joshua, and the depictions of Israel after Joshua. Joshua evidently prepared no successor. There was no consistent, strong leadership in Israel during the time following his leadership. What are our biblical depictions of the life of Israel during this period?

> Another generation grew up after them, who did not know the Lord or the work that he had done for Israel. (Judg. 2.10)

> Then the Israelites did what was evil in the sight of the Lord. (Judg. 2.11: see also 3.7, 12; 4.1; 6.1; 10.6; 13.1)

> In those days there was no king in Israel; all the people did what was right in their own eyes. (Judg. 17.6; see also 18.1; 19.1; 21.25)

The story of Israel after Joshua is a story of the failure of leadership. Joshua did not provide for the leadership of future generations, nor did the judges. The same cycle of sin and punishment plays out over and over. Israel falls away from the commitment to Yahweh after the death of Joshua and his generation (Judg. 2.10-11), after the death of Ehud (4.1), after the death of Jair (10.6), after the death of Abdon (13.1). In none of these cases, nor in any other case, are we told of any provision for succession of leadership after the death of these or other leaders. No one followed the example of Moses, and—from the perspective of Judges—Israel suffered for the lack of leadership as a result.

Equally interesting and instructive is the case of Samuel. Samuel led Israel well, but did not train up his sons to be good leaders. His sons were corrupt, and Israel refused to be led by them, opting instead for a human king. Again, a crisis was brought about by a failure to provide for a healthy succession of leadership.

Good Christian leadership, both in the Church and in para-church organizations, is necessary for the health of the Church. Healthy succession of leadership is essential if the Church and its ministries are to enjoy consistently good leadership past the effective career of the individual Christian leader.

Third, use of succession shows an awareness of the beneficial power of symbol, ceremony, liturgy, and sacrament. American Protestantism has largely forgotten this benefit. It has taken postmodernism to point us back to what the ancients knew: of course, the more liturgical churches have never forgotten this power. Ceremony and symbol remind believers that they are part of something larger and more powerful than what can be perceived with the five senses. Succession ceremonies, properly planned, can give the members of a church or the partners in a ministry greater confidence in the direction of the organization, and greater confidence in and commitment to their own calling and service.[5] Notice again the example of Moses, who brought Joshua before the people and with solemn ceremony placed his hands on Joshua, transferring some of his own power to his successor, commissioning

---

5. See Dan Kimball, *Emerging Worship: Creating Worship Gatherings for New Generations* (Grand Rapids: Zondervan/emergentYS, 2004), pp. 80-86, for a description of the power of symbol in worship.

him publicly. What did this symbol and ceremony achieve? As Josh. 1.5 and 1.17 suggest, they helped both Joshua and the Israelites to have confidence that God was with Joshua just as he had been with Moses, and the Israelites would thus continue to be well led.

Fourth, use of succession demonstrates an awareness of the necessity of training and preparing emergent leaders for their task. The work of the Kingdom of God is too vital and too difficult for leaders simply to assume that the mantle will be picked up when they no longer hold it. Today's leaders cannot assume that tomorrow's leaders are qualified, or that they have been successfully trained by osmosis. Again, predecessors must carefully and intentionally raise up and mentor their successors.

3. *Avenues for Future Research*

My work in this monograph will lead me into further work in two broad areas, further work in succession and further work in the Pastoral Epistles. With regard to succession, at least the following work needs to be done. First, my textbase will continue to expand. As I continue to read and examine ancient Mediterranean texts that describe transitions in leadership, my overall understanding of how succession worked will grow. Does literary genre affect the way succession was depicted and understood? What terms other than those outlined above (p. 16) are commonly used to describe the various aspects of succession? Are ἀπόστολος and πιστόω (and cognates) used in succession contexts? These and other questions I aim to answer as I continue my research.

Second, the question of the functions of succession requires further investigation. Are the functions that I have described the only ways that succession works in ancient Mediterranean texts? What other things might the phenomenon have brought to the table, in terms of the choices ancient authors could make? Are there other functional categories than those outlined in this study?

Third, the description of the interaction of actants requires further refinement. For example, I have shown that with some functions, the successor is always (so far, at least) the receiver. Are there special implications when the successor is not the receiver?[6]

With regard to the Pastoral Epistles, this study leads to further work in three general areas, literary, historical, and theological. Let me examine each of these in turn.

Literary. First, scholars working in the Pastorals need to undertake full narrative-critical and reader-response analyses of the Pastoral Epistles, beginning

---

6. I am indebted to Mikeal Parsons for bringing this particular point to my attention.

with something of the nature of R. Alan Culpepper's *Anatomy of the Fourth Gospel*.[7] The Pastoral Epistles create their own closed, self-contained narrative universe. What can we learn from studying the Pastoral Epistles' characterization, use of narrative time, order of events, the interplay of implied author and implied reader, and other narratological issues? What is the plot of the Pastoral Epistles, and how does that plot intersect with the letters' theology? Further, these literary aspects of the Pastorals must be compared with the parallel aspects of the other Pauline letters.

Second, the relationships between the letters of the Pastoral Epistles need to be evaluated thoroughly. Is each letter to be taken on its own merits, or can the three be glossed together and treated as a single document? If we take the letters as separate but deeply interrelated documents, how do we account for the differences between them and how should these differences affect our formulations of, say, 'THE theology of the Pastoral Epistles'? How do the letters differ in rhetorical strategies, depictions of characters, and so on? These differences seem to go beyond the implied readers and epistolary genres involved, but how deep do they go? There is work to be done here on all kinds of levels, rhetorical, historical, theological, and literary.

A third line of literary inquiry that needs to be made is further study of the nature of ancient epistles, their use of rhetoric, and other literary conventions beyond epistolary nature and awareness of succession. How do advances in socio-scientific and other criticisms increase our understanding of these literary conventions?[8] Also, the ways Paul is depicted in the disputed Paulines (and in the non-disputed letters) need to be compared with the ways leaders and philosophers were depicted by themselves and by others in ancient Mediterranean literature.

Historical. Current work on the Pastorals still seems to be obsessed with the issue of authorship, and tied to a setting at least a generation removed from Paul's death. Pseudonymity remains an open question, regardless of the position of critical orthodoxy. During the writing of this study, four major English language commentaries on the Pastorals were published, those of Marshall,

---

7. R. Alan Culpepper, *Anatomy of the Fourth Gospel: A Study in Literary Design* (Philadelphia: Fortress Press, 1983). Two other studies offer promising examples of what can be done by applying narrative criticism to Paul's letters: Norman Petersen, *Rediscovering Paul: Philemon and the Sociology of Paul's Narrative World* (Philadelphia: Fortress Press, 1985), and David Trobisch, 'Let the Context Interpret: A Narrative Critical Approach to the Letters of Paul' (paper presented at the annual meeting of the Society of Biblical Literature, San Antonio, TX, 23 November 2004).

8. The work of Dale B. Martin provides an excellent model of this type of analysis: see his *Slavery as Salvation: The Metaphor of Slavery in Pauline Christianity* (New Haven: Yale University Press, 1990), and *The Corinthian Body* (New Haven: Yale University Press, 1995).

Mounce, Johnson, and Collins.⁹ Three of the four view the contents of the Pastorals as directly (Johnson, Mounce) or indirectly (Marshall) Pauline. Only Collins accepts and proceeds from the party line of pseudonymous, late first- or early second-century authorship.

In this study, I have attempted to show that it is possible to set that issue aside for a time to examine the ways that the Pastoral Epistles would have functioned for ancient auditors apart from a historical author and his specific *Sitz im Leben*. Generally speaking, future work on the Pastorals needs to proceed from an awareness that, whatever one concludes regarding authorship, both the historical audience and the authorial audience received these letters as Pauline.

On the other hand, the authorship of the Pastorals should not be disregarded. Succession's function in these letters demands a full evaluation of the possibility that Timothy is the actual author of the Pastorals, acting as both Paul's successor and tradent. One component of this evaluation is the question of how ancient authors described themselves when they were characters in their own stories, and how those self-descriptions compare with Timothy's role in these letters.

Theological. The most obvious area of theological inquiry in the Pastorals is in the area of ecclesiology: how can we understand and apply (or refute) what the Pastorals have to say about the nature of ministry, authority in the Church, transitions in ministry, training for ministry, women's roles in the Church, and other such issues? These areas are currently under intense investigation, but more ink remains to be spilled.

Other theological themes also promise reward for students of the Pastorals. These letters provide rich material for investigating New Testament Christology, soteriology, teaching on the nature of humanity, and so on. The interplay between the Pastorals' (supposed) waning eschatological fervor (what of 2 Tim. 4.1-5?) and the other theological themes needs to be thoroughly reexamined. What exactly is the eschatological outlook of the Pastoral Epistles?

Further, do the letters present a unified theological outlook, in terms of eschatology or their understandings of human nature, the purpose of suffering, the nature of ministry? Or do they differ significantly on these and other points? If so, what do those differences suggest about the situations from which the letters come?

These questions are but the beginning. The Pastoral Epistles are a rich and fertile field, promising abundant harvest to those who invest time and research here.

9. Marshall, *Pastoral Epistles*; Mounce, *Pastoral Epistles*; Johnson, *First and Second Letters to Timothy*; R. Collins, *1 & 2 Timothy and Titus*.

BIBLIOGRAPHY

Primary Sources

The Ante-Nicene Fathers (ed. Alexander Roberts and James Donaldson; 10 vols.; 1885–87 [reprinted edn, Peabody, MA: Hendrickson, 1994]).

The Apostolic Fathers (ed. Michael W. Holmes; trans. J.B. Lightfoot and J.R. Harmer; Grand Rapids: Baker Book House, 1989).

Aristotle, *Aristotle, with an English Translation* (trans. H. Rackham; LCL; 23 vols.; Cambridge, MA: Harvard University Press, 1932–38).

—*Politics* (trans. Benjamin Jowett; Oxford: Clarendon Press, 1921).

—*Sophistical Refutations* (trans. E.S. Forster; LCL; Cambridge, MA: Harvard University Press, 1955).

Athenagoras, *Legatio and De resurrectione* (trans. and ed. William R. Schoedel; Oxford: Clarendon Press, 1972).

Aulus Gellius, *Attic Nights* (trans. John C. Rolfe; LCL; 3 vols.; Cambridge, MA: Harvard University Press, 1948).

Baptism, Eucharist & Ministry 1982–1990 (Faith and Order Paper, 149; Geneva: WCC Publications, 1990).

Baptism, Eucharist, and Ministry (Faith and Order Paper, 111; Geneva: World Council of Churches, 1982).

Caesar, Julius, *The Gallic War* (trans. H.J. Edwards; LCL; Cambridge, MA: Harvard University Press, 1979).

Calvin, John, *Institutes of the Christian Religion* (trans. John Allen; 4 vols.; Philadelphia: Presbyterian Board of Christian Education, reprinted edn, 1986).

Clement of Alexandria, *Stromateis* (trans. John Ferguson; Fathers of the Church, 85; 2 vols.; Washington, DC: Catholic University of America Press, 1991).

Cyprian, *The Letters of St. Cyprian of Carthage* (trans. G.W. Clarke; Ancient Christian Writers, 43; New York: Newman, 1984).

Demosthenes, *Works* (trans. A.T. Murray; LCL; 7 vols.; Cambridge, MA: Harvard University Press, 1936).

Dio Cassius, *Roman History* (trans. Earnest Cary; LCL; 9 vols.; Cambridge, MA: Harvard University Press, 1955).

Dio Chrysostom, *Dio Chrysostom, with an English Translation* (trans. H.L. Crosby; LCL; 5 vols.; Cambridge, MA: Harvard University Press, 1964).

Diodorus of Sicily, *Bibliotheca historica* (trans. Charles L. Sherman, Charles H. Oldfather and C. Bradford Welles; LCL; 12 vols.; Cambridge, MA: Harvard University Press, 1952).

Diogenes Laertius, *Lives of Eminent Philosophers* (trans. R.D. Hicks; LCL; 2 vols.; London: Heinemann, 1966).

Eusebius, *Ecclesiastical History* (trans. Kirsopp Lake; LCL; 2 vols.; Cambridge, MA: Harvard University Press, 1944).

Herodotus, *Herodotus, with an English Translation* (trans. A.D. Godley; LCL; 4 vols.; Cambridge, MA: Harvard University Press, 1963).
Iamblichus, *On the Pythagorean Way of Life* (trans. John Dillon and Jackson Hershbell; Texts and Translations, Greco-Roman Religion Series; Atlanta: Scholars Press, 1991).
Josephus, *Josephus, with an English Translation* (trans. H. St. J. Thackeray *et al.*; LCL; 10 vols.; Cambridge, MA: Harvard University Press, 1956).
Livy, *Livy, with an English Translation* (trans. Frank Gardner Moore; LCL; 6 vols.; Cambridge, MA: Harvard University Press, 1940).
Lucian, *Lucian, with an English Translation* (trans. A.M. Harmon *et al.*; LCL; 8 vols.; Cambridge, MA: Harvard University Press, 1968).
Luther, Martin, *Luther's Works* (ed. Jaroslav Pelikan; trans. George Schick; 55 vols.; St Louis: Concordia Publishing House, 1958).
Lysias, *Lysias, with an English Translation* (trans. W.R.M. Lamb; LCL; Cambridge, MA: Harvard University Press, 1930).
Philo, *Philo, with an English Translation* (trans. F.H. Colson and G.H. Whitaker; LCL; 10 vols.; Cambridge, MA: Harvard University Press, 1929).
Plato, *Dialogues* (trans. Benjamin Jowett; 4 vols.; Oxford: Oxford University Press, 3rd edn, 1892).
—*Laws* (trans. R.G. Bury; LCL; Cambridge, MA: Harvard University Press, 1952).
Pliny, *Natural History* (trans. W.H.S. Jones; LCL; 10 vols.; Cambridge, MA: Harvard University Press, 1963).
Pope Leo XIII, *The Great Encyclical Letters of Pope Leo XIII* (New York: Benziger Brothers, 1903).
St Leo the Great, *Sermons* (trans. Jane Patricia Freeland and Agnes Josephine Conway; Washington, DC: Catholic University of America Press, 1996).
Second Vatican Council, *The Documents of Vatican II* (ed. Walter M. Abbott; New York: Guild, 1966).
Septuaginta (ed. A. Rahlfs; Stuttgart: Deutsche Bibelgesellschaft, 1982).
Strabo, *The Geography of Strabo* (trans. Horace Leonard Jones; LCL; 8 vols.; Cambridge, MA: Harvard University Press, 1928).
Tacitus, *Tacitus, in Five Volumes* (trans. John Jackson; LCL; 5 vols.; Cambridge, MA: Harvard University Press, 1937).
Thesaurus linguae graecae (Thesaurus Linguae Graecae; Irvine, CA: University of California, Irvine, 1996).
Thurian, Max (ed.), *Churches Respond to BEM*. II. *Official Responses to the 'Baptism, Eucharist and Ministry' Text* (Faith and Order Paper, 132; Geneva: World Council of Churches, 1986).
—*Churches Respond to BEM*. IV. *Official Responses to the 'Baptism, Eucharist and Ministry' Text* (Faith and Order Paper, 137; Geneva: World Council of Churches, 1987).
Xenophon, *Xenophon with an English Translation* (trans. C.L. Brownson; LCL; 4 vols., Cambridge, MA: Harvard University Press, 1947).

Secondary Sources

Alexander, Philip S., 'Enoch, Third Book of', in *ABD*, II, pp. 522-26.
Ascough, Richard S., *What are they Saying about the Formation of Pauline Churches?* (New York: Paulist Press, 1998).

Aune, David, *The New Testament in its Literary Environment* (LEC, 8; Philadelphia: Westminster Press, 1987).
Bakke, Odd Magne, *'Concord and Peace': A Rhetorical Analysis of the First Letter of Clement with an Emphasis on the Language of Unity and Sedition* (Tübingen: J.C.B. Mohr [Paul Siebeck], 2001).
Balch, David L., *Let Wives Be Submissive: The Domestic Code in 1 Peter* (SBLMS, 26; Chico, CA: Scholars Press, 1981).
Balch, David L., and Carolyn Osiek, *Families in the New Testament World: Households and House Churches* (Louisville, KY: John Knox Press, 1997).
Balz, Horst, and Gerhard Schneider (eds.), *Exegetical Dictionary of the New Testament* (trans. John W. Mendenorp; Grand Rapids: Eerdmans, 1990).
Barclay, John M.G., 'The Family as the Bearer of Religion', in Halvor Moxnes (ed.), *Constructing Early Christian Families: Family as Social Reality and Metaphor* (London: Routledge, 1997), pp. 66-80.
Barnard, Leslie W., *Athenagoras: A Study in Second Century Christian Apologetic* (Paris: Beauchesne, 1972).
Barnett, Albert E., *Paul Becomes a Literary Influence* (Chicago: University of Chicago Press, 1941).
Barrett, C.K., *Signs of an Apostle* (London: Epworth, 1970).
Bartlett, John R., *Jews in the Hellenistic World: Josephus, Aristeas, the Sibylline Oracles, Eupolemus* (Cambridge: Cambridge University Press, 1985).
Bassler, Jouette M., *1 Timothy, 2 Timothy, Titus* (Abingdon New Testament Commentaries; Nashville: Abingdon Press, 1996).
Bauckham, Richard J., 'Pseudo-Apostolic Letters', *JBL* 107 (1988), pp. 469-94.
Beker, J. Christiaan, *Heirs of Paul* (Philadelphia: Fortress Press, 1991).
Bergmann, Marie Theresa, 'Magic in Pliny's *Natural History*' (MA thesis, Washington University, 1940).
Bilde, Per, *Flavius Josephus between Jerusalem and Rome: His Life, his Works and their Importance* (JSPSup, 2; Sheffield: JSOT Press, 1988).
Boer, Martinus C. de, 'Images of Paul in the Post-Apostolic Period', *CBQ* 42 (1980), pp. 359-80.
Boesche, Roger, 'The Politics of Pretence: Tacitus and the Political Theory of Despotism', *History of Political Thought* 8 (1987), pp. 189-210.
Bookman, J.T., 'The Wisdom of the Many: An Analysis of the Arguments of Books III and IV of Aristotle's "Politics"', *History of Political Thought* 13 (1992), pp. 1-12.
Bowe, Barbara Ellen, *A Church in Crisis: Ecclesiology and Paraenesis in Clement of Rome* (Minneapolis: Fortress Press, 1988).
Brown, John, *Apostolical Succession in the Light of History and Fact* (London: Congregational Union of England and Wales, 1898).
Brown, Raymond E., *The Churches the Apostles Left Behind* (New York: Paulist Press, 1984).
Brox, Norbert, *Die Pastoralbriefe* (RNT; Regensburg: Friedrich Pustet, 1963).
Buck, P. Lorraine, 'Athenagoras's Embassy: A Literary Fiction', *HTR* 89 (1996), pp. 209-26.
Buell, Denise Kimber, *Making Christians: Clement of Alexandria and the Rhetoric of Legitimacy* (Princeton, NJ: Princeton University Press, 1999).
Bultmann, Rudolf, 'πιστόω', in *TDNT*, VI, pp. 178-79.
Burtchaell, James T., *From Synagogue to Church: Public Services and Offices in the Earliest Christian Communities* (Cambridge: Cambridge University Press, 1992).

Campbell, R. Alastair, *The Elders: Seniority within Earliest Christianity* (Edinburgh: T. & T. Clark, 1994).
Campenhausen, Hans von, *Ecclesiastical Authority and Spiritual Power in the Church of the First Three Centuries* (trans. J.A. Baker; Stanford, CA: Stanford University Press, 1969).
Caulley, Thomas Scott, 'Fighting the Good Fight: The Pastoral Epistles in Canonical-Critical Perspective', *Society of Biblical Literature Seminar Papers, 1987* (SBLSP, 26; Atlanta: Scholars Press, 1987), pp. 550-64.
Chesnut, Glenn F., 'Hegesippus', in *ABD*, III, pp. 110-11.
Collins, John J., *Daniel, First Maccabees, Second Maccabees* (Wilmington, DE: Michael Glazier, 1988).
Collins, Raymond, *1 & 2 Timothy and Titus: A Commentary* (NTL; Louisville, KY: Westminster/John Knox Press, 2002).
—*Letters that Paul Did Not Write: The Epistle to the Hebrews and the Pauline Pseudepigrapha* (Good News Studies, 28; Wilmington, DE: Michael Glazier, 1988).
Countryman, L. William, *The Rich Christian in the Church of the Early Empire: Contradictions and Accommodations* (New York: Edwin Mellen Press, 1980).
Culpepper, R. Alan, *Anatomy of the Fourth Gospel: A Study in Literary Design* (Philadelphia: Fortress Press, 1983).
Danker, Fredrick W., *Benefactor: Epigraphic Study of a Graeco-Roman and New Testament Semantic Field* (St Louis: Clayton, 1982).
Daube, David, *The New Testament and Rabbinic Judaism* (London: Athlone Press, 1956).
Davies, Margaret, *The Pastoral Epistles* (Epworth Commentaries; London: Epworth, 1996).
—*The Pastoral Epistles* (New Testament Guides; Sheffield: Sheffield Academic Press, 1996).
Davies, W.D., and Dale C. Allison, *A Critical and Exegetical Commentary on the Gospel according to Saint Matthew* (ICC; 3 vols.; Edinburgh: T. & T. Clark, 1991).
Davis, Michael, *The Politics of Philosophy: A Commentary on Aristotle's Politics* (Lanham, MD: Rowman & Littlefield, 1996).
Dibelius, Martin, and Hans Conzelmann, *The Pastoral Epistles* (Hermeneia; Philadelphia: Fortress Press, 1972).
DiLella, Alexander A., 'Wisdom of Ben-Sira', in *ABD*, VI, pp. 931-45.
Donelson, Lewis R., *Pseudepigraphy and Ethical Argument in the Pastoral Epistles* (Hermeneutische Untersuchungen zur Theologie, 22; Tübingen: J.C.B. Mohr [Paul Siebeck], 1986).
—'The Structure of Ethical Argument in the Pastorals', *BTB* 18 (1988), pp. 108-13.
Donovan, Mary Ann, 'Irenaeus', in *ABD*, III, pp. 457-61.
Duff, Jeremy, 'P46 and the Pastorals: A Misleading Consensus', *NTS* 44 (1998), pp. 578-90.
Easton, Burton Scott, *The Pastoral Epistles* (New York: Charles Scribner's Sons, 1947).
Ehrhardt, Arnold, *The Apostolic Succession in the First Two Centuries of the Church* (London: Lutterworth, 1953).
Farrer, Austin M., 'The Ministry in the New Testament', in Kenneth E. Kirk (ed.), *The Apostolic Ministry: Essays on the History and Doctrine of Episcopacy* (London: Hodder & Stoughton, 1946), pp. 113-83.
Fee, Gordon D., *1 and 2 Timothy, Titus* (New International Biblical Commentary on the New Testament; Peabody, MA: Hendrickson, rev. edn, 1988).

—*God's Empowering Presence: The Holy Spirit in the Letters of Paul* (Peabody, MA: Hendrickson, 1994).
Feldherr, Andrew, *Spectacle and Society in Livy's History* (Berkeley: University of California Press, 1998).
Feldman, H., 'Josephus', in *ABD*, III, pp. 981-98.
—*Josephus and Modern Scholarship* (Berlin: W. de Gruyter, 1984).
Ferguson, Everett, 'Apostolic Succession', in *idem* (ed.), *Encyclopedia of Early Christianity* (2 vols.; New York: Garland, 2nd edn, 1997), pp. 94-95.
Fiore, Benjamin, *The Function of Personal Example in the Socratic and Pastoral Epistles* (AnBib, 105; Rome: Biblical Institute Press, 1986).
Fischer, Thomas, 'First and Second Maccabees', in *ABD*, IV, pp. 439-50.
Floor, L., 'Church Order in the Pastoral Epistles', *Neotestamentica* 10 (1976), pp. 81-91.
Floyd, W.E.G., *Clement of Alexandria's Treatment of the Problem of Evil* (London: Oxford University Press, 1971).
Garland, David E., *Reading Matthew: A Literary and Theological Commentary on the First Gospel* (Reading the New Testament; New York: Crossroad, 1993).
Gerhardsson, Birger, *Memory and Manuscript: Oral Tradition and Written Transmission in Rabbinic Judaism and Early Christianity, with Tradition and Transmission in Early Christianity* (Biblical Resource Series; repr., Grand Rapids: Eerdmans, 1998).
Grant, Michael, *Readings in the Classical Historians* (New York: Charles Scribner's Sons, 1992).
Grant, Robert M., *Irenaeus of Lyons* (New York: Routledge, 1997).
Gunn, David M., *The Story of King David: Genre and Interpretation* (JSOTSup, 6; Sheffield: JSOT Press, 1978).
Guthrie, Donald, *The Pastoral Epistles* (Tyndale New Testament Commentaries; Downers Grove, IL: Intervarsity Press, 1983).
Hägg, Tomas, Philip Rousseau, and Christian Høgel, *Greek Biography and Panegyric in Late Antiquity* (Berkeley: University of California Press, 2000).
Halton, T., 'Hegesippus in Eusebius', *Studia patristica* 17 (1982), pp. 688-93.
Hammond, N.G.L., *Three Historians of Alexander the Great: The So-Called Vulgate Authors, Diodorus, Justin, and Curtius* (Cambridge: Cambridge University Press, 1983).
Hanson, A.T., *The Pastoral Epistles* (NCBC; Grand Rapids: Eerdmans, 1982).
Harding, Mark, *Tradition and Rhetoric in the Pastoral Epistles* (Studies in Biblical Literature, 3; New York: Peter Lang, 1998).
—*What are they Saying about the Pastoral Epistles?* (New York: Paulist Press, 2001).
Hasler, Victor, *Die Briefe an Timotheus und Titus* (Zürich: Theologischer Verlag, 1978).
Hirsch, Steven W., *The Friendship of the Barbarians: Xenophon and the Persian Empire* (Hanover: University Press of New England, 1985).
Holford-Strevens, Leofranc, *Aulus Gellius* (Chapel Hill: University of North Carolina Press, 1989).
Holladay, Carl R., 'Eupolemus', in *ABD*, II, p. 671.
Holmberg, Bengt, *Paul and Power: The Structure of Authority in the Primitive Church as Reflected in the Pastoral Epistles* (Philadelphia: Fortress Press, 1980).
Hornblower, Simon, and Antony Spawforth (eds.), *Oxford Classical Dictionary* (Oxford: Oxford University Press, 3rd edn, 1996).
Horrell, David G., *The Social Ethos of the Corinthian Correspondence: Interests and Ideology from 1 Corinthians to 1 Clement* (Edinburgh: T. & T. Clark, 1996).

Jacobson, Howard, *A Commentary on Pseudo-Philo's* Liber Antiquitatum Biblicarum, *with Latin Text and English Translation* (2 vols.; Leiden: E.J. Brill, 1996).
Jauss, Hans Robert, *Toward an Aesthetic of Reception* (Minneapolis: University of Minnesota Press, 1982).
Jeffers, James S., *Conflict at Rome: Social Order and Hierarchy in Early Christianity* (Minneapolis: Fortress Press, 1991).
Johnson, Luke Timothy, *1 Timothy, 2 Timothy, Titus* (Knox Preaching Guides; Atlanta: John Knox Press, 1987).
—'2 Timothy and the Polemic against False Teachers: A Re-examination', *Ohio Journal of Religious Studies* 6/7 (1978-79), pp. 1-26.
—*The First and Second Letters to Timothy* (AB, 35A; New York: Doubleday, 2001).
—*Letters to Paul's Delegates* (The New Testament in Context; Valley Forge, PA: Trinity Press, 1996).
Judge, Edwin A., *The Social Pattern of Christian Groups in the First Century: Some Prolegomena to the Study of New Testament Ideas of Social Obligation* (London: Tyndale Press, 1960).
Karris, Robert J., 'The Background and Significance of the Polemic of the Pastoral Epistles', *JBL* 93 (1973), pp. 549-64.
—*The Pastoral Epistles* (Wilmington, DE: Michael Glazier, 1979).
Käsemann, Ernst, *New Testament Questions of Today* (trans. Wilfred F. Bunge; London: SCM Press, 1969).
—'Paul and Early Catholicism', in idem, *New Testament Questions of Today*, pp. 236-51.
Kelly, J.N.D., *A Commentary on the Pastoral Epistles* (Black New Testament Commentary; London: A. & C. Black, 1963).
Kennedy, George, *The Art of Persuasion in Greece* (Princeton, NJ: Princeton University Press, 1963).
—*The Art of Rhetoric in the Roman World, 300 BC–AD 300* (Princeton, NJ: Princeton University Press, 1972).
Kidd, Reggie, *Wealth and Beneficence in the Pastoral Epistles* (SBLDS, 122; Atlanta: Scholars Press, 1990).
Kimball, Dan, *Emerging Worship: Creating Worship Gatherings for New Generations* (Grand Rapids, MI: Zondervan/emergentYS, 2004).
Knight, George W., *The Pastoral Epistles: A Commentary on the Greek Text* (New International Greek Testament Commentary; Grand Rapids: Eerdmans, 1992).
Küng, Hans (ed.), *Apostolic Succession: Rethinking a Barrier to Unity* (Concilium, 34; New York: Paulist Press, 1968).
Lawton, Robert B., 'Saul, Jonathan, and the "Son of Jesse"', *JSOT* 58 (1993), pp. 35-46.
Lips, H. von., *Glaube–Gemeinde–Amt: Zum Verständnis der Ordination in den Pastoralbriefen* (Göttingen: Vandenhoeck & Ruprecht, 1979).
Lucks, Henry A., *The Philosophy of Athenagoras: Its Sources and Value* (Washington DC: Catholic University of America Press, 1936).
Macdonald, Margaret Y., *The Pauline Churches: A Socio-Historical Study of Institutionalization in the Pauline and Deutero-Pauline Writings* (SNTSMS, 60; Cambridge: Cambridge University Press, 1988).
MacKenzie, R.A.F., *Sirach* (Wilmington, DE: Michael Glazier, 1983).
Malherbe, Abraham J., *Ancient Epistolary Theorists* (SBLRBS, 19; Atlanta: Scholars Press, 1988).
—*The Cynic Epistles* (SBLRBS, 12; Atlanta: Scholars Press, 1986).

—'Hellenistic Moralists and the New Testament', in H. Temporini and W. Haase (eds.), *Aufstieg und Niedergang der römischen Welt: Geschichte und Kultur Roms im Spiegel der neueren Forschung* (37 vols.; Berlin: W. de Gruyter, 1993), II, pp. 267-333.
—*Paul and the Popular Philosophers* (Minneapolis: Fortress Press, 1989).
Marshall, I. Howard, *Kept by the Power of God: A Study of Perseverance and Falling Away* (Carlisle: Paternoster Press, 3rd edn, 1995).
—'Salvation, Grace, and Works in the Later Writings in the Pauline Corpus', *NTS* 42 (1996), pp. 339-58.
Marshall, I. Howard, with Philip H. Towner, *A Critical and Exegetical Commentary on the Pastoral Epistles* (ICC; Edinburgh: T. & T. Clark, 1999).
Martin, Dale B., *The Corinthian Body* (New Haven: Yale University Press, 1995).
—*Slavery as Salvation: The Metaphor of Slavery in Pauline Christianity* (New Haven: Yale University Press, 1990).
Martin, Seán Charles, *Pauli Testamentum: 2 Timothy and the Last Words of Moses* (Rome: Gregorian University Press, 1997).
McKenzie, Stephen L., 'The So-Called Succession Narrative in the Deuteronomistic History', in Albert de Pury and Thomas Römer (eds.), *Die sogenannte Thronfolgegeschichte Davids* (Göttingen: Vandenhoeck & Ruprecht, 2000), pp. 123-35.
Meade, David G., *Pseudonymity and Canon* (WUNT, 39; Tübingen: J.C.B. Mohr [Paul Siebeck], 1986).
Meeks, Wayne A., *The First Urban Christians: The Social World of the Apostle Paul* (New Haven: Yale University Press, 1983).
Mejer, Jørgen, *Diogenes Laertius and his Hellenistic Background* (Wiesbaden: Steiner, 1978).
Metzger, Bruce M., 'Literary Forgeries and Canonical Pseudepigrapha', *JBL* 91 (1972), pp. 3-24.
Minns, Denis, *Irenaeus* (London: Geoffrey Chapman, 1994).
Moore, J.M., *Aristotle and Xenophon on Democracy and Oligarchy* (Berkeley: University of California Press, 1975).
Mounce, William, *The Pastoral Epistles* (WBC; Nashville: Thomas Nelson, 2000).
Murphy-O'Connor, Jerome, *Paul the Letter-Writer: His World, his Options, his Skills* (Collegeville, MN: Liturgical Press, 1995).
O'Brien, Mark A., 'The Portrayal of Prophets in 2 Kings 2', *Australian Biblical Review* 46 (1998), pp. 1-16.
Oberlinner, Lorenz, *Die Pastoralbriefe: Kommentar zum ersten Timotheusbrief* (HTKNT, XI/1; Freiburg: Herder, 1994).
—*Die Pastoralbriefe: Kommentar zum zweiten Timotheusbrief* (HTKNT, XI/2; Freiburg: Herder, 1995).
Odeberg, Hugo, *3 Enoch* (New York: Ktav, 1973).
Patte, Daniel, *The Religious Dimensions of Biblical Texts: Greimas's Structural Semiotics and Biblical Exegesis* (Atlanta: Scholars Press, 1990).
Pervo, Richard, 'Romancing an Oft-Neglected Stone: The Pastoral Epistles and the Epistolary Novel', *Journal of Higher Criticism* 1 (1994), pp. 25-48.
Petersen, Norman, *Rediscovering Paul: Philemon and the Sociology of Paul's Narrative* (Philadelphia: Fortress Press, 1985).
Pöhlmann, W., 'μορφόω', in *EDNT*, II, pp. 443-44.

Pomeroy, Sarah B., *Goddesses, Whores, Wives, and Slaves: Women in Classical Antiquity* (New York: Schocken Books, 1995).
Porter, J.R., and John I. Durham (eds.), *Proclamation and Presence: Old Testament Essays in Honour of Gwynne Henton Davies* (Richmond, VA: John Knox Press, 1970).
Priest, John F., 'Moses, Testament of', in *ABD*, IV, pp. 920-22.
Prior, Michael, *Paul the Letter-Writer and the Second Letter to Timothy* (JSNTSup, 23; Sheffield: JSOT Press, 1989).
Quinn, Jerome D., 'The Pastoral Epistles', *Bible Today* 23 (1985), pp. 228-38.
Quinn, Jerome D., and William Wacker, *The First and Second Letters to Timothy* (Eerdmans Critical Commentary; Grand Rapids: Eerdmans, 1999).
Rabinowitz, Peter J., *Before Reading: Narrative Conventions and the Politics of Interpretation* (Ithaca, NY: Cornell University Press, 1987).
—'Truth in Fiction', *Critical Inquiry* 4 (1977), pp. 121-41.
—'Whirl without End: Audience-Oriented Criticism', in G. Douglas Atkins and Laura Morrow (eds.), *Contemporary Literary Theory* (Amherst, MA: University of Massachusetts Press, 1989), pp. 81-100.
Rahner, Karl, and Joseph Ratzinger, *The Episcopate and the Primacy* (trans. Kenneth Barker, *et al.*; Quaestiones disputatae; New York: Herder & Herder, 1962).
Rajak, Tessa, *The Jewish Dialogue with Greece and Rome: Studies in Cultural and Social Interaction* (Leiden: E.J. Brill, 2001).
Reed, Jeffrey T., 'To Timothy or Not? A Discourse Analysis of 1 Timothy', in Stanley E. Porter and D.A. Carson (eds.), *Biblical Greek Language and Linguistics: Open Questions in Current Research* (JSNTSup, 80; Sheffield: JSOT Press, 1993), pp. 90-118.
Rich, J.W., *The Augustan Settlement: Roman History 53–59/Cassius Dio* (Warminster: Aris & Phillips, 1990).
Richards, William A., *Difference and Distance in Post-Pauline Christianity: An Epistolary Analysis of the Pastorals* (Studies in Biblical Literature, 44; New York: Peter Lang, 2002).
Roloff, Jurgen, *Der erste Brief an Timotheus* (Zurich: Benziger, 1988).
Romm, James, *Herodotus* (New Haven: Yale University Press, 1998).
Rosen, Edward, 'How the Shackles Were Forged and Later Loosened', *Journal of the History of Ideas* 38 (1977), pp. 109-17.
Schlarb, Egbert, *Die gesunde Lehre: Häresie und Wahrheit im Spiegel der Pastoralbriefe* (Marburg: Elwert, 1990).
Schlatter, Adolf, *Die Briefe an die Thessalonicher, Philipper, Timotheus und Titus* (Erläuterungen zum Neuen Testament; Stuttgart: Calwer Verlag, 1964).
—*Romans: The Righteousness of God* (trans. Siegfried Schatzmann; Peabody, MA: Hendrickson, 1995).
Schwarz, Roland, *Bürgerliches Christentum im Neuen Testament?* (Klosterneuburg: Österreichesches Katholisches Bibelwerk, 1983).
Simms, Lawrence Joseph, 'Tacitus on Seneca: An Interpretation' (MA thesis, University of North Carolina, 1969).
Skeat, T.C., '"Especially the Parchments": A Note on 2 Timothy IV.3', *JTS* 30 (1979), pp. 173-77.
Spicq, Ceslas, *Saint Paul. Les Epîtres pastorales* (Etudes bibliques; Paris: J. Gabalda, 4th edn, 1969).

Stählin, G., 'χήρα', in *TDNT*, IX, pp. 440-65.
Stalley, R.F., *An Introduction to Plato's Laws* (Indianapolis: Hackett, 1983).
Steger, Carlos Alfredo, *Apostolic Succession in the Writings of Yves Congar and Oscar Cullmann* (Andrews University Seminary Doctoral Dissertation Series; Berrien Springs, MI: Andrews University Press, 1993).
Stewart-Sykes, Alistair, 'The Original Condemnation of Asian Montanism', *Journal of Ecclesiastical History* 50 (1999), pp. 1-22.
Stiefel, Jennifer H., 'Women Deacons in 1 Timothy: A Linguistic and Literary Look at "Women Likewise..." (1 Tim 3.11)', *NTS* 41 (1995), pp. 442-57.
Stirewalt, Martin L., 'The Form and Function of the Greek Letter-Essay', in Karl P. Donfried (ed.), *The Romans Debate* (Peabody, MA: Hendrickson, rev. edn, 1991), pp. 147-71.
Stowers, Stanley K., *Letter Writing in Greco-Roman Antiquity* (LEC, 5; Philadelphia: Westminster Press, 1986).
Stylianou, P.J., *A Historical Commentary on Diodorus Siculus, Book 15* (Oxford: Clarendon Press, 1998).
Talbert, Charles H., and Perry L. Stepp, 'Succession in Mediterranean Antiquity, Part 1: The Lukan Milieu', and 'Succession in Mediterranean Antiquity, Part 2: Luke–Acts', in *Society of Biblical Literature Seminar Papers, 1998* (SBLSP, 37; 2 vols.; Atlanta: Scholars Press, 1998), I, pp. 148-68 and 169-79.
Talstra, E., 'Deuteronomy 31: Confusion or Conclusion? The Story of Moses' Threefold Succession', in Marc Vervenne and Johan Lust (eds.), *Deuteronomy and Deuteronomic Literature: Festschrift for C.H.W. Brekelmans* (Leuven: Peeters, 1997), pp. 87-110.
Thrall, Margaret, 'The Pauline Uses of ΣΥΝΕΔΗΣΙΣ', *NTS* 14 (1967–68), pp. 118-25.
Thurston, Bonnie B., *The Widows: A Women's Ministry in the Early Church* (Philadelphia: Fortress Press, 1989).
Towner, Philip H., 'Gnosis and Realized Eschatology in Ephesus (of the Pastoral Epistles) and the Corinthian Enthusiasm', *JSNT* 31 (1987), pp. 95-124.
—*The Goal of our Instruction* (JSNTSup, 34; Sheffield: JSOT Press, 1989).
Trobisch, David, 'Let the Context Interpret: A Narrative Critical Approach to the Letters of Paul' (paper presented at the annual meeting of the Society of Biblical Literature, San Antonio, TX, 23 November 2004).
—*Paul's Letter Collection* (Minneapolis: Fortress Press, 1994).
Tromp, Johannes, *The Assumption of Moses: A Critical Edition with Commentary* (Leiden: E.J. Brill, 1993).
Verner, David C., *The Household of God: The Social World of the Pastoral Epistles* (SBLDS, 71; Chico, CA: Scholars Press, 1983).
Wacholder, Ben Zion, *Eupolemus: A Study of Judaeo-Greek Literature* (Cincinnati: Hebrew Union College–Jewish Institute of Religion, 1975).
Warkentin, Marjorie, *Ordination—A Biblical-Historical View* (Grand Rapids: Eerdmans, 1982).
Welborn, Laurence L., 'Clement, First Epistle of', in *ABD*, I, pp. 1055-60.
Wild, Robert A., 'The Image of Paul in the Pastoral Letters', *Bible Today* 23 (1985), pp. 239-45.
Winter, Bruce, 'Providentia for the Widows of 1 Timothy 5.3-16', *TynBul* 39 (1988), pp. 83-99.

Wolter, Michael, *Die Pastoralbriefe als Paulustradition* (Göttingen: Vandenhoeck & Ruprecht, 1988).
Young, Frances M., 'On ΕΠΙΣΚΟΠΟΣ and ΠΡΕΣΒΥΤΕΡΟΣ', *JTS* NS 45 (1994), pp. 142-48.
—'The Pastoral Epistles and the Ethics of Reading', in Stanley E. Porter and Craig A. Evans (eds.), *The Pauline Writings: A Sheffield Reader* (Biblical Seminar, 34; Sheffield: Sheffield Academic Press, 1995), pp. 268-82.
—*The Theology of the Pastoral Epistles* (Cambridge: Cambridge University Press, 1994).

INDEXES

INDEX OF REFERENCES

Old Testament
Genesis
12	61
20	61
36	20
36.33-39	20, 61
36.33-36	62

Exodus
14	63
18.13-26	94
24.13	63
29.29	68
33.11	63

Numbers
20.25-28	61
27.12-23	1, 62, 64, 81, 89, 90, 194, 203
27.12-13	95, 185
27.16-17	63
27.17	62
27.18-20	62

Deuteronomy
10.6	69

Joshua
1.1	63
1.2-9	62, 64, 81, 89, 95, 185, 194, 203
1.3	63
1.5	63
1.17	63

3	63
3.7	63
4.14	63

Judges
2.10-11	204
2.10	204
2.11	204
3.7	204
3.12	204
4.1	204
6.1	204
10.6	204
13.1	204
17.6	204
18.1	204
19.1	204
21.25	204

1 Samuel
7.7-14	64
8	65
8.20	65
9–18 LXX	64, 67, 89, 90, 193, 194
9–18	64, 67, 89, 90, 193, 194
9	66
9.16	65, 66
10.1-10	65
10.1-8	65
11	65
13	65
14.1-15	65
14.45	65
14.47	65

14.52	65
15.1-33	65
16.1-13	65
16.13	65
16.14	65
17	65
17.38-39	65
18.1-4	65
18.6-7	65, 66
18.27	65
19.8	65
20.15	66
20.42	66
23	65
31.2	66
31.4-6	66

2 Samuel
5	65
7	67, 68
7.11-16	67, 70
8	65
10.1	69

1 Kings
1–2 LXX	67, 69, 89-91, 194, 195
1–2	61, 67, 69, 74, 75, 82, 89-91, 194, 195
1.13	68
1.30	68
1.40	68
1.48	68
2	68

Index of References

2.15	68	8	71	33.25	69
2.24	68, 113	8.12	70	36.8	69
2.24 LXX	113	8.19	70		
11.43	69, 70, 90, 195	8.24	69	*Esther*	
		9	71	10.3	61, 181
11.44	69	10.32	70		
11.44 LXX	69, 70, 90, 195	10.35	69	*Ecclesiastes*	
		12.21	69	2.12	68
14.20	69	13.7	70		
14.31	69	13.9	69	Apocrypha or Deutero-	
15.4	70	13.24	69	Canonical books	
15.8	69	14.6	69	*Ecclesiasticus*	
15.24	69	14.29	69	44–51	73
16.6	69	15.7	69	46.1	61
16.28	69	15.22	69	47	73
18	72	15.38	69	47.11-13	73, 74, 82, 90, 195
19	70, 72, 81, 89, 90, 95, 193, 195	16.20	69		
		19.34	70	47.11	73, 74
		20.6	70	47.12-13	73
19 LXX	70, 72, 81, 89, 90, 95, 193, 195	20.21	69	47.12	74
		21.18	69	48.8	61
		21.24	69		
		21.26	69	*1 Maccabees*	
		24.6	69	2	76
19.15-18	72			2.17	76
19.16	70, 71	*1 Chronicles*		2.24-25	76
19.19	71	1.44-50	61, 62	2.42-48	76
19.21	71	18.17	61, 181	2.49-68	76
22.40	69	19.1	69	2.65-66	76
22.50	69	27.7	61, 68	2.65	90, 195
		27.34	61, 68	3.1	76, 90, 195
2 Kings		29.28	69		
2	70-72, 81, 89, 90, 95, 193, 195			3.33	77
		2 Chronicles		6	78
		9.31	69	6.12-13	77
		12.16	69	6.14-15	77, 78, 90, 195
2 LXX	70, 72, 81, 89, 90, 95, 193, 195	14.1	69		
		17.1	69	6.55-61	77
		21.1	69		
		24.27	69	*2 Maccabees*	
2.8	71	26.11	61, 181	4.29	61, 181
2.9-10	71	26.23	69	4.31	61, 181
2.11-12	71	28.7	61, 181	9	78
2.13 LXX	71	31.12	61, 181	9.13-18	78
2.13-15	71	32.33	69	9.19-27	78
2.24	153	33.20	69		

2 Maccabees (cont.)

9.22-27	78, 79, 89, 90, 194, 195			1.18-19	122, 126, 132, 133, 136, 138, 140, 147, 148
14.26	61, 181			1.18-19a	124
				1.18	4, 123, 124, 135-37, 139, 156, 175, 202

New Testament

Matthew

		Romans			
		2.20	172		
		16.1	200		
16.13-20	91, 93, 108, 110, 195	*Philippians*			
		1.1	200		
		Colossians			
		1.24	154, 164		
		1.29	119		
16.18-19	92	*1 Timothy*		1.19-20	136
28.18-20	202	1.1-11	114, 133	1.19b-20	131, 133
		1.1	113-15, 118, 121	1.19	124
				1.20	171

Luke

1.1-4	104, 110, 196	1.3-11	186	2.1-7	126, 133
		1.3-5	117, 142, 148	2.1-4	127, 143, 148, 203
5.17-26	93				
6.19	94	1.3-4	120, 133	2.1-2	126
7.11-17	94	1.3	114, 116, 118, 121-23, 133, 135, 136, 138, 140, 147, 148, 151, 156, 174	2.2	127
22.28-30	93-95, 110, 117, 195			2.4	127
				2.5-6a	119, 133
				2.6b	127
				2.7	113, 114, 121, 134, 136, 153
				2.8-15	120, 126, 128, 133, 143, 148

Acts

1.7-8	115				
1.8	202				
3.1-10	94	1.4	119, 139, 143, 203		
5.15	94				
6–7	94-96, 108, 110, 183, 193, 195	1.5	123, 136	2.12	120, 122, 129, 133, 141, 147, 148, 150, 151
		1.7a	116		
		1.8-11	116, 122, 160		
6	94	1.8	140, 148		
6.1	94	1.9	113	3	202
6.2-4	94	1.11	113, 114, 118, 121, 138, 154, 167	3.1-13	130, 132, 133, 147
6.6	95			3.1-7	133
9.36-43	94			3.2-12	145
20.29-31	141			3.2-7	144, 148
20.29	172	1.12-16	125, 131, 133	3.2	122, 133, 151
21	96				
23.12-22	96	1.12-15	114, 121		
24–25	195	1.12	113, 153	3.5	151
24.27	96, 97, 110	1.13	131	3.8-15	133
		1.15	119, 133	3.8-13	145, 148
25.9	96, 97, 110	1.16	136	3.9	124

Index of References   221

3.11	145	5.17	137, 139,	1.4	176	
3.14-15	11, 126,		144, 151	1.5	167	
	130, 132,	5.19-25	132, 133	1.6-9	169, 176	
	133, 142,	5.19-20	136	1.6-7	159, 167,	
	143, 148,	5.20-22	147		176	
	199	5.20	130, 133,	1.6	137, 139,	
3.15	126		146		159, 167,	
3.16	119, 133	5.21	133, 135		169, 174	
4.1-5	120, 133	5.22	132, 136,	1.7	156, 167,	
4.1	124, 203		147, 148,		176	
4.4-6	119, 133		150	1.8	162, 164,	
4.6-11	141, 148	5.22a	146		167, 170,	
4.6	124	5.22b-25	130, 133		173, 174,	
4.7-11	119, 121,	5.24-25	147		176	
	133	5.24	132	1.9b-10	158, 164	
4.7-10	120, 121,	6.1-2	143, 148	1.9	156, 167,	
	133	6.1-2a	129, 133		176, 202	
4.8	119	6.2b-4	118, 133	1.11-12	153-56,	
4.10	119	6.2b	133		162, 164,	
4.10b	119	6.10	124		176	
4.11-16	137, 142,	6.11-15	123, 138	1.11	157, 164,	
	148	6.12-15	133, 140,		167, 176	
4.11-14	136		147, 148	1.12-14	4	
4.11	130, 133	6.12	124, 135	1.12	154, 155,	
4.12	130, 133,	6.13-21	174		174	
	136, 142,	6.13-15	161	1.13-14	159, 165,	
	202	6.13-14	135		175-77	
4.13-15	139, 147	6.14-20	136	1.13	157, 164,	
4.13	11, 136	6.14	123, 136		174, 177	
4.14	136, 151,	6.17-19	129, 142,	1.14	154, 167,	
	159, 168,		143, 148		169, 174-	
	202	6.17-18	133		76	
4.16	130, 133	6.17	148	1.15	162, 164	
5.1–6.2a	119	6.19	148	2.1-2	174, 177	
5.1-2	129, 133,	6.20	123, 124,	2.1	170, 176	
	143, 148		133, 135,	2.2	158, 160,	
5.3–6.2a	118		136, 138,		161, 164,	
5.3-16	129, 133,		140, 147,		165, 167,	
	141, 142,		148, 154,		168, 175,	
	148, 151		175		176, 199,	
5.5	151	6.21	124, 151		202	
5.8	124			2.3	162, 164,	
5.10	151	*2 Timothy*			167, 173,	
5.14-15	143, 148	1.1	156		174, 176	
5.17-20	146, 147	1.2-3	167	2.4-7	161, 164,	
5.17-19	148	1.3	176		170, 176	

Reference	Pages	Reference	Pages	Reference	Pages
2 Timothy (cont.)		4.1-2	161, 167, 174, 176	**Pseudepigrapha**	
2.4	168, 176			*3 Enoch*	
2.8-10	162, 164	4.1	169	48D.6-10	90, 196
2.8	158, 159, 164, 174, 175, 177	4.2-5	167, 176	48D6-10	86, 87
		4.3-4	158, 162, 164, 172, 176	*4 Maccabees*	
2.11-13	158, 164			4.15	61
2.11	154	4.5	161, 162, 164, 167, 173, 174, 176		
2.12	162-64, 167, 173, 176			*Pseudo-Philo*	
				19.16	79
				20.2	80
2.14-17a	171	4.6-8	163, 167, 176	20.3	80
2.14	160, 161, 171, 174			20.5	80
		4.6-7	157, 164	25.3	80
2.15-18	161	4.7-8	173, 174, 176		
2.15-17a	176			*Testament of Moses*	
2.15	159, 175, 177	4.7	124	1.6-10	81, 82, 90, 195
		4.9-13	168, 169		
2.17	161	4.9-11	176	1.919-34	81
2.20-26	161, 171, 176	4.9-10	162, 164	10.15	81, 90, 195
		4.14-15	162, 164, 173, 174		
3.1-13	173				
3.1-9	158, 162, 164, 172, 176	4.14	167	**Ancient Jewish Authors**	
		4.16-18	163	*Josephus*	
		4.17	156	*Antiquities*	
3.6	173			4.165	63
3.8	124	*Titus*		7.14.2+337	82, 83, 90, 195
3.10-12	163	1	202		
3.10-11	157, 158, 164	1.1-3	179, 180	8.7+353	71
		1.3	179	9.2.1+18	82
3.10	124, 164, 165, 176, 202	1.5-7	200	9.2.2+27-28	82, 83, 90, 195
		1.5	180, 199		
		1.13	124		
3.12-13	162, 164	2.2	124	*Apion*	
3.12b-13	172, 176	2.3-5	151	1.1+15	84
3.12	162, 164, 165, 167, 176	2.7-8	180, 202	1.7+31	87-90, 193, 197
		2.15	180		
		3.12-15	181, 199	1.8+41	85, 86, 89, 90, 193, 196
		3.12	198, 199		
3.13	173				
3.14-17	160, 176, 177	*Philemon*		1.17+110	84, 85, 90, 195
3.14	167, 168, 176	8–9	130	1.41	85
3.16-17	158, 164	*Hebrews*			
4.1-5	164, 167, 207	13.23	165		

Index of References

Life		Cyprian		Aristotle	
1.1+3	87-90, 193, 197	*Letters*		*Athenian Constitution*	
1.1+6	87-90, 193, 197	3.3.1	4	28.1-4	26, 27, 29, 31, 56, 58, 193, 194
		66.4.2	4		
1.76+428-29	84, 90, 195	Eupolemus		28.1	26
		Preparation for the Gospel		28.3	26
Philo		9.30	75	28.4	28
Virtues		9.30+447c-d	74, 75		
68–70	63			*Politics*	
		Eusebius		12.93a.13-30	58
Christian Authors		*Ecclesiastical History*		1293.13-20	
Athenagoras		4.21-22	100, 101	§§4.5.6	26
Legatio		5.14-19	102, 103	1293a-13-30	
4–30	105	5.17	102	§§4.5.6	25
28	105, 110, 196	4.21.1	101	1293a.13-30	25, 27
		4.22.3	101	1293a.21-26	
28.5	105	5.17.4	103	§§4.5.7	26
37	99, 100, 108, 110, 194, 195			1293a23-30	
		Irenaeus		§§4.5.7-8	26
		Against Heresies		1923a.13-30	193, 194
37.2-3	99, 128	3.2.1-2	106, 110, 196		
				Sophistical Refutations	
		3.2.2	3, 106	34.27-35	
1 Clement		3.3.1-3	107, 110, 196	§§183b.28-32	47
20.10	128				
42–44	2, 6, 97, 98, 108, 110, 193, 195, 201	3.3.1	3, 107	34.27-35	47, 48, 59
		3.3.3	107		
				Aulus Gellius	
42	175	St Leo the Great		*Attic Nights*	
42.1-2	98	*Sermons*		13.5	1, 39, 40, 58
42.4	98	3.3	5		
43	98				
43.1–44.1	98	Tertullian		Caesar	
44.1	98	*Prescription against Heretics*		*Gallic Wars*	
44.2-3	98			6.13	20
60.4	128	20–21	3		
		21	4	Demosthenes	
Clement of Alexandria		25	4	*Aphobus*	
Stromateis				2.19	51, 52, 56, 57, 59
1.21.109	101	Classical Authors			
1.21.109.2-4	101	Appianus		25	197
1.21.110.4–111.2	102	*Syriaca*			
		343.1	1		

Dio Cassius		4.67	41, 42, 53, 58, 195	Pausanius	
40.14.2.5	1			*Description of Greece*	
53	38, 57, 58, 194			7.12	36, 58, 194
		9.115	41, 42, 56, 58, 195	7.12.2	36
53.30-31	38				
53.30.2	38	10.9	43, 58, 195	Plato	
53.31.1	38			*Laws*	
53.31.3	113	10.17	43	5.740b	52, 53, 59, 197
53.31.4	38				
53.32.1	38	Herodianus		6.769	23, 56, 194
54.11.6	38	6.2.6.7	1		
				6.769c	23-25, 56, 58, 193
Dio Chrysostom		Herodotus			
64	37, 56	*Histories*			
64.20-22	32, 37, 45, 58, 194	3.53	20-23, 55, 56, 58, 193, 194	Pliny the Elder	
				Natural History	
		5.90-92	21-23, 31, 56, 58, 193, 194	30.2.4-5	48, 49, 59
64.20-21	37			Plutarch	
64.22	37			*Alexander*	
				72.3	31
Diodorus Siculus					
10.30.1-2	53, 54, 197	Iamblichus			
15.8-11	28, 29, 56, 58, 194	*On the Pythagorean Way of Life*		*Demetrius*	
				5.1.4	1
		36	44, 58		
15.93.1	30, 58, 95, 181, 185, 194	36.265	44	Strabo	
		36.266	44	*Geography*	
				11.13.9	32, 33, 58, 194
17–18	31, 32, 37, 45, 58, 194	Livy			
		23.27.9-12	34, 35, 58, 194	13.1.3	33, 34, 58, 194
17.117.3-4	31				
17.117.4	1	Lucian		Tacitus	
17.118.2	31	*Alexander the False Prophet*		*Annals*	
18.3-4	1			15.48-71	49
18.4.1	1, 31	5	54, 55, 59, 197	15.62	49, 50, 56, 59, 125
18.4.3	31				
18.4.6	31				
		Lysias			
Diogenes Laertius		*Pension*		Xenophon	
1.20	43	6	45, 59, 95, 181, 183, 196	*Anabasis*	
2.108-109	43			1.5.2	46, 47, 59
4.65-67	41				
4.65	41				

INDEX OF AUTHORS

Alexander, P.S. 86
Allison, D.C. 92
Aune, D. 10

Bakke, O.M. 97
Balch, D.L. 128, 130
Barclay, J.M.G. 130
Barnard, L.W. 99
Bartlett, J.R. 74
Bassler, J.M. 120
Bauckham, R.J. 200
Beker, J.C. 128
Bergmann, M.T. 49
Bilde, P. 82
Boer, M.C. de 125
Boesche, R. 50
Bookman, J.T. 26
Bowe, B.E. 97
Brox, N. 120, 146, 163, 175
Buck, P.L. 99
Buell, D.K. 101
Bultmann, R. 167
Burtchaell, J.T. 144

Calvin, J. 6
Campbell, R.A. 145
Campenhausen, H. von 2, 144, 145
Caulley, T.S. 115
Chesnut, G.F. 101
Collins, J.J. 76
Collins, R. 120, 123-26, 128, 131, 132, 137, 143, 145, 146, 157, 161, 164, 166-68, 170, 171, 175, 179, 207
Conzelmann, H. 120, 124, 125, 127, 138, 146, 160, 161
Countryman, L.W. 142
Culpepper, R.A. 206

Danker, F.W. 142
Daube, D. 137
Davies, W.D. 92
Davis, M. 26
Dibelius, M. 120, 124, 125, 127, 138, 146, 160, 161
DiLella, A.A. 73
Donelson, L.R. 125
Donovan, M.A. 106
Durham, J.I. 62

Easton, B.S. 166, 173

Fee, G.D. 124, 153, 168
Feldherr, A. 35
Feldman, H. 82
Ferguson, E. 5, 8
Fiore, B. 125
Fischer, T. 76
Floyd, W.E.G. 101

Garland, D.E. 92
Grant, M. 29
Grant, R.M. 106
Gunn, D.M. 68
Guthrie, D. 157, 175

Hägg, T. 44
Halton, T. 101
Hammond, N.G.L. 31
Hasler, V. 168, 169
Hirsch, S.W. 46
Høgel, C. 44
Holford-Strevens, L. 39
Holladay, C.R. 74
Horrell, D.G. 97

Jacobson, H. 80
Jauss, H.R. 8, 9
Jeffers, J.S. 97
Johnson, L.T. 118, 120, 123-25, 127, 128, 130, 132, 136, 143, 146, 150, 153, 155, 157, 160, 161, 166-68, 170, 171, 175
Judge, E.A. 128

Karris, R.J. 120
Käsemann, E. 115, 128, 144
Kelly, J.N.D. 157, 170
Kennedy, G. 37, 51
Kidd, R. 129, 142
Kimball, D. 204
Knight, G.W. 118, 121, 123, 124, 131, 136, 137, 145, 146, 153, 161
Küng, H. 2

Lawton, R.B. 64
Lips, H. von 118, 139, 146
Lucks, H.A. 99
Lust, J. 62
Luther, M. 5

MacKenzie, R.A.F. 73
Malherbe, A.J. 120, 135
Marshall, I.H. 115, 117, 118, 120-28, 131, 132, 136, 137, 140, 142, 143, 145, 146, 151, 154, 156, 157, 160, 161, 163, 164, 166-68, 170, 171, 173, 175, 207
Martin, D.B. 206
McKenzie, S.L. 68
Mejer, J. 41
Minns, D. 106
Moore, J.M. 28
Mounce, W. 115, 118, 119, 123-25, 128, 140, 142, 144, 146, 151, 153, 207

Oberlinner, L. 119, 135, 137, 156, 170, 175
O'Brien, M.A. 71
Odeberg, H. 86
Osiek, C. 130

Patte, D. 18
Petersen, N. 206
Pöhlmann, W. 172
Pomeroy, S.B. 151
Porter, J.R. 62
Priest, J.F. 81
Prior, M. 161, 164

Quinn, J.D. 115, 117, 122-24, 131, 137, 145, 146, 151, 184

Rabinowitz, P.J. 8, 9
Rajak, T. 82
Reed, J.T. 199
Rich, J.W. 38
Richards, W.A. 10, 11, 155, 158, 185
Roloff, J. 115-17, 119, 121, 125, 136, 137, 139, 146
Romm, J. 21
Rosen, E. 50
Rousseau, P. 44

Schlarb, E. 116, 120
Schlatter, A. 172
Schoedel, W.R. 99
Simms, L.J. 50
Skeat, T.C. 121
Spicq, C. 117, 120, 138, 167
Stählin, G. 151
Stalley, R.F. 24
Steger, C.A. 3
Stepp, P.L. 1, 15, 16, 19, 63, 93, 112, 114, 117, 180
Stewart-Sykes, A. 103
Stiefel, J.H. 145
Stirewalt, M.L. 11
Stowers, S.K. 10
Stylianou, P.J. 29

Talbert, C.H. 1, 15, 16, 19, 63, 93, 112, 114, 117, 180
Talstra, E. 62
Thrall, M. 126
Thurian, M. 7
Thurston, B.B. 151

Towner, P.H. 115, 120, 129
Trobisch, D. 206
Tromp, J. 81
Verner, D.C. 128, 129
Vervenne, M. 62

Wacholder, B.Z. 74
Wacker, W. 115, 117, 122-24, 131, 137, 145, 146, 151

Warkentin, M. 168
Welborn, L.L. 97
Wild, R.A. 183
Winter, B. 130, 151
Wolter, M. 115, 125, 154, 168, 180

Young, F.M. 145

www.ingramcontent.com/pod-product-compliance
Lightning Source LLC
Chambersburg PA
CBHW071709160426
43195CB00012B/1625